NO SIMPLE HIGHWAY

EDMUND J. SULLIVAN. 1909.

NO SIMPLE HIGHWAY

A CULTURAL HISTORY OF

GRATEFUL DEAD

PETER RICHARDSON

St. Martin's Press
New York

www.stmartins.com

Library of Congress Cataloging-in-Publication Data

Richardson, Peter, 1959–author.
  No simple highway : a cultural history of the Grateful Dead / Peter Richardson.
    p. cm.
  ISBN 978-1-250-01062-9 (hardcover)
  ISBN 978-1-250-02133-5 (e-book)
 1. Grateful Dead (Musical group) 2. Rock musicians—United States—Biography. 3. Rock music—Social aspects. I. Title.
  ML421.G72R53 2015
  782.42166092'2—dc23
  [B]   2014036345

First Edition: January 2015

10 9 8 7 6 5 4 3 2 1

Contents

There is a road,
no simple highway,
between the dawn
and the dark of night.

"Ripple," lyrics by Robert Hunter

Introduction

Five decades ago, the Grateful Dead emerged from a vibrant San Francisco arts scene to claim national attention. Along with a supportive community and plenty of psychoactive drugs, they pioneered a new and ecstatic form of expression called the rock concert. For a brief time, they helped make San Francisco a center of the rock music world, and almost three decades after that, they were the nation's most popular touring band. While many of their peers flashed brilliantly across the American scene, the Grateful Dead became one of the counterculture's most distinctive and durable institutions. This book raises a deceptively simple question: why?

The best answer probably won't be found in the Grateful Dead's substantial studio output. Although their songbook contains many gems and reflects a rich array of American idioms, the Dead acknowledged that their recordings were neither consistently excellent nor broadly popular. The albums sold well over time, but the Dead never had a number one song, and they cracked the top ten only once—more than two decades after their formation. Nor was the Dead's success due to their showmanship. Their live performances were their calling card, they cared about the audience's experience, and their sound system was legendary, but they put almost no energy into the usual rock theatrics. They skipped the stagy strutting, flashy costumes, and special effects. In fact, they usually skipped the set list. The presentation was so stripped down that a single smile from lead guitarist Jerry Garcia could delight the audience.

What, then, accounts for the Dead's long-standing popularity? Their image was certainly a factor. Hip, funny, and articulate, they seemed to create effortlessly and without artifice. Their authenticity also satisfied a countercultural ideal. For many, the Grateful Dead were cool because they gave mainstream American culture a wide berth and still managed to flourish. In this sense, they were living proof that hippies could make it on their own preferred terms. Wherever the Grateful Dead played, the Summer of Love lived on, long after the original San Francisco hippies headed for the hills and their Haight-Ashbury neighborhood descended into squalor.

But the Grateful Dead's status as counterculture heroes masks an even more important source of their popularity. Although they offered a fully formed alternative to America's sober, God-fearing, and profit-maximizing ways, a large part of their appeal arose not from their resistance to American culture, but rather from their uncanny ability to tap its inexhaustible utopian energies. Garcia, in fact, regarded the Dead as the American experiment in action. "We're basically Americans, and we like America," he said. "We like the things about being able to express outrageous amounts of freedom." Always more than a series of shows, Grateful Dead tours were mobile social laboratories, chances to experiment and innovate, not only musically but also personally and even spiritually. Living on the edge of novelty, inventing their own ways and means, the Dead absorbed and supplemented a rich strain of American culture that included literature and the visual arts as well as music. But even compared to their key influences, the Dead pushed their utopian ideals to another level in their music, organization, and community.

Utopian communities are usually organized around religious, political, or social goals, and though these aspirations hovered around the Dead and their tribe, they never quite defined them. The Dead declined to systematize or justify their enterprise publicly, and they often downplayed any form of intentionality. "Nobody's making any real central decisions or anything," Garcia said in 1969. "Everything's just kind of hashed out. It stumbles. It stumbles, then it creeps, then it flies with one wing, and then it flies with one wing and bumps into trees and shit." Garcia's remark was accurate as far as it went; the Dead usually lacked a formal business plan and collectively adapted to changing circumstances. It also reflected the Dead's hippie *sprezzatura*; they carefully wrapped their aspirations in studied nonchalance and self-deprecation. But if their enterprise was neither a traditional utopian community nor a conventional corporation, the Dead often discussed and consistently enacted the chief characteristic of all utopian practice: the transformation of the everyday. Their project was an attempt to free themselves and their community from ordinary, straight, "normal" life. The Dead called that liberation getting high, and they sought to transcend ordinary experience through continuous experimentation and improvisation in their music and lives.

Rather than argue for the centrality of the Dead's utopian ideals, I've used them to organize the band's unique story. The first part of *No Simple Highway* explores the Dead's commitment to ecstasy—not the drug, but the urge to transcend—which was always at the heart of their project. A subjective experience of total rapture, ecstasy has a long, diverse, and cross-cultural history, but it often involves music, dancing, psychotropic drugs, and altered states of consciousness. Ecstatic experiences and their interpretation often change the subject's values and worldview permanently, and the Grateful Dead regularly described their project in those terms. "The Grateful Dead is not for cranking out rock and roll, it's not for going out and doing concerts or any of that stuff, I think it's to get high," Garcia said in 1972. "I'm not talking about unconscious or zonked-out, I'm talking about being fully conscious." Garcia's statement also reflects a historically specific understanding of what it was to be an artist, one that placed enormous value on intense and transformational experience. The first section of the book traces that understanding to the Dead's cultural milieu, their major influences, and the rapturous events that transformed a bar band into nationally recognized artists.

The Dead were devoted to mobility as well as to ecstasy, and the book's second section reflects their life on—and songs about—the open road. Making a virtue of necessity, the Dead put touring ahead of recording, and their lyrics elevated geographical and psychic journeys to mythic importance. Their key influences also associated mobility with freedom and discovery, but the Dead supercharged that impulse, created a larger social space for its expression, and modeled two generations of youthful wanderlust. When thousands of fans began following the Dead's tours, Garcia suggested that the Dead's nomadic culture was that generation's archetypal American adventure, the equivalent of joining the circus or riding freight trains. The middle section of the book recounts the Dead's transition from a Haight-Ashbury icon to a touring simulacrum of the 1960s counterculture.

Finally, the Dead were dedicated to community. This commitment, arguably the most important for understanding their achievement, organizes the final section of the book. From the outset, the Dead's enterprise was tribal as well as utopian. Their inner circle consisted of the musicians, managers, lyricists, and crew members who lived together in various configurations, shared their earnings more or less equally, and made decisions more or less democratically. As the touring operation grew, so did the core group of employees, friends, and family. Connected by the Dead's annual migrations, newsletter, and later its website, a growing cohort of Dead Heads swelled the progress. By the early 1980s, Dead Heads dominated the Dead's media coverage. Despite its gypsy image, the Dead Head community always included a professional (and preprofessional) element; the Dead's record company estimated that three-quarters of their audience was college educated, and the band regularly received glowing reviews in elite campus newspapers. Indeed, some Dead Heads—including a US vice president and two senators—became downright respectable. The Dead's communal impulse also informed their corporation, which was headed by a crew member and eventually grossed more than $30 million annually in touring revenue alone. Again, many of the Dead's precursors and peers emphasized community, but the Dead were uniquely successful at fostering it: so successful, in fact, that the Dead community is still thriving two decades after the band's dissolution.

These three ideals animated the Dead's project at every level, but to describe them as utopian doesn't mean that the results were always happy. As the Dead pursued their vision, they confronted a series of daunting artistic, organizational, and personal challenges that hampered their creative development, imperiled their enterprise, and claimed several lives. Like the Dead's achievements, those challenges can't be fully understood apart from the utopian ideals that propelled their overall project. The Dead's attempts to enact their ideals met with resistance from various sources in the mainstream culture, including the music business, and many of the Dead's most intractable problems, I would argue, arose from tensions that emerged over time between their utopian impulses. Even so, the Dead never renounced their aspirations, and their lived experience with their most cherished ideals was complex, layered, and paradoxical. In short, theirs was no simple highway.

Although the Dead disbanded in 1995, their iconic status remains secure. A visit to their website confirms what Dead Heads already know: a large, active, and deeply connected audience still reveres the band's music and lore. Box sets are doing brisk business, satellite and terrestrial radio programs reach millions of listeners, and the Dead's Facebook page counts more than 1.8 million followers. A growing body of scholarly literature has explored the Dead's music, history, business practices, and community. Memoirs by insiders have furnished a richly informative and consistently entertaining portrait of the band's experience, and as the fiftieth anniversary of the band's formation approaches, we will see even more reflections on that experience and its significance.

For all of its strengths, however, this work hasn't convinced broader audiences that the Grateful Dead deserve their attention. There is more to this failure than Garcia's famous observation that the Dead resembled licorice: not everyone likes it, but those who do *really* like it. Much of the indifference to, and sometimes disdain for, the Dead and their project can be traced to simple intellectual inertia. For decades now, a large fraction of the mainstream media has depicted the Grateful Dead as grizzled hippie throwbacks with a cult following of burned-out stoners. Never especially accurate, this stereotype has become a handy synecdoche for the 1960s, the musical part that stands for the countercultural whole. It also acts as a marker in the continuing and sometimes heated debates over that decade and its significance. Whatever purposes this cartoon version of the Dead has served over the years, it has also discouraged any serious reconsideration of their legacy and obscured the combination of talent, range, intelligence, and authenticity that made them so appealing in the first place.

No Simple Highway is meant to replace the stereotype with a fresh portrait. It situates the band in their time and place, explores the origins of their unique project, and documents its remarkable reception. Drawing on a wide range of sources, it also argues that the Dead's success cannot be separated from the utopian chords their project struck among two generations of American youth. By organizing the Dead's story around this claim and its implications, I hope to place the Dead's achievement in the broader sweep of American cultural history. If that purpose sounds exalted for a dance band, at least the critical stakes are clear.

My own interest in the Grateful Dead doesn't follow the usual track. While growing up in the San Francisco Bay Area during the 1960s, I was well aware of the Dead and their milieu. My oldest brother was a fan, and their music was our household's sonic wallpaper. As often happens, that familiarity worked against a deeper understanding of the Dead's project, and by the mid-1970s, my friends and I were inclined to dismiss them as relics. But after a chance meeting several years ago with author, radio host, and musician David Gans, I realized that the band's story chimed well with the key themes of a course I taught at San Francisco State University. When I invited David to visit my class, I discovered that students with little or no prior knowledge of the Grateful Dead responded enthusiastically to the band's long, strange trip.

Intrigued, I began to ponder the riddle of the Dead's appeal. I contacted Professor Fredric Lieberman at the University of California, Santa Cruz. He had created a course on the Dead's music and collaborated with percussionist Mickey Hart on three books. Professor Lieberman recommended a list of readings with Dennis McNally's history at the top. After inhaling those, I met with Dennis, the band's longtime publicist, and then Nicholas Meriwether, the founding director of the Grateful Dead Archive at the University of California, Santa Cruz. Nick encouraged me to submit a conference paper to the Grateful Dead Scholars Caucus, which I began attending in 2011. The panels there resembled an academic version of a Dead concert—communal, uneven, full of peak moments. As for camaraderie, the caucus easily eclipsed anything I had experienced in my academic life, and our colloquies helped me identify and explore my interests in the Dead and their history.

I attended the Grateful Dead Archive's official opening in 2012 and returned the next summer to explore its contents. Renting a home on campus, I hiked up the sere hill each day to McHenry Library, which houses the archive. As I entered the stand of coastal redwoods and oaks that surrounds the library, its canopy cooled and refreshed me for my afternoon's work. After two weeks of that routine, I realized that my daily hike resembled Jerry Garcia's description of the Grateful Dead. In the great forest of music, he reportedly told Sam Cutler, you wander through the trees until you stumble upon a glade. In the center of that clearing, you find delicate flowers, radiant in their perfection. "Those flowers," Garcia said, "so fragile and insubstantial, so manifest and yet so vulnerable, are the Grateful Dead." As it was with the Dead, so it was with their archive. But I came to believe that its most valuable treasure was Nick Meriwether, who not only guided me through the material I needed for this project, but also shared his personal library and encyclopedic knowledge of the Dead and their bohemian milieu.

Much like my previous book, a history of *Ramparts* magazine, *No Simple Highway* is an attempt to understand the Bay Area milieu into which I was born. As a youth, I naturally mistook that world for a universal and permanent reality. I now realize that it must be understood on its own peculiar and historically specific terms. Even more obviously than *Ramparts*, the Grateful Dead helped establish those terms—and then stuck to them for better or worse. I would be interested in the Dead's story even if its importance were only a regional affair. Since their experience was much more than that, I hope others will find value in it as well.

PART 1

ECSTASY

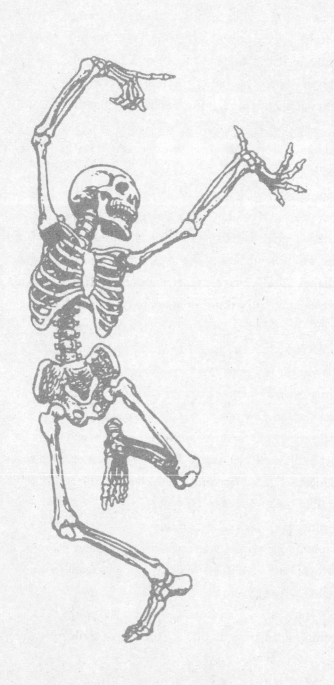

n the spring of 1965, they got their chance.

Jerry Garcia and his wife, Sara Ruppenthal, were eager to try psychedelic drugs. As teenagers in the suburbs south of San Francisco, each had smoked marijuana; in fact, one of Garcia's friends, Robert Hunter, had given Ruppenthal her first "funny cigarette." She thought marijuana brought out her husband's irresponsible side, but she was curious about LSD. "I had always wanted to do psychedelics," she recalled later. "I'd read Aldous Huxley's *Doors of Perception* when I was a teenager and really wanted to expand my consciousness."

If hers was an unusually literary introduction to psychedelics, *The Doors of Perception* was an unusual book. Published in 1954, it recounted a single day in the life of the English intellectual tripping on mescaline in and around his Hollywood home. The book's title echoed a passage from William Blake's *The Marriage of Heaven and Hell*. "If the doors of perception were cleansed, every thing would appear to man as it is, Infinite," Blake wrote. "For man has closed himself up, till he sees all things thro' narrow chinks of his cavern." Ingesting mescaline, which was legal, would put Huxley in direct contact with that insight. Intrigued by the links between drugs, consciousness, and art, Huxley knew that mescaline had been isolated from peyote in the late 1890s, that British physician Havelock Ellis had experimented with it in the 1920s, and that Ellis had supplied poet William Butler Yeats with peyote. Yeats reported that he had seen "the most delightful dragons, puffing out their breath straight in front of them, like rigid lines of steam."

At age fifty-nine, Huxley had already led a remarkable life. Born into a family of prominent writers, scientists, and physicians, he studied literature at Oxford and established himself as a successful novelist, poet, and journalist. His fifth novel, the dystopian *Brave New World*, appeared in 1932. It was both a jab at the earlier utopian works of H. G. Wells and a complex response to the fast-paced, unreflective, and technology-obsessed mass society that Huxley saw around him, especially in America. In that novel, an overweening state encourages its citizens to drink soma, a hallucinogen that pacifies its users and provides a measure of temporary transcendence and communion. *Brave New World* brought Huxley even more notoriety, but his outspoken pacifism in the 1930s alienated him from his British peers, and he decided to move to the United States.

In 1937, Huxley arrived in Hollywood and soon began mixing screenwriting assignments with fiction and nonfiction. After the Republican Party took control of the House of Representatives in 1946, the House Committee on Un-American Activities subpoenaed the Hollywood Ten, the so-called unfriendly witnesses who declined to answer questions about their alleged membership in the Communist Party. Four years later, Congress launched a second investigation of leftists in the film industry, and this time, Huxley was identified as a Communist fellow traveler. His film career collapsed after a cover story in *Counterattack,* a right-wing magazine, described him as a Communist dupe.

In 1953, Huxley persuaded Humphry Osmond, the British psychiatrist who invented the term *psychedelic,* to dose him with mescaline. On the morning of May 4, Osmond mixed less than half a gram of white crystals into a glass of water, which Huxley drank. After thirty minutes, Huxley noticed that the flowers in his study melted into wavy patterns. Osmond began to quiz him about spatial relationships. They were altered, but Huxley found that he could move around the room normally. The more interesting change, he thought, was that his books were glowing with living light. When the psychiatrist asked about time, Huxley replied, "There seems to be plenty of it." After ninety minutes, Huxley was asked if his experience was agreeable. "It just *is,*" he said, laughing. As his daily concerns evaporated, Huxley looked around his home, and he noticed that "a sense of special significance began to invest everything in the room. . . . A plain wooden chair was invested with a 'chairliness' which no chair ever had for me before."

In the afternoon, Huxley wandered down to the local drugstore seven blocks from his Hollywood home. There he made his way through the aisles of toys, greeting cards, comic books, and cooking utensils. Nearly blind since his teenage years, Huxley was transfixed by the art books he discovered there. "This is how one ought to see," he told his companions repeatedly, but he also felt panic. "Suddenly I had an inkling of what it must feel like to be mad," he recalled. That sensation gave way to a more peaceful one that he called "contemplation at its height." Reflecting on his experience, Huxley didn't equate it with authentic enlightenment, but he stressed its intellectual benefits.

All I am suggesting is that the mescalin [sic] experience is what Catholic theologians call "a gratuitous grace," not necessary to salvation but potentially helpful and to be accepted thankfully, if made available. To be shaken out of the rut of ordinary perception, to be shown for a few timeless hours the outer and the inner world . . . this is an experience of inestimable value to everyone and especially to the intellectual.

Reviewers panned *The Doors of Perception* and castigated Huxley, but he was unfazed. He continued to trip several times a year for the rest of his life, and his book spread the word about the virtues of psychedelic drugs.

Garcia's interest in psychedelics was less bookish than Ruppenthal's—not surprising, perhaps, given that she attended Stanford University, where her father taught, and he dropped out of high school. But Garcia and his friends were no dullards. Ruppenthal met them at Kepler's Books, the Menlo Park store where local intellectuals and activists gathered. Garcia, Hunter, and David Nelson spent their days playing music in the back room, and they impressed Ruppenthal with their energetic banter. At the time, Garcia and Hunter were living at a boardinghouse called the Chateau near the Stanford campus. Inhabited by bohemians and eccentrics, the Chateau was a step up from the East Palo Alto vacant lot where Garcia and Hunter had previously lived in their automobiles. But Garcia's room at the Chateau was primitive. "I think it had a dirt floor," Ruppenthal said. "He'd stuck a bed in there, and there was a box with a candle on it, and that was it. There was no electricity. There were spiders. It was really funky."

A few weeks after Ruppenthal and Garcia began dating, she was pregnant. They married, moved into a small apartment, and tried to manage on his meager earnings from the local music store, where he taught guitar and banjo. Their prospects weren't bright, but at twenty-three, Jerome John Garcia was just getting started.

Like many residents in and around Palo Alto, Jerry Garcia was a newcomer. He grew up thirty miles north in the famously freewheeling city of San Francisco. His father, Jose, emigrated from Spain with his family at sixteen. A clarinetist, Joe formed a small band that played on cruise ships shuttling between San Francisco and Los Angeles. Joe later joined the Orpheum Circuit, a chain of vaudeville theaters based in San Francisco, and toured for several years before settling in Hollywood and playing clubs and occasionally for the movies. Returning to San Francisco to be near his family, he married Ruth Clifford, a registered nurse. They had two sons, Clifford (known as Tiff) and Jerry, who grew up to the sound of woodwinds. "The clarinet had that lovely wood quality, especially in the middle register. And that sound is very present in my ear," Jerry recalled. "Some people can recall smells. I can recall specific sounds—I can hear a sound and all of a sudden it will transport me to places."

Four years after the repeal of Prohibition, Joe and Ruth opened a bar called Garcia's at the corner of First Street and Harrison Street on Rincon Hill. It was close to the city's docks, skid row, and the recently completed Bay Bridge, which connected San Francisco to Oakland.

Business was good, but family life soon took a turn for the worse. When Jerry was four, he lost half of his right middle finger while Tiff was chopping wood. The next year, his father drowned while fishing on the rugged Northern California coast. Ruth took over the bar, remarried, and eventually moved the family to the peninsula suburbs. By that time, the bar had exposed Jerry to professional music and life on the city's bustling waterfront. At Garcia's, Jerry found a community receptive to his outgoing nature and enthusiasms. "I've always wanted to be able to turn on people, and also I've taken it for granted that if I like something, that other people will like it, too," he said. "The bar world established that kind of feeling; it engulfed me like a little community."

The docks near Garcia's were also a key part of San Francisco's identity. Ever since the city's furious growth during the Gold Rush, the waterfront had been a busy node in the global economy. By the time Garcia's opened, San Francisco supported the nation's largest population of sailors, and 5 percent of the city's employed males worked as seafarers, longshoremen, or warehousemen. More than two-thirds of the district's population was male, half of them were foreign-born, and many lived in hotels. The neighborhood around Garcia's was known for its bars, gambling dens, and bordellos, and such vice districts had been integral parts of San Francisco's social fabric for generations. The same year Garcia's opened, an FBI agent told a San Francisco grand jury that the city's police force received at least $1 million in graft each year to keep the party going. Despite periodic calls for reform, especially from clergy, crackdowns were a low priority, as even the FBI agent acknowledged: "We were aware that the bulk of the people wanted a so-called open town, and that the history of San Francisco reflected a public attitude of broad-mindedness, liberality, and tolerance comparable to only two other American cities, namely New York and New Orleans."

The docks also shaped San Francisco's political culture. For decades, organized labor had been a key component in local politics. Garcia's maternal grandmother, who helped raise him after his father's death, organized the laundry workers' union in San Francisco and served as its secretary-treasurer. But the city's pro-labor disposition was tested in a series of dramatic showdowns less than a decade before Garcia's birth. In 1934, militant longshoremen led a general strike that shut down San Francisco for months. That lethal conflict, which played out around the site of Garcia's, transformed labor relations in and around the ports and established the longshoremen's union as a potent political force on the West Coast. Its leader, however, became a target of federal probes that dragged on for decades. The government claimed that Harry Bridges, a native of Australia, had lied about his Communist Party membership in his immigration documents. But prosecutors couldn't prove that claim, and Bridges's feisty lawyer, Vincent Hallinan, helped fend off the attacks. While doing so, Hallinan was convicted of contempt and spent six months in prison. Eventually federal prosecutors dropped the Bridges case, and though local authorities continued to pressure and prosecute dissidents of all stripes, San Francisco became known as a haven for radicals and free spirits.

The Second World War, which the United States entered shortly before Garcia was born, changed the Bay Area profoundly. Some 240,000 workers built and repaired ships at various Bay Area locations, and defense-related activities drew the first sizable black population to the region from Texas, Louisiana, and Arkansas. Another 1.6 million soldiers and sailors traveled through San Francisco on their way to and from the Pacific theater, and after the war, many settled in the Bay Area. Some veterans used their GI Bill benefits to earn college degrees and swelled the region's professional ranks. Others took a different path. A small but highly visible faction of veterans formed motorcycle gangs that maintained large chapters in and around San Francisco. Rogue bikers were at the center of a 1947 incident in Hollister, where four thousand motorcyclists attended a rally and overwhelmed the small town south of San

Jose. Their brawling led to dozens of injuries and arrests, and the spectacle served as the basis for the 1953 film *The Wild One* with Marlon Brando.

In the 1960s, Hunter S. Thompson's bestselling book *Hell's Angels* focused national attention on the region's most notorious motorcycle gang, which derived its name and insignia from military units in previous wars. "Like the drifters who rode west after Appomattox," Thompson noted, "there were thousands of veterans in 1945 who flatly rejected the idea of going back to their prewar pattern." But well before Thompson's book appeared, the Hells Angels were famous in the Bay Area. According to Laird Grant, Garcia's boyhood friend, the motorcycle gang fired their young imaginations. "We knew about the beatniks, and we knew about Hells Angels and were fascinated by both of these cultures," Grant said. "We'd see the bikers, the Hells Angels, coming up from San Jose or read about the runs that would happen in Monterey. The movie *The Wild One* with Brando came out in '53, I think, and that was incredible. At that point, all of us wanted to wear leather jackets and ride Harleys." Law enforcement cast the motorcycle gang as a threat to public safety and order, but the Hells Angels saw themselves as pursuing the good life: a combustible admixture of heavy drinking, road trips, and a powerful if frequently extralegal form of fellowship.

As Grant's comment about beatniks suggests, the war also changed the local arts community. Although San Francisco was beautifully situated and commercially connected, it was culturally isolated. Perhaps for this reason, the avant-garde played a different role in the city than it did elsewhere. Poet Kenneth Rexroth, the éminence grise of midcentury San Francisco letters, described the city's underground arts scene as "dominant, almost all there is." This postwar scene was by no means the first bohemia. The French, who coined that term in the nineteenth century, based it on the Central European region through which the Romany people, or Gypsies, entered Western Europe. Greenwich Village had served as New York City's bohemia for generations, and in California,

Bret Harte wrote as "The Bohemian" as early as the 1860s. When other local journalists, including Mark Twain, began to identify themselves that way, they founded the Bohemian Club in 1872. Its members had a clubhouse in downtown San Francisco and eventually acquired a camp in the redwood forests of Sonoma County for their summer revelries, which featured music, plays, and heavy drinking.

Living on the nation's geographical and artistic margin, and with no culturally important cities for thousands of miles in any direction, San Francisco artists were constantly in the position of making their own party. Though small, that party was lively. The earlier San Francisco literature created by Jack London and others was populist, bohemian, and rowdier than its Eastern counterparts. After the war, San Francisco artists built on that legacy in new and interesting ways. Politically radical, attracted to the Romantic and prophetic traditions, and drawing on esoteric spirituality, writers of the so-called San Francisco Renaissance dreamed of more connected and fulfilling communities.

After settling in San Francisco in 1953, Lawrence Ferlinghetti began attending the Friday-night soirées at Rexroth's apartment over Jack's Record Cellar in the predominantly black Fillmore district. "Local and itinerant poets and other flickering literary lights would show up," Ferlinghetti recalled, "usually loaded in more ways than one but mainly with the latest poetry." The poets were "passionate, erudite, disputative conversationalists," Ferlinghetti recalled, and he thought it best to keep his mouth shut, drink the dago red, and let the brilliant raps wash over him. When he opened City Lights Bookstore that year with Peter D. Martin, Ferlinghetti helped make the North Beach neighborhood the center of San Francisco's literary activity.

The underlying impulses of many San Francisco writers—elegiac, nostalgic, and utopian—responded to the violence and dislocation of the war, but much of their work also arose from a profound sense of insularity. "In the spiritual and political loneliness of America in the fifties, you'd hitch a thousand miles to meet a friend," poet Gary Snyder recalled. "West Coast of those days, San Francisco was the only city; and of San Francisco, North Beach." The coteries formed by local poets reflected the need for community that was otherwise lacking—not only among artists, but also in postwar American society generally. Stan Brakhage, whose experimental films would later influence Martin Scorsese and Oliver Stone, remembered the city's arts community as a welcoming place. "You sensed that everybody was very active and very creative and needed the support of others," Brakhage said.

Several San Francisco poets hosted programs on KPFA, the nation's first listener-supported radio station across the bay in Berkeley, but most had little or no financial support for their work. Meeting in bars or at informal dinner parties to talk politics, religion, and art, they presented their work not as literary artifacts but as dramatic performances intended for (and sometimes aimed at) close friends. Those encounters, which could include up to one hundred persons, were intellectually acute but also fully embodied. Sensuality and excess, as represented by the Greek god Dionysus, were regarded as artistically useful. "My view of the Dionysian," San Francisco poet William Everson wrote, "is that you gain more through a certain quality of imprecision . . . a certain openness or vulnerability to sensation."

In that spirit, Robert Duncan occasionally disrobed during readings. Fellow poet Michael McClure recalled one such instance at a 1955 comic masque. "When it ended, Duncan, trembling and cock-eyed with pleasure, stood up, took off his pants, and showed the nakedness of the poet," McClure said. "All of us knew we'd done something outrageous, something that took a little courage in the silent, cold gray . . . chill fifties of suburban tract homes, crew cuts, war machines, and censorship." Allen Ginsberg noted Duncan's exhibitionism in his journal and reenacted it the following year at a reading in Los Angeles. Responding to a heckler, Ginsberg shed his clothing and shouted, "A poet always stands naked before the world!"

Duncan's audacity reflected another aspect of San Francisco's historical roots. A century earlier, the Gold Rush had drawn a population that not only tolerated risk, but also actively sought it out. Like their Gold Rush precursors, San Francisco artists felt no need to play it safe. If a painter decided to work on a single piece for six years, as Jay DeFeo did with *The Rose,* so be it. If she applied hundreds of pounds of paint so that the piece resembled a sculpture, even better. And if the paint inside never quite dried, or if the piece fell apart when moved, or if the whole thing turned to goo when stored, those risks were worth taking. Fear of failure mattered less than the artist's commitment to her evolving vision. "Only by chancing the ridiculous," DeFeo said, "can I hope for the sublime."

In the mid-1950s, the Beats arrived in San Francisco and energized the local arts scene. "We had been trying for a whole decade to get something like the Beat Generation going," William Everson recalled. "As it turned out, Allen Ginsberg and Jack Kerouac provided the ingredients. They came to San Francisco and found themselves, and it was *their* finding that sparked us. Without them, it never would have happened." Ferlinghetti described the encounter more pointedly. The Beat poets were "wild-ass carpetbaggers from Back East like Allen Ginsberg who proceeded to take over the scene."

For a young Jerry Garcia, the most influential Beat figure was Kerouac, a Columbia University dropout whose westward drift informed his picaresque fiction. Kerouac's most acclaimed novel, *On the Road,* was set in the late 1940s and featured cross-country car trips and spirited adventures, some of them in and around San Francisco. His fictional odyssey through the nation's social margins glorified spontaneous and intense experience often fueled by alcohol, Benzedrine, marijuana, and morphine. Bebop jazz, with its soaring improvisations, provided the sound track, and Kerouac consciously adapted its methods to his own writing. For many readers, his America was an exotic continent waiting to be explored. It was right now, just over the horizon, and Kerouac populated it with his thinly disguised friends. Even the narrator's name, Sal Paradise, signaled the novel's utopian theme. "I was a young writer and I wanted to take off," Paradise says. "Somewhere along the line I knew there'd be girls, visions, everything; somewhere along the line the pearl would be handed to me."

On the Road's hero, Dean Moriarty, was based on Neal Cassady, a charismatic hustler and erstwhile car thief from Denver. To Kerouac, Cassady's combination of energy, raw appetite, and thirst for experience represented a romantic frontier ideal. Moriarty was "a sideburned hero of the snowy West," and his energy was "a wild yea-saying overburst of American joy; it was Western, the west wind, an ode from the Plains, something new, long prophesied, long a-coming." In real life, the cross-country car trips bonded Kerouac and Cassady, and their frantic jags with a speedy Cassady at the wheel prompted a compositional style that captured the spirit of their journeys. After extensive planning and out-lining, Kerouac banged out the manuscript for *On the Road* in a series of Benzedrine-powered raptures.

On the Road challenged mainstream American values in several ways. Its key relationships aren't found in nuclear families but in male friend-ships forged by shared adventures. In their bohemian exuberance, Sal and his friends ignore or flout almost everything Main Street might recognize as worthy, including sobriety, common sense, hard work, mo-nogamy, conventional forms of spirituality, and patriotism. Their goal is rapture, not respectability, and they pursue it ardently. But for all their high spirits, Sal realizes that his paradise lacks something: "'I want to marry a girl,' I told them, 'so I can rest my soul with her till we get old. This can't go on all the time—this franticness and jumping around. We've got to go someplace, find something.'" Later Sal admits, "I had nothing to offer anybody but my own confusion." Even after witnessing an ecstatic jazz performance, he and his friends feel empty. "This mad-ness would lead nowhere. I didn't know what was happening to me, and

I suddenly realized it was only the tea [marijuana] we were smoking."
But Sal sets his misgivings aside when the next adventure beckons. "We
were all delighted, we all realized we were leaving confusion and nonsense behind and performing our one and noble function of the time,
move."

Published in 1957, *On the Road* failed to please many critics, but it
found a large and appreciative audience, especially among young people
bored by the mainstream American culture of the 1950s. Garcia fit that
profile perfectly. His family's move down the peninsula was part of a
larger pattern of suburbanization and white flight enabled by the national expansion of the freeway system under President Eisenhower.
"My mother remarried when I was about ten or eleven or so," Garcia
recalled, "and she decided to get the kids out of the city, that thing, go
down to the Peninsula, and we moved down to Menlo Park for about
three years, and I went to school down there." The nearby community
of Palo Alto, which had been known for fruit orchards and Stanford
University, became a suburban showcase. Another local institution, *Sunset* magazine, blossomed in the postwar period by offering advice on
homes, gardens, food, travel, and tasteful Western living. Nothing could
be less interesting to Garcia. For him, *On the Road* and its promise of
adventure was the antidote to suburban life.

Kerouac's fiction also connected Garcia to the more intriguing world
he experienced in San Francisco, not only on the embarcadero, but also
in nearby North Beach, the Beat epicenter and home of City Lights.
Adjacent to the Barbary Coast, another vice district with a colorful history, North Beach was teeming with bars and strips joints catering to
GIs and tourists. Its residents were primarily working-class Italians,
who populated its cafés, restaurants, delicatessens, and Catholic churches.
Raised on circuses, small theater groups, and anarchist politics in the
old country, many North Beach residents were remarkably open to their
new bohemian neighbors. The same cannot be said of the mainstream
media, which quickly stereotyped and lambasted the Beats. Even pro-

gressive magazines got their shots in, casting Kerouac as a mindless, apolitical primitive. But critics couldn't blunt the novel's appeal to Garcia and others who longed for something more exciting than the Great American Barbecue of the Eisenhower era. Garcia was soon attending poetry readings in and around North Beach and generally absorbing the neighborhood's bohemian atmosphere. "We'd hang out in front of the Anxious Asp," Laird Grant said, "the Green Street Saloon, the Co-Existence Bagel Shop, Coffee & Confusion, and we'd go to parties here and there—there was a lot of action around."

Although the Beats brought national attention to North Beach, they weren't permanent fixtures. In 1958, Kerouac bought a home on Long Island and returned to San Francisco occasionally. That same year, Cassady was arrested for selling two marijuana cigarettes to an undercover police officer in San Francisco. Cassady's sentence was five years to life in San Quentin, the notorious state prison a few miles north in Marin County. He was released in 1960, but the Beat frenzy had already peaked, and he began searching for a new scene.

On the Road changed Jerry Garcia's life, but he discovered it only by pursuing another interest. A capable illustrator, he enrolled in a summer and weekend program at the California School of Fine Arts (CSFA) when he was fifteen years old, the same year he received his first guitar and smoked his first joint. Garcia's studies at CSFA, whose campus was perched on a hill just above North Beach, immersed him more deeply in the Beat milieu. His teachers included Elmer Bischoff, whose figurative work bore some of the immediacy and exuberance of the abstract expressionists. Rexroth and another poet, Jack Spicer, also taught there. Spicer, whose college friends from Berkeley included Robert Duncan and science fiction writer Philip K. Dick, accepted the CSFA teaching position only after refusing to sign the University of California's anticommunist loyalty oath and thwarting his mainstream academic career.

Garcia's main mentor at CSFA was Wally Hedrick, whose example appealed directly to a teenager looking for more. Growing up in Southern California, Hedrick had been interested in hot rods, bridge, and the beach, but after learning that he could avoid gym class by helping an art teacher, he received solid training at Pasadena Junior College. As the Cold War began in earnest, Hedrick and his friends called their group the Progressive Art Workers, thereby connecting themselves to the area's small but vocal radical tradition once embodied by resident muckraker and two-time gubernatorial candidate Upton Sinclair. Hedrick recalled the political climate after the war. "This was when they were coming down hard on Communists and all that stuff, but we didn't know that from a hole in the ground," he said. "I mean, the closest I got to it was maybe singing folk songs. We'd sit around and sing 'Freiheit' or something and really feel like we were on the verge of something." On the advice of a local artist, Hedrick and his friends headed north to investigate CSFA. By the time they arrived, Mark Rothko, Richard Diebenkorn, Ansel Adams, Edward Weston, and Dorothea Lange had already come and gone, but the San Francisco Renaissance was only beginning to attract national attention.

The Korean War protracted Hedrick's studies; he had joined the National Guard to avoid the draft, but his unit was called up. Despite his decorations and the GI Bill benefits that supported his studies, Hedrick detested his military experience. He returned to civilian life painting American flags before Jasper Johns did so; during the Vietnam War, Hedrick painted them black in protest. After completing his studies at CSFA, he signed on as an instructor and began to produce assemblage and funk art that grew out of the futurist, surrealist, and Dada traditions. Reviewing his work of that period, author Rebecca Solnit noted that it managed to be "lurid, mystical, and sarcastic all at once."

For Hedrick, making art was primarily an act of pleasure. "There is, no doubt, an element of hedonistic selfishness in the act of my painting, for I enjoy it," he wrote in a 1956 brochure about his work. "I *like* to paint. Much of the time there is a complete freedom from harassment, from even awareness of the world. There is no time, no place. It is in the act of painting that I find my keenest sense of self and of 'being.'" His work routinely lampooned conceit, self-deception, and authority, including in the art world. Garcia took to heart Hedrick's final comment in that early brochure: "In painting, it is not what you paint that is important, it is what you paint out that counts." Years later, Garcia gave the same advice almost verbatim to Jorma Kaukonen about playing the guitar.

Garcia learned from Hedrick that art is not only something you do, but something you are as well. Garcia's bohemian models at CSFA opened up a world of new possibility—not only in his thinking about art, but also in how to live like an artist. Hedrick and his wife, Jay DeFeo, had a flat at 2322 Fillmore Street in a four-unit building known as Painterland. Their neighbors included poets Michael and Joanna McClure, painter Joan Brown, and Dave Getz, who studied painting at CSFA and later played drums for both Big Brother & the Holding Company and Country Joe & the Fish. Hedrick and DeFeo's flat served as a touchstone for their colleagues and visiting artists. "Wally and Jay's house on Fillmore was the unofficial first stop on any art itinerary—anyone important in the art world—national or international—theirs was the first stop," recalled CSFA faculty member Carlos Villa. In that maze of studios and apartments, DeFeo worked steadily on *The Rose*, which took up an entire wall of the apartment.

The CSFA scene also included the Studio 13 Jass Band, with Hedrick on banjo and Bischoff on trumpet. Hedrick's banjo was the first one Garcia had ever seen. Later, Garcia noted that the banjo informed his taste in music. "I like to hear every note," he said. "I like the clarity and separation of notes." The Studio 13 Jass Band played at CSFA parties, which were known for their bohemian excess. Laird Grant recalled one such Halloween party when he and Garcia were sixteen years old: "This big limo pulled up in front of the California School of Fine Arts.

This chick got out in this fur coat and left it there. She was totally stark naked with a raisin in her navel. She came as a cookie. She was one of the art-student models who modeled in the nude all the time. To her, it was nothing at all. But in '56 or '57, it was quite unusual."

In addition to drinking heavily, many CSFA artists smoked marijuana and hashish and ate peyote to heighten their perceptions. One issue of *Semina,* an underground journal connected to CSFA, was originally titled *Cannabis Sativa.* While visiting Michael McClure in 1958, Wallace Berman described the Native American uses of peyote and left behind some buttons in the apartment. McClure ingested them and wrote a poem about the experience for the journal. A few artists were also using heroin. A 1957 issue of *Semina* included two photographs of poet Philip Lamantia injecting it and an excerpt from Alexander Trocchi's novel about his experiences as an addict. Hedrick and his colleagues also explored esoteric traditions, including tarot, theosophy, the *Kama Sutra,* and the kabbalah. Never expecting to make money from their art, Garcia's teachers worked without concern for posterity or publicity. Influenced by their example, Jack Spicer later refused to seek copyrights for his poetry and invented new ways to narrow its distribution.

With Spicer and four others, Hedrick founded the Six Gallery at 3119 Fillmore Street in 1954. That decision solved the basic problem of where to show their work. "There was no market for art," Bruce Conner said later. "The Six Gallery would have an opening and everybody would have a lot of beer and wine and get drunk and maybe Wally Hedrick and Dixieland friends would play music. . . . Why have a show? Just have a party." At one such party in 1955, Allen Ginsberg read "Howl" for the first time in public. It was a raucous scene and signal event in Beat history. Kerouac, who wore a gas mask for the occasion, drank from a bottle of burgundy and scatted during Ginsberg's performance. Kerouac also offered a fictionalized version in *The Dharma Bums,* which was published in 1958. By that time, Lawrence Ferlinghetti had been cleared of obscenity charges arising from his publication of Ginsberg's "Howl." (The poem's most legally troubling line mentions those "who let themselves be fucked in the ass by saintly motorcyclists, and screamed with joy.") There would be more San Francisco obscenity trials, most notably that of comedian Lenny Bruce, who cast himself as a stand-up version of a jazz soloist, free-associating on sex, politics, race, and religion. But Ferlinghetti's legal victory in 1957 was regarded as another advance for liberty, San Francisco style.

The same year, the second issue of *Evergreen Review* ran a cover story called "The San Francisco Scene." Kenneth Rexroth wrote the introductory essay, and Gary Snyder, Michael McClure, and Henry Miller contributed poems and articles. In her piece, art critic Dore Ashton claimed that San Francisco was second only to New York City as a source of avant-garde painting. Two years later, Hedrick and DeFeo were included in a Museum of Modern Art exhibit called *Sixteen Americans,* which also served as the museum debut of Jasper Johns and Robert Rauschenberg. Hedrick and DeFeo didn't attend what turned out to be the pinnacle of his artistic career. In 1962, Hedrick contributed an assemblage piece called *Xmas Tree* to a group show at the San Francisco Museum of Art. *Xmas Tree* was composed of bed rails, record players, radios, and lights as well as a blasting cap, bullhorn, siren, and fan, all wired to washing-machine timers. When activated, one of the phonographs spun Bing Crosby's "White Christmas," while the other played a blues song about a poor man pawning possessions to buy holiday gifts. Before the exhibition, Hedrick set the timers, alerted the museum to his plan, and left town. When the appliances kicked in during a private showing, the fan snagged a startled trustee's fur. She screamed, the piece's lights and sirens added to the commotion, and a museum employee finally severed the electrical cord with an ax.

It was Hedrick who introduced Garcia to Kerouac and *On the Road.* For Garcia, much of the novel's appeal lay in its musicality and romantic depiction of travel.

Then in the next couple of years I read Kerouac, and I recall in '59 hanging out with a friend who had a Kerouac record, and I remember being impressed—I'd read this stuff, but I hadn't heard it, the cadences, the flow, the kind of endlessness of the prose, the way it just poured off. It was really stunning to me. His way of perceiving music—the way he wrote about music and America—and the road, the romance of the American highway, it struck me. It struck a primal chord. It felt familiar, something I wanted to join in. It wasn't like a club; it was a way of seeing.

On the Road was so transformative that Garcia later had difficulty distinguishing his identity from Kerouac's. "It became so much a part of me that it's hard to measure; I can't separate who I am now from what I got from Kerouac," he said. "I don't know if I would ever have had the courage or the vision to do something outside with my life—or even suspected the possibilities existed—if it weren't for Kerouac opening those doors."

If Kerouac's fiction was a key influence, Garcia's contact with San Francisco bohemians during this period also shaped his broader understanding of art and the people who made it. Their emphasis on ecstasy, spontaneity, and community offered him a conceptual platform that was enticing and flexible, and their example encouraged him to experiment with new forms of expression, high and low, without weakening his core convictions about what was worth doing. His eclectic interests—which included painting, film, comic books, and science fiction—reflected Lawrence Ferlinghetti's advice to keep an open mind, but not so open that your brains fall out. Garcia's emerging artistic sensibility also mirrored a cardboard sign that painter and collagist Jess Collins, who was Robert Duncan's partner, posted in his San Francisco studio.

THE SEVEN DEADLY VIRTUES OF CONTEMPORARY ART
ORIGINALITY
SPONTANEITY

SIMPLICITY

INTENSITY

IMMEDIACY

IMPENETRABILITY

SHOCK

Garcia's chance encounter with the midcentury art scene furnished him with the core principles for his lifelong project. "I wanted to do something that fit in with the art institute, that kind of self-conscious art—'art' as opposed to 'popular culture.'" That aspiration can be traced to the interval between his fifteenth and sixteenth birthdays. He would later acknowledge the significance of this annus mirabilis, when he received his first guitar, smoked his first joint, signed up for art classes, and discovered Kerouac.

Inspired by San Francisco's bohemian scene, Garcia still wasn't sure how to find his way. After dropping out of high school, he enlisted in the army. "I wanted so badly to see the world," he said. "It was the only hope I had." But the world would have to wait; Garcia was assigned to the Presidio in San Francisco. He frequently missed roll call, was court-martialed for going AWOL, and was discharged in December 1960.

Two months later, Garcia and his friends were bombing around the peninsula in a Studebaker after a party. The car hit a guardrail, fishtailed, and rolled into a field. Garcia, who was hurled through the windshield with such force that he lost both of his shoes, broke his collarbone. His good friend Alan Trist suffered a compressed fracture of the back. The driver received a gash on his abdomen, and the car landed on Paul Speegle, a fellow Chateau resident and talented artist, crushing almost every bone in his body and killing him. Garcia recalled the accident as a turning point for him. "That's where my life began," he said. "Before then, I was always living at less than capacity. I was idling. That was the slingshot for the rest of my life. It was like a second chance."

Later, he kept a reminder of that opportunity close at hand by hanging one of Speegle's paintings in the Grateful Dead rehearsal studio.

Although Garcia steeped himself in Beat fiction, his true passion was American roots music. He studied the banjo and guitar, eagerly mastered the bluegrass songbook, and joined a lively folk music scene in and around Palo Alto. Reaching back to the prewar period, the folk revival offered an alternative to 1950s mainstream culture, which increasingly valued technology, mass production, and progress. But there was nothing new or improved about folk music. It was handcrafted, authentic, and, according to folk singer John Sebastian, unapologetically local in nature. One New York bluegrass player later cited folk music's cult appeal. "It was not merely *not* commercial music. It was *anti*-commercial music," he said. "When you met anyone else who was into it, you were members of the same club, and I still thought of it as a very small club."

With its emphasis on outcasts, anti-heroes, and socially marginal groups, folk music was also a vehicle for dissent. Like Woody Guthrie, who had been shaped by the Dust Bowl and Popular Front politics of the 1930s, many folk musicians were involved in the labor union, civil rights, and peace movements. Guthrie played for Communist Party meetings in Los Angeles as well as for Harry Bridges's union, the International Longshoremen's and Warehousemen's Union (ILWU), in San Francisco. After moving to New York City in the 1940s, Guthrie joined the Almanac Singers, who specialized in antiwar, antiracist, and pro-labor songs. Guthrie's example would preoccupy the young Bob Dylan, who read Guthrie's *Bound for Glory* in 1960 and even absorbed his hero's speech patterns. When Dylan arrived in New York for the first time, he announced to his audience that he had been "travelin' around the country, followin' in Woody Guthrie's footsteps."

Pete Seeger also played with the Almanac Singers; later, he cofounded the Weavers, who named themselves after a nineteenth-century uprising of German linen workers. His father had founded the music program at the University of California, Berkeley, but was forced to resign because of his outspoken pacifism during World War I. Pete Seeger's leftist politics also hampered his musical career. Between 1950 and 1952, the Weavers sold more than 4 million records, but after appearing before the House Committee on Un-American Activities in 1955, Seeger was blacklisted from broadcast radio and major music venues. He began playing schools, community centers, and union halls as well as for private organizations sympathetic to his views. When Seeger played a Bay Area high school in the mid-1950s, Stanford student Dave Guard attended and bought a copy of his book, *How to Play the 5-String Banjo*. Three years later, Guard formed the Kingston Trio, whose members Garcia had met and played with during his brief stint in the army. The trio's extended engagement at the Purple Onion nightclub in San Francisco led to a recording deal and several hit songs, including "Tom Dooley," a nineteenth-century ballad about the hanging of a Confederate veteran who murdered his lover.

The folk revival was especially popular in the Bay Area, and Garcia and his friends were part of it. Beginning in 1961, Garcia and Robert Hunter played folk festivals at Stanford, at San Francisco State College, and in Monterey. The lineups and band names were fluid; the two folkies and their friends appeared as the Wildwood Boys, the Black Mountain Boys, or the Hart Valley Drifters. They also played local clubs and coffeehouses, including the Folk Music Theater in San Jose, which was renamed the Offstage in 1962. Paul Kantner and David Freiberg helped manage the Offstage, and other musicians who gathered and played there included Jorma Kaukonen, David Crosby, Janis Joplin, and Ron McKernan.

In the early 1960s, however, the local scene's brightest star was Joan Baez, a Palo Alto High School graduate who had attended the same Pete Seeger concert as Dave Guard. A friend of Ruppenthal's and only a year older than Garcia, Baez had already recorded a bestselling album, appeared on the cover of *Time* magazine, and raised Bob Dylan's profile by inviting him to appear with her at the Newport Folk Festival in 1963. Although Baez's breakthrough occurred in Cambridge, Massachusetts, she returned to California to live in the Carmel Highlands, an artist community near Big Sur. Her political mentor, Ira Sandperl, was a longtime employee at Kepler's, and in the mid-1960s, the pair cofounded the Institute for the Study of Nonviolence.

According to Ruppenthal, Garcia resented Baez's success and dismissed her guitar playing. Later, however, Garcia recalled her influence on him. "When Joan Baez's first record came out," he said, "I heard it and I heard her fingerpicking the guitar, I'd never heard anything like that before, so I got into that and started getting into country music, into old-time white music. Mostly white spiritual stuff, white instrumental music, and I got into finger style, the folk music festival scene, that whole thing." Garcia wasn't attracted to political songs, one of Baez's specialties. "When I got into folk music, I never got into it behind the lyrical content. I was never into protest songs," Garcia said. "What first attracted me was the sound of it and those modal changes and so forth and the sound of Joan Baez's voice and the sound of her guitar and then into the more complex forms and finally what I got into was the instrumental parts." Garcia didn't mention it, but Baez's national celebrity also suggested that the Palo Alto folkies weren't laboring in a remote vineyard.

The folk revival pointed Garcia and Hunter back to prewar America for inspiration. On that point, they resembled many writers of the San Francisco Renaissance, but their main portal to that lost world was Harry Smith's *Anthology of American Folk Music*, a six-album collection of Appalachian folk, fiddle, gospel, hillbilly, blues, and Cajun music released by Folkways Records in 1952. Its utter weirdness captivated Hunter and Garcia as well as Bob Dylan, with whom the Palo Alto folkies would eventually join forces. Smith himself was a classic West Coast oddball. Raised in the Pacific Northwest by parents steeped in theosophy and freemasonry, he studied anthropology and did fieldwork with Native American tribes. But his life took a different turn in the

1940s, when a trip to Berkeley introduced him to Woody Guthrie and marijuana. He later downplayed the significance of Guthrie's performance. "It could have been at some longshoremen's hall," he recalled vaguely. "I'm sure it was, like, Communists. But I didn't like his singing. It was too sophisticated and too involved in social problems, I felt. It wasn't the sort of stuff I was interested in."

Soon Smith was living in a small Berkeley apartment attached to the home of Professor Bertrand Bronson, an expert on Francis James Child, the nineteenth-century Harvard folklorist who had cataloged Scottish and English ballads. With Jack Spicer and others, Smith scoured the East Bay for vintage records. He also explored avant-garde film, which introduced him to Robert Duncan. A gay hunchback, Smith became an enthusiastic drug user. He drank heavily, used amphetamines and barbiturates, smoked weed incessantly, and took peyote, which he acquired from the Sears Roebuck catalog. In his view, anything that "changed consciousness was to some degree useful."

In 1952, Smith moved to New York City, took up residence in the Hotel Chelsea, and approached Moe Asch, who had recorded Woody Guthrie for Folkways. Smith's original idea was to sell his record collection to Folkways, but Asch persuaded him to fashion an anthology from it. Smith ignored field recordings and focused instead on commercial songs released in the late 1920s and early 1930s. His selections suggest live performances rather than finished studio products. The singers, for example, frequently shout out instructions to invisible dancers. Despite that sense of immediacy, the social world that gave rise to these performances remained strangely inaccessible. Smith's records were only twenty years old when his anthology appeared, but both the music and the world they evoked already felt ancient and remote. The nineteenth-century source material was even more peculiar. Smith later noted its "amazing subject matter, all connected with children freezing to death." Smith added a twenty-eight-page booklet filled with idiosyncratic liner notes, woodcuts, record-sleeve art, and faded photographs of the artists.

The anthology's cover illustration showed what Smith called the celestial monochord, a single-stringed instrument of ancient origin, being tuned by the hand of God.

Hunter and Garcia couldn't afford their own copy of Smith's anthology, but a friend owned one. "We would visit her apartment constantly with hungry ears," Hunter recalled. "When she was at work, we'd jimmy the lock to her apartment or crawl through the window if the latch was open. Had to hear those records." Garcia was enthralled: "For me it was the Harry Smith anthology that showed me that there was this vital, rich, primitive form with all these guys sawing away on their fiddles and banjos and singing in these creaky old voices. That was very exciting for me." The anthology's entire package—recordings, liner notes, and cover art—became a talisman for Hunter and Garcia. It connected them to what Greil Marcus would later call Smith's "invisible republic"—a shadow world of obscure heroes, rogues, doomed love affairs, suicides, murderous exploits, and half-forgotten legends. Riffing on what Kenneth Rexroth had called the old, free America, Marcus also called this realm the Old, Weird America. For a young Bob Dylan, that nation and its strangeness practically defined folk music, which Dylan described as "roses growing right up out of people's hearts . . . seven years of this and eight years of that, and it's all really something that nobody can touch."

Harry Smith eventually befriended Allen Ginsberg and Patti Smith, donated his enormous paper-airplane collection to the Smithsonian Institution's National Air and Space Museum, served as shaman-in-residence at the Naropa Institute, earned a Grammy for lifetime achievement, and received $10,000 per year for living expenses from the Grateful Dead's charitable foundation. But for Garcia and Hunter in the late 1950s, Smith's weirdness was all. They were astonished that such music had been made in America within living memory, and they explored it ardently. When Hunter eventually turned to songwriting, Smith's invisible republic became a touchstone.

• • •

Harry Smith's anthology was strange, but it was Hunter's part-time work that truly pushed back the frontiers of weirdness. He volunteered as a government test subject at Stanford, where he ingested psychoactive drugs under clinical conditions. The drugs were quite pure, Hunter recalled: "I have *never* had better acid than they gave me, or better mescaline, or better psilocybin—boy, *they* had the stuff!" The experience proved to be a revelation. "I, for the first time on this earth of all men, finally realized the *full* truth of just what was going on, you know, the powers of the mind," Hunter recalled. When a clinician came to draw blood and test his motor skills, Hunter was overwhelmed. "I was sitting in the chair, and he was running these tests, and suddenly great tears starting running down my face. He asked me what was happening, and I explained to him that I wasn't crying; that I was inhabiting the body of this great green Buddha who had a pool in his lap, and the pool was running through my eyes."

Like Huxley, Hunter wanted to write about these experiences, but unlike his precursor, he was unaware of the experiment's true purpose. "I couldn't figure out why they were paying me to take these psychedelics," Hunter recalled. "What they wanted to do was check if I was more hypnotizable when I was on them. It was hard to pay attention to what the hell they were talking about, much less be hypnotized." The CIA, which sponsored much of the early research on psychedelic drugs, concluded that they weren't helpful in extracting state secrets from foreign agents. But the US military, which had dosed a willing Robert Duncan with mescaline in the early 1950s, still thought psychedelics could be used to pacify enemy populations, perhaps by spiking water supplies or spraying the drugs in aerosol form.

If Hunter's personal project was Dionysian, a new version of Arthur Rimbaud's systematic derangement of the senses, the Pentagon's mission was both Apollonian and Martian. Certainly the officer in charge of developing chemical weapons regarded his research program as the height of enlightened warfare. The alternative to these weapons, he noted in a 1959 magazine article, would be even more savage:

> I do not contend that driving people crazy—even for a few hours—is a pleasant prospect. But warfare is never pleasant. And to those who feel that any kind of chemical weapon is more horrible than conventional weapons, I put this question: Would you rather be temporarily deranged, blinded, or paralyzed by a chemical agent, or burned alive by a conventional fire bomb?

So went the dark logic of the Cold War. When it came to the arms race, the US government wasn't taking any chances, except with the minds of its test subjects. Meanwhile, the Pentagon was funding a vast array of other research programs, including the development of more powerful nuclear weapons, in the San Francisco Bay Area. The drug research was a tiny part of this effort, but it produced the most unlikely outcome of all. In less than a decade, this exotic form of defense spending would ignite the 1960s counterculture.

Curious about Hunter's experience, Garcia and David Nelson took him out for coffee and pressed him for details. Hunter reported only one hallucination—a chair had barked at him. But another illusion was more nightmarish. He imagined that a demon was chasing him with a dagger. Finally Hunter faced his assailant, wrested the dagger out of his hand, stabbed himself in the heart, and licked the blood off the dagger. "God," Garcia said, "I've *got* to have some of that."

At a Chateau party in the fall of 1959, Garcia met Phil Lesh, who was studying music at the nearby College of San Mateo. Lesh found Garcia singing folk songs, but when Lesh identified himself as a jazz musician, Garcia offered to introduce him to other members of the Palo Alto jazz scene. A Berkeley native and jazz trumpeter, Lesh had already befriended fellow student Bobby Petersen, whom Lesh described as a "mad beatnik" and "a product of the quasi-criminal subculture." Petersen was born in Oregon, grew up in Sacramento, and served time in the state prison system for robbery. He also introduced Lesh to marijuana and a wide range of twentieth-century literature.

After his junior-college stint, Lesh enrolled at the University of California, Berkeley, to continue his music studies. There he met pianist Tom Constanten, who shared Lesh's interest in avant-garde composition. Uninspired by the program's emphasis on musicology, Lesh quickly dropped out and began auditing the graduate-level composition course at Mills College in Oakland. Lesh's teacher there was Luciano Berio, whose experimental compositions and pioneering work in electronic music were attracting notice in the avant-garde community. When Berio became composer in residence at the Ojai Festival in 1962, Lesh traveled south to mix the tape sections of *Differences*, Berio's piece for chamber quintet and tape.

Lesh and Constanten hoped to study with Berio in Europe, but Lesh's plan perished for lack of funds, and Berio went on to teach at Juilliard and Harvard. Drawing liberally from literature, linguistics, and ethnomusicology, Berio's writings stressed music's immateriality and impermanence. Precisely because music didn't endure beyond its own performance, he argued, musical institutions became "shrines to memory." The rapid development of recording technology was an important step in that direction. Recordings enhanced musical memory and durability, but Berio claimed that they had two other important effects as well. First, recordings created a kind of "acoustic amnesia," a separation of music from the culture that produced it. Second, they enabled bold experimentation by composers, who could use technology to combine and transform received materials. Berio's teaching simultaneously privileged the moment of performance and emphasized the experimental possibilities afforded by technology. Neither insight was lost on Lesh.

Back in Berkeley, Lesh also volunteered at KPFA, where he learned about microphones, control boards, and tape manipulation. KPFA famously aired unorthodox political views throughout the McCarthy era, but the station also featured experimental music and established a studio at the San Francisco Tape Music Center. Founded in 1961, the Tape Music Center explored combinations of avant-garde musical techniques, especially improvisation, with new forms of technology. It was closely connected to other local art groups, especially after cofounder Ramon Sender and his colleagues decided that every concert would be a collaboration with some other group in the city. The Tape Music Center's first event was Robert Duncan's *Halloween Masque,* which also featured Jess Collins's paintings. The center went on to work with the San Francisco Mime Troupe, which produced politically edgy outdoor plays in the commedia dell'arte tradition. Yet another Tape Music Center happening, *City Scale,* transported the audience in trucks through a car ballet in North Beach, a trombone performance in the Broadway tunnel, a light show in the Mission, and a book-returning ceremony at City Lights. (The ceremony was atonement for all the books that had been lifted from the store since its opening.) The purpose of *City Scale,* Ramon Sender said, was to encourage the audience to wonder whether a particular event was staged or occurring naturally. That theme reflected the San Francisco art scene's heavy emphasis on both improvisation and audience participation.

In addition to its work with the Tape Music Center, KPFA produced a popular folk music program called *The Midnight Special.* Senior board operators were unwilling to give up their Saturday nights to produce the live show, and Lesh landed the job. At a Palo Alto party in 1964, Lesh suggested to Garcia that they produce a demo tape for the program, which soon hosted a segment called "The Long Black Veil and Other Ballads: An Evening with Jerry Garcia." The title referred to a 1959 country song, first recorded by Lefty Frizzell, which became a staple in Garcia's growing repertoire. The KPFA appearance raised Garcia's profile among Bay Area bluegrass players and helped consolidate his partnership with Lesh.

Despite his various activities, Lesh was restless. He and Constanten took jobs in Las Vegas, where Constanten's stepfather worked at the Sands Hotel, to raise cash for their European studies with Berio. When that plan dissolved, Lesh returned to the Bay Area and moved into the Chateau. Garcia, who was living in the pump room, impressed Lesh with his banjo playing. "He would walk around the Chateau in the afternoon playing the most astonishing shit," Lesh recalled, "and *he never seemed to repeat himself.*" After the owner sold the property, Lesh shared a house in Palo Alto with another former Chateau resident, Page Browning. During this time, Lesh developed a reputation as an avant-garde wild man. "Lesh lived down the street with a friend of my brother," recalled Peter Albin, who later played for Big Brother & the Holding Company. "I'd go over there and see these charts that Lesh had written. I couldn't believe this weird shit. Like a symphony for fifty guitars. They were all circular. It was a circular chart. A bizarre-looking thing. How do you read this?"

One of Page Browning's friends, Ken Kesey, was a student in the creative writing program at Stanford University. Kesey grew up on a dairy farm in Springfield, Oregon, where he read westerns, watched John Wayne movies, and became a high school wrestling champion. He married his girlfriend, whom he'd met in junior high school, enrolled at the University of Oregon, and studied journalism and theater. At Stanford, his unusually gifted classmates included Larry McMurtry, Edward Abbey, Wendell Berry, Robert Stone, and Thomas McGuane. Under the direction of novelist Wallace Stegner, many of them were busily reimagining the literary West, which for generations had been dominated by frontier myth and legend. Kesey's fiction fit that larger project, and his first published novel, *One Flew Over the Cuckoo's Nest,* became a commercial and critical success in 1962.

Kesey's relationships at Stanford were volatile, in part because he was determined to be the star of the program. "Ken was a competitive writer when I first met him," Larry McMurtry recalled. "He really had to be the stud duck." Kesey was capable of irking his teachers, too. In a later interview, he claimed that Wallace Stegner's soft berth at Stanford had dulled his talent. Stegner never forgave him. A popular teacher whose work and outlook were more traditional than Kesey's, Stegner had no problem with Kesey's fiction but took a dim view of his "extracurricular activities." Those activities shifted into high gear when Kesey volunteered to ingest psychedelic drugs under clinical conditions at the local VA hospital. He later described the routine.

> Eight o'clock every Tuesday morning I showed up at the vets' hospital in Menlo Park, ready to roll. The doctor deposited me in a little room on his ward, dealt me a couple of pills or a shot or a little glass of bitter juice, then locked the door. He checked back every forty minutes to see if I was still alive, took some tests, asked some questions, left again. The rest of the time I spent studying the inside of my forehead, or looking out the little window in the door.

Despite the sterile, almost nightmarish setting, Kesey valued the experience. After completing the tests, he became a night attendant in the hospital's psychiatric ward. Soon he and his bohemian friends were regularly tripping on LSD and other psychoactive drugs.

Kesey drew on his hospital experience to produce *Cuckoo's Nest*. Narrated from the perspective of Chief Bromden, a Native American schizophrenic, Kesey's dystopian novel inverted Kerouac's fictional adventures. Its protagonist, Randle P. McMurphy, enters an Oregon mental hospital and immediately challenges its joyless, static, and isolating regime. Like Dean Moriarty, McMurphy is a boisterous rambler. After a conviction for statutory rape, he feigns madness to escape hard labor at a correctional institution. Dulled by medications, his fellow patients slowly rally behind his insurgency. In the end, the emasculating Combine embodied by the Big Nurse defeats McMurphy, but not before he inspires Chief Bromden to escape. To channel his narrator's madness, Kesey wrote the first three pages while under the influence of peyote.

After submitting the manuscript for *Cuckoo's Nest*, Kesey returned to Oregon in the summer of 1961 and began to research his next novel. When he and his wife returned to Palo Alto, they found Neal Cassady, who had recently completed his prison term, in their front yard working on a car. Kesey, whose earlier unpublished novel featured North Beach bohemians, idolized the Beats. "Everybody I knew had read *On the Road,*" Kesey said, "and it opened up the doors to us just the same way drugs did." While Cassady was serving time, Kerouac and Ginsberg drifted back east, leaving Cassady without his usual wingmen. Despite their age difference, Kesey welcomed Cassady into his social circle.

With his earnings from *Cuckoo's Nest*, Kesey bought a home with acreage in La Honda, a tiny burg in the nearby coastal mountains, and invited his friends to live and revel in the woods there. Later called the Merry Pranksters, the group was a key part of Kesey's project. Vic Lovell, the psychologist to whom *Cuckoo's Nest* was dedicated, noted that Kesey's charisma was transactional; he needed a group to activate his extraordinary energy. In later interviews, Kesey cast himself as the group's quarterback; he wanted to call the plays and lead the team. In La Honda, the Merry Pranksters began the real drug experiments, this time without VA supervision. It was just as well, Kesey said, since the VA personnel "didn't have the common *balls* to take the stuff themselves." Their adventures would require music, Robert Stone noted later. "Many of the bands came around to provide background music for the strange blending of literary and chemical techniques the Pranksters hoped would lead them beyond the New Beginning to some Dionysian Jerusalem," Stone wrote. "The imminent heaven that seemed to pulse just beneath California's sunny surface might be turned loose by happening on the right magic. Gratuitous grace would abound. Of course, you would need the right music. The bands would be there to provide the anthems."

In 1964, the Merry Pranksters set off on a cross-country trek in a refurbished 1939 school bus called Further (or, less often, Furthur). The official destination was the New York World's Fair. With Cassady at the wheel, the trip was in many ways a reenactment of Kerouac's adventures in *On the Road*, but there were important differences. The Pranksters' journey wouldn't feed Kesey's fiction; instead, Kesey planned to produce a film from the footage shot on the trip. Another difference was pharmaceutical. Along with red wine, speed, and marijuana—Kerouac's drugs of choice—the Pranksters brought LSD and other psychedelics. Their modus operandi was also more theatrical and high-tech than the subterranean Beat style. Wired for sound, brimming with equipment, and painted with swirling Day-Glo colors, Further created a scene wherever it went. Finally, the Pranksters' enterprise was more communal than Kerouac's. The Beats were a band of brothers, the Pranksters a psychedelic tribe on the move, and the active presence of women tempered the homosocial and homoerotic aspects of the Beat scene. On the bus, the romantic pairings shifted frequently as the Pranksters performed an extended heterosexual square dance.

When the Pranksters finally arrived in New York City, Cassady introduced Kesey to Kerouac and Ginsberg. The alcoholic Kerouac wasn't inspired by their craziness, one Prankster noted, and another found him "kind of a sad character." But Kesey cast the encounter in heroic terms. "We had been accepted by the old gunfighters," he said. "These are the real heavies in our mythologies—Kerouac, Cassady, Ginsberg." The World's Fair was also anti-climactic. Dedicated to the future, the event would soon become passé, and the tripping Pranksters made filming difficult by scattering themselves over the fairgrounds. While they were in New York, Ginsberg referred Kesey to Timothy Leary, the Harvard psychologist who was working with Ginsberg to promote the spiritual and artistic uses of psychedelics. The Pranksters pointed the bus to Millbrook, the mansion outside of Poughkeepsie, where Leary and his community were living. But the reception there was somber. The East Coast spiritual scientists wanted nothing to do with the West Coast revelers, who set off a smoke bomb in the driveway upon their arrival. Disappointed by the subdued tone of the encounter, Kesey and the Pranksters loaded up the bus and returned to the Bay Area.

In effect, Kesey and the Pranksters had reversed the direction of Kerouac's mythical quest. Instead of heading west, they brought their provincial exuberance to the nation's cultural center with mixed results. Decades later, Kesey reflected on his group's drug adventures, which he compared to exploring a new frontier. "I thought this was as American as you could get because we were exploring a new territory—just the same way we went to the moon or sent the Lewis and Clark expedition here to Oregon," he said. In his view, that impulse "was part of our American personality," and the drugs he ingested "were opening the door to new landscapes" that represented infinite possibility. "You become tremendously excited and want to do what you can to explore it, because you could look around and you saw that there weren't human footprints all over this landscape." In Kesey's view, this frontier experience was the key to his work. "All of the themes in my work have to do with America," he said. "Traveling across this land, coming to this edge, and then what?"

Kesey's question tapped one of the deepest wellsprings of American identity. Beginning with Frederick Jackson Turner, some US historians had argued that the frontier was the hallmark of American culture, and that its disappearance at the end of the nineteenth century represented a kind of national identity crisis. Countless authors, journalists, illustrators, and painters had capitalized on the frontier's mystique, especially as it was vanishing, and its appeal helped make Buffalo Bill Cody, creator of the popular Wild West exhibition, an international celebrity. In the twentieth century, artists responded to the frontier's disappearance in various ways. Ansel Adams's wilderness photography, for example, gave little indication that the frontier had closed at all. In contrast, Kesey's breakthrough novel dramatized the crisis; the mental hospital and the Combine showed what happened when Americans could no longer light out for the territories. But Kesey also supplied the solution to this problem. With the help of LSD, he and the Pranksters discovered a new psychic territory to explore, thereby refreshing the frontier ethic and America's core identity.

Younger than Kesey and the Pranksters, Garcia and his friends tried in vain to crash their parties on Perry Lane, the bohemian neighborhood near Stanford University where the acid dropped freely. When a fellow roommate said he could score some LSD, Garcia and David Nelson pooled their money with friends who also hadn't tripped before. They ingested capsules with white powder and wandered off before reconvening. "Everybody looks like animals," Nelson observed. "Like the human version of their animal." The swarthy Garcia resembled a brown bear, and Ruppenthal looked like a swan or goose. Later that evening, the group decided to play basketball. The ball had a jet trail about six feet long, Nelson recalled. "It made it easier to hit the basket and definitely easier to catch. Because it had this trail, you could see like a big pointer. It was like Disneyland. It was the first-time realization that we could go to Disneyland anytime, man."

Still high later that night, they wondered whether they might be in danger. They decided to visit Hunter, who was experienced with LSD. They woke him and explained their situation. "Are you always in the habit of jumping out of planes without parachutes?" Hunter asked. They looked at each another anxiously. "No, no," Hunter said. "Relax. Sit down." Ruppenthal was relieved. "Everything was okay," she recalled later. "That revelation saved our lives."

In 1964, the same year Kesey and the Pranksters pointed Further toward New York City, Garcia undertook an odyssey of his own. He and fellow folkie Sandy Rothman drove to Indiana to meet their hero, Bill Monroe, the father of bluegrass music. Garcia and Monroe seemed to have little in common. Born in Kentucky in 1911, Monroe grew up in a farming community a world away from the San Francisco docks and peninsula suburbs. Unlike the affable Garcia, Monroe could be aloof and prone to grudges, but his distinctive music—rooted in Appalachian fiddle tunes, blues, church music, and ballads from the British Isles— appealed to the young Californian. Monroe's band, the Blue Grass Boys, supported his high lead vocal lines and mandolin with close harmonies and fiddle, banjo, guitar, and upright bass. By the time Garcia and Roth-man set out, two of Monroe's former sidemen, Lester Flatt and Earl Scruggs, were enjoying commercial success as the Foggy Mountain Boys. Riding the crest of the folk revival, Flatt and Scruggs recorded "The Ballad of Jed Clampett," the theme song for *The Beverly Hillbillies,* a tele-vision comedy about a backwoods Tennessee family that discover oil and move to the luxurious Southern California community. That tune be-came a top country single in 1962.

Garcia's immediate goal was to tape Monroe's music and perhaps play with him; the fantasy was that Monroe would recognize his talent and offer him a job. Hunter and Nelson had moved to Los Angeles to investi-gate the Church of Scientology, and Garcia and Rothman made that city their first stop on their cross-country trek. There they hooked up with the Kentucky Colonels, a bluegrass band heading east to play the Newport Folk Festival and other gigs. Driving east along Route 66, they made their way to Indiana, where Monroe was playing a summer festival. Gar-cia and Rothman spent more than a week there and taped performances, but they never asked to play for or with Monroe. They also made a side trip to Florida and Alabama and were shocked by the racial segregation they witnessed during Freedom Summer. Garcia and Rothman weren't civil rights activists, three of whom would be slain in Mississippi the month after they passed through; but as a precaution, Garcia cut his hair and shaved his goatee, and he later described reactions to their California

license plates and foreign-sounding names as creepy. Garcia and Rothman also made stops in New York City, Massachusetts, Ohio, and Pennsylvania, where Garcia met David Grisman, a mandolin player from New
Jersey. Finally Garcia told Rothman that he needed to return to the Bay
Area, where Sara had given birth to their daughter, Heather.

After his return, Garcia landed a job transcribing Lenny Bruce's
stand-up performances. The controversial comedian had been charged
with obscenity, and his attorneys used the transcripts to defend him.
Bruce kept those lawyers busy; in two years, he was arrested fifteen
times in various cities, leading one irreverent San Francisco nightclub
manager to waive the cover charge for patrolmen in uniform. In the
end, Bruce won a landmark victory in San Francisco, where he was prosecuted for using the word *cocksucker* onstage at the Jazz Workshop in
North Beach. But in April 1964, Bruce was busted twice in Greenwich
Village and defended himself in the six-month trial. Despite support
from Woody Allen, Norman Mailer, Bob Dylan, and James Baldwin,
Bruce was convicted.

Meanwhile, Bruce was writing his autobiography, *How to Talk Dirty
and Influence People*. *Playboy* magazine, which ran excerpts, hired editor
and satirist Paul Krassner to work with Bruce on the manuscript. When
Krassner first met the comedian, who was a heavy drug user, he noticed
that Bruce typically shot up in the hotel bathroom with the door closed.
Over time, however, Bruce began casually injecting himself on the bed
while they chatted. He also sampled the new offerings from the emerging psychedelic scene. Hugh Romney of the Committee, a San Francisco improvisational comedy group, left two hits of LSD in Bruce's
North Beach room along with some DMT, a powerful hallucinogenic.
The accompanying note read, "Please smoke this until the jewels fall out
of your eyes." After ingesting all of it at once, Bruce fell out of the window of his second-floor hotel room, fracturing his pelvis and both ankles. As his legal and health problems mounted, Bruce had trouble
arranging gigs, and when he did, he often bored audiences by rehears-

ing the details of his court cases. Even so, Garcia considered his work on Bruce's behalf part of his informal education. "I learned so much, it was incredible," he said. "What a mind."

Music remained Garcia's focus, however, and he soon formed Mother McCree's Uptown Jug Champions, the latest in a series of makeshift folk and bluegrass bands. This time, Garcia recruited two other Palo Alto friends, Ron McKernan and Bob Weir. Nicknamed Pigpen after the hygienically challenged character in the comic strip *Peanuts*, McKernan was a Lightnin' Hopkins devotee who frequented the black clubs in East Palo Alto clad in a beat-up cowboy hat, motorcycle boots, and greasy clothes. His father, who hosted a rhythm-and-blues radio show in Berkeley, later became an engineer at the Stanford Research Institute (SRI). McKernan developed harmonica and keyboard chops as well as impressive street credentials. Weir was a delicately handsome high school student and space cadet taking guitar lessons from Garcia. A resident of Atherton, a premier peninsula address, Weir struggled in school due to undiagnosed dyslexia. His musical influences, besides Garcia, included Joan Baez and Jorma Kaukonen, a folk and blues guitarist in nearby San Jose. Weir taped Kaukonen's coffeehouse performances, discussed each one with Kaukonen, and studied the tapes at home.

Even as the jug band was coming together, however, the folk revival was in decline. The hottest musical act by far was the Beatles, who in April 1964 occupied the top five slots on the *Billboard* singles chart—an unprecedented achievement. "The Beatles were why we turned from a jug band into a rock-and-roll band," Weir said later. "What we saw them doing was impossibly attractive. I couldn't think of anything else more worth doing." Garcia appreciated the Fab Four's irreverence and penchant for fun, not only in their music, but also in their films. "The movies were a big turn-on," Garcia said. "They were making people happy. That happy thing—that's the stuff that counts—was something we could all see right away." The Beatles' songs were too light and clean-cut for Lesh, but the film *A Hard Day's Night,* which he happened to watch with a throng of teenage girls, was another matter. It hit him like "a big soft pillow at about nine hundred miles an hour," Lesh recalled. The audience reaction, which he described as "pink clouds of raw hormonal anguish," also inspired him. "The first thing I did when I got home," he wrote later, "was to take a shower and comb my hair forward over my forehead."

By this time, Lesh was living in San Francisco, where he delivered mail and shared a house with Constanten. He hadn't earned a degree or found a suitable vehicle for his musical aspirations, and throughout that year, he "toiled in a fog of depression and gloom." Some of that gloom was dispelled by the advent of LSD.

> I was twenty-four years old, a college dropout with no girlfriend, working at a nowhere job, not making music of any kind. The Kennedy assassination had hit me hard, and I was feeling very much at loose ends. I was definitely in the proper frame of mind, looking for a change, anything, when one day after work I was handed a foil-wrapped cube by one of my coworkers. "Here ya go," he whispered. "Two hundred fifty mikes."

For Lesh, who split the dose with Constanten, LSD was a turning point. With his first psychedelic experience, his depression lifted, and he sought out less solitary forms of creative activity. At that point, Lesh recalled, "Things started happening." His classmate at Mills College, Steve Reich, was composing for the San Francisco Mime Troupe, and Lesh began to contribute music to their performances.

Another turning point for Lesh was Garcia's decision, prompted by McKernan in 1965, to form an electric blues band called the Warlocks. Much to the disappointment of his folk and bluegrass friends, Garcia switched to electric guitar. "I gotta make a buck," he told his brother. Garcia tapped Weir to handle the rhythm guitar duties and recruited drummer Bill Kreutzmann, another Palo Alto youngster, whose station wagon could accommodate their equipment. Kreutzmann was no folkie; he played with a rhythm-and-blues band that covered James Brown and Ray Charles at local dances. Like Garcia, he was already married, a father, and an instructor at the local music store. Although he was still too young to enter bars, Kreutzmann handled the band's business arrangements and dealt with club owners. To avoid problems, he carried a fake draft card under the name Bill Sommers.

The Warlocks began to play local gigs, but Garcia wasn't satisfied with the lineup. In between sets at Magoo's, a Menlo Park pizza parlor, he asked Lesh to join the band as its bass player. Lesh agreed on the condition that Garcia give him a lesson, which Garcia furnished at his home while Sara and Heather slept in the other room. "See this guitar, man? The bottom four strings on the guitar are tuned the same as the four strings of the bass, so borrow a guitar from somebody and practice scales on it until you can get down here, and we'll start rehearsing."

Recruiting Lesh was a bold move on Garcia's part. By replacing the band's original bassist, whose father was his employer at the music store, Garcia risked his paltry income and even his guitar, which was a loaner from the store. One of Garcia's boyhood friends, Marshall Leicester, considered that move especially significant. "Jerry took a real leap there," he said. "I remember some of us chicken bourgeois types being afraid he'd lose his job at Morgan's by firing his boss's son. But Lesh was adamant about that. I think some of us went to Phil at one point and said, 'Would you back off a little? We're worried about whether Jerry's going to be able to survive.' And Lesh said, 'No way. I've waited too long for this.'"

At the time, Garcia's aspiration and Lesh's resolve outstripped their musical skills. Still learning to play their instruments, the Warlocks deferred to McKernan's showmanship. "Pigpen was the only guy in the band who had any talent when we were starting out," Garcia said later. "He was the guy who really sold the band, not me or Weir. Back then, Weir was almost completely spaced; he was just barely there. And I was crazy. I could talk to anybody until hell froze over, but I wasn't really what made the band work. Pigpen is what made the band work." Even with McKernan, however, the Warlocks weren't ready for prime time. Scheduled to play for two nights at Frenchy's Bikini-A-Go-Go in the East Bay backwater of Hayward, the Warlocks opened before a crowd of three, two of them their female friends. After marching through their limited repertoire, the band returned the next night to discover that management had replaced them with an elderly trio playing clarinet, upright bass, and accordion.

Over the next several months, the Warlocks cleared one forgettable venue after another before landing a steady gig at the In Room, a bar in the peninsula suburb of Belmont. Performing six nights per week and five sets per night, they began experimenting with long jams. Lesh's jazz background encouraged that experimentation, and after watching bluegrass fiddler Scotty Stoneman stretch a number to twenty minutes at a live performance, Garcia was transported. "That's the first time I had the experience of being high," Garcia said, "getting high from him, going away from it like, 'What happened?' and just standing there clapping till my hands were sore." And because more was always better, the Warlocks pushed the concept further. One night, they played Wilson Pickett's "In the Midnight Hour" for an entire forty-five-minute set.

LSD changed the way the Warlocks lived and made music. In between gigs, most of them tripped freely. Only McKernan, who preferred alcohol, refrained. As the band's front man, he served as its anchor; when the drugs kicked in, the other musicians knew they could take their cues from him. Garcia later recalled the way LSD, which was still legal, satisfied his appetite for new and intense experience: "When LSD hit the streets finally, that was like, 'You're looking for more? Here it is. This is more. This is more than you can imagine.'" LSD also altered his ideas about the future. "After that, for me, in my life, there was no turning back. There was no back, not just a turning back, but the idea of backness was gone. It was like all directions were forward from there."

The Warlocks talked enthusiastically about their LSD experiences; under its influence, they claimed, they could see through people. But energy and irreverence were their most striking qualities. "When I first saw the Warlocks, they came in like a band of Gypsies, long hair flowing and wearing crazy clothes," said one contemporary, Sam Salvo. "I had been around musicians in bars for a few years by that time, but they were like none I had ever seen. Even the crew had this wild energy about them, and they all seemed to be in their own world." Salvo also recalled their playful performances. "I remember them playing the Rolling Stones song 'Get Off of My Cloud,' except they reworded that line to 'Hey, you, get the fuck off of my cow.'" The first two sets would be fine, another spectator recounted; by the third, the band was high. By the fifth set, they were "barbaric."

While the Warlocks were playing the In Room, they auditioned for a San Francisco hippie commune called the Family Dog, a quartet of young people—Luria Castell, Ellen Harmon, Alton Kelley, and Jack Towle—who were determined to host dance concerts in the city. They approached Ralph J. Gleason, the *San Francisco Chronicle* music critic, with their idea in October 1965. The forty-eight-year-old Gleason was a respected observer of the local scene. A graduate of Columbia University and former contributor to *Down Beat* magazine, Gleason had turned his attention to Elvis Presley, Bob Dylan, the Beatles, and the Rolling Stones after many years of astute jazz criticism. The city had to give young people a place to dance, Kelley told Gleason. "That's what's wrong with the Cow Palace shows," he said, referring to the Daly City venue where the Beatles played in 1964. "The kids can't dance there."

By that time, the Family Dog had also connected with the Charlatans, who were headed by George Hunter. Though not an accomplished musician, Hunter was an influential tastemaker who relished the Victorian era and its look. A native of Southern California, he found life as a beatnik difficult at Canoga Park High School and followed a girlfriend to San Francisco State College, where he tried to assemble a futuristic band of men and women with identical outfits and haircuts. While standing in an unemployment line, Hunter met piano player Michael Ferguson, who ran a shop on Divisadero Street called the Magic Theater for Madmen Only, where he sold Victorian knickknacks, pipes, cigarette papers, and weed. "George was the first hippie I ever saw in San Francisco," Ferguson said. "George was the one who turned everyone on at San Francisco State, and he turned on the Haight."

In the summer of 1965, the Charlatans landed a long-term gig in an unlikely location: Virginia City, Nevada, a silver-mining town that Mark Twain had featured almost a century earlier in *Roughing It*. A small group of music and LSD enthusiasts refurbished the Comstock House, a decrepit gambling hall, and dubbed their new venue the Red Dog Saloon. To recruit musical talent, the bartender traveled to San Francisco and discovered two members of the Charlatans on the street in North Beach. "Are you the Byrds?" he asked, mistaking them for the Los Angeles group that had scored a hit with Bob Dylan's "Mr. Tambourine Man" earlier that year. The Charlatans saw an opportunity, and the proto-hippies spent the summer in vintage drag playing music, dancing, and tripping on the arid eastern slope of the Sierra Nevada mountain range.

Hunter and Ferguson lined up carpenters to build a stage and expand the room. "We completely decorated the place," Hunter said. "We brought rugs and Victorian tapestries from the city. We were re-creating the Wild West, pretending it had never gone away." To complete the tableau, the revelers also carried loaded pistols, at least one of which was discharged in the saloon. Alton Kelley created the first psychedelic poster, eventually known as *The Seed*, to promote the Charlatans at the Red Dog Saloon. Kesey and the Pranksters loaded up the bus to investigate, but by the time they arrived, the summer mayhem was coming to a close. After an extended psychoactive party, the saloon's owner padlocked the club. No one suspected that the Red Dog Saloon experience would be the first of three ecstatic summers with far-reaching consequences for San Francisco's arts scene.

That fall, the Family Dog began hosting weekend house parties at their San Francisco digs at 2125 Pine Street. When those parties outgrew their home, they began booking union halls. In October, the Family Dog hosted the first adult rock dance at Longshoremen's Hall, which the ILWU had built near Fisherman's Wharf in 1958. The event, "A Tribute to Dr. Strange," featured the Charlatans, Jefferson Airplane, and the Great Society, which included Grace Slick, the sultry-voiced debutante and model who chose San Francisco bohemia over high society. One of the organizers, Chet Helms, borrowed a strobe light from the Tape Music Center to heighten the visual effects. "About four hundred or five hundred people showed up—it was *such* a revelation," Kelley recalled. "Everybody was walking around with their mouths open, going, 'Where did all these freaks come from? I thought my friends were the only guys around!'" Avant-garde composer Ramon Sender recalled that the participants were "also, now, getting more *ecstatically* dressed." According to Ralph Gleason, the apparel that night ranged from "velvet Lotta Crabtree to Mining Camp Desperado, Jean Lafitte leotards, I. Magnin Beatnik, Riverboat Gambler, India Imports Exotic to Modified Motorcycle Rider Black Leather-and-Zippers."

The Family Dog wanted their events to be profitable, but the communards bore no resemblance to the businessmen who had promoted such dances and concerts. "They entered into the occasion as participants, not as organizers," Gleason noted. "They danced along with the rest. Luria Castell's Benjamin Franklin glasses were misty with perspiration, her long beads swung around her heaving bosom and a gown designed for the nineties trailed on the floor as she danced." After the dance, Gleason drove back to Berkeley and noted the caravan of cars packed with long-haired youth, their Volkswagens festooned with

SNCC and Free Speech Movement bumper stickers. It was the same weekend as the Berkeley Vietnam Day March to the Oakland induction center. Lawrence Ferlinghetti, Robert Duncan, and Michael McClure read to the crowd before the march, Kesey and the Pranksters were on hand, and Country Joe McDonald sang from a flatbed truck with the Instant Action Jug Band. The Hells Angels were also there—to assault the peace marchers as they tried to cross the Oakland city limit.

The Warlocks weren't invited to play at Longshoremen's Hall, but when the Family Dog convened another show two weeks later featuring the Lovin' Spoonful and the Charlatans, the Warlocks were in attendance. Having spent the afternoon stoned on Mount Tamalpais in Marin County, they heard about the event on their car radio and were eager to participate. After their arrival, Lesh pulled Luria Castell aside and said, "Lady, what this little séance needs is us." He had a point, but the converse was also true. The Warlocks had learned as much as they could from their steady gig at the In Room. Toward the end of their run there, the club's manager offered a prediction: "You guys will never make it. You're too weird."

In December 1965, that weirdness found its ideal audience. The Pranksters' Saturday-night parties had outgrown Kesey's La Honda home, and they decided to initiate a series of off-site events called the Acid Tests. (For their psychedelic project, the Pranksters repurposed the Gold Rush–era term for distinguishing gold from other metals.) The first Acid Test took place in Santa Cruz and was smaller than intended. Looking for ways to increase the turnout, Page Browning suggested that Kesey meet with the Warlocks. The band had missed most of Kesey's parties because they were working almost nightly. But after they were fired from their steady gig, Browning arranged a confab at Kesey's house, and the Warlocks were invited to the second Acid Test in San Jose. Performing in a small living room, they played too loudly for comfort, and the host tried to charge them for the electricity they used. But the Pranksters welcomed their experimentation, and the Warlocks appreciated the opportunity to hang out with Neal Cassady. The San Jose event also drew several new faces, including Jann Wenner, a student at the University of California, Berkeley.

The *San Jose Mercury* cast the Acid Test as a "drug orgy," but Lesh realized that the combination of LSD and music was the tool he was seeking. Garcia was more ambivalent, at least at the outset. "Actually, Jerry didn't love that scene up there at Kesey's right away," recalled Tiff Garcia. "It took him a while to fit into it. He was always telling me, 'These people are up there in the woods getting ripped and doing this . . .' Like it was beneath him to do that." Garcia's wife, Sara, was also leery, in part because of the other guests. While researching his Hells Angels book, Hunter S. Thompson introduced Kesey to the San Francisco chapter of the motorcycle gang, and after attending an epic wingding at La Honda, some of its members became regulars at Kesey's parties. As a young mother protective of her family life, Ruppenthal gave those events a wide berth. "The idea of dealing with motorcycle gang members while stoned on acid was not my idea of fun," she said.

Later, Garcia noted the differences between his friends and Kesey's. "We were younger than the Pranksters. We were wilder. We weren't serious college people. We were on the street," he said. "But they liked us because we were so out there. Our music scared them. It scared them at first, but then as soon as they realized it was not going to hurt them, they liked it. Like a scary roller coaster." Despite their differences, the Warlocks appreciated the Pranksters' support. "They were our first and best audience," Garcia recalled. "They were the first ones to get off on us." The two groups had a great deal in common. Both had absorbed the Beat emphasis on adventure and intense experience. Both were uninterested in the straight world and uninspired by the folk world's leftist pieties. Members of each were married and had families, but they were also attracted to communal life. Finally, both groups enjoyed partying with the Hells Angels, who were even scarier and less collegiate than the Warlocks.

Garcia especially relished the spontaneity and open-endedness of the Acid Tests. "When it was moving right, you could dig that there was something that it was going toward, something like ordered chaos, or some *region* of chaos," he said. "Everybody would be high and flashing and going through insane changes during which everything would be *demolished*, man, and spilled and broken and affected, and after that, another thing would happen, maybe smoothing out the chaos, then another, and it'd go all night till morning." No one mistook the events for musical performances, and Garcia appreciated that freedom. "It wasn't a *gig*, it was the Acid Tests, where everything was okay." The chaos offered the band an extraordinary opportunity—the chance to fail safely. Because it wasn't a show as such, they could try anything without fear of ruining the moment. As one insider noted later, the freedom to fuck up was a gift they accepted from the Acid Tests.

Soon after the San Jose Acid Test, Lesh discovered that another band was recording as the Warlocks, and the group met at his house to develop a new name. Garcia, who had smoked DMT earlier that day, began flipping through a Funk & Wagnalls dictionary and discovered the term *grateful dead*, which denotes a common folklore theme; in it, the hero facilitates the proper burial of a corpse and later accomplishes an impossible task with the help of the dead man's spirit. "Everything else on the page went blank, diffuse, just sort of oozed away," Garcia recalled, "and there was *Grateful Dead*, big black letters edged all around in gold, man, blasting out at me, such a stunning combination." Weir thought the name was too morbid, but Lesh loved it, and the band accepted Garcia's suggestion.

As the Acid Test house band, the Grateful Dead now had a profile, and the next two months were especially important to the band's development. Six days after the San Jose Acid Test, the Dead played a benefit for the San Francisco Mime Troupe, whose members had been convicted for performing in a park without a permit. Their real offense, many felt, was disturbing members of the park commission with their frank and politically oriented theater. Unable to pay their attorney, the Mime Troupe decided to host an Appeal Party to raise money. The first benefit was held in the troupe's Howard Street loft and featured Lawrence Ferlinghetti, Allen Ginsberg, and Jefferson Airplane. That event exceeded expectations, and a second one was scheduled for the Fillmore Auditorium at 1805 Geary Boulevard. Built in 1910 in what had since become a predominantly African-American neighborhood, the Fillmore served as a dance school and roller-skating rink before hosting rhythm-and-blues acts in the early 1950s. The Fillmore benefit received extra publicity when Bob Dylan, who was in the Bay Area for a series of concerts, held up the promotional poster at his San Francisco press conference.

The Mime Troupe's manager, Bill Graham, organized the benefits. A refugee from Nazi Germany and a New York City transplant, Graham had a long-standing interest in music and theater nurtured by his stint as a Borscht Belt waiter in the Catskill Mountains. Despite his work with the Mime Troupe, he was largely unprepared for the emergent San Francisco counterculture. When the Family Dog said they wanted to help with the benefit, Graham was agreeable. But when they arrived, he asked them where their dogs were; he had assumed they were an animal act.

The Fillmore benefit drew several spectators who became mainstays in the Dead community. One was Rock Scully, a graduate student at San Francisco State College who was also promoting the Charlatans. His partner, Danny Rifkin, ran a rooming house at 710 Ashbury Street, where Luria Castell lived before forming the Family Dog commune. Scully and Rifkin had scheduled a Family Dog event on the night of the Mime Troupe benefit, but they also wanted to check out the Dead at the Fillmore. Scully liked what he saw. "The band went on, and this fierce-looking biker-guy dude, Pigpen, got up there and started belting out these blues," Scully recalled. "Garcia was also high. His eyes were all dilated. He started to swoop around the room with his picking. . . . He was running all over the place. Pig was trying to be the leader and bring them back."

Garcia's guitar work made a deep impression on Scully. "We'd never seen anyone play like that before," he said. "Jerry was lifting the roof. To be frank about it, we were tripping, so it seemed like there was no roof on the house. Every now and then, he'd look down at his guitar, and I thought he was seeing some kind of monster. He was all surprised, looking over his hand down the neck of his guitar, like, 'Wait a minute. Where is the end of this thing?'" This was no folk festival. "We'll have to wipe the mikes off after they play," Grace Slick commented to a friend. But it wasn't easy to determine when, exactly, their set ended. "Garcia sort of put down his guitar," Scully said, "and everybody kind of ambled offstage and came back to the beer bar. And that was the end of the set."

Also present at the Fillmore benefit was Augustus Owsley Stanley III, who was busily cooking up the Bay Area's best LSD. The grandson of a US senator from Kentucky, Owsley Stanley had studied engineering at the University of Virginia and served in the air force before enrolling at the University of California, Berkeley. He met Melissa Cargill, a chemistry student, and persuaded her to produce one hundred grams of methedrine for a class project. Later, the two were arrested at their Berkeley lab on Virginia Street. The police were looking for methamphetamine but found only its components, which were legal. After recovering their equipment from the police, Stanley and Cargill headed south for Pasadena. There he created a dummy company, the Bear Research Group, and ordered five hundred grams of lysergic acid from a Los Angeles supplier. (One hundred grams was enough to produce 5 million doses.) Stanley paid $20,000 for the first order and soon acquired another three hundred grams. Back in the Bay Area, he introduced himself to Kesey in August 1965, the same day the Beatles performed at the

Cow Palace. He soon became the Pranksters' main LSD supplier. For Stanley, that connection was transformative. "Kesey was the kind of guy that reached out, took your knobs, and tweaked them all the way to ten," Stanley said. "All of them. And the whole scene was running at ten all the time."

Stanley was no stranger to weirdness, but the Grateful Dead's performance at the Fillmore frightened him. "I was standing in the hall, and they were playing, and they scared me to death," he said. "Garcia's guitar terrified me. I had never before heard that much power. That much thought. That much emotion. I thought to myself, 'These guys could be bigger than the Beatles.'" Stanley approached Lesh and said he wanted to work for the band. Lesh said they didn't have a manager, but Stanley demurred. Lesh said they also lacked a sound engineer, and Stanley was hired.

The night after the Fillmore benefit, the Dead played an Acid Test at the Big Beat Club in Palo Alto. Festooned with movie screens, speakers, microphones, strobe lights, and slide projectors, the club had a small stage and a control tower manned by Kesey, who projected images and directed the revelers to *"Get nekkid! Freak freely! Kiss your brains goodbye! Fuck sanity, go crazy!"* After the Dead finished playing, Stanley introduced Scully to the band. In his memoir, Scully recalled that initial encounter in the present tense: "Close up, the bizarre nature of the tatterdemalion group is more glaring than ever. Bob Weir looks like a sixteen-year-old kid who had no business being in a place that serves drinks, much less acid. And with the exception of Pigpen, they are all totally zonked." Stanley mentioned Scully's connection to the Family Dog and recommended him for the position of band manager. By the end of that strange night, Scully had the job.

The San Francisco scene was taking on momentum. The comparatively sedate folk revival and fugitive Beat scene were quickly giving way to something far more psychedelic, spectacular, and ecstatic. Bill Graham saw an opportunity. He urged the Mime Troupe to host benefits on a regular basis, but founder Ronnie Davis was unconvinced, and Graham lost the ensuing vote. He resigned as the Mime Troupe's manager and began promoting his own events.

In January 1966, Graham helped organize the Trips Festival, a three-night happening at Longshoremen's Hall. It was billed as "a non-drug re-creation of psychedelic experience" featuring "the Trip—or electronic performance—a new medium of communication and entertainment." Conceived by Stewart Brand of the Pranksters, Ben Jacopetti of the Open Theater, and Ramon Sender of the Tape Music Center, the Trips Festival combined experimental theater, dance, music, and light shows. In addition to being the largest Acid Test, the Trips Festival featured virtually every significant avant-garde art group in the Bay Area, including the Committee, the San Francisco Mime Troupe, and the Dancers' Workshop. Michael McClure read poetry, and Bruce Conner showed films. It was, according to one music scholar, "a watershed event in the history of the underground arts scene in San Francisco."

Stewart Brand, who had studied at CSFA (by then renamed the San Francisco Art Institute), described the Trips Festival as a brief intersection between that scene and the emerging counterculture. The crowd, however, clearly preferred ecstatic dancing to avant-garde experimentation. The other performances were fine, Brand recalled; people applauded politely, but then they wanted to dance. "It was the beginning of the Grateful Dead and the end of everybody else," Brand said. Ralph Gleason was less charitable about what happened the first night: "Nothing. A bust, a bore, a fake, a fraud, a bum trip." Halfway through the evening, one participant took the microphone and said, "This is a bore even on acid." Later, Gleason overheard someone say, "Let's go out to the car and listen to the radio." But once the music started on Saturday night, the Trips Festival achieved liftoff. "The truth about the Trips Festival is that it was a three-night, weekend-long rock 'n' roll dance with light effects," Gleason observed. "When the dull projections took over, it was nowhere. When the good rock music wailed, it was great."

At least one new art form survived the Trips Festival and even flourished. The light show was pioneered by Seymour Locks, an art professor at San Francisco State College, who used an overhead projector with hollow slides and plastic dishes filled with pigments; by swirling them, he created moving patterns of light that could be projected against a screen or wall. When combined with the Dead's music, the light show at the Trips Festival created a powerful effect. "And so the Grateful Dead was blasting away, and images were blasting away somewhat in sync with them on the wall," Brand said. "That whole aspect of the show was so much more effective than anything else. That's what took off. And so then, within a couple weeks, Bill Graham was taking over the Fillmore and advertising shows that included 'the sights and sounds of the Trips Festival.'"

The light shows were a visual analogue to the blues-based psychedelic rock, and the combined effect at the Trips Festival was especially powerful and transporting. For many spectators, however, the event was most notable not for the music or light shows, but rather for its participatory quality. The Trips Festival was an early opportunity for hippies to see each other at their weirdest. They were energized by their own forms of self-display, which became an integral part of the entertainment. The Dead encouraged that ethic, which blurred the line between performers and spectators, and it quickly became a hallmark of the Haight-Ashbury scene.

The Trips Festival was Graham's first contact with the Pranksters, and his initial reaction was shock. "I remember the Merry Pranksters were there, and they were pretty spaced-out," he said. "Very decent people, but just *out there*. I had not seen the acid thing in full force. That night, I did. It shocked me. They might as well have been offering hand grenades to people." Graham's other reaction was anger, especially when he noticed Kesey admitting people through the back door. "There was a guy standing there in a space suit. A full-body space suit with a helmet on top," Graham recalled. "I ran to him, and I looked at him, and I said, 'Why are you letting these people in? Are they working here?' The space helmet turned toward me with the visor up. . . . He looked at me again, and he just kept on letting people in." Graham's temper flared. "Then I started yelling. I said, *'Would you mind answering me? What the HELL are you doing HERE?'* Inside the helmet, it was Kesey's face. . . . Without saying a single word, he flipped the visor of his space helmet down. That's how we met."

The Trips Festival was also Graham's first encounter with Garcia. Wandering around the venue, Garcia was relishing the chaos: "Everything was going on at once," he recounted. "There was no focus of attention. Everybody was just partying furiously. There were people jumping off balconies into blankets and then bouncing up and down. I mean, there was just *incredible* shit going on." Because the Acid Tests weren't gigs in the normal sense, Garcia felt free to absorb the experience.

> I had some sense that the Grateful Dead was supposed to play sometime maybe. But it really didn't matter. We were used to the Acid Tests, where sometimes we'd play, and sometimes we wouldn't. Sometimes we would get up onstage, play for about five minutes, and all freak out. And *leave*. You know? That was the beauty of it. People weren't coming to see the Grateful Dead, so we didn't feel compelled to perform. If we wanted to, we got together and played. Sometimes it was great. Sometimes it was horrible. Sometimes we freaked out and didn't go through with it.

Garcia spotted Graham, who didn't fit the Acid Test profile: "And here's this guy running around with a clipboard, you know," Garcia recalled. "I mean, in the midst of total insanity. I mean total, wall-to-wall, gonzo lunacy. Everybody in the place is high but Bill." While watching one of the oversize screens, Garcia noticed a message: JERRY GARCIA,

PLUG IN! As Garcia pondered what seemed to be an oddly personal message, it dawned on him that it was time to play. But when he found his guitar, he saw that its bridge had been flattened. He showed the shattered guitar to Graham, who immediately fell to the ground and tried to fix the instrument. "I just thought it was the most touching thing I'd ever seen," Garcia said. "Here's this guy who doesn't know a thing about guitars, and he's trying to fix mine."

For Garcia, the Trips Festival was a peak experience. Despite the chaos, he saw little to fear: "Thousands of people, man, all helplessly stoned, all finding themselves in a roomful of other thousands of people, none of whom any of them were afraid of." He later described the Trips Festival, the largest of the Acid Tests, as "magic, far-out, beautiful magic."

The Family Dog events, Mime Troupe benefits, and Acid Tests launched a new form of ecstatic expression—the rock concert. By the 1970s, its distinctive combination of rock music, light shows, and freestyle dancing was a central and seemingly permanent ritual in American youth culture. In 1964, however, it didn't exist. Even as late as August 1966, when the Beatles performed their last live concert at Candlestick Park, they wore matching suits and tore through their usual twenty-five-minute set. Across town, hippies were creating something far more participatory, open-ended, and transcendent.

The significance of those events wasn't lost on Ralph Gleason, who covered them in his *San Francisco Chronicle* column. In July 1966, he described the Fillmore Auditorium as the city's new center for the performing arts, whether or not most residents were aware of it. In September, he also reviewed a Dead show favorably. Recounting a twenty-minute version of "In the Midnight Hour," Gleason reported that McKernan was the star of the show, "stabbing the phrases out into the crowd like a preacher, using the words to riff like a big band, building to climax after climax, coming down in a release and soaring up again." In Gleason's opinion, McKernan was already one of the best blues singers of his generation, and his performance equaled Mick Jagger's on "Goin' Home." By 1967, Gleason was describing the San Francisco concerts as Dionysian. There was no alarm in his report; to the contrary, he welcomed the innovation and even quoted German philosopher Friedrich Nietzsche on the Athenian festivals and orgiastic movements that left their traces in music. In Gleason's view, the local scene's vitality derived from its unique cultural stew, whose three main ingredients were "the three B's of the Bay Area": Harry Bridges, Berkeley, and the beatniks.

The Dead's shows at the Fillmore Auditorium and Avalon Ballroom were especially festive. "Going to the Fillmore and the Avalon and all those places was probably the most fun I ever had in my life," recalled Florence Nathan, Lesh's girlfriend at the time, who later took the name Rosie McGee. "Considering that I personally probably knew a couple of hundred people at the Fillmore on a given night, the shows seemed more like parties than concerts, and there was a wonderful sense of community, and great music, obviously." Dick Latvala, who later managed the Dead's tape vault, was also swept up by the energy. "I went to shows every night. In '66, I didn't do anything *but* go to shows," he said. "Because I thought, 'This is what I'm supposed to do—take acid and go see this music.'" Garcia appreciated the kinetic, informal vibe. "The best thing about it was that the audience all danced," he recalled. "We were part of that world. We were not performers. We were playing for our family, in a sense. It kind of had that feel, that kind of informality. The times when someone came in and gave a show, it seemed freakish. It was like, 'Well, what's *he* doing up there?'"

As enjoyable as these happenings were for Garcia and others, many besides Graham had trepidations, especially about the drugs. Even Robert Hunter, who missed the first Acid Tests, was dubious. "I wasn't into acid in *that* way, as a show," he said. "I was into it as a kind of personal trip because I'd been through those things at the Stanford Hospital.

I was the only one I knew who had taken the stuff, and I was a bit surprised that they took it to that level." But an epiphany at the Trips Festival converted him.

> I was thinking, "This is hell, this is the worst thing I've ever seen." Then Kesey was writing on an overhead projector, and on the ceiling it said, "Outside is inside, how does it look?" I went "Aaaahhhhhh . . ." because it was true, and I was seeing hell projected out there, and all of a sudden I did that whole little flip around. That's been one of my little guiding mottoes ever since, because it became very, very ecstatic and very groovy after I stopped projecting my own hell out there.

If Hunter considered himself a convert, Owsley Stanley continued to warn Kesey about the Acid Tests. "Hey, you're messing with ancient stuff," Stanley recalled telling Kesey. "And without any maps! You may need to be careful about this." Stanley later offered an anthropological comparison.

> Supposing some guy was a Yanomami Indian or something, and he comes out of the forest for the first time. And the first thing he does is somebody puts him on a roller coaster. He's never even seen civilization, and somebody puts him on a roller coaster. He'll get off that thing and say, "That's very dangerous. That's scary." And yet other people go around and around, again and again and again.

By this time, Kesey's own roller coaster was going off the rails. In 1965, he was arrested twice for marijuana possession; on the second occasion, his girlfriend and fellow Prankster, Carolyn "Mountain Girl" Adams, was also busted on the roof of Stewart Brand's apartment building in North Beach. With his trial date approaching, Kesey staged a fake suicide and departed for Mexico. Adams, who was pregnant with Kesey's child, later joined him and gave birth to their daughter, Sunshine, in Mexico. Adams had already paid a fine for marijuana possession, but Kesey correctly expected tougher treatment for himself. He returned to the United States in 1966, and aided by attorney Patrick Hallinan, whose father had defended Harry Bridges, Kesey spent much of that year preoccupied with his legal problems.

While Kesey and several friends were in Mexico, the remaining Pranksters scheduled more Acid Tests, this time in Los Angeles. With financial support from Stanley, the Dead headed south to play there. Stanley rented a large pink house on Third Avenue, and the musicians were grateful for his help. "It was patronage in the finest sense: he never once thought about the money," Lesh said. "We were able to be the Grateful Dead, and if they hired us, great. But we could at least eat." Stanley also determined what they ate. He believed that humans were natural carnivores and that vegetables caused cancer. Back in the Bay Area, he once complained that his companions were trying to poison him with apple pie. He hadn't had any "plant food" in his system for years, he said, and he predicted that his digestion would be "fucked-up for a month." In Los Angeles, the Dead's diet consisted mostly of steak and milk.

The Dead played seven gigs in Los Angeles, but the most notorious was their second event, the Watts Acid Test, which was held at the Youth Opportunities Center in Compton. For the first time, the Pranksters prepared Kool-Aid spiked with LSD and offered it to their guests without revealing its contents. In fact, the Pranksters accidentally spiked the Kool-Aid twice, and many participants had bad experiences. When the police arrived, they brought the festivities to a close. Amid the commotion, Ruppenthal and Garcia, whose marriage had been on the rocks, decided to split up. After the party, Garcia and Carolyn Adams began chatting for the first time while sweeping out the community center. "We were mostly just bullshitting each other and goofing off and saying funny stuff and commenting on what had been going on," Adams said. "I was eight months pregnant, and I didn't feel very attractive."

On the way back to the house, the band rolled by the Watts Tower, the hundred-foot composite sculpture decorated with found objects. As he pondered it, Garcia had two epiphanies about his own art. First, it would be intangible; it would exist in the moment and leave behind no material artifacts. Second, the Dead would be communal and leaderless. Watching the Pranksters form around Kesey and then crumble without him may have reinforced Garcia's insight; in any case, his epiphany changed his orientation to the Grateful Dead. Paradoxically, the realization that the band should be leaderless helped Garcia focus his efforts. "This isn't strictly recreational," Garcia concluded. "This is really important. And that's when I started paying attention." Rock Scully noticed the change in Garcia's outlook. "He was very professional about it," Scully said. Musically, Lesh was a perfectionist, but it was Garcia who told the band that they had to be on time and play their best. Garcia's emergent professionalism didn't include more attention to their finances. Rather, his goal was to ensure a steady supply of transcendence. While sharing some weed with a group of close friends, he said, "I want to make enough money to stay high like this forever."

The urge to remain leaderless was already in the air, especially after Lesh encouraged the band members to read Theodore Sturgeon's *More Than Human,* a science fiction novel whose characters found they could "blesh" (blend and mesh) their minds to create a superior collective being. The Dead would later compare themselves to Sturgeon's characters and remark on the way LSD helped them produce a single musical mind. "For any reader of science fiction in the early 1960s," one scholar later noted, "this theme would have been difficult to avoid, especially after having been sensitized to it through shared psychedelic experience." At least one Bay Area science fiction writer was also sharing that experience. Philip K. Dick, whose *Man in the High Castle* received the Hugo Award in 1962, experimented with LSD two years later. During his first trip, he imagined he was a Roman gladiator who witnessed Christ being shot to heaven from a crossbow. Dick eventually became a Dead fan and mentioned the band in *VALIS*, the last major work published before his death.

Garcia, Lesh, and Hunter were fascinated by the utopian and dystopian possibilities of science fiction, which was thriving in the Bay Area. The editors of *The Magazine of Fantasy and Science Fiction*, Anthony Boucher and Francis McComas, formed a kind of salon that revolved around a regular poker game; Boucher was also Dick's mentor and hosted an opera program on KPFA. Frank Herbert, Jack Vance, and Poul Anderson worked and socialized in the area as well, making it one of the major forces in science fiction at that time. A fellow musician recounted Garcia's attraction to that genre. "We both loved science fiction," Ozzie Ahlers told Garcia biographer Blair Jackson. "Jerry was very impressed that I'd met Theodore Sturgeon. He wanted to know everything he could about my twenty-minute meeting with him." While traveling with Garcia, Ahlers noticed that Garcia's luggage contained almost no clothing. "He'd just brought two suitcases," Ahlers said, "almost entirely filled with science fiction books."

Kurt Vonnegut, a Garcia favorite, also mined the what-if premise of science fiction. The Dead eventually named their publishing company Ice Nine, after the fictional material at the center of *Cat's Cradle* (1963). Garcia was even more enamored of Vonnegut's *The Sirens of Titan*, which appeared in 1959 and was nominated for a Hugo Award. Decades later, when Garcia had more means, he purchased the novel's film rights. "It's one of the few Vonnegut books that's really sweet, in parts of it, and it has some really lovely stuff in it," Garcia told one interviewer. "It's the range of it that gets me off."

By March 1966, Stanley was running low on cash. He decided to tablet some four thousand hits of LSD in the attic of the pink house and sold some of them to a female acquaintance. Loading them into a peanut butter jar, she took them to Canter's, a popular deli and lounge on Fairfax Avenue. There at "Capsule Corner," she announced to the assembled street dealers—and photographer Lawrence Schiller—that she had acquired a batch of Owsley's finest. *Life's* next cover story, accompanied by Schiller's photographs, appeared under the headline "The Exploding Threat of the Mind Drug That Got Out of Control: LSD." Not especially grateful for that kind of attention, the Dead played their last Los Angeles show and returned to the Bay Area.

While the Dead were away, the San Francisco music and arts scene continued to develop. Jefferson Airplane, the city's most prominent band, became the first to sign a recording contract with a major label. RCA had handled many top acts, including Elvis Presley, but it had no significant presence in the emerging rock scene, and the San Francisco upstarts seemed like a good place to start. Meanwhile, Bill Graham was scheduling regular concerts, as was Chet Helms, who arrived in San Francisco in 1962. A child evangelist at fifteen, Helms became a civil rights activist and joined the Young People's Socialist League at the University of Texas before trying to crack the Beat poetry scene in San Francisco. He turned to organizing jam sessions in his apartment at 1090 Page Street, a six-bedroom Victorian in the Haight. Later, he returned to Austin to fetch his friend Janis Joplin, who, he thought, "would knock these people on their ass." Joplin played Bay Area coffeehouses and even sang on KPFA's *Midnight Special,* but after she developed a nasty methedrine habit, Helms put her on a Greyhound bus bound for Austin. Helms began managing Big Brother & the Holding Company, and when Luria Castell decamped for Mexico, he took over the Family Dog events and later recruited Joplin for Big Brother.

The Haight-Ashbury district, where much of the new artistic energy was centered, also continued to evolve. It was originally an affluent neighborhood of large Victorian homes that survived the 1906 earthquake, but in response to an acute housing shortage after the Second

World War, many homes were divided into flats, and the Haight became a plentiful source of low-cost rental housing, especially for students at nearby San Francisco State College. Many residents also took advantage of the Haight's easy access to Golden Gate Park, with its one thousand acres of woodlands, meadows, lakes, gardens, and recreation areas.

The Haight was to the hippies what North Beach had been to the Beats, but its animating spirit differed from its precursor's. Like the Beats, the hippies valued intense experience, Eastern mysticism, and the redemptive power of nature, but they were less alienated and much more optimistic than their predecessors. By that time, half of America's population was under the age of twenty-five, postwar prosperity had created a significant economic cushion for millions of American families, and higher education in California was virtually free. The Vietnam War, the draft, and the specter of nuclear destruction tempered their optimism, but most young people felt that they could live richer lives than their parents—if not materially, then spiritually. That improvement would begin with social and artistic experiments that reflected their values.

Rock music was an important but by no means the only vehicle for that experimentation. San Francisco writer Richard Brautigan, whose mentor was Jack Spicer, became famous for his experimental novel *Trout Fishing in America*. Composed in 1961, that book appeared in 1967 and sold more than 4 million copies. But the Haight was even better known for its poster art. That medium had been largely dormant since the Second World War, but another serendipitous Bill Graham discovery advanced its development. In 1966, Graham was tacking up promotional posters along Telegraph Avenue in Berkeley when he realized that people were collecting the posters as fast as he was putting them up. Soon Graham was distributing posters for free at his Fillmore Auditorium concerts. To design them, he and Chet Helms turned to the so-called Big Five: Alton Kelley, Wes Wilson, Stanley "Mouse" Miller, Victor Moscoso, and Rick Griffin. Wilson, a former student at San Francisco State College, had designed the promotional materials for both the Trips Festival and the Beatles concert at Candlestick Park. Griffin, a native of Palos Verdes in Southern California, saw the Dead at the Watts Acid Test, migrated north in 1966, and began producing posters for the Family Dog. Of the Big Five, only Moscoso had significant formal training. Having studied at Cooper Union and Yale University, he enrolled at the San Francisco Art Institute, where he later taught.

Taking inspiration from the opulence and decadence of art nouveau posters, the Big Five experimented with intense colors, revolving patterns, and wild typography. They downplayed legibility, long considered the central requirement of poster art, to create hallucinatory effects. The rock poster's broad appeal was an unexpected bonus for Graham and Helms, but for the artists, it was also deeply intentional. Although they were often required to produce posters on a few days' notice, they preferred posters to other forms because their work was displayed quickly and distributed widely. The interest generated by these posters wasn't lost on political activists, who began using posters to promote their benefits (often rock concerts) and other causes. In effect, local San Francisco artists converted a medium traditionally used for government purposes into a vehicle for dissent. Rock posters also exerted a profound effect on album art, thereby consolidating their connection with the music emerging from San Francisco. The artists drew inspiration from various sources, not the least of which was LSD. But many artists also found the Grateful Dead's name a rich source of ideas. "You can throw anything at it," Garcia said in 1987. "That's one of the reasons the artists loved it."

Stanley Mouse was one such artist. The son of a former Disney animator, he arrived in San Francisco from Detroit just as the Trips Festival was getting under way. His friend, Big Brother guitarist Jim Gurley, was Alton Kelley's roommate. Partnering with Kelley, Mouse helped the Dead cultivate their own distinctive iconography. Its key elements were conceived the day Mouse and Kelley entered the San Francisco

Public Library in search of inspiration. Chet Helms had hired them to produce a poster for a 1966 Dead concert at the Avalon Ballroom, and this time they were determined to spell the band's name correctly. (Their first effort for the "Greatful Dead" featured the head of Franken-stein's monster.) Inside an 1859 book, Kelley found the perfect image: an illustration of a skeleton adorned with a crown and wreath made of roses. "I was just thumbing through some books," Kelley recalled, "and I had *The Rubaiyat of Omar Khayyam* with the illustrations by Edmund J. Sullivan, and I came to that picture. I said, 'Look at this, Stanley. Is that the Grateful Dead or is that the Grateful Dead?'" The *Rubaiyat*'s language, too, was consistent with the Dead's project. A twelfth-century mathematician and astronomer, Khayyam was also an ecstatic poet. Verse after verse of the *Rubaiyat* urged his audience to drink wine, enjoy music, make love, ignore distant events, and otherwise live for the moment before they went the way of all things.

Because Sullivan's illustration was in the public domain, Kelley and Mouse simply redrew it, added trippy lettering and other adornments, and made the overlays. "We didn't really know what it was going to look like," Kelley said, "but when it came out, it just floored us." The result was *Skeleton and Roses,* one of the most important posters of the psyche-delic era. Initially unaware of the illustration's provenance, Garcia con-sidered the poster "brilliant." Chiming perfectly with both the band's name and Haight-Ashbury flower power, skeletons and roses became fixtures in the band's poster art and album covers.

Rock posters featured scores of local and national acts, but the Grate-ful Dead consistently attracted the best artists to their projects. The band's name was a key factor, as was Garcia's training and interest in the visual arts. But his enthusiastic reaction to *Skeleton and Roses* can also be traced to one of his own aesthetic preoccupations—fear. Later in life, Garcia explained his early interest in horror films, which began when his mother took him to see *Abbott and Costello Meet Frankenstein.* He was both frightened and riveted, and he talked at length about its emotional effect: "It was sheer panic. It was like the first time you're on a roller coaster," he said. "It scared me, really, out of my wits. But it scared and fascinated me. I was six years old. My father had died the previous year, in '47. So that also made it kind of a heavy time in my life emotionally, so that was another thing, a big effect, a big reason for my clamping on to it." As a visual artist, too, Garcia was drawn to the look of such films. "For me, the iconography—the Frankenstein's monster, Dracula, and the Wolf Man—became figures of tremendous fascination for me," he said. "I think part of it had to do with the thing of being afraid the first time I saw it. I think there was some desire on my part to embrace that, to not let that control me that way."

Fear also figured in Garcia's attraction to psychedelics. "Some of the scarier [trips] were the most memorable," he said. "I had one where I thought I died multiple times. It got into this thing of death, kind of the last scene, the last scene of hundreds of lives and thousands of incarnations and insect deaths and these, like, kinds of life where I remember spending some long bout, like eons, as kind of sentient fields of wheat, that kind of stuff." One anthropologist noted that most commentary on the Grateful Dead has lacked a sufficient consideration of fear, and it was no accident that many early listeners cited terror as their first reaction to the Dead's music. Several frightening aspects of the psychedelic experience, including the dissolution or fluidity of ego boundaries, contributed to that effect. The antique *danse macabre* iconography also expressed a basic fascination with the darker side of life that lay behind the band's name. In this sense, skeletons and roses weren't adornments, but rather central elements in the Dead's project and its reception.

Returning to the Bay Area from Los Angeles, the Dead spent a week crashing on couches before exploiting a novel housing solution. Rosie McGee and Melissa Cargill, who had been sent north to reconnoiter, discovered that the entire tribe could rent a large adobe house with an expansive lawn and swimming pool at Rancho Olompali, a property thirty minutes north of San Francisco in bucolic Marin County. Originally a large settlement of Coast Miwok Indians, Olompali was nestled in a grassy swale dotted with oak trees that lay on the eastern slope of the coastal mountains. The Olompalis occupied it continuously from AD 500 until the early 1850s. During that time, they had contact with Europeans; archaeologists later found an Elizabethan coin minted in 1567, about a decade before English explorer Sir Francis Drake landed in what became Marin County. In 1828, the Spanish established a mission in nearby San Rafael, and the Olompalis adopted their construction methods to build adobe homes, including the large one occupied by the Dead. In 1852, the Olompali leader sold most of the property. After several more ownership changes, the University of San Francisco bought the property and rented it out.

The Dead could scarcely believe their good fortune and immediately began sharing it. They hosted two large parties and countless smaller ones for their San Francisco friends. Jorma Kaukonen, by then the lead guitarist for Jefferson Airplane, looked forward to his visits. "It was a really fun place. To get out of town, go up there and take a guitar, hang out for a day, two days, whatever. Play, socialize. It didn't get much better than that," Kaukonen said. "Before we knew what rock star heaven was, they were defining rock star heaven." Rock Scully also recalled it as a peak experience. "It was the height of our folly," he said. "This was a time when girls were taking off their clothes. It was wonderful. It was idyllic and a very happy time."

The parties were freestyle affairs. "Two or three hundred people would come," recalled George Hunter, "and of course, most of them probably took LSD. This was around the time that a lot of new ground was being broken, socially, and it seemed like a third to a half of the people at these parties would be naked, hanging around the pool." Hunter also recounted the outdoor jam sessions. "In between the house and the pool, the Dead would set up their equipment and play from time to time," he said. "Usually there'd be members of other bands there, too, like the Airplane and Quicksilver [Messenger Service], and there'd be little jams with people who wanted to play." Hunter also recalled that when the Dead played, Neal Cassady did "this strange little dance—it was almost like break dancing, very fluid." The party seemed to be continuous. "I don't know if it was twenty-four hours a day," Hunter said later, "but every time I was there, it was going."

Garcia was in heaven. Olompali was "completely comfortable, wide-open, high as you wanted to get, run around naked if you wanted to, fall in the pool, completely open scenes. Everything was just supergroovy. It was a model of how things could really be good," he said. "It was good times, unself-conscious and totally free." Many of his most profound LSD trips occurred at Olompali. "We all took a big hit of acid and a hit of mescaline at the same time, and I lay down and closed my eyes—but I could see, it was like my eyes were still open," he said. His visual horizon "started to open like an old-time coffee can with a key, that metal band, and my vision opened out until I had 360-degree vision." The experience "effectively opened out into some kind of totally 'otherly' dimension beyond time and beyond physical reality," Garcia recalled. "During that day, more happened to me than would happen to me in a thousand lifetimes. I'm still mulling over that, you know?" The event affected him deeply. "Psychedelics were probably the single most significant experience in my life," he said. "Otherwise I think I would be going along believing that this visible reality is all that there is." The drugs also shaped his music. "I was a person looking for something, and psychedelics and music are both part of what I was looking for. They fit together, although one didn't cause the other."

According to Rock Scully, not all of Garcia's trips that summer were blissful. "Jerry freaked out there on an overdose of LSD," Scully said. "He blamed it on the ghosts of the Tamal Indians." Scully said Garcia found a giant oak tree and began communicating with it. The next time Scully saw Garcia, he was under the dining-room table, huddled up and shivering. "It had been a tough day," Scully recalled. "I couldn't get Jerry out from under the table." When Garcia finally emerged, he reportedly said he "started having feelings about the Spanish coming to California and what happened to the natives that were here, and I just felt their ghosts. I felt a ghost and it scared me." During one of Lesh's trips that summer, he also felt he made contact with the Native American spirits, who asked him, "What are you doing here, white boy?"

Despite those harrowing trips, Rancho Olompali was the place to be that summer, just as the Red Dog Saloon had been the previous year. Other visitors included Grace Slick, Janis Joplin, David Freiberg of Quicksilver Messenger Service, and Barry Melton of Country Joe & the Fish. Owsley Stanley furnished plenty of acid, which kept the festivities at the correct altitude. By that time, he had partnered with Tim Scully, who was studying mathematical physics and working at the Radiation Laboratory at the University of California, Berkeley. That summer, Stanley, Melissa Cargill, and Scully set up a lab in Point Richmond, a small community north of Berkeley and across the bay from Marin County. There they fabricated carefully measured tablets of LSD, which was still legal, and sold them for $2 per dose. They shared their signature products—White Lightning, Blue Cheer, and Window Pane—with a network of distributors, including Terry the Tramp of the San Francisco chapter of the Hells Angels. Eventually Stanley and his partners produced 4 million hits, much of which they gave away. For Tim Scully, making and distributing LSD was a social mission as much as anything else. "Every time we'd make another batch and release it on the street, something beautiful would flower, and of course we believed it was all because of what we were doing," he recalled. "We believed that we were the architects of social change, that our mission was to change the world substantially, and what was going on in the Haight was a sort of laboratory experiment, a microscopic example of what would happen worldwide."

The Dead's second major party that summer was thrown for the ben-efit of the BBC, which had dispatched a film crew to cover the emerging San Francisco scene. According to Rock Scully, the film crew was greeted by Hells Angels at the property's entrance and forced to walk their equipment to the house. The BBC crew began "taking in the local color, hippies dressed like light-opera pirates and hussars, pantomime outlaws and cowboys and Indians and galoots," but they were vexed by the ubiq-uitous nudity. "Everywhere they turn," Scully recalled in his memoir, "there are people in the nude jumping in the swimming pool, naked couples making love on the grass and kissing in the trees. Kissing the *trees*, actually." The crew asked Scully to instruct everyone to dress so they could start filming. When that plan backfired, they proposed that all the naked people enter the pool. That solution worked fine until the Dead started playing; then the nudes emerged from the pool and flocked to the stage. Scully buttonholed one of the revelers, attorney Brian Rohan, for advice. Already down to his shorts, Rohan was prepared to reason with the BBC. "They're about to pack up their equipment and walk away," Scully told him. "Brian, see if you can convince them to do the shoot and just keep the tits out of the frame, if that's what they're worried about." Scully saw that Rohan was perplexed. "Get rid of the *tits*?" Rohan exclaimed. "Get *rid* of the tits? Why would they want to do that?"

The ecstatic Olompali experience was fleeting. By midsummer, the Dead moved to Camp Lagunitas, a set of rustic cabins between the West Marin towns of Fairfax and Point Reyes Station. Janis Joplin and her band, Big Brother & the Holding Company, lived up the hill, and Quicksilver Messenger Service was staying in nearby Olema. The bands trekked into San Francisco for shows, rehearsals, and studio sessions. In late July, the Dead left the Bay Area for their first out-of-town gigs, and when autumn rolled around, they began looking for a permanent resi-dence in San Francisco.

. . .

That fall was a political season, and Bay Area youth played a significant role in the statewide elections. Although many hippies ignored politicians, the converse wasn't true. The Republican challenger for California governor, Ronald Reagan, made "cleaning up the mess" at Berkeley a key part of his campaign. By 1966, the Free Speech Movement there had successfully challenged limits on campus political activism and morphed into an antiwar campaign. Behind the scenes, and with help from FBI director J. Edgar Hoover and his informants, Reagan was gathering information on student activists, campus administrators, and liberals on the university's Board of Regents.

It wasn't the first time Reagan had worked with the FBI to persecute leftists. Two decades earlier, when the House Committee on Un-American Activities (HUAC) began to investigate Communists in the film industry, the FBI contacted Reagan in his capacity as president of the Screen Actors Guild. Despite his duty to guild members, Reagan secretly turned over names of film-industry leftists to FBI agents, who fed them to HUAC. The Hollywood blacklist that followed the HUAC investigations spoiled many film careers, including Aldous Huxley's. As Reagan began his gubernatorial campaign, however, he shifted his sights away from leftist screenwriters to students who smoked weed and danced to rock music and light shows.

By raising fears about anarchic youth on campus, Reagan was also targeting a premier public university. Like Hollywood, another liberal habitat, the University of California had endured the Red Scare of the 1950s, when right-wing regents pressured the administration to impose new and more specifically anticommunist loyalty oaths designed to purge leftists from the faculty. The institutional crisis that followed that effort, which Hoover aided, was eventually resolved, but the trauma continued to inform the administration's cautious approach to political speech on campus. That caution fueled the Free Speech Movement, whose leaders felt that campus speech regulations consigned students to sandbox politics.

To make his case about the mess at Berkeley, Reagan held a press conference at the Cow Palace, where he had made his political debut at the 1964 GOP national convention. In his address to the GOP delegates, some of whom pelted local African-American journalists with food and garbage inside the hall, Reagan had argued that the United States should cut taxes, balance the federal budget, and win the Cold War. Returning to the scene of his triumph in 1966, Reagan called attention to the youthful perversions in Berkeley, where "a small minority of beatniks, radicals, and filthy-speech advocates" brought shame on the university. The campus, Reagan maintained, had become "a rallying point for Communists and a center of sexual misconduct. Some incidents in this report are so bad, so contrary to our standards of decent human behavior, that I cannot recite them to you in detail." Nevertheless, Reagan managed to produce a few tidbits about a Jefferson Airplane concert held in Harmon Gym. "The hall was entirely dark except for the light from two movie screens," Reagan said. "On these screens the nude torsos of men and women were portrayed from time to time in suggestive positions and movements. Three rock-and-roll bands played simultaneously. The smell of marijuana was thick throughout the hall. There were signs that some of those present had taken dope. There were indications of other happenings that cannot be mentioned here," he hinted darkly.

For Reagan, targeting Berkeley students was a political gold mine. His moral indignation shifted the media focus from the students' concerns—especially free speech on campus, racism and civil rights, and a disastrous war—to the horrors of rock music, dancing, silhouettes of nude torsos, and marijuana. The fact that most college students were under twenty-one years old, the minimum voting age at the time, lowered the electoral cost of the tactic.

Reagan's campaign had two other things going for it. The first was white backlash after the summer of 1965, when a routine arrest of a drunk driver in the predominantly black Los Angeles neighborhood of Watts spun out of control. Six days of rioting, looting, and arson left thirty-four residents dead, more than one thousand injured, and the neighborhood's business district in flames. Robert Hunter, who was serving in the National Guard reserves, was called down to the scene and received a campaign ribbon for his service. Vacationing in Greece, Governor Pat Brown was unable to provide leadership during the crisis, and the state's white residents became even more anxious than usual about residential integration. Reagan pounced on that opportunity, telling an audience of California realtors that the state's 1963 fair housing law was an unconscionable breach of private property rights, which were the essence of freedom. Responding to the dog whistle, the realtors gave Reagan a standing ovation.

Reagan's other advantage was a national push to ban LSD, which played to his antihippie message. In the spring of 1966, the US Senate Subcommittee on Juvenile Delinquency called for an end to the recreational use of LSD. Senator Thomas Dodd, the Democratic committee chair from Connecticut, denounced "pseudo-intellectuals who advocate the use of drugs in search for some imaginary freedoms of the mind and in search of higher psychic experiences." Those pseudo-intellectuals included Timothy Leary, the erstwhile Harvard University psychologist, and Allen Ginsberg, who had quietly worked with Leary to promote the use of LSD among a small group of artists. Both men testified before Dodd's subcommittee. Leary called for a one-year moratorium on LSD use, and Ginsberg emphasized the peaceful and artistically productive aspects of psychedelics. By way of example, he explained to the senators that he had written the second part of "Howl" on peyote. But legislators were more concerned about media reports stressing bad trips, which were frequent, and unsubstantiated claims about chromosome damage resulting from LSD use.

One month before California's gubernatorial election, the state outlawed the possession and use of LSD. The same day, the Dead played the Love Pageant Rally in the panhandle of Golden Gate Park, where hundreds of hippies protested the new law by dropping acid together. Allen Cohen, publisher of the *San Francisco Oracle,* read "A Prophecy of the Declaration of Independence." Among the inalienable rights it declared were "the freedom of body, the pursuit of joy, and the expansion of consciousness." At the same time, Kesey and Pranksters were planning the Acid Test Graduation, which was supposed to feature the Dead at the Winterland Arena on Halloween. The theme, Kesey told local media, was "trip or treat." But Graham was persuaded to cancel the Winterland event on the grounds that Kesey might have been planning to dose the state's Democratic Party leadership, which was scheduled to meet there the next day. Kesey, whose legal problems were still unresolved, suggested he might run for governor to pardon himself. As it turned out, the Dead played a Halloween gig at California Hall, and the Pranksters held a small event at a downtown warehouse that turned out to be their last stand.

Less than a week later, Reagan crushed Pat Brown in the November election. His victory showed, among other things, that running against students and hippies was a winning strategy. As governor, he routinely drew laughs by denigrating antiwar protesters: "Their signs say, 'Make love, not war,' but it didn't look like they could do either." Hippies were another favorite target. "We have some hippies in California," Reagan told out-of-state audiences. "For those of you who don't know what a hippie is, he's a fellow who dresses like Tarzan, has hair like Jane, and smells like Cheetah."

By the time Governor Reagan took office, the Grateful Dead had settled into a large Victorian rooming house at 710 Ashbury Street. Managed by Danny Rifkin, the house was located three blocks away from Golden Gate Park. Garcia, Weir, McKernan, and Scully joined Rifkin there. Lesh and Kreutzmann rented a small house in nearby Diamond Heights; later, they rented an apartment on Belvedere Street, where they were joined by Weir.

Before long, Neal Cassady was spending a good deal of time at the mother ship, and Garcia relished his company. "Neal, man! He was our inspiration," Garcia recalled. "He was the most amazing human being of the century, and all in ways that have yet to be understood." Cassady brought that energy to 710 Ashbury. "Nothing was more incredible than getting high on acid and spending a day with Neal Cassady," Garcia said. "Nothing. He would blow your mind so totally and never ever lock you up or put a rope around you, a border around you, or anything. But always as far-out as you wanted to get." Jon McIntire, who later became the band's manager, recalled Cassady's attraction to the Dead's pad. "I think Cassady just went where the juice was," McIntire said, "and this is where he felt it." The Beat icon stayed in the attic, which lacked a floor. "I remember at one point," said McIntire, "Cassady's foot came through the ceiling. He slipped and his foot came down into Pigpen's room."

The house wasn't a commune in the classic sense. "The reason they lived at 710," said McIntire, "was because it made economic sense to do so. There wasn't any money. And so, yes, there was a commitment to community, to family, to the living situation as a commune, but it wasn't some sort of political ideal that was being lived out and realized, as in, 'Ah, yes, we will become a commune.'" Music was their main preoccupation, but the Dead were also surrounded by other creative activity. Kelley and Mouse produced their posters across the street, and Allen Cohen, the Brooklyn schoolteacher turned poet, hosted psychedelic salons at his nearby apartment. Cohen's extravagant and short-lived publication, the *San Francisco Oracle*, was funded in part by Owsley Stanley and helped set the visual and literary mood for the neighborhood. Bruce Conner and Rick Griffin designed some of the *Oracle*'s psychedelic covers, and the paper featured work by Ginsberg, Snyder, Ferlinghetti, and McClure.

When Kesey and the Pranksters returned to San Francisco from Mexico, they realized that the Grateful Dead's fortunes had risen in their absence. "Suddenly they were the stars, and we weren't," Carolyn Adams said. "And we were kind of miffed, actually." But the Dead still weren't the biggest act in town. That honor went to Jefferson Airplane, who added singer Grace Slick in October 1966 and recorded their first hit single, "Somebody to Love," for their second album, *Surrealistic Pillow*. The lyrics for the album's other hit single, "White Rabbit," mixed Lewis Carroll's *Alice's Adventures in Wonderland* with the spirit of the San Francisco drug culture. Written by Slick while she was still with the Great Society, the song describes the perception-altering effects of various pills and ends with the exhortation, "Remember what the dormouse said: Feed your head." Garcia joined Jefferson Airplane for the recording sessions in Los Angeles and helped on various fronts. "Jerry was a leader," said Jefferson Airplane guitarist Jorma Kaukonen. "When he worked with us on *Surrealistic Pillow*, he really helped discipline us. Because he had come from a band, and as a bandleader and an arranger, he just really knew what was important." Garcia also furnished the album's title in a passing remark. To acknowledge Garcia's help, Jefferson Airplane listed Garcia on the album credits as musical and spiritual adviser.

Garcia's connections to Jefferson Airplane also raised the Dead's profile, and soon they had an offer from Warner Bros. Records. It was an unlikely fit between band and label. Established in 1958, Warner Bros. Records was only beginning to make its mark in the music business. One of its top recordings was a comedy album, *The Button-Down Mind of Bob Newhart*, but through its subsidiaries and acquisitions, the label signed or landed the rights to albums by Frank Sinatra, the Everly Brothers, and Peter, Paul and Mary, a leading folk act. Warner Bros. Records needed to recruit new talent, but its managers felt no strong connection with the Haight-Ashbury musicians they wanted to sign. When Joe Smith traveled to San Francisco to scout the Dead, he discovered "kids lying around painting each other's bodies." He immediately felt uncomfortable. "Even the name was intimidating," Smith recalled. "What did it mean? No one knew." Smith told his longtime friend and San Francisco music impresario, Tom Donahue, that he didn't think Jack Warner would ever understand this. "I don't know if I understand it myself," Smith added. But Donahue was adamant. "You've got to sign them," he told Smith, "because this is where it's going."

Backstage at the Avalon Ballroom, Donahue made the introductions. He was a big man, literally and figuratively, in the San Francisco music scene. "Big Daddy" Donahue ("three hundred pounds of solid sounds") was a former disc jockey at KYA, a Top 40 AM station, as well as a coproducer of the Beatles concert at Candlestick Park. He owned a psychedelic nightclub in North Beach called Mother's and cofounded Autumn Records, a small label that employed Sylvester Stewart (later known as Sly Stone) as a producer. Donahue vouched for Smith, but the executive had trouble connecting to the musicians. "Garcia was the most visible, but he refused to speak for the group," Smith said. "Pigpen never said ten words, and Lesh was very nasty, constantly negative, because I was a record company guy and he was a serious musician."

With Donahue's help, Smith finalized the record deal with the Dead. When Smith met with Scully and Rifkin at Donahue's Telegraph Hill home to sign the contract, the young managers urged him to take LSD so he could understand the Dead's music. Smith refused, and the band signed anyway for a $10,000 advance against royalties.

In January 1967, the Dead played at the Human Be-In, the "gathering of the tribes" announced by issue #5 of the *San Francisco Oracle*. Jefferson Airplane and Quicksilver Messenger Service also performed, and the speakers included Timothy Leary, Allen Ginsberg, Gary Snyder, Lawrence Ferlinghetti, and Jerry Rubin. To the surprise of many, the event drew more than twenty thousand people to Golden Gate Park. The Hells

Angels also attended and helped look after lost children. There were no drunks, Ralph Gleason noted, but many in the audience were stoned. Michael Bowen, who organized the event, had coined its name in a chance remark at the Love Pageant Rally a few months earlier. A word play on *human being*, the name also echoed the sit-ins and teach-ins of the civil rights and antiwar movements. The popularity of the San Francisco event led to even more verbal adaptations, and within a year, *Rowan & Martin's Laugh-In*, an up-tempo comedy program with a signature 1960s look, became a hit show on network television.

By drawing significant national attention, the Human Be-In set the stage for yet another summer of revelry, but the Dead had little time to savor the experience. Less than a week later, they drove to Los Angeles to produce their first album, *The Grateful Dead*, which was recorded in four days and issued in March 1967. At the release party in North Beach's Fugazi Hall, the culture clash between the hippies and the music-industry executives came to the fore when Joe Smith addressed the assembled supporters. "I just want to say what an honor it is to be able to introduce the Grateful Dead and its music to the world," Smith announced. Garcia couldn't resist the opening, replying, "I just want to say what an honor it is for the Grateful Dead to introduce Warner Bros. Records to the world."

At first, Garcia was happy with the debut album. "It sounds like one of our good sets," he said before the album's release. A few years later, he was less satisfied. "So we went down there," he recalled, "and what was it we had? Dexamyl? Some sort of diet-watcher's speed, and pot, and stuff like that. So in three nights, we played some hyperactive music. That's what's embarrassing about that record now: the tempo was way too fast." Although the songs reflected their electric-blues and jug-band repertoire, Lesh thought "Viola Lee Blues" was "the only track on the record that sounds at all like we did at the time." The lyrics for that song and "New, New Minglewood Blues" were credited to Noah Lewis, whose work also appeared in Harry Smith's anthology. A Tennessee native born in the nineteenth century, Lewis died of gangrene brought on by frostbite only six years earlier. Besides "Viola Lee Blues," "Good Morning Little Schoolgirl," a blues standard first recorded by Sonny Boy Williamson, was the only other long track. Its lyrics about the seduction of a young girl contrasted with the feel-good vibe of "The Golden Road (to Unlimited Devotion)," an up-tempo number that captured the barefoot-hippie spirit in the Haight. Hoping for a hit single, Warner Bros. Records released two candidates, "The Golden Road" and "Cream Puff War." Neither hit the charts, and both quickly disappeared from the band's live repertoire. The marketing effort, which included a Pigpen look-alike contest, also fizzled.

But all was not lost. The release of *The Grateful Dead* coincided with yet another innovation hatched in San Francisco. A struggling local radio station, KMPX, gave its midnight slot to guitarist Larry Miller, who mixed his favorite folk-rock tunes with the station's foreign-language programming. According to Joe Smith, KMPX was one of those stations "so far off to the right end of the dial that they fell into your glove compartment." But the word got out that something new was on the air, and Tom Donahue proposed an unprecedented format to KMPX: free-form, album-based rock music. Management accepted Donahue's proposal, and he began broadcasting in the 8:00 p.m. slot in April 1967. Almost immediately, Donahue brought Garcia and Lesh into the studio for a chat. He also mixed cuts from the Dead's new album with their favorite tunes by Charles Mingus, Blind Willie Johnson, Ray Charles, James Brown, Bob Dylan, and Aretha Franklin. Donahue's format proved so successful that KMPX went to it full-time four months later.

The Dead's debut album impressed Ralph Gleason, whose columns for the *San Francisco Chronicle* were amplified by his work for *Ramparts* magazine, where he was a contributing editor. Founded on the peninsula in 1962 as a Catholic literary journal, *Ramparts* moved to North Beach and morphed into a New Left muckraker whose circulation and cachet were soaring on the strength of blockbuster stories about Viet-

nam, the Black Panthers, and the CIA. But Gleason was especially interested in the emerging local music scene. "The bands in San Francisco
are wild," he told jazz musician and historian Frank Kofsky privately.
"You should get the Grateful Dead on Warner Bros. and listen to that
guitar player and listen to that bass player." Gleason also saw unique
cultural significance in the scene as a whole:

> I find the San Francisco groups incredibly important, and one of
> the reasons is that unlike Los Angeles—where everything is aimed
> toward the recording studio, and where there are no dances (cer-
> tainly not in the sense that there are in San Francisco), or like New
> York, which is also aimed at concert appearance [sic] and recording
> studios—the San Francisco bands, which are almost all of them
> cooperative bands in the fullest sense of the word, with no leaders
> and living together in a communal sense, these bands are all play-
> ing two and three times a week for dances. They've got a tremen-
> dous personal following and tremendous personal rapport with
> their audience. They function together, and the bands and the au-
> dience create something. They create it together.

For Gleason, that communal dynamic was almost unprecedented. "There
has been no point in American history that I know of, except the street
bands of New Orleans, where music has had such a direct role in the
culture of any area as it has in San Francisco at this point in our history,"
he wrote Kofsky. "And it seems to me that far from tending to die out,
it's becoming increasingly important."

Gleason presented those ideas in a February 1967 speech given at the
University of California, Santa Cruz. A new campus, it was designed as
an alternative to the "knowledge factory" model that Mario Savio had
deplored during Berkeley's Free Speech Movement only a few years before. Gleason opened his speech with a reference to the news of the day,
a *Ramparts* whistle-blower story on the CIA's clandestine support for

US cultural organizations and publications. "I am not now, and never have been, subsidized by the CIA," Gleason joked. His wide-ranging remarks covered politics, race, the music industry, drugs, and money, but mostly he celebrated the youth culture's appetite for ecstasy. As "prisoners of logic," he argued, leftist intellectuals were especially prone to misconstrue that desire. Those intellectuals included his colleagues at *Ramparts* magazine, which he described as "the white hope of the square left."

When *Ramparts* profiled the Haight-Ashbury scene the following month, Gleason was outraged. As San Francisco braced for the Summer of Love, *Ramparts* editor Warren Hinckle turned a gimlet eye to his new neighbors, the hippies. The youthful Hinckle's colorful leadership was a key part of the magazine's success, but the native San Franciscan was no flower child. His cover article, "The Social History of the Hippies," offered a sweeping and sometimes critical take on the local scene, including the Grateful Dead. Bob Seidemann's cover photograph showed Stanley Mouse dressed in Sgt. Pepper–style jacket, an iron cross dangling from his neck, and a small pipe in his hand. The photograph was accompanied by an enigmatic caption, which Chet Helms had originally coined for an Avalon Ballroom happening: "May the Baby Jesus Shut Your Mouth and Open Your Mind."

In his article, Hinckle claimed the San Francisco Beat scene had two distinct political strains that predated and influenced the hippies. The majority strain, represented by Allen Ginsberg and Lawrence Ferlinghetti, sought to challenge the mainstream culture's complacency and conventional wisdom. (This was also how *Ramparts* understood its own purpose.) The other strain, Hinckle argued, was a "distinctly fascist" one embodied by Jack Kerouac. "It is into the fascist bag," Hinckle wrote, "that you can put Kesey and his friends, the Hell's Angels, and in a more subtle way, Timothy Leary." That brand of fascism, according to Hinckle, "can be recognized by a totalitarian insistence on action and nihilism, and is usually accompanied by a Superman concept."

Hinckle's definition of fascism wasn't especially clear or common, but his claim hinged on Kesey's relationship with the Hells Angels. The gang members weren't known for their politics, but many were veterans, and some made their opinions crystal clear on the subject of the Vietnam War. In October 1965, a group of Hells Angels led by Sonny Barger assaulted peaceful antiwar protesters on a march from Berkeley to Oakland. In the middle of that scene, one Angel shouted, "Go back to Russia, you fucking Communists!" A month later, Kesey persuaded the Angels to stay away from a similar antiwar march by furnishing them with a generous supply of beer.

But where Hinckle saw fascists, Kesey and the Dead saw fellow travelers. By the time Hinckle's article appeared, the Hells Angels had become regulars at Kesey's parties and Grateful Dead concerts. The motorcycle gang's bond with the Dead was forged in January 1967, when the Hells Angels threw a party in Golden Gate Park for the Diggers, a group of improvisational actors and radical community activists. Like the Dead, the Diggers sought to break down the barriers between performers and audiences. In an effort to challenge the money economy that they thought had disfigured American society, the Diggers offered residents free food, much of which they salvaged from restaurants and groceries, as well as free furniture, clothing, and shelter. They also organized street theater and free concerts and established a community news service. Their work, Digger Peter Coyote later said, wasn't meant to be an economic blueprint; rather, it was a "three-year art project" designed to inspire new ways of thinking. On December 17, 1966, the Diggers held an event called "The Death of Money," during which one Hells Angel was arrested. The Diggers posted his bail, and the Angels wanted to repay the favor with their own party. When the Dead played the event on New Year's Day, the Hells Angels became fixtures at their concerts in and around the Bay Area.

The Hells Angels connection wasn't lost on Hinckle, who closed his *Ramparts* article by returning to his political point:

The danger in the hippie movement is more than overcrowded streets and possible hunger riots this summer. If more and more youngsters begin to share the hippie political posture of unrelenting quietism, the future of activist, serious politics is bound to be affected. The hippies have shown that it can be pleasant to drop out of the arduous task of attempting to steer a difficult, unrewarding society. But when that is done, you leave the driving to the Hell's Angels.

Hinckle was correct that the hippies had little interest in steering society. As Garcia would later say, the Dead saw themselves as "signposts to new space," not political activists or social engineers. Like many of their heroes and peers, the Dead rarely commented on politics as such, and though they played scores of benefits for various causes, they were consistently and pointedly uninterested in speeches, elections, and most forms of conventional political activity. Garcia cast his last vote in 1964, and eight years later the Dead declined to help George McGovern's presidential campaign after the Democratic nominee balked at their suggestion to legalize marijuana.

In a 1982 interview with *Playboy* magazine, Garcia confirmed his aversion to the political speeches he witnessed in the mid-1960s. "I remember once being at a be-in or one of those things, and the Berkeley contingent—Jerry Rubin and those guys—got up on stage and started haranguing the crowd," Garcia said. "All of a sudden it was like everybody who had ever harangued a crowd. It was every asshole who told people what to do. The words didn't matter. It was that angry tone. It scared me; it made me sick to my stomach." Garcia also wondered why students had tried to reform their universities in the 1960s. He considered "all that campus confusion laughable," and asked:

Why enter this closed society and make an effort to liberalize it when that's never been its function? Why not just leave it and go

somewhere else? Why not act out your fantasies, using the positive side of your nature rather than just struggling? Just turn your
back on it and split—it's easy enough to find a place where people
will leave you alone.

In a 1989 *Rolling Stone* article, Garcia was even more emphatic: "For
me, the lame part of the sixties was the political part, the social part.
The real part was the spiritual part." Garcia's distaste for politics even
affected his musical judgments. In 1972, for example, he said he admired the singing of Crosby, Stills, Nash & Young but noted that they
were "into a political bag, which I don't like that much."

Garcia's remarks also reflected the insular, do-it-yourself ethos of
San Francisco's midcentury arts community. Changing the straight world,
which was sending thousands of American youth to kill and be killed in
Vietnam, was an uphill climb to the bottom, but it was still possible to
create something new and interesting in one's own community. That
message was the thrust of the Dead's first newsletter, *The Olompali Sunday Times,* which appeared in March 1967. "We inherited the evil and
wars," the first issue noted, "but chose to ignore them to death rather
than try to kill off everyone who does not see Utopia as we do. The
movement of Joy is spreading, and we are glad to be a part of it." That
message was consistent with Kesey's speech at an antiwar rally in Berkeley two years earlier. "You know, we're not going to stop this war with
this rally, by marching," Kesey said. "That's what *they* do." There was a
more effective gesture in such circumstances, he claimed. "And that's
everybody just look at it, look at this war, and turn your backs and
say . . . 'Fuck it.'"

Although Ronald Reagan and others elided the differences between
activists and hippies, the split between the two groups was widely noted
at the time and has been well documented since. There were tensions galore, SDS activist and sociologist Todd Gitlin noted, between radical political strategy and the countercultural ideal of living fully in a community

of kindred spirits. Ralph Gleason was in a perfect position to observe that split. A sophisticated political observer as well as a music critic, he had a large network that included Harry Bridges, I. F. Stone, Ken Kesey, Allen Ginsberg, and Marxist historian Eric Hobsbawm, who wrote jazz criticism under a pen name. Gleason also witnessed the Lenny Bruce saga, wrote liner notes for Bruce's comedy albums, testified in his San Francisco obscenity trial, and kept Bruce's friends up-to-date on his news until the comedian died of an overdose in 1966. Gleason was a man of the left, but in a 1963 letter to lawyer Alexander Hoffman, he wrote that "the square, myopic, UNHIP left antagonizes me like the bandilleras in the bull." In Gleason's opinion, young people in particular were way ahead of leftist intellectuals and activists in making the social revolution, which he believed would have manifold political effects. "You make the social revolution first and politicize it, don't you?" he asked Hoffman rhetorically in that letter.

In another private communication, Gleason noted the futility of politicizing the San Francisco hippies. By way of example, he explained to musician and historian Frank Kofsky that *Ramparts* editor Robert Scheer, who almost defeated an East Bay congressman in the 1966 Democratic primary, wasn't a natural leader of the hippie community. Age twenty-nine when he decided to run, Scheer was a former Berkeley graduate student, City Lights employee, beatnik, and jazz aficionado. His campaign speeches called for an end to the war in Vietnam, more attention to poverty and racism in the East Bay, and the legalization of marijuana and abortion. His extemporaneous addresses were notable for their lucidity and power, and his friendship with Bill Graham gave him access to San Francisco hippies. Yet Gleason was adamant about the mismatch between Scheer and the Haight-Ashbury counterculture. "I don't think there is any possibility whatsoever of Bob Scheer ever becoming a leader of the hippies," Gleason claimed. "In the first place, the hippies don't listen to speeches." Reflecting on the Human Be-In, Gleason reported that the addresses were a drag. "Nobody wants to hear political speeches," he told Kofsky. "These kids will not listen to political speeches, and Bob Scheer doesn't swing and he doesn't move and he doesn't get to them." Gleason thought that the New Left in general would have difficulty mobilizing the San Francisco hippies. "I don't think that they can be politicized in the sense that Scheer is a political person," he continued. "And I think that looking at what they are doing with a view toward politicizing or not politicizing them is discussing them in the wrong framework."

Gleason's point certainly applied to the Dead. As Garcia told Jorma Kaukonen, it's not what you play, it's what you don't play that's important, and the Dead's repertoire didn't include political pronouncements. When asked to describe their project in social or political terms, they often stressed what didn't interest them. "What we're thinking about is a peaceful planet," Garcia said in a 1967 CBS documentary called *The Hippie Temptation*.

> We're not thinking about anything else. We're not thinking about any kind of power. We're not thinking about any of those kinds of struggles. We're not thinking about revolution or war or any of that. That's not what we want. Nobody wants to get hurt. Nobody wants to hurt anybody. We would all like to be able to live an uncluttered life. A simple life, a good life, you know. And think about moving the whole human race ahead a step.

In the same interview, Rock Scully noted the spiritual benefits of drugs, and Lesh added, "I think, for me personally, that the more people turn on, the better world it's gonna be." Garcia's quick nod indicated his agreement, but he later shied away from the view that the Grateful Dead were trying to save the world. Instead, he said, they were "trying to make things groovier for everybody so that more people can feel better more often, to advance the trip, to get higher, however you want to say it. But we're musicians, and there's just no way to put that idea, 'save the world,' into music; you can only *be* that idea, or at least make manifest that idea as it appears to you and hope others will follow."

If getting high wasn't a political program, Garcia found it personally transformative. "To get really high is to forget yourself," Garcia said. "And to forget yourself is to see everything else. And to see everything else is to become an understanding molecule in evolution, a conscious tool of the universe. And I think every human being should become a conscious tool of the universe. That's why I think it's important to get high." For him, getting high didn't mean tuning out. "I'm not talking about unconscious or zonked-out," he explained. "I'm talking about being fully conscious." That consciousness included acknowledging the challenges posed by the Dead's new lifestyle. "We're kinda like a signpost," he said, "and we're *also* pointing to danger, to difficulty, we're pointing to bummers."

Despite Hinckle's thesis, no one familiar with the Grateful Dead thought they aided the forces of fascism, but the Hells Angels were another matter. In his 1966 bestseller, Hunter Thompson wrote that the gang's assault on the peace marchers in Oakland was "completely logical. The Angels' collective viewpoint has always been fascistic." Describing a gang member named Tiny, Thompson wondered about his fit with the times: "Tiny hurts people. When he loses his temper he goes completely out of control and his huge body becomes a lethal weapon. It is difficult to see what role he might play in the Great Society." Both Garcia's youthful fascination with the Angels and Kesey's affiliation with them had created an unlikely coalition based on a shared interest not in the arts, but in wild parties. To the world at large, that coalition reinforced everything scary about the Grateful Dead, including its name and iconography.

Incensed by Hinckle's article, Gleason resigned from *Ramparts* and turned his attention to another publication. At a Jefferson Airplane concert, he met Jann Wenner, who by that time was a rock columnist at the UC Berkeley newspaper. Gleason landed Wenner a job at the *Sunday*

Ramparts, the magazine's spin-off newspaper, but when Hinckle shut that down in 1967, Wenner found himself out of work. With Gleason's help, and using a spare room at the *Ramparts* office, Wenner began planning a new magazine called *Rolling Stone.*

As Hinckle's *Ramparts* article betokened, San Francisco became the epicenter of a unique season, the so-called Summer of Love. The turnout for the Human Be-In six months earlier had astonished even many hippies, and the national media coverage of that "gathering of the tribes" alerted millions of American youth to the happenings in the Haight. In the spring of 1967, the city was expecting an influx of one hundred thousand young people for at least part of the summer. Two hit singles served as Top 40 invitations: John Phillips's "San Francisco (Be Sure to Wear Flowers in Your Hair)" and Eric Burdon and the Animals' "San Franciscan Nights." (In Great Britain, the B-side of Burdon's single was "Gratefully Dead.") Those songs urged young people not only to embrace Flower Power, but also to travel to San Francisco to experience it. Garcia later described Phillips's song, which Scott McKenzie recorded, as the lamest possible rendition of the Haight-Ashbury experience.

City officials strongly discouraged the migration, which seemed only to increase its appeal. Members of the Family Dog, the Straight Theater, the Diggers, and the *San Francisco Oracle* formed a Council for the Summer of Love to prepare for the deluge. The council's purpose was to counteract the city's negative response and to emphasize the potential spiritual benefits of the Summer of Love. The Diggers, for example, welcomed the larger audience. Peter Coyote recalled their utopian vision. "We thought culture was much more important than politics," he said. "Let's just start getting people living the way they want to live. You want to live in a world where you don't have to work? Let's make it. You want to live in a world where you can get food for free? Let's make it. You want to live in a house with, you know, lots of women and men, and live the way you want? Let's do it. Let's make the world that you imagine real by acting it out. And if you can act it out, it's real."

The Summer of Love's main attraction was the chance to sample or create a new life based on transcendence. Experimental filmmaker Ben Van Meter later offered a personal example:

There's a kid in Iowa, Kansas, in the summer of '67, and he's an outcast kid. He's got long hair, he smokes dope. . . . The football team beats him up once in a while. And he's an outcast. He knows he doesn't fit in in Kansas, he doesn't think he fits in anywhere in the world. And he reads in *Life* magazine that something's happening in San Francisco called the Summer of Love. So he hitchhikes out, goes to the Haight-Ashbury, meets a girl, they smoke pot, drop acid, make love.

And that night she takes him to the Avalon Ballroom, and they pay their money, and they run up the stairs, they run into the ballroom, and it's like nothing he's ever seen before. The music is overwhelming, overpowering him. And the lights envelop him. They're on the band, they're on the walls, they're on the ceiling, they're on the floors, they're on all the other dancers, they're on the girl he's with, they're on him. And he reaches out his hand, he looks at it, and it becomes difficult to see the point where he ends and everything else begins. And he's got a moment of enlightenment there that'll come back to him for the rest of his life periodically. Because he realizes there *is* no point where he ends and everything else begins.

Van Meter's account registers the combination of drugs, sex, dance, and light show as a subjective experience of total rapture. For him and others, that "moment of enlightenment" was transformational. *San Francisco Chronicle* music critic Joel Selvin recalled the Grateful Dead's role in that transformation. "I cannot explain to you what it's like to be in a crowd of five thousand people on LSD with the Grateful Dead, also on LSD, leading the crowd through a series of improvisations," Selvin said. "And before that, rock-and-roll songs were three minutes. Period, paragraph, we're out of here." Later in his career, Garcia identified such moments as the key to the Dead's success. When the Grateful Dead took the stage, they wanted "to be transformed from ordinary players into extraordinary ones, like forces of a larger consciousness," he said. "And the audience wants to be transformed from whatever ordinary reality they may be in to something a little wider, something that enlarges them."

Although those transformations were strongly associated with the San Francisco music scene, bands in other regions were pushing many of the same boundaries in their performances and recordings. The Doors, for example, formed in Los Angeles the same year as the Dead, and two songs on their debut album, "Light My Fire" and "The End," ran seven and twelve minutes, respectively. The former was a huge hit and another ode to rapture. On the strength of that song, the Doors were invited to appear on *The Ed Sullivan Show* on CBS. A former theater and gossip columnist, Sullivan was an important national tastemaker. Appearances on his Sunday-evening program, which had been running since 1948, boosted the fortunes of Elvis Presley, the Beatles, and the Rolling Stones. Almost comically stiff onstage, Sullivan considered even the modest slice of ecstasy in "Light My Fire" too much for national television. His producer told singer Jim Morrison to replace the line "Girl, we couldn't get much higher" with "Girl, we couldn't get much better." Morrison agreed but sang the original lyric; afterward, he told the enraged producer that he had forgotten his instructions. When the producer said the Doors would never do the *The Ed Sullivan Show* again, Morrison replied, "We just *did* the *Sullivan Show!*"

Morrison's response was a sign of the times. Like the Dead and Kesey, Morrison was impatient with repetition, and his appetite for new and intense experience was far stronger than his desire for Ed Sullivan's

approval. But even for many contemporaries, that appetite was unnerv-
ing. Joan Didion described Morrison as a twenty-four-year-old UCLA
graduate "who wore black vinyl pants and no underwear and tended to
suggest some range of the possible just beyond a suicide pact." Narra-
tion, Didion's stock-in-trade, depended in large part on repetition and
predictability. "We live entirely, especially if we are writers, by the im-
position of a narrative line upon disparate images," Didion wrote, "by
the 'ideas' with which we have learned to freeze the shifting phantas-
magoria which is our actual experience." But Didion's actual experience
in Los Angeles between 1966 and 1971 was an ordeal. Her disjointed
personal life, she wrote, was an "adequate enough performance as
improvisations go."

> The only problem was that my entire education, everything I had
> ever been told or had told myself, insisted that the production was
> never meant to be improvised: I was supposed to have a script,
> and had mislaid it. I was supposed to hear cues, and no longer
> did. I was meant to know the plot, but all I knew was what I saw:
> flash pictures in variable sequence, images with no "meaning"
> beyond their temporary arrangement, not a movie but a cutting
> room experience.

To the extent that Morrison and others refused the safety of repetition
and predictability, Didion regarded them as threats to social and psy-
chological order. She wasn't alone. As historian David Farber noted, the
counterculture posed a significant threat to business as usual in American
society because it affected far more families than other social movements
of the same period.

If Didion wasn't a Morrison fan, neither were most San Francisco
musicians. Many took a dim view of the entire Los Angeles scene, despite the shared interest in Kerouac and psychedelics, and New York
music critic Robert Christgau picked up on the intercity rivalry. The

Los Angeles musicians, he reported in *Esquire,* "have mixed feelings about San Francisco; most of them admire the music but distrust the mystique. San Franciscans respond with brickbats." Part of the problem, Christgau thought, was that the San Francisco scene wasn't sufficiently urbane. "When it has to deal with uptight New York or plastic Los Angeles," he wrote, "it loses its vaunted cool." Garcia thought the Doors had more style than substance and described Los Angeles unflatteringly. "They don't have any dance things in LA," he told Ralph Gleason. "The extent of the dancing in Los Angeles is ten feet off the floor in a glass cage. Everybody watches, like the movies. Except you go there to be watched as well." Another major difference was automotive: "Your car is where you live in LA. The car radio is where it's at. Because if you don't have an automobile, you're not even alive in Los Angeles." Finally, there was the difference in community: "And their scene is real isolated, you know. They don't have a community in LA," he said. "For the millions of people down there, there is no place where you can go and cool it and just, like, be there and not have to worry about what you're doing there."

In the end, the Summer of Love's most important musical event occurred in yet another California city. Earlier that year, John Phillips of the Mamas & the Papas and his label's president, Lou Adler, began organizing the Monterey International Pop Music Festival. Its models were the successful Monterey Jazz Festival, which had begun in 1958, and the Monterey Folk Festival, which had featured Joan Baez and Bob Dylan in 1963. Phillips and Adler, who both worked out of Los Angeles, believed they needed the blessing of the San Francisco music community to succeed, and they courted Ralph Gleason, the Grateful Dead, Jefferson Airplane, Quicksilver Messenger Service, and Big Brother & the Holding Company. All four bands agreed to play, but suspecting that the Los Angeles slicks were exploiting them, they declined to sign releases for the film rights. In the Digger spirit, Danny Rifkin and the Dead pushed for a free concert but didn't prevail.

Scheduled for June, the Monterey Pop Festival brought together a wide range of talent, including Otis Redding, Ravi Shankar, Hugh Masekela, the Byrds, Buffalo Springfield, and the Butterfield Blues Band. Performing with Big Brother & the Holding Company, Janis Joplin electrified the crowd. Bob Dylan's manager soon added her to his list of clients, and Big Brother signed a contract with Columbia Records on the strength of their performance. The Dead found themselves playing between two relatively unknown acts, the Who and the Jimi Hendrix Experience. Fresh from London, the Who closed with a high-powered version of "My Generation." As smoke bombs detonated, Pete Townshend smashed his guitar against the stage and stabbed his amplifier with its neck. Keith Moon finished the set by kicking over his drums to raucous cheering. As it dawned on the Dead that they had to follow this mayhem, Kreutzmann threw up.

The Dead, who often needed time to find their groove, made no attempt to match the Who's maniacal energy. Encouraging the audience to dance, they marched through a so-so set. *Down Beat* magazine's review of the festival took the band's measure. The Dead were "a curiously down-homey bunch that has become enshrined as the king group of West Coast acid rock," the review noted. "It is a formidable outfit, with two of the coast's top freakout musicians, guitarist Jerry Garcia and a bearlike organist known only as Pigpen." But their music was a work in progress. "The Dead's shorter arrangements are brilliant, but its longer tunes have a habit of ending up in the same way. Uncontrolled cascades of notes over tonic drone build up to the threshold of pain. Then, suddenly, everything stops and they go back to the beginning. Certainly it mesmerizes the freaks (which is what the Dead get paid for doing), but it's kind of a slipshod, lazy way to play music."

The Dead yielded the stage to Jimi Hendrix, who equaled Townshend's intensity with a torrid rendition of "Wild Thing." After a series of sexual gyrations, he finished by setting his guitar on fire, smashing it, and throwing parts of it into the audience. "If the Who had not done some of this before," *Down Beat* speculated, "there might well have been a riot." Like the Dead, the Mamas & the Papas had no answer to such theatrics and closed out the festival with a perfectly adequate and largely forgotten performance. The Dead's decision not to sign releases for D. A. Pennebaker's documentary ensured that their appearance would be even less memorable. The other San Francisco bands reconsidered their initial opposition and were eventually included in the film, which was a critical and commercial success.

Robert Hunter missed San Francisco's Summer of Love entirely. In April 1967, he left the Bay Area for New Mexico, in part to recover from his methedrine problem and hepatitis, which earned him the nickname Yellow Angel. There he began writing song lyrics for the first time. His interest in literature had blossomed after he discovered Beat poet Lew Welch's *On Out*, which he plucked randomly from a girlfriend's bookshelf. Later, Hunter recalled the poems and their effect on him. "There was a beautiful line in one of them, 'Trails go nowhere, they end exactly where you stop.' There was a lot of wisdom in it, and an easiness, and a fluidity of language," he said. "Very, very appealing. I would say that was my beginning turn-on. I was ready to get bonked over the head with something, and that book was there for it."

Another early inspiration was James Joyce. "I had been writing unpublishable poetry," Hunter recalled. "Joyce was my primary influence; it was really heavy Joycean stuff. I guess it made Joyce look more conservative, though—he didn't have acid." Even without LSD, Joyce had pushed the modern novel to its narrative and linguistic limits, first in *Ulysses*, a stylistic tour de force, and then in *Finnegans Wake*, one of the most complex works in the English language, complete with nonce words and puns fashioned out of sixty or more other languages. Hunter found Joyce's most elaborate fiction intoxicating. "Before I was writing songs, I was a stoned James Joyce head, *Finnegans Wake* head," he said. "I can still recite the first page and last couple of pages of that thing. There was something in the way those words socketed together, and the wonderful feel of reciting them, that very, very deeply influenced me."

But it was Bob Dylan, not James Joyce, whose work prompted Hunter to write his first song lyrics. "I first started waking up to the possibilities of rock lyrics being serious with *Blonde on Blonde*," Hunter recalled. "It opened up everything; it said it was okay to be as serious as you wanted in rock." Dylan's seventh album was released in the spring of 1966 and included "Rainy Day Women #12 and 35" and its famous refrain, "Everybody must get stoned." Although that song became Dylan's most popular single, many agreed with critic Mark Marqusee that two other numbers, "Visions of Johanna" and "Stuck Inside of Mobile with the Memphis Blues Again," were "beyond category. They are allusive, repetitive, jaggedly abstract compositions that defy reduction." Later, the same description would apply to many of Hunter's lyrics.

Hunter and Dylan had something else in common: a shared interest in Harry Smith's Old, Weird America. Dylan spent most of 1967 holed up in and around Woodstock producing the so-called Basement Tapes, which circulated in bootleg form until some songs were released as an album in 1975. The Basement Tape sessions were "palavers with a community of ghosts," Greil Marcus noted, "once gathered in a single place: on the *Anthology of American Folk Music*." Smith exerted a profound influence on Dylan. "In 1959 and 1960," Marcus claimed, "the *Anthology of American Folk Music* was Bob Dylan's first true map of a republic that was still a hunch to him." Soon Hunter would augment that invisible republic with the new and psychedelic frontier that was unfolding before him and his peers.

In the summer of 1967, Hunter mailed the lyrics for "Saint Stephen," "China Cat Sunflower," and "Alligator" to Garcia, who invited him to join the band in San Francisco. On his last night in New Mexico, Hunter took LSD. The next morning, he began to wend his way home. "I hitchhiked west with twenty dollars in cash and high hopes," he said. "The trip took six weeks with a surreal layover in Denver. By the time I hit Nevada, I had a dime in my pocket, which I put in a slot machine and parlayed into enough to make a phone call and tell the guys I was on my way. I arrived in San Francisco with walking pneumonia and the clothes on my back." Lesh met the bedraggled Hunter in San Francisco, and the two drove north to Rio Nido, the Russian River hamlet where the band was performing. Soon after his arrival, Hunter began writing lyrics. "I was in my cabin," Hunter recounted. "They were rehearsing in the hall, and you could hear them from there. I heard the music and just started writing 'Dark Star' while lying on my bed. I wrote the first half of it, and I went in, and I think I handed what I'd written to Jerry. He said, 'Oh, this will fit just fine,' and he started singing it." Later, Garcia noted that the music for "Dark Star" was shaped by Hunter's lyrics. "The reason the music is the way it is, is because those lyrics did suggest that to me," he said. "They are saying, 'This universe is truly far out.' . . . For me, that suggestion always means, 'Great, let's look around. Let's see how weird it really gets.'"

To that point, the Dead's lyrics had been uneven at best. "Caution (Do Not Stop on Tracks)" featured McKernan's blues persona and an up-tempo jam, but the lyrics were thin soup: "I went down one day / I went down to see a gypsy woman just one day; yes I did / I wanna find out / What's wrong with me and my baby." Garcia's "Can't Come Down" was more promising: "I'm flying down deserted streets / Wrapped in mother's winding sheets / Asbestos boots on flaming feet / Dreaming of forbidden treats." Written quickly after the band had composed the music, Garcia's lyrics captured some of the dangers of the ecstatic life he and his friends had embraced. But Garcia later admitted that his lyrics were a slapdash affair. He composed them, he said, "only by default. I felt my lyric writing was woefully inadequate." Songs with his lyrics were quickly dropped from the Dead's active repertoire.

Hunter's first batch of lyrics coincided with an emergent interest in all things psychedelic. In February 1967, Jefferson Airplane released

Surrealistic Pillow, which charted in March and stayed there for a year, peaking at number three. In June, the Beatles rolled out *Sgt. Pepper's Lonely Hearts Club Band,* which included "Lucy in the Sky with Diamonds." Later that year, the Rolling Stones released *Their Satanic Majesties Request.* When some critics panned that album, the Stones concluded their psychedelic phase. But with the first verse of "Dark Star," the Dead went galactic: "Dark star crashes / pouring its light / into ashes / Reason tatters / the forces tear loose / from the axis." Hunter was also raising the literary stakes. While "White Rabbit" riffed on Lewis Carroll, Hunter's lyric ("Shall we go / you and I / while we can / Through / the transitive nightfall / of diamonds") echoed the opening of T. S. Eliot's "The Love Song of J. Alfred Prufrock," a touchstone of high modernism.

The lyric for "China Cat Sunflower"—a rich mix of oxymorons and images drawn from Asian culture, comic strips, and playing cards—also strains the limits of coherence.

Look for a while at the China Cat Sunflower
Proud walking jingle in the midnight sun
Copper-dome bodhi drip a silver kimono
Like a crazy-quilt star gown through a dream night wind.

Originally a seven-verse ballad, "China Cat Sunflower" grew out of an especially intense rapture on Lake Chapala in Mexico. "I had a cat sitting on my belly," Hunter said, "and I was in a rather hypersensitive state, and I followed this cat out to—I believe it was Neptune—and there were rainbows across Neptune, and cats marching across this rainbow. . . . I wrote part of it in Mexico and part of it on Neptune." He later joked, "Nobody ever asked me the meaning of this song. People seem to know exactly what I'm talking about. It's good that a few things in this world are clear to all of us."

In fact, clarity was never a priority. "Some songs are trying to make sense," Hunter said, "and others are just dreams." For his part, Garcia considered opacity an asset, and Hunter complained that his partner's merciless editing drained the sense out of the lyrics. But Garcia was confident that such edits improved the overall effect. Because of his background in folk music, he liked songs that "hint at either a larger story or something behind the scene, shifting around. Maybe something not quite nameable. The raw lyric might be out front, but what we'll end up with is something slightly more mysterious." In another interview, Garcia reaffirmed his preference for rich ambiguity. "It was the power of the almost expressed, the resonant," Garcia said. "It seemed to speak at some other level than the most obvious one, and it was more moving for that reason." When those lyrics worked, Garcia thought, they had the "scary power that the Mass used to have in Latin." But if Garcia's folk background encouraged such mystery, Hunter's cosmic imagery was a radical departure from the tradition that he and Garcia had explored so passionately. When embedded in the most protean jam in the Grateful Dead's repertoire, the "Dark Star" lyrics accelerated the Dead's evolution from jug band to something far more ambitious.

The Dead performed "Dark Star" for the first time in Rio Nido, but "Alligator" was the first Hunter song recorded by the band. With a $250 advance on his royalties, Hunter bought a used car and headed for Seattle. The car broke down, and after discovering that he couldn't support himself by restringing beads for a friend's boutique, he hitchhiked back to San Francisco and "decided to hang in there with the Dead." He soon realized that the band was a suitable vehicle for his artistic aspirations. Those opportunities were scarce; as he later noted, "There was no place else on God's green earth that I, for one, fitted." Nevertheless, he began to think big. "My own improbable dream," he recalled, "was to aid and abet a unified indigenous American, or at least Western, music, drawing on all bona fide traditional currents, including pop. Tall order for a bunch of white kids."

Hunter's dream tapped his erudition and negative capability,

Romantic poet John Keats's term for the ability to remain "in uncertainties, mysteries, doubts without any irritable reaching after fact and reason." Even before Garcia edited Hunter's lyrics, they were dense and unruly. "Madly in love with metaphor," Hunter recalled, "I took a lover's liberties with it, crushing unlikely relations into strange situations, letting it summon a sense of its own, or none, to be continued." He realized that his "attempt to speak on as many levels at once as is humanly possible" invited "the worried concern of more orderly minds." One of those minds belonged to Jürgen Fauth, who argued that Hunter's lyrics illuminated the meaning of the Dead's music "by not meaning anything at all." Focusing on the Dead's concerts, rather than the printed page, as the primary site of lyrical meaning, Fauth claimed that each Dead performance activated "a different set of potential meanings that are inherent in the piece." The result was "an ever-changing, fluctuating whole that contains familiar parts while never yielding completely to reason." Fauth's remarks about meaninglessness and nonsense drew an uncharacteristic response from Hunter. Begrudgingly, he discussed his methods for composing "Franklin's Tower" (1975) to show that his lyrics were elusive not because they were meaningless, but because their associative patterns produced a surfeit of meaning.

If Hunter's lyrics resisted simple reduction, he returned again and again to signature themes and images. Nursery rhymes, the ultimate in traditional lyrics, figured heavily in his work, as did specific objects. "I like a diamond here, a ruby there, a rose, certain kinds of buildings, vehicles, gems," Hunter said. "These things are all real, and the word evokes the thing. That's what we're working with, evocation." His entire project, he also claimed, was shaped by the band's name, "the master metaphor for our group situation" that "called sheaves of spirits down on us all." His method was to channel those spirits to produce the "exstasis [*sic*] of a song lyric."

Hunter's ecstasies didn't resemble the feel-good sentiments of Top 40 hits. There would be no surfing safaris or warm San Franciscan nights in his work. To the contrary, his lyrics often featured foul weather, and both he and Garcia were interested in the darker tones they associated with the folk tradition. "Jerry favors a certain type of folk song," Hunter said. "He loves the mournful, death-connected ballad, the Child ballad stuff. This is a venerable source which has always spoken to him, and to me as well, which is one reason we got together writing songs—because of that haunting feel that certain traditional songs have." Hunter was less averse to political songs than Garcia; he sometimes wrote a dozen per year and promptly discarded them. "I keep doing them, though, because I feel 'protesty' about things," Hunter said. He also knew Garcia had a limited appetite for love songs, a staple of popular music. "Most songs are basically love songs," Garcia said, "and I don't feel like I'm exactly the most romantic person in the world. So I can only do so many love songs without feeling like an idiot." Scholar Brent Wood estimates that nearly three-quarters of the songs Garcia performed with the Grateful Dead featured lyrics about suffering, and nearly half of those directly addressed death. The downbeat lyrics contrasted sharply with the band's festive concerts and broadened the band's repertoire and emotional range. They also connected the Dead to American roots music in a way that escaped many casual listeners and critics.

The Summer of Love was the final incandescent moment for the Haight. The youthful throngs and national media attention crushed the fledgling art and music scene. Decades later, Bob Weir recalled the early signs of the Haight's swift descent into squalor.

Even before the summer of '67, the strangers coming in were starting to outnumber the rest of us. We weren't quite getting the riffraff yet—people with missing teeth and stuff like that. But the folks who lived in our youth ghetto in Haight-Ashbury in '65 and

'66 were of an artistic bent, almost all of them. Everyone brought something to the party. By the time of the Be-In, people were coming just to be at the party, not bringing anything. I could see the whole thing tilting.

Garcia's hippie parlance, which stressed the "drag energy" in the Haight, was more charitable, but Hunter Thompson shared Weir's assessment. "By the end of '66," Thompson wrote, "the whole neighborhood had become a cop-magnet and a bad sideshow." Rosie McGee was even pithier. "It was too many people and too much chaos, too many people with no place to go and being taken advantage of," she later told Blair Jackson. "The streets got really, really dirty. It was just insane."

Like many other residents, Garcia regarded the Haight's rapid decline as an ecological disaster. When asked whether the youth influx had been mishandled by the city, Garcia replied, "Yeah, and also by us. I mean, had we been more perceptive at that time, when we were too young and foolish to be, we would have just not said anything to *Time* magazine. We should have said, 'Oh, nothing's happening here,' and cooled it for a while." Responding to the public health threat, the Diggers taught a survival course to help destitute young people obtain food, shelter, and proper health care. But hard drugs, rising crime rates, and general mayhem turned the neighborhood into a place where Charles Manson felt right at home. Fresh out of prison in March 1967, Manson and his growing tribe settled in at 636 Cole Street. Attorney Brian Rohan, who had helped the Dead negotiate their record deal, recalled meeting Manson during that time. "He was a little troll," Rohan said. "He kept his girls on drugs all the time; they didn't know what they were doing." One of those women, Susan Atkins, reportedly dropped acid at least three hundred times during her time with Manson.

On October 6, 1967, exactly one year after the Love Pageant Rally, the San Francisco Mime Troupe staged another event, the Death of Hippie, signaling an end to the festivities. Even the Psychedelic Shop, which had quickly become a Haight-Ashbury institution, was calling it quits. "We're getting rid of all these possessions," cofounder Ron Thelin said, "in the spirit of Thoreau." By that time, the Dead were regarded as pillars of their unique but troubled community. Rock Scully noted that their home had become "the Haight's unofficial community center." At 710 Ashbury, the Dead received a steady stream of hippie neighbors, especially on weekends, as well as out-of-town visitors and impromptu dinner guests. They also played benefits for good causes and performed many small kindnesses for their neighbors. When one neighbor contracted hepatitis, she refused to enter the hospital but instead contacted McKernan, who posted a sign-up sheet on her door to make sure she was fed and cared for. Some nights he slept on her sofa, and she recalled waking up to find band members and Hells Angels chatting at the foot of her bed.

The Dead's notoriety also drew the attention of the State Narcotics Bureau and San Francisco Police Department. Four days before the Death of Hippie ceremony, police raided 710 Ashbury and arrested everyone on-site for possession of a pound of marijuana and a small amount of hashish. For legal help, the band turned to Michael Stepanian and Brian Rohan, two attorneys in Vincent Hallinan's law office who had formed the Haight-Ashbury Legal Organization. HALO performed free legal work for runaways, draft dodgers, and drug users. Much of its funding came from benefit concerts featuring the Dead and their friends, and their office was the downstairs apartment at 710 Ashbury. A New York transplant and Stanford Law School graduate, Stepanian played rugby with the senior Hallinan and had developed a reputation for toughness. But the Human Be-In, which Stepanian observed from his rugby match in Golden Gate Park, moved him. "The sun was shining, the kids were beautiful, the music was magic," he said. "That was the beginning of my education."

The Dead's drug bust was big news. Baron Wolman, *Rolling Stone* magazine's first chief photographer, visited the bail bondsman's office and subsequent press conference. The Dead were unfamiliar with the magazine, which had yet to publish its first issue, but Wolman managed to group the Dead on the front steps for the shots Jann Wenner wanted. One photograph shows Kreutzmann clowning for the camera, a somber McKernan brandishing a shotgun, and Scully cradling another one on his shoulder. That photograph appeared in *Rolling Stone*'s premiere issue the following month. "Busted!" the headline blared. "The Grateful Dead Did Get It." The headline referred to a quote from the arresting officer. "That's what ya get for dealing the killer weed," he remarked after rounding up McKernan, Weir, Scully, Danny Rifkin, Rosie McGee, and six others in the kitchen.

At the press conference, Stepanian maintained that the occupants of 710 Ashbury were arrested precisely because they were symbols of the Haight. "If they lived on Russian Hill, they wouldn't be busted," he said. "If they lived on Pacific Heights, no officer would go near the house." Danny Rifkin read a statement written by his friend Harry Shearer, who would later become famous for his work on *Saturday Night Live, This Is Spinal Tap*, and *The Simpsons*. "The arrests were made under a law that classifies smoking marijuana along with murder, rape, and armed robbery as a felony. Yet almost anyone who has studied marijuana seriously and objectively has agreed that marijuana is the least harmful chemical used for pleasure and life enhancement," Rifkin said. "The law creates a mythical danger and calls it a felony. The people who enforce the law use it almost exclusively against individuals who threaten their ideas of the way people should look and act." The marijuana laws, Rifkin claimed, were "seriously out of touch with reality." Although originally booked on felony charges, Scully and Bob Matthews each pled guilty to a misdemeanor charge of maintaining a residence where marijuana was used; both were fined $200. McKernan and Weir paid $100 fines for being in a place where marijuana was used. All were placed on probation for one year. The three women ("girls," in the newspaper report) along with two other men received similar sentences.

Rifkin's press statement served immediate legal and publicity needs, but it was also prophetic. There was, in fact, little scientific evidence that cannabis was a dangerous drug. In the nineteenth century, British and American doctors prescribed it for a wide variety of ailments, but as the medical profession turned increasingly to opiates, which were toxic but easier to dose precisely, cannabis became known as a recreational drug. California was the first state to prohibit its use, not long before the federal government also outlawed alcohol. The cannabis issue was also racialized; in the popular press, early proponents of prohibition associated weed with Mexicans, blacks, and East Indians. (The term *marijuana*, which the press popularized during this period, underscored the Mexican connection.) When marijuana use became widespread among white youth in the 1960s, the crackdown began in earnest. By 1974, marijuana arrests constituted one-quarter of all felony arrests in California. The following year, the state legislature passed the Moscone Act, which made possession of small amounts of marijuana a misdemeanor. The year after that, San Franciscans overwhelmingly voted to legalize its medical use, but state and federal law trumped that measure. Another two decades would pass before California voters reauthorized the medical use of cannabis.

The Dead were ahead of their time on marijuana, but harder drugs had also infiltrated the band's inner circle. Cocaine was common, speed was ubiquitous, and at the suggestion of Peter Coyote and his fellow Digger Emmett Grogan, Rock Scully shot heroin for the first time at 710 Ashbury. "I feel this incredible hot rush," Scully recalled in his memoir, "and the next thing I know Pigpen's in the room screaming and yelling at me. I guess I must've passed out. . . . I wake up with Grogan slapping my face and Pigpen's on top of him, ready to kick his kidneys in. And that's my first brush with smack. Scared me to death."

As the Summer of Love turned to fall, the Dead decided to take more control over their touring operation. It was a natural impulse, especially given the local art scene's do-it-yourself ethos, but the band realized they needed help. Scully hired his friend Ron Rakow to arrange a Pacific Northwest tour with Brian Rohan, whom Rakow soon outflanked in the Dead's organization.

The son of a New York City garment manufacturer, Rakow had moved to San Francisco to manage a small finance company after a decade of working on Wall Street, where he started as a runner on the floor of the New York Stock Exchange. He met Scully and Rifkin in San Francisco when they applied for a $12,000 loan to buy equipment. When Rakow said he didn't know anything about the music business, they replied, "You'll hear all about it—you listen to the Beatles, the Rolling Stones?" Rakow replied that he listened to Frank Sinatra and Tony Bennett. Scully and Rifkin invited him to a concert, where Rakow was offered a Coca-Cola dosed with LSD. "After about an hour," Rakow recalled, "I got this twitch in my face, and my eyes started to tear, and I had this incredible need for tissues and shit like that. And I really got off on the music—*really* got off on it. I solved a lot of my own personal problems, just right there at the end of some of Garcia's guitar licks. So I just started to come around, and I gave them the money—I didn't lend it to them, I gave it to them, 'cause it was obvious that they were never going to be able to pay it back." Soon Rakow was spearheading a new partnership between the Grateful Dead, Jefferson Airplane, and Quicksilver Messenger Service. Dubbed Headstone Productions, it was created to operate the Carousel Ballroom in downtown San Francisco. Located over a rug showroom on the corner of Van Ness Avenue and Market Street, the new music venue opened its doors in February 1968.

The same month, Neal Cassady died in San Miguel de Allende, Mexico. He had traveled there to avoid several traffic warrants, but as he approached his forty-second birthday, he was also questioning his routines. "I get in a group," he told his wife, "and everyone just stares at me, expecting me to perform . . . and my nerves are so shot, I get

high . . . and there I go again, I don't know what else to do." He also
rued his life decisions. "Twenty years of fast living—there's just not
much left, and my kids are all screwed up," he reportedly told one of his
companions. "Don't do what I have done." After leaving a wedding party
where he ingested tequila and Seconal, he took a walk along a railroad
track, collapsed, and died an hour after arriving at a local hospital. Cassady's demise was consistent with the emptiness and frantic questing
that Kerouac's narrator described in *On the Road*. Living with his mother
in Florida, Kerouac would succumb the following year while drinking
and watching daytime television. He began to hemorrhage and died in a
local hospital.

Back in San Francisco, Ron Rakow quickly developed a reputation
as a hustler. Weir recalled that Rakow introduced the word *scam* into
the Dead's working vocabulary. Paradoxically, Rakow's flexible ethics
enhanced his authority with the Dead. Many hippie bands felt they
needed aggressive managers to protect them from music industry pred-
ators. David Crosby, for example, believed that his new group needed a
shark, and a young David Geffen was theirs. Playing to that view, Rakow convinced the Dead that Bill Graham was taking advantage of
them. It wasn't a difficult case to make. Graham had already developed
a reputation for taking meticulous care of the talent but trimming on
the financial side. Graham had his own view of Rakow: "He'd been in
the world where I came from, but then he'd gotten hip and soulful,"
Graham said. "One of the ways these kind of people always endeared
themselves to the Dead was to say, 'We can handle Bill.' What they really meant was, 'We're going to prove to you that we can be a bigger
crook than him.' And they always were."

The Headstone venture attracted other new faces to the Dead scene.
One was Jon McIntire, a San Francisco State College student who managed the Carousel's concessions. Another was Betty Cantor, who was
working with the Family Dog before she started selling hot dogs at the
Carousel. She was dating Bob Matthews, Weir's high school friend and

a former member of Mother McCree's Uptown Jug Champions. Matthews worked on the Carousel's sound system, and Cantor began her apprenticeship as a sound engineer there. Bill "Kidd" Candelario performed odd jobs and eventually joined the Dead's crew. The Carousel also reassembled some of the old cohort. Laird Grant became the stage manager. Sue Swanson, another Weir classmate who had attended the Warlocks' first rehearsals and published the *Olompali Sunday Times*, sold tickets with Connie Bonner, her friend and longtime band supporter. Owsley Stanley was the Carousel's house sound engineer. He was out on bail after an arrest in Orinda, an upscale suburb on the east side of the Berkeley hills; the police claimed he tableted 217 grams of LSD—about 750,000 doses. The Carousel work was a healthy distraction for him. "I had a little problem in December," he recalled in an interview, "and in January or February, I was really itching to do something."

Lacking a business plan, the Carousel operation was messy from the beginning. That much was foreseen by Janis Joplin, who told Scully, "It's like turning over the Bank of America to a bunch of six-year-olds. I give you guys six months at best. A bunch of hippies high on acid running a business—my Lord!" Bill Graham was also skeptical and later described Rakow's modus operandi. "Ron Rakow was a wheeler-dealer who convinced the Dead and other Bay Area groups that he could run the hall for them," Graham said. "In terms of being my competition, he was mainly playing to their ego. If I would offer a band, say, seven hundred and fifty dollars, he would go to fifteen hundred. I would go to seventeen. He would go to two thousand. *Pass!* Because even at capacity, he would lose money paying that much." In Graham's view, the Carousel's management also shared a fatal flaw with Chet Helms, who admitted too many friends for free to his shows. "The band had so many guests? They *all* got in with no questions asked," Graham said. "And then the band would want to know *why* they hadn't gotten paid."

By summer, the Carousel was out of business, and Graham flew to Ireland to meet the building's owner. Over a breakfast of steak, eggs, and bourbon, they negotiated a three-year lease. Graham closed the Fillmore Auditorium as a full-time rock venue and reopened the Carousel as Fillmore West. Graham's lease on the Fillmore Auditorium ran to March 1973, but *Rolling Stone* reported that he planned to put the hall "at the disposal of the Fillmore community, at no profit to him, for Black-run political events and musical and theatrical productions." That fall, Graham also launched a booking agency, and the Dead joined Graham's roster of clients. As his operation took off, others were closing their doors. In October, the Dead played their last shows for the Family Dog at the Avalon. Chet Helms had lost his license after a series of hearings before the Board of Permit Appeals. The chairman of that august body, Ralph Gleason noted, "indicated that he had never been [to the Avalon], would not go, and thought everybody ought to be in bed at 9 p.m. and that he had heard that people smoked LSD there!"

Having rushed through the production of their debut album, the Dead took a more deliberate approach to *Anthem of the Sun,* which appeared in July 1968. The album's title derived from a fanciful 1926 book by James Churchward called *The Lost Continent of Mu.* A former British officer and plantation owner in Ceylon, Churchward claimed to have discovered and translated, through psychic inspiration, ancient tablets that described an advanced civilization that sank in the Pacific Ocean sixty thousand years ago. His book, which found its way to 710 Ashbury, described an instrument made out of a skull that was used to perform the "Anthem of the Sun."

By the time *Anthem* appeared, concept albums by the Beatles (*Sgt. Pepper*) and the Beach Boys (*Pet Sounds*) had become critical and commercial successes. Always inclined to innovate, the Dead gave full expression to the avant-garde energies circulating in San Francisco during that time. Lesh later noted that *Anthem* was "an attempt to convey the experience of consciousness itself, in a manner that fully articulates its simultaneous, layered, multifarious, dimension-hopping nature." For him, the album was an important work. "I've always felt that as an artistic statement, *Anthem of the Sun* was our most innovative and far-reaching achievement on record." The album also solidified Lesh's artistic and personal bond with Garcia. "Both of us were seekers, brimming with intellectual and spiritual curiosity; both of us were always actively search-ing for the next wave, or what was around the next corner, or what was hidden behind the surface of appearances," Lesh recalled in his memoir. "To be sure, this obsession sometimes drove the other members of the band crazy, but boy, did Jerry and I have fun."

For all its innovations, *Anthem of the Sun* had three things in com-mon with its precursor. It didn't sound like the band in concert, none of the songs worked as singles, and it didn't sell well. Warner Bros. Rec-ords shipped sixteen hundred copies and sold five hundred. The critical reception was mixed. "Each side of this album is a mish-mash of self-indulgent formlessness," *High Fidelity* magazine charged in its July 1968 issue. "There's really no excuse for this kind of junk, but there is an ex-planation. Drugs. The album is essentially background music for pot par-ties (or Methedrine or LSD)." The reviewer didn't have anything against drugs as such. "Pot can enhance the listener's experience; it can make something good sound great, but it can also make something trite sound meaningful," he maintained. "It is within the latter category that this album belongs, and I'm sorry that the Dead have fallen victim to the delusion of the complete psychedelic experience." *Boston After Dark* drew a very different conclusion. *Anthem of the Sun* was "an important album in the history of jazz, rock, and modern music in general. It is also a delight to listen to. . . . The Dead's use of understatement, the soft, and the subtle gracefully form every moment. Their free use of time, complex, intelligent bridging, and their use of straight electronic music make the Grateful Dead virtually unique in the rock world." Likewise, *Rolling Stone* called the album "an extraordinary event."

Anthem of the Sun was also the first Grateful Dead album to include drummer Mickey Hart. A Brooklyn native, Michael Steven Hartman was the only band member not born and raised in the Bay Area. Both of his parents were drummers, but Hart had little contact with his father, Lenny, after his parents divorced. Mickey enlisted in the air force because, he said, "that's where the great drummers were." After leaving the military, he moved to San Carlos, a peninsula suburb, where his father ran a drum store. Mickey took LSD for the first time there and saw the drums come alive. At a Count Basie concert at the Fillmore, Hart met Kreutzmann; afterward, the pair visited the Matrix, a club cofounded by Marty Balin in the Marina district of San Francisco, to hear Big Brother & the Holding Company. "The din was incredible," Hart recalled. "And just as the noise was starting to get unbearable, up to the mike stepped a singer who opened her mouth and split my head with a thunderous cry. It was Janis Joplin." Before the night was over, he and Kreutzmann were in sync. A month later, Hart sat in with the Dead at a local gig; by the end of that night, he was in the band.

As *Anthem of the Sun* made its way into the world, the nation was experiencing a political crisis that had been brewing for years. Policy failures, assassinations, social ruptures, and a divisive war had all taken their toll. While American soldiers decimated the Vietnamese population and perished by the thousands, the major political parties refused to acknowledge what Washington insiders already knew—that military victory was impossible. Opinion polls showed that more and more Americans opposed the war, but even in relatively liberal San Francisco, most citizens supported the effort despite mounting evidence that the US government had been untruthful about the war's origins and prospects.

After years of organizing, many antiwar leaders felt they had exhausted the opportunities provided by conventional politics, and some promoted direct action. That trend gave rise to an especially theatrical form of protest developed by the yippies, who issued a press release before the Democratic Party's national convention in Chicago vowing to "piss and shit and fuck in public . . . we will be constantly stoned or tripping on every drug known to man." There were also rumors that LSD would be slipped into Chicago's water supply. When thousands of protesters converged on the city, police flayed provocateurs, peaceful protesters, and observers alike. Even a seasoned journalist such as Hunter Thompson, who was bludgeoned by Chicago police while trying to return to his hotel, recoiled from the scene. The police brutality, he said later, was ten times worse than anything he had seen the Hells Angels do. "I went from a state of Cold Shock on Monday, to Fear on Tuesday, then Rage, and finally Hysteria—which lasted for a month," he recalled. "I went to the Democratic convention as a journalist and returned a raving beast."

The Dead continued their program of ignoring politics to death, but much like the nation as a whole, they were in disarray. As their new album tanked, the Dead and their partners were forced to close the Carousel. Even the band's comparatively stable lineup became a source of consternation. In August, the Dead met to discuss the ejection of Weir and McKernan. Garcia and Lesh were exasperated with Weir's rhythm-guitar work and felt that McKernan wasn't keeping up with the band's musical experimentation. At one especially tense meeting, Scully and Garcia outlined the problem but never called the question. A spaced-out Weir had difficulty forming a response. "I'm losing control of words here," he said. "They are falling apart in my mouth." Hoping to adjourn, Hart said he was prepared to make a motion. "A motion?" Weir asked. "What's that?" The meeting ended without a clear decision. McKernan skipped a few gigs, and the band recruited Tom Constanten, who had finished his hitch in the air force, to play keyboards for their studio recordings. But otherwise the personnel crisis blew over.

By the fall of 1968, the Dead had cleared out of 710 Ashbury and set up shop in Marin County. Garcia and Adams were the first to depart, leaving the Haight within weeks of the drug arrest they had narrowly avoided. But the Dead had been considering a move as early as March 1967, when the *Chronicle* reported that they had their eye on Santa Fe, New Mexico. They would always be associated with San Francisco, where they resided for only two years, but their new home shaped their project and its reception almost as much as the Haight did.

Only a few miles north of the city, Marin County was a very different kind of community. Most residents lived in small towns strung along Highway 101, but Marin was also home to several bohemian enclaves in its redwood forests and along its rugged coastline. The county's ample open space was a major part of its appeal as well as the focus of protracted political conflict. With the completion of the Golden Gate Bridge in the 1930s, the county's population quickly doubled. The Sierra Club had failed to stop the bridge's construction, but local conservation groups, led by well-connected society ladies, helped blunt the forces of development. In 1972, San Francisco congressman Phillip Burton augmented their efforts by authoring the bill to establish the Golden Gate National Recreation Area. Capitalizing on a wave of decommissioned military bases clustered around the Golden Gate, Burton's bill was later described as "the most outrageous move in the history of the Bay Area greenbelt." In one legislative stroke, the GGNRA protected seventy-five thousand acres of coastal lands from development. Stinson Beach and Bolinas, where Garcia and other musicians would occasionally make house, remained isolated burgs instead of the popular seaside destinations that state planners envisioned.

The Dead's move to Marin County coincided with the early days of the back-to-the-land movement, which was as utopian as the Haight-Ashbury scene that had preceded it. With the despoliation of that neighborhood, many San Francisco hippies decamped to fashion simpler and more rustic lifestyles in California's northern counties. The movement's underlying impulses were organic extensions of Beat and Prankster values. Kerouac and Gary Snyder had featured the California hinterlands in their work, but Mount Tamalpais and Muir Woods in Marin County were also touchstones for both writers. Kesey had pre-figured the back-to-the-land ethic in La Honda, but after serving time in the San Mateo County jail for marijuana possession, he retreated to the family dairy farm in rural Oregon. Mixing light literary production with occasional public appearances, Kesey became a psychedelic gentle-man farmer.

In a piece for *The New York Times Magazine*, Hunter Thompson con-nected the dots between the Beats, Diggers, American Indians, tribal-ism, and the back-to-the-land movement. "The Digger ethic of mass sharing goes along with the American Indian motif that is basic to the Hashbury scene," Thompson explained. "The cult of 'tribalism' is regarded by many of the older hippies as the key to survival. Poet Gary Snyder, a hippy guru, sees a 'back to the land' movement as the answer to the food and lodging problem. He urges hippies to move out of the cities, form tribes, purchase land, and live communally in remote areas."

The movement was by no means limited to the Bay Area. New En-gland produced its essential literature, starting with Henry David Thoreau's *Walden* (1854). "I went to the woods because I wished to live deliberately," Thoreau wrote, "to front only the essential facts of life, and see if I could not learn what it had to teach, and not, when I came to die, discover that I had not lived." Published a century after Thoreau's classic, Helen and Scott Nearing's *Living the Good Life: How to Live Sanely and Simply in a Troubled World* described their modern-day home-steading experience in Vermont and became another guidepost. Those works stressed the spiritual benefits of simple living, reflection, and eco-nomic self-sufficiency. The hippie back-to-the-landers picked up on those themes, but many were more interested in community than in rug-ged individualism or solitary contemplation.

As the Dead's interest in Santa Fe suggested, northern New Mexico was seen as another promising site for communal living. It became the proposed site of Earth People's Park, a seventy-thousand-acre hippie habitat that Phil Lesh mentioned approvingly in interviews. The community never materialized, in part because many native New Mexicans resisted it from the outset, but hippies established several communes in the area, including the Hog Farm, which was linked to the Grateful Dead through Hugh Romney. The comedian had left the Committee and moved to the outskirts of Los Angeles, where he hosted a passel of Pranksters at his one-bedroom cabin. He was promptly evicted but became a caretaker at a nearby hog farm; over time, the Hog Farm became a "bizarre communal experiment" where the "people began to outnumber the pigs."

Southern California's other back-to-the-land efforts often grew out of licit or illicit enterprises that had strong spiritual and psychedelic underpinnings. The Source Family, for example, ran a popular health-food store on Sunset Strip; its members lived in the Hollywood Hills before moving to Hawaii in 1974. Its founder—a former marine and Hollywood stuntman who also served as the lead singer in their psychedelic rock band—died the next year in his first hang-gliding attempt, and the community collapsed shortly thereafter. Likewise, the Brotherhood of Eternal Love was a group of Orange County surfers who produced LSD, dealt hashish, and lived on a commune in the mountains near Palm Springs. One of its members, Mike Hynson, was best known as the costar of *Endless Summer*, the popular 1966 film that followed two surfers as they circumnavigated the globe in search of the perfect wave. In 1969, the Brotherhood's founder died of a synthetic-psilocybin overdose, and the following year they paid the Weather Underground $25,000 to spring Timothy Leary from federal prison and smuggle him to Algeria. The Brotherhood cratered in 1972, when most of its members were arrested on drug charges. Two members who escaped arrest were nabbed in San Francisco while waiting in line for the Dead's 1973 New Year's Eve show.

Most back-to-the-land projects were far less flamboyant and consisted of small-scale efforts to live harmoniously and intentionally outside urban areas. But at least one group of San Francisco hippies enacted the new utopian vision in their patented way: they loaded up the bus and hit the road. In 1971, Stephen Gaskin, a popular lecturer at San Francisco State College, led a caravan of hippies to the Farm, a 175-acre parcel in the Tennessee backwoods. Their goal, one founding member said, was to extend "the visions of the psychedelic world into the straight every-day world." They were also "trying to be tribal," another recalled. "To get back to something that white Euro/American culture had lost . . . Trying to get real close real fast, so we can get on with the trip." In Tennessee, Gaskin's teaching included a dose of San Francisco ecstasy. "Stephen Gaskin gets people high by telling the truth," the Farm's promotional literature maintained.

Other San Francisco hippies, such as Digger and Mime Troupe veteran Peter Coyote, helped establish communes that dotted the land-scape between Marin County and California's northern border. Coyote was part of the Black Bear Ranch, an eighty-acre former gold mine in Dunsmuir, California, which was purchased by the Free Family for $22,000. After submitting a down payment, Coyote and others began a fund-raising effort that tapped their celebrity contacts in Los Angeles. According to one founding member, the original concept was to create a "mountain fortress in the spirit of Che Guevara, where city activists would be able to come up, hide out, practice riflery and pistol shooting, have hand grenade practice, whatever." When they arrived at the prop-erty, however, Coyote found "people already camping there who refused to budge. It was, after all, free land, wasn't it?"

A key figure in the Bay Area back-to-the-land movement was Stew-art Brand, the Prankster and American Indian enthusiast who co-organized the Trips Festival in 1966. Almost immediately after that event, he conceived another project while tripping on the roof of his North Beach apartment building. Brand was pondering Buckminster Fuller's notion that people regarded the earth's resources as unlimited, in part because they thought of the earth as flat. If so, Brand concluded, a photograph of Earth taken from space would alter their collective sense of the planet and its resources. He linked that brainstorm to the fact that many of his friends were establishing rural communes. Timothy Leary had also picked up on and endorsed that idea. In his brief remarks at the Human Be-In, Leary encouraged the crowd to "get Western man out of the cities and back into tribes and villages." He amplified that notion in a later exchange, the so-called Houseboat Summit, with Allen Ginsberg, Gary Snyder, and philosopher Alan Watts. Sponsored by the *San Francisco Oracle* and held on Watts's boat in Marin, the Houseboat Summit led Leary to dream openly of MIT scientists taking LSD, buying a little farm out in Lexington, and using their creativity "to make some new kind of machines that will turn people on instead of bomb them."

Brand thought such communards would need tools for their project, and he decided to create a catalog in the L.L. Bean tradition and pair it with a "road show." Specifically, he would tour the communes and offer his collection of tools, many of them books, for living off the land. One of Brand's earliest clients was Ramon Sender, his partner in organizing the Trips Festival. Sender was already well versed in experimental living. His wife's great-grandfather was the founder of the Oneida Community, a nineteenth-century religious commune with unorthodox sexual views and practices. In the 1950s, Sender and his wife joined the Bruderhof, an international Christian community, but he decamped in 1959 and settled in San Francisco, where he filed for divorce, resumed his music studies, and founded the Tape Music Center. At the Trips Festival, he met Lou Gottlieb, a former singer with the Limeliters and owner of Morning Star ranch, a thirty-two-acre parcel in Sonoma County north of Marin. Soon they were planning to present that property as open land, a utopian community without hierarchy or government. Gottlieb's "old lady," Rena Morning Star, described her attraction to communal living. "Having a baby, having a family, living with God in the country," she said. "Just being free to trip as I want to. That's what Morning Star gives me."

As Sender and Gottlieb shaped up Morning Star ranch, Sender visited Rancho Olompali after the Dead had decamped and found the hippie resort insufficiently radical. "We looked down our noses at them," Sender recalled, "because it wasn't 'open' land." But by that time, the Olompali community had more urgent problems than Sender's disdain. "Stoned hippies going ten mph had to enter sixty mph traffic, which was not good," Sender remarked. "Then the horses escaped and got out on the freeway and somebody hit one. Then two children drowned in the pool. It was looking like the adults were not exactly there. Shortly after, the main house caught fire and the Novato fire chief died of a heart attack on the way to the fire." The only other casualty of that fire, Sender added, was a Chihuahua. Rancho Olompali had become unhealthy for children and other living things, and the commune folded after twenty months.

In the spring of 1968, Brand printed a six-page list of 120 items, loaded his Dodge pickup truck, and visited communes in New Mexico and Colorado. He sold only $200 worth of merchandise, but the catalog quickly became a much bigger affair. By 1971, the *Last Whole Earth Catalog* grew to 448 pages, sold 1.2 million copies, and landed a National Book Award. The tools it featured included mechanical devices, outdoor recreational gear, home-weaving kits, potter's wheels, bamboo flutes, and reports on the science of plastics. Just as Henry David Thoreau had chosen to live off the land at Walden Pond, the *Whole Earth Catalog*'s implied audience could experience full, rich, and meaningful lives off the grid. But the catalog's look and feel didn't evoke Brook Farm or other New England experimental communities. Its diction and iconography were thoroughly Western, complete with cowboys and Indians. Eventually, Brand himself decided to live off the land—literally. He purchased a sixty-four-foot tugboat, docked it in a Marin County marina, and began living there with his wife, a Chippewa Indian, in 1982.

In its various incarnations, Brand's *Whole Earth Catalog* expressed a distinctively American blend of utopian aspiration and pragmatism. "We *are* as gods," the first edition claimed in its opening sentence, "and might as well get good at it." Topics ranged from the establishment of space colonies to septic-tank practices. One scholar described the catalog's how-to orientation and Western provenance as a countercultural version of *Sunset* magazine. Like *Sunset* (and the Dead), Brand avoided political topics as such, preferring to focus on how to change the games people play. In the preface to the *Last Whole Earth Catalog*, he articulated his strategy. "You don't change a game by winning it or losing it or refereeing it or observing it," he claimed. "You change it by leaving and going somewhere else and starting a new game from scratch."

Over time, the *Whole Earth Catalog* also proved to be an important bridge between the Bay Area's counterculture and cyberculture. Kevin Kelly, who later became the founding executive editor of *Wired* magazine, edited and published the *Whole Earth Catalog* and described it as "a great example of user-generated content, without advertising, before the Internet." In his view, "Brand invented the blogosphere long before there was any such thing as a blog." In a 2005 commencement speech at Stanford University, Apple cofounder Steven Jobs called the *Whole Earth Epilog* "one of the bibles of my generation" and "sort of like Google in paperback form, thirty-five years before Google came along. It was idealistic and overflowing with neat tools and great notions." In 1972, Brand wrote an article for *Rolling Stone* that featured the first use of the term *personal computer* in print. "Ready or not, computers are coming to the people," Brand announced. "That's good news, maybe the best since psychedelics."

For all of Brand's futurism and avant-garde credentials, however, his project was also deeply nostalgic. Both the *Whole Earth Catalog* and the back-to-the-land movement tapped a set of long-standing and powerful

American myths and symbols. If the frontier was an essential part of the American character, the domestication of the land that lay behind the frontier was even more central to the nation's sense of itself. Since the colonial period, the small farmer had occupied a special place in the American political imagination. The lowly European peasant was venerated but oppressed, and the South's plantations were built on slave labor, but the small farmer was his own man; he produced wealth, moved American civilization westward, and possessed the economic and moral independence indispensable to a healthy democracy. The yeoman reflected both a Jeffersonian ideal and a political fantasy at the center of nineteenth-century Republican doctrine: namely, that free land in the West would serve as a safety valve for social and economic tensions in the industrialized East. President Lincoln, who signed bills to expand homesteading and agricultural research, hoped that westward expansion would create the Garden of the World.

The master symbol of the garden created a new cast of heroic figures and defined the promise of American life. By the end of the nineteenth century, however, that ideal bore little resemblance to the situation on the ground. "Free land" in the West required the violent dispossession of the Native Americans and Mexicans who lived there, and it didn't prevent decades of bitter labor conflicts back East. Drought, overgrazing, mining, commercialized farming, poor soil conservation, and the completion of the transcontinental railroad were quickly converting the American West into something far less pastoral than the original vision. Despite these challenges, the myth endured and even flourished. In a famous 1956 article, historian Richard Hofstadter argued that the more commercial American society became, the more it clung nostalgically to noncommercial agrarian values. Even as the myth of the happy yeoman became less descriptive, it retained the power to evoke a simpler and more organic society. For Walt Whitman, that society was "the real genuine America," and Brand's *Whole Earth Catalog* was a love letter to that nation.

The back-to-the-land movement also found expression in light popular culture. *The Beverly Hillbillies,* a situation comedy that drew some of its imagery from John Ford's *The Grapes of Wrath,* turned out to be a major success. CBS followed up with *Petticoat Junction* and *Green Acres,* which were set in overlapping rural communities. *Green Acres* turned the hillbilly scenario on its head by featuring a New York City couple that moves to a rural town to fulfill the husband's lifelong dream of becoming a farmer. Like other programs with rural settings and themes, including *The Andy Griffith Show, Green Acres* found a large audience. Most of these programs contained at least an implicit critique of modern consumer society, but that perspective didn't serve the needs of the advertising industry that underwrote the programs. In 1971, CBS canceled *Green Acres* and other related programs as part of its "rural purge." One *Green Acres* actor recalled 1971 as "the year the network canceled everything with a tree—including *Lassie.*"

If the back-to-the-land movement was an exercise in nostalgia, it also had real-world consequences. One was the creation of a new generation of small farmers in California's backcountry. The state's family-farming tradition had always been weak; even before the Gold Rush, the Spanish and Mexican land grants had been huge, and after California became a state, its farmers quickly embraced industrialized farming. Big agriculture produced what author Carey McWilliams called "factories in the field" and the labor conflicts featured in *The Grapes of Wrath.* But after a series of fits and starts, the Haight-Ashbury refugees, who originally sought to create a less materialistic and more spiritual subculture in the California hinterlands, realized that their new habitat, with its rugged terrain and sparse population, was well suited to the cultivation of a profitable commodity. Despite a series of crackdowns and eradication efforts, cannabis quickly became one of California's top cash crops, and its growers bore more than a passing resemblance to Jeffersonian yeomen, not to mention the moonshiners in Harry Smith's invisible republic.

• • •

Although the Dead's move to Marin County chimed well with the back-to-the-land movement, they weren't exactly roughing it. From their office in Novato, they had easy access to San Francisco—and from there, everywhere else. But they could also spread out on prime Marin acreage and live the Western lifestyle. Mickey Hart rented a thirty-two-acre ranch from the city of Novato for $250 a month. Not far from Rancho Olompali, Hart's ranch became a focal point for the band, crew, and extended family, including the Hells Angels. After gigs, Hart relaxed by dosing his horse and riding the trails. "The only thing you'd notice," Hart recalled, "was his hair used to stand up on end. And when you stopped, sometimes he rolled, like a pussycat."

Garcia, Carolyn Adams, and Sunshine Kesey set up house in nearby Larkspur, where he worked with Hunter on a new batch of songs. Janis Joplin and Bill Graham also lived in Larkspur, and some of Joplin's band members settled in Olema, the West Marin hamlet where Peter Coyote and others had established a commune. Over the years, the Dead shifted about restlessly within Marin County; Lesh settled in Fairfax, a hippie village west of San Rafael. McKernan shared a house with Constanten in Novato, Weir had a ranch in Nicasio and later a home in Mill Valley, and Kreutzmann maintained a ranch in Novato.

The musical migration wasn't lost on *Rolling Stone*, which noted in 1970 that Marin County was "where all good San Francisco musicians go when they've made it, or even before." By that time, Quicksilver Messenger Service, the Sons of Champlin, former Charlatan Dan Hicks, and Steve Miller were living there. The migration would continue, *Rolling Stone* predicted, because it was better to go hungry in Marin than in New York or Chicago. The article also claimed hyperbolically that the concentration of musicians had become demographically significant: "Maybe half of Mill Valley is composed of rock musicians and the dope dealers they support, and the lawyers they support, and the attendant narcs and politicians."

The Dead's living arrangements became a topic of interest to the media. Pat O'Haire, a *New York Daily News* columnist, quizzed Jon McIntire about the Dead's lifestyle in Marin County. "I asked how many there were in the commune," O'Haire wrote, "and I almost lost control of the car when he answered, 'About fifty.'" Although McIntire explained that they thought of themselves as a family, not a commune, O'Haire struggled with the concept. He asked McIntire how fifty grown people lived together, how anything got decided, and whether there was a leader. "We make decisions every possible way—sometimes by voting, other times all it takes is an agreement," McIntire replied. "As to money, well, the band supports the family, but everyone does something. We own the horse farms, land in Marin County, and other things. Band members and technicians all draw salaries. We work a lot—we have to, I guess—and it seems we're always on the road." As for the group dynamic, McIntire returned to the family concept. "Sure, we argue, just like any blood family," he told O'Haire. "And we make up, like people have to do."

In an interview with *CREEM* magazine, an upstart rock publication edited by Lester Bangs, the Dead discussed their living arrangements, finances, and family responsibilities. "I would say there are about fifty in the family," Lesh said, but Weir noted that they also tried to support the scene around them. "Not just our family," Weir said, "but the hippie craftsmen and artists and stuff like that. And we have electronics crews who are exploring new horizons in sound. And they need support, and we're just about the only people who can give it to them, us and the Airplane. And that's expensive." When asked whether those groups all depended on the band, Garcia replied, "Well, we depend on us a lot, and each of us has at least some small scene to cover . . . more or less. But essentially we are in debt, and we've been working to get out of that.

And to get a little ahead of ourselves. Mostly to buy ourselves time so we don't have to work so fucking much." Quizzed about their pay, Weir called it a "working-class salary. Nothing spectacular." Lesh added that they weren't making top scale, and McKernan went straight to the number: $90 per week (about $556 in 2014 dollars).

As the back-to-the-land movement peaked, the Dead made a remarkable appearance on Hugh Hefner's television show, *Playboy After Dark*, which staged cocktail parties at a studio version of the magazine publisher's penthouse. The urbane setting and cool-jazz aesthetic contrasted sharply with the Dead's hippie ethos. Clad in a black tuxedo, hair slicked down, and smoking a pipe, Hefner personified a Kennedy-era masculine ideal that now seemed decidedly square. Hefner asked Garcia, who wore a brightly colored poncho for the occasion, about the Haight-Ashbury scene, which the Dead had already abandoned. Garcia replied that the media had latched onto the location and missed the point. When Hefner asked why the Dead had two drummers, Garcia joked, "Mutual annihilation." They didn't compete, he explained, but rather chased each other around, and he compared that activity to a serpent eating its own tail. Garcia then invited Hefner to stand between them to experience the drums making "figure eights on their sides in your head." Hefner politely declined and asked whether the Dead would play a number for them. "Absolutely not," Garcia answered playfully before stepping out from behind the wet bar and leading the Dead through "Mountains of the Moon" and "Saint Stephen."

Later, a rumor circulated that someone in the Dead's entourage dosed the set's coffeepot and Hefner's Pepsi. "Things began to get odder and odder," Dennis McNally reported. "Technicians began to stare up into the lights. The male extras began to loosen their ties, and women started to loosen their tops, their make-up melting along with their inhibitions." While the credits rolled, Pigpen belted out "Love Light," and the penthouse's cool-jazz vibe began to heat up. As Lesh and Kreutzmann were leaving, a bright-eyed Hefner stopped them and said, "I want to thank you for your special gift."

The Dead's move to Marin put them in closer touch with David Crosby, who lived on his own Novato ranch. Crosby had crossed paths with Garcia and his friends on the folk circuit even before they formed the Warlocks. Two years after leaving the Byrds, Crosby formed a new band with Graham Nash of the Hollies and Stephen Stills of Buffalo Springfield. The resulting trio released its first album on Atlantic Records in May 1969. The cover photograph featured the band members in jeans, work shirts, and boots, sitting on a tattered sofa in front of a dusty frame house. In the gatefold photograph, which was shot near Big Bear Lake in the rugged mountains of Southern California, the three men appeared in fur parkas with a sunset in the background. Their acoustic guitars, sweet harmonies, and folksy iconography were a winning combination, especially after Neil Young, another Buffalo Springfield alumnus, joined their tour later that summer. *Crosby, Stills & Nash,* their eponymous debut album, was an immediate critical and commercial success, charting at number six with two Top 40 singles.

That success coincided with two other countercultural benchmarks: the release of *Easy Rider* and the Woodstock Music & Art Fair. Directed by Dennis Hopper, *Easy Rider* carried forward the Beat and Prankster emphasis on mobility and freedom. But the film had a sharper political message, and alienation and disaffection set its downbeat mood. The film's protagonists, Wyatt and Billy, are modern-day cowboys, riding their chopped motorcycles across the Southwest flush with cash after a successful drug deal. Along the way to Mardi Gras in New Orleans, Wyatt and Billy visit a back-to-the-land commune in northern New Mexico modeled on the Hog Farm. Furnished with LSD and invited to stay, they decide to continue their trek. In effect, the two men reverse the migration depicted in *The Grapes of Wrath,* in which sharecroppers reluctantly abandon their agrarian way of life to make a new start in California. But Wyatt realizes that ecstasy, mobility, and community are inadequate, and their search for freedom ends when two rednecks murder them, literally on the road. The low-budget film surprised the industry by becoming the third-highest-grossing film of 1969. As a result, Hollywood moguls more comfortable with *Hello, Dolly!* than with the counterculture began to approve films by Francis Ford Coppola, George Lucas, Robert Altman, Martin Scorsese, and other maverick directors.

The Woodstock festival, which took place at Max Yasgur's six-hundred-acre dairy farm in upstate New York, was less jadedly imagined as a return to a lost Eden. Joni Mitchell's "Woodstock" became a hit for Crosby, Stills, Nash & Young that year, and the lyrics ("And we got to get ourselves back to the garden,") became an anthem for the back-to-the-land movement at its peak.

In the case of Woodstock, getting back to the garden meant thirty-two acts performing for 450,000 spectators. Traffic snarled for miles, thunderstorms turned Yasgur's farm into a vast mudscape, and food, sanitation, and first aid were in short supply. Hugh Romney and other Hog Farm members were a high-profile source of relief, but the county declared a state of emergency, and Governor Nelson Rockefeller almost dispatched ten thousand National Guardsmen to prevent the concert from devolving into chaos. Even the performers were unprepared for the scale and spectacle of Woodstock. Playing for only the second time before a live audience, Crosby, Stills & Nash were visibly nervous; from the stage, Stephen Stills admitted to the throngs that he and his colleagues were "scared shitless."

The Grateful Dead joined the Woodstock party in progress on Friday. By that time, 175,000 spectators were on-site, and many motorists had abandoned their cars and walked to Yasgur's farm. Arriving at the Holiday Inn in nearby Liberty, the Dead joined Joan Baez, Sly Stone,

Ravi Shankar, and Janis Joplin in the line for room keys. The next day, the Dead's management chose not to sign the film release, and they were absent from the documentary that grossed $50 million and received the Academy Award for Best Documentary Feature in 1970. Given the Dead's performance, it may have been just as well. Their equipment was too heavy for the revolving stage, and the electrical grounding was flawed. Owsley Stanley tried to solve the latter problem before the band performed, which delayed their set. Even worse, his solution didn't work. When the band finally stepped up to their microphones Saturday at midnight, they received powerful shocks. Weir was essentially electrocuted and thrown back against the drums. His girlfriend recalled seeing "a blue arc go from the mike to his top lip. . . . He had a huge blister, awful, when the song was over." Lesh's speaker picked up radio chatter from the helicopter pilots overhead, and the wind blew the light-show screen so hard that the crew had to slash holes in it. The Dead's sixty-minute set sounded fine to many observers, but the band considered it another blown opportunity.

Despite their ordeal, the Dead valued the Woodstock experience. Together, the musicians and audience had overcome many challenges, both natural and logistical, and exemplified the peaceful and ecstatic life they envisioned. The next day, the Dead were evacuated by helicopter with $2,250 in earnings. Although the Dead embodied the spirit of Woodstock perhaps as fully as any other group of that era, their compensation roughly reflected their position in the rock hierarchy at that time. Another Bay Area band, Creedence Clearwater Revival, received four times that much. Jefferson Airplane collected $15,000, and Jimi Hendrix was the biggest earner at $18,000.

Back in San Francisco, Ralph Gleason applauded Woodstock and free concerts generally. "The idea of giving away something you can sell is quite revolutionary in the context of the American society," Gleason wrote in the *Chronicle*. "It means that the society's main straitjacket is no longer useful." The challenge posed by free concerts wasn't necessarily political in the usual sense or even intentional. "Consciously or subconsciously, by their free concerts the pop musicians are rejecting the value system of The Establishment," he claimed. "When the love of money weakens, can the roots of evil survive?"

Gleason also tried to support that effort locally. Along with other notables—including Tom Donahue, Bill Graham, Rock Scully, Jann Wenner, and Jefferson Airplane manager Bill Thompson—Gleason served on the San Francisco Music Council, which was trying to organize its own free three-day event that summer. The Wild West Festival was scheduled for August in Golden Gate Park, and the plans were fantastical. When organizers met with community groups, however, they were caught flat-footed, and Graham became embroiled in a profane yelling match with a black neighborhood activist. Graham's famous temper was running especially hot. Light-show artists were on strike for higher wages, and Garcia wouldn't cross their picket line. The strike was called off when Graham took a hard line, but his outbursts undermined the festival's chances and revealed the fragility of San Francisco's vaunted music community.

In the meantime, Gleason continued to tout the Dead. "Garcia is really a remarkable musician," he wrote a month before the Wild West Festival collapsed. "No one I can think of, with the possible exception of Wes Montgomery and Barney Kessel, has had such an individual sound in his guitar playing. Garcia is paradoxical. His sound is butter-soft and mellow, but it cuts through." Garcia's voice was also improving, Gleason noted, and sometimes served as "a truly impressive instrument." He also complimented Lesh's play, which reminded him of saxophonist Paul Desmond "in one of those long dialogues with Brubeck or maybe Miles Davis in musical conversation with Tony Williams." A few days later, Gleason attended a free show in Golden Gate Park with the Dead and Jefferson Airplane. "Out in the sunlight, the people looked happy and wild and strangely beautiful as they always do," he reported. That beauty was enhanced by the Dead and the Airplane, who worked "in a truly spiritual way. They make you feel good."

The New York critics also felt the good vibrations. Writing for the *Village Voice*, Lucian Truscott IV held up the Dead as a model of peaceful comportment during an especially turbulent period in American public life.

> The forces of "law and order" in this city and elsewhere might do well to take note of the Dead's approach to and solutions of the problem that plagues every large gathering of people. It's a low-key approach with a sure-fire solution. Ask no favors of the crowd; rather, let the musical, physical, and spiritual presence of the Dead themselves fill the atmosphere with vibrations as directional as they are all pervasive.

In his piece for the *New York Times*, Robert Christgau opened with a more skeptical view of the Dead and the San Francisco scene. Noting that eight San Francisco groups "copped some instant hype" at the Monterey Pop Festival, Christgau reported that within two years "the success trip has shattered six of the eight." The main problem was youthful West Coast naïveté. "At the beginning it seemed so simple: everyone loved everyone, and everyone dug music," he wrote. "But the communal thing has collapsed. The only exceptions are Jefferson Airplane, biggest of the groups commercially, which persists and grows amid rumors of dissension, and the Grateful Dead, which has managed to evade success altogether." The Dead had the best buzz, but they were "basically a blues band without a blues singer—Pigpen tried but never made it, and Garcia didn't even try."

Yet Christgau also detected and praised an underlying authenticity in the Dead's project. "It was not so much music then as a gestalt: they really did love everyone, and they really did transcend showbiz," he conceded. "Merely by being themselves they projected an almost cosmic benevolence." Christgau also applauded the band's versatility. In his view, their western and soul numbers were warm-ups for the longer jams that closed the show. Those jams were "the Dead's true music," which "always aims toward spiritual exaltation." Even as they spurned rock's predictable beat, the Dead produced music that worked kinetically. "But if rock is music that makes you dance," Christgau concluded, "then they may make the best rock of all."

The Dead also had *Rolling Stone* in their corner, and shortly after Woodstock, a cover story by Michael Lydon featured them. A Boston native, Lydon had reported on the civil rights movement and the London music scene before *Newsweek* transferred him to San Francisco, where he quickly went native. He grew his hair, quit *Newsweek*, and joined *Rolling Stone*. His cover story, which the Dead considered one of the better descriptions of their project, showed them in a state of furious muddle. By that time, they had parted ways with Bill Graham's booking agency and hired Lenny Hart, Mickey's father, as their new manager. The article described how a single campus show in Santa Barbara devolved into a logistical clusterfuck. But the Dead were nothing if not resilient, and their next show at an Oregon honky-tonk was smoking hot. Lydon presented the touring operation as a work in progress, but he also captured the Dead's intelligence, energy, openness, and dedication to the music. His article began with a suggestive passage from Mark Twain's *Adventures of Huckleberry Finn*: "But I reckon I got to light out for the Territory ahead of the rest, because Aunt Sally she's going to adopt me and sivilise me and I can't stand it. I been there before." The implication was that the Dead were archetypal American explorers of wild psychic frontiers.

Lydon's *Rolling Stone* piece preceded the release of *Live/Dead*, a double album the Dead recorded earlier that year at the Fillmore West and Avalon Ballroom. In his *Chronicle* column, Ralph Gleason raved about one of those shows:

The Grateful Dead are the Grateful Dead, which is to say they are absolutely wonderful. They have one of the most individual sounds of any band and its tone is set by the soft butter feeling of Jerry Garcia's lead guitar. . . . To hear their long instrumental passages with Garcia and Phil Lesh (on bass) weaving lines above the tremendous rhythms of two drummers, Bill Sommers [*sic*] and Mickey Hart, is a joy.

Rolling Stone complimented the new album. Journalist Lenny Kaye, who would soon become Patti Smith's guitarist and producer, noted that *Live/Dead* "explains why the Dead are one of the best performing bands in America, why their music touches on ground that most other groups don't even know exists." The album received praise from East Coast critics as well. "Finally, a great album from the Dead," wrote Dave Marsh in *CREEM*. Robert Christgau gave the album an A+ and a stellar capsule review: "Side two of this four-sided set contains the finest rock improvisation ever recorded, and the rest is gently transcendent as usual. Beautifully recorded, too." That success would have been a fitting end to an eventful year, but 1969 wasn't done with the Grateful Dead.

The Rolling Stones, who had missed Woodstock, accepted a suggestion from Rock Scully, Danny Rifkin, and Emmett Grogan to finish their 1969 tour with a free concert in the Bay Area. Partly designed to blunt criticism of the band's ticket prices, the original concept was a relatively modest affair in Golden Gate Park. But the Stones, who were also filming a documentary, had something grander in mind. Mick Jagger described the free concert they were planning as a Christmas and Hanukkah gift for America's youth, and promoters billed it as "Woodstock West." When San Francisco officials heard that announcement, they nixed Golden Gate Park as a venue. The Sears Point Raceway in Sonoma County was the second option. Built into the bare hills a few miles east of Rancho Olompali, the raceway was a far cry from the lush glades of Golden Gate Park. But its parent company, Concert Associates, also

promoted rock events, and it had unexpectedly lost the rights to promote the Stones concerts in Los Angeles. Concert Associates wanted
a piece of the documentary-film revenues, but the Stones wouldn't
cede it.

As the parties tried to finalize the deal, a major news story emerged
from Southern California: Charles Manson and his followers were arrested for murder. After leaving the Haight and plying the Western
highways in their black school bus, the Manson Family had resettled in
Los Angeles. There they visited the Hog Farm commune, where Manson tried to exchange one of his women for Hugh Romney's wife. While
hitchhiking, two female members of the Manson Family also met
Dennis Wilson, the Beach Boys' drummer. Wilson left the women at
his house that afternoon, and when he returned, Manson emerged to
meet him in the driveway. "Are you going to hurt me?" Wilson asked.
"Do I look like I'm going to hurt you, brother?" Manson replied. He
then dropped to his knees and kissed Wilson's feet. Eventually, Wilson
paid the group's medical bills and arranged for studio time so Manson
could record his own songs; when Neil Young heard some of them, he
recommended Manson to his label.

Wilson's manager finally ordered the Manson Family out of the
house, but Manson's interest in the music business continued. Obsessed
by the Beatles' *White Album,* especially "Helter Skelter," Manson told
his followers that his own album would trigger social chaos. Manson
tried to interest music producer Terry Melcher in his work. Melcher,
who had produced albums for the Beach Boys and the Byrds, was initially
receptive, but when he passed on Manson's project, Manson directed his
followers to visit the home Melcher had shared with his girlfriend, actress
Candice Bergen. By that time, film director Roman Polanski was renting
the house with his pregnant wife, Sharon Tate. Manson's orders were to
kill everyone on-site and "leave a sign . . . something witchy." Polanski
was out of town, but Manson's minions brutally murdered Tate and her
guests. When Tate begged for her and her unborn baby's lives, one of

the female executioners told her, "Look, bitch, I don't care about you. . . . You're going to die, and I don't feel anything about it." Later, she told a fellow inmate, "You have to have a real love in your heart to do this for people." The other victims that night included San Francisco socialite and coffee heiress Abigail Folger. By coincidence, Folger's mother volunteered at the Haight-Ashbury Free Medical Clinic, where the Manson Family had received treatment.

The next night, Manson Family members entered the Los Feliz home of supermarket executive Leno LaBianca and his wife, Rosemary. The Manson Family's connection to the LaBiancas was even slighter than the one to Tate; the year before, the Family had attended a party at the house next door. Upon entering the LaBianca home, they tied up the couple, bayoneted them to death, carved the word *war* into his abdomen, and used her blood to write *Rise* and *Death to pigs* on the walls and *Healter Skelter* [*sic*] on the refrigerator.

The police broke the case in November 1969 when a member of the Straight Satans, a Southern California motorcycle gang, told police that Manson had mentioned the homicides to him. Earlier, Manson had tried to hire the gang to provide security at his Death Valley commune. The arrests preceded the Altamont concert by four days, and to many, the Manson Family story read like a ghoulish inversion of Haight-Ashbury flower power. Psychedelic drugs, communal living, crackpot spirituality, rock music, and motorcycle gangs weren't producing a peaceful world but instead a chaotic and senselessly violent one.

As the nation absorbed the Manson Family horror show, the Sears Point deal collapsed. Ralph Gleason's attempts to report on the concert arrangements reflected the chaos. "Are the Rolling Stones seriously going to appear free next weekend?" Gleason wondered. "Your guess is as good as mine, at this point." It seemed unlikely, but Gleason thought the Stones might have been spooked by the San Francisco Mime Troupe's demand, issued the day before, that all the television and film money be directed to a defense fund established for the Weather Underground, which had split from Students for a Democratic Society earlier that year. "There doesn't really seem to be time enough to get it on in some other facility," Gleason wrote. "It has really been masterfully mismanaged. The Stones' tour this year has been handled like that."

Gleason's next column, which ran the day before the scheduled concert, tried to offer helpful advice to spectators: "If you're going to Sears Point Raceway tomorrow to see the Rolling Stones in their free concert, don't worry about wearing a flower in your hair. Just be sure to have food, water, and transportation, baby." In a later edition of that day's newspaper, he followed up with a fresh column about the concert and its organization. He felt something was wrong, but couldn't identify it. "I don't know what, really, just bad vibes," he wrote. "So when I got home, it wasn't really a surprise to get the succession of phone calls that indicated the raceway people had withdrawn their permission." The free-concert concept Gleason had applauded that summer was in complete disarray. "Behind it all was a long torturous tale of confusion and bad communication," Gleason wrote. "As late as yesterday afternoon, it was not set just who Mick Jagger would permit to share the stage with the Stones, other than the Grateful Dead."

Determined to follow through, the organizers looked to the windswept hills of the far East Bay. The treeless grasslands of eastern Alameda County were mostly used for cattle grazing, but a businessman had recently built the Altamont Raceway there, and he thought the publicity would help his new enterprise. The final lineup was certainly impressive: Santana would open, followed by Jefferson Airplane, the Flying Burrito Brothers, and Crosby, Stills, Nash & Young. After the Dead's set, the Rolling Stones would close the show and film their performance for the documentary. But the last-minute relocation made it impossible to provide adequate facilities for what turned out to be three hundred thousand spectators. Security was also a question mark, but the Dead never needed much of that for their spontaneous Golden

Gate Park gigs, and Woodstock had shown that good vibrations could overcome poor logistics. At Emmett Grogan's suggestion, the Rolling Stones' manager, Sam Cutler, offered the Hells Angels $500 worth of beer to sit near the stage and help out as needed. As organizers frantically prepared for the event, Grogan scrawled a prophetic message on the office blackboard: *Charlie Manson Memorial Hippie Love Death Cult Festival.*

When the big day arrived, all the predictable problems came to pass along with some novel ones. As spectators made their way to the make-shift venue, traffic knotted up. Many trampled through the fields, tore down fences, scattered livestock, and caused thousands of dollars of damage. After sunset, they used disassembled barns and sheds as firewood to protect themselves from the December chill. In his memoir, Cutler described the tableau the next morning: "Dawn broke at Altamont on December 6, 1969, and from the stage it looked like I was observing the camp of some dreadful invading army." That stage, less than one meter high, had been built for the Sears Point site; now it sat at the bottom of a hill, where it looked even less substantial. To secure it, crews erected a chain-link fence around the front of the stage and parked a phalanx of trucks behind it.

When the Hells Angels arrived, they placed their motorcycles between the stage and the chain-link fence. But when the music started, the crowd surged toward the stage, took down the fence, and besmirched the choppers. Valuing their motorcycles over all else, the Hells Angels retaliated with pool cues, bottles, and fists. Hoping to pacify them, Southern California drug dealers near the stage shared their Orange Sunshine, a brand of powerful LSD, with the raging gang members. "I remember filling up a bottle of cheap wine with Sunshine LSD, and another guy I was with handed it to the Hells Angels," one of them recalled. "They punched him in the face and took the wine and drank it." Cutler watched the bloody skirmishes with mounting horror. "Before me was the ugly truth of what we had collectively wrought, manifested in greed, blood, drug overdoses, spilled guts, and hatred. The peace-and-love generation was smashing itself to bits."

In the middle of Jefferson Airplane's set, singer Marty Balin left the stage to help an audience member under attack from Hells Angels. "I had my eyes closed," Balin recounted, "and I heard a commotion. I opened my eyes, and the Hells Angels are beating this guy with pool cues. I saw the whole crowd, this mass, just back up and allow it to happen. I said, 'To hell with the song, this guy needs some help.' So I went down there and started fighting, helping the guy out." Another Angel, nicknamed Animal, knocked Balin unconscious, and Grace Slick announced from the stage, "The Hells Angels just knocked out my lead singer." Sam Cutler approached Animal to explain that the show required conscious musicians. "That motherfucker insulted my people," Animal replied. "He talks like that about my people, he's going to get it." Hoping for reconciliation, Cutler led Animal to a groggy Balin, but when Animal offered to shake his hand, Balin cursed him. Animal immediately knocked him out again and told Cutler, "I tried." The Hells Angels intimidated other musicians as well. One gang member threatened Jefferson Airplane's Paul Kantner, and another poked Stephen Stills with a bicycle spoke until he bled. Yet another wouldn't let the Dead out of their truck and physically threatened Lesh.

Later, Garcia recalled the scene. "I've worked out the essence of the way it was that day, and it was so *weird*, man," he said. "I took some STP, and you just don't know. . . . Phil and I, we got off the helicopter and we came down through the crowd, and it was like Dante's Inferno. It was spreading out in concentric waves." He was reluctant to attribute the weirdness to the Hells Angels alone. "It wasn't just the Angels. There were weird kinds of psychic violence happening around the edges that didn't have anything to do with the blows. Shit, I don't know—spiritual panic or something. And then there were all of those anonymous, borderline, violent street types, that aren't necessarily heads—they may take dope, but that doesn't mean they're heads—and there was of course, you know, the top-forty world."

The Dead decided not to play at all, and because the Rolling Stones weren't ready to go on, that meant no music at all for two hours. Tension mounted, and when the music resumed at nightfall, the violence intensified. As the Stones began their seventh number, a young black man named Meredith Hunter rushed the stage and was rebuffed. He brandished a gun and was swarmed by Hells Angels; one of them, Alan Passaro, stabbed him, and several others stomped him as he lay dying. The Stones appealed for calm, but the show went on. They played seven more songs before ending the concert with "Street Fighting Man." Many spectators had no idea what had transpired in front of the stage; for them, Altamont was an epic show. But the documentary film, *Gimme Shelter*, caught much of the violence on film, and police used the footage to identify Passaro, who was eventually acquitted on grounds of self-defense.

In his memoir, Lesh cast Altamont as the atavistic dark side of the Woodstock utopia, and Stewart Brand connected the Haight's Dionysian spirit to both the primitivism at Altamont and the Manson Family atrocities: "If you're going to have a Ken Kesey, you're going to have a Charles Manson—the one basically gave permission to the other," Brand said. "I went to Altamont and thought it was terrific. The hubris of hiring the Angels to work as security was both ballsy and bad judgment, but that's what the period was all about—exploring the limits of bad judgment." Given the spirit of the times, Brand saw nothing unusual about the violence at Altamont. "It seemed entirely appropriate that there'd be people beating each other to death in the midst of all that. Dionysus leads people to being shredded and eaten. Those were the death-defying leaps we were about in those days, and some people die in the process."

Brand's reference to Dionysus wasn't gratuitous. The ancient Athenian festivals, and contemporary responses to them, bore a striking similarity to the Grateful Dead's project and its reception. As god of the grape harvest, Dionysus symbolized ecstasy, chaos, danger, and irrationality. Some ancient Greeks criticized his festival's wild music and dancing; in Plato's *Laws*, for example, Philostratus rebukes the Athenians for their "lascivious jigs" and brightly colored clothing. After witnessing a Grateful Dead concert, mythologist Joseph Campbell remarked on the similarity. "The first thing I thought of was the Dionysian festivals, of course," he said. "This is Dionysus talking through these kids." But Campbell found no fault with the Grateful Dead event he attended; indeed, he was happy to see the Dionysian spirit alive and well in modern American culture. "This is a wonderful, fervent loss of self in the larger self of a homogeneous community. This is what it's all about!" For Campbell, the concert he witnessed represented thousands of people "tied at the heart."

No one described Altamont that way. Sol Stern, a *Ramparts* magazine veteran, called the disaster "Pearl Harbor to the Woodstock Nation." Before the concert, Stern and his friends fantasized about marching en masse from Altamont to the nearby Alameda County jail to free the prisoners. "The reality was that when we beat a hasty retreat from Altamont," Stern wrote, "we left behind the body of Meredith Hunter, one of our people, a kid many of us had probably nodded to on Telegraph Avenue." Ralph Gleason, who once praised the scene's Dionysian spirit, used his *Chronicle* column to ruminate on the disaster. "Is this the new community? Is this what Woodstock promised?" Gleason asked rhetorically. "Gathered together as a tribe, what happened? Brutality, murder, despoliation, you name it." Gleason found plenty of blame to go around. "I think we have to remember that it wasn't just the Stones and it wasn't just the Angels, it was all of us. The Angels were dupes and so in a way are the Stones and so are we. And it's time to get it all straight."

Unlike Brand and Lesh, Gleason didn't see Altamont as the dark side of countercultural utopianism but rather as its death knell. The following year, he wrote a related article for *Esquire*. "If the name 'Woodstock' has come to denote the flowering of one phase of the youth culture," he concluded, "'Altamont' has come to mean the end of it." The underground press, which proliferated during the late 1960s, drew a similar conclusion. "STONES CONCERT ENDS IT," read the front-page headline of the *Berkeley Tribe*. Altamont "exploded the myth of innocence for a section of America." Jagger resembled a "diabolical prince," and the entire event was a metaphor for a more general social disintegration. "Clearly, nobody is in control. Not the Angels, not the people. Not Richard Nixon, or his pigs. Nobody."

Sensing trouble, Robert Hunter had skipped Altamont and watched *Easy Rider* instead. But in response to Gleason's *Chronicle* column, he wrote "New Speedway Boogie," which debuted at a live performance two weeks after Altamont. Hunter's lyric begins with a pointed request to a tiresome interlocutor.

> *Please don't dominate the rap, Jack*
> *if you got nothing new to say*
> *If you please, go back up the track*
> *This train got to run today.*

The speaker's initial impatience opens out to a more complex moral deliberation. He acknowledges the gravity of the Altamont debacle ("Who can deny? Who can deny?") but also notes the difficulty of interpreting events in the heat of the moment: "Things went down we don't understand / but I think in time we will." For Hunter, Altamont was part of a longer journey, not all of which he expected to be blissful. That much is clear from another verse, which substitutes the opening locomotive trope with an automotive one.

You can't overlook the lack, Jack
of any other highway to ride.
It's got no signs or dividing lines
and very few rules to guide.

It was an apt summary of the Dead's quandary. Despite mystery, moral ambiguity, and potential peril, they would continue their journey.

PART 2

MOBILITY

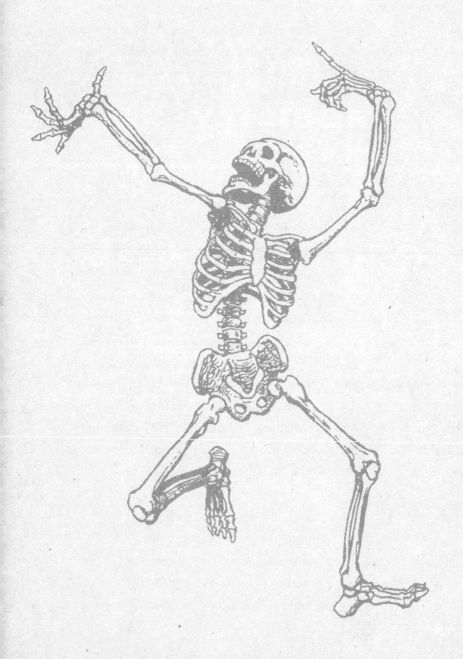

Two months after the Altamont disaster, the Grateful Dead entered the Pacific High Recording Studio in San Francisco to begin work on a new album. They completed their sessions in only nine days, a tempo determined by their substantial debt—about $180,000—to Warner Bros. Records. Their third album, *Aoxomoxoa*, had taken eight months to finish, and though it included many keepers, including "Saint Stephen" and "China Cat Sunflower," it was expensive to produce and sold poorly. *Live/Dead*, which appeared in November 1969, was more successful on both fronts, but the band was still in the red.

The Dead decided to try another approach. "So I was thinking," Garcia said later, "when we go into the studio next time, let's try a real close-to-the-bone approach, like the way they record country and western records—a few instruments, relatively simple and easy-to-record songs." The streamlining also represented a shift in the Dead's self-understanding. "We were into a much more relaxed thing about that time, and we were also out of our pretentious thing," Garcia said. "We weren't feeling so much like an experimental music group, but were feeling more like a good old band." The Dead's fashion choices reflected the new direction their music was taking; denim shirts and cowboy hats were replacing louder hippie costumes from the Haight. David Nelson, who hadn't seen Garcia for two years, recalled the outward change. Garcia had "gone through a transformation," Nelson said. "He had the full beard and he was wearing the Levi shirt and that poncho all the time. He looked beatified. I thought he looked like an angel. Like an angel with a bad streak."

Unlike its precursor, the new album featured acoustic guitars, pedal steel, and traditional song structures. Weir began contributing country-western cover songs, but according to Hunter, "The others were a little worried about the folk direction, but agreeable." Lesh favored experimental, open-ended jams, but even he admitted that the band's previous work was "too explosive. It took too much out of us, for one thing." Hart felt similarly. "The electric side was so fun and so stimulating and so rewarding and so energetic, and then all of a sudden we were starting to explore the soft side of the GD," he said. "And I thought, what a beautiful thing—acoustic guitars. It was cold out there in the feedback, electric GD world."

The Dead weren't the only musicians moving in that direction. "I was very much impressed with the area [Robbie] Robertson was working in," Hunter later said about the Band's lead guitarist. "I took it and moved it to the West, which is an area I'm familiar with." Hunter's chief influence, Bob Dylan, was mining a similar vein. After his Basement Tape sessions with the Band, Dylan traveled to Nashville to record *John Wesley Harding*. Playing acoustic guitar and backed by studio musicians, he quickly laid down the album's twelve tracks. "That's really the way to do a recording," he told Jann Wenner in 1969, "in a peaceful, relaxed setting, in somebody's basement. With the windows open and a dog lying on the floor." *Rolling Stone* later maintained that Dylan's effort "had the result of stopping the psychedelic movement cold." Dylan's influence on Garcia and Hunter was a given; both admired his songwriting and thought he gave rock music a modicum of respectability and authority. "He took [rock music] out of the realm of ignorant guys banging away on electrical instruments and put it somewhere else altogether," Garcia said later.

The Dead's new tracks also coincided with the success of Crosby, Stills & Nash, with whom they were spending more time in and out of the studio. The Dead adopted some of their friends' musical techniques, especially on the vocal tracks, and began exploring their own countrified sound. "Hearing those guys sing and how nice they sounded together, we thought, 'We can try that. Let's work on it a little,'" said Garcia. Hart was more emphatic about that influence. "Crosby, Stills and Nash came along and changed us tremendously. Stills lived with me for three months around the time of their first record, and he and David Crosby really turned Jerry and Bobby onto the voice as the holy instrument," Hart said. "They turned us away from pure improvisation and more toward songs." Shortly after the Dead completed their recordings, Crosby, Stills, Nash & Young released *Déjà Vu*. The cover art, photographed at Crosby's Novato ranch, was even folksier than the debut album's, and *Déjà Vu* sold even better, briefly reaching number one and settling at number eleven for the year. Garcia, whose steel-guitar riff opened "Teach Your Children," contributed directly to that success.

Even before the Dead's new album appeared, Garcia's growing interest in country music was leading to other creative endeavors. One of them began when he rekindled a friendship with John "Marmaduke" Dawson, an original member of Mother McCree's Uptown Jug Champions. After that group dissolved, Dawson played with David Nelson in several other bands, including the Mescaline Rompers, before moving to Los Angeles to study at Occidental College. Dawson relished the Bakersfield style of country music, especially the work of Merle Haggard and Buck Owens, and after returning to the Bay Area, he began practicing country tunes with Garcia. Dawson arranged a regular gig at the Hofbrau House in Menlo Park. "I'd play for a couple of hours for the people eating their roast-beef sandwiches," said Dawson. Garcia joined him there with his pedal steel. "There wasn't any money involved," Dawson said, "and there was no importance to the thing. But it got to be pretty good." They also worked on their country chops in Weir's living room and Hart's barn.

Adding David Nelson to the lineup, Dawson and Garcia formed a new country-rock band, the New Riders of the Purple Sage, which began opening for the Dead in May 1970. It was another example of working closer to the knuckle. Because the New Riders already included Hart, Lesh, and Garcia, adding Nelson and Dawson to the tour added a new musical layer but only a small increase in the total nose count. "We gave them an opening act for cheap," Dawson said. "For the price of two tickets, [Garcia] got a new five-piece band to open for the Dead."

The show was a good value for fans as well. The first set of the evening's entertainment usually featured the New Riders, the second set show-cased the Dead's new acoustic numbers, and the third was an all-electric set that usually ran more than two hours. "Jerry would be onstage all night long," Nelson said. "In those days, the show wasn't over at two in the morning. Sometimes, it was over at six in the morning. Not every gig. But sometimes." The longer sets, which became a Dead signature, were related to their acid consumption. "In the first days," Dawson said, "the length of the sets was due to the LSD because that gave you that unlimited amount of energy. You didn't even know when you were tired, and you couldn't go to sleep."

The New Riders soon signed with Columbia Records, whose presi-dent, Clive Davis, was eager to put Garcia under contract. The New Riders' first album appeared in 1971; their fourth, *The Adventures of Panama Red*, appeared in 1973 and went gold. The title track, written by Peter Rowan, portrayed a smuggler named after a popular strain of marijuana. Robert Hunter also contributed a song, "Kick in the Head," to that album. He had already composed "Friend of the Devil" with Dawson. When the pair first played that song for Garcia, he pointed out the need for a bridge; Hunter composed it quickly, and Garcia added the music for that section. Somewhere along the line, "Friend of the Devil" became a Grateful Dead classic instead of a New Riders number.

The Dead's folk-country turn put Garcia and Hunter at the center of the band's creative process. For their new album, Garcia cowrote seven of the eight new tracks and sang lead on five. McKernan sang one num-ber, "Easy Wind," which Hunter wrote in the spirit of old-school blues-man Robert Johnson. The album's first track, "Uncle John's Band," also had a folksy feel, and in the wake of Altamont, its initial question ("What I want to know / is are you kind?") was especially soothing. Hunter's lyric for "Cumberland Blues," a rambling bluegrass number about Appalachian miners, may have received the highest compliment of all. Assuming that the San Francisco hippies were covering a traditional song, a coal miner asked Hunter what the original lyricist would have thought of the Dead's misappropriation.

Although Hunter's lyrics tapped traditional forms, his themes were grounded in contemporary experience. "Dire Wolf" and its refrain ("Please don't murder me") reflected the fear that many Bay Area residents felt between December 1968 and October 1969, when the so-called Zodiac Killer murdered four men and three women and then mailed a series of taunting letters to the press. "Every night I was coming home from the studio," Garcia told Paul Krassner, "and I'd stop at an intersection and look around, and if a car pulled up, it was like, this is it, I'm gonna die now. It became a game. Every night I was conscious of that thing, and the refrain got to be so real to me. 'Please don't murder me, *please* don't murder me.'"

"Black Peter," a lament from a man on his deathbed, grew out of an especially heavy LSD trip Hunter experienced the previous year at the Carousel. Having accidentally consumed a megadose of LSD and mescaline, Hunter endured multiple imaginary deaths over a long evening. The same night, Janis Joplin read Stanley the riot act. "Janis Joplin came in while I was starting to rush on it," Hunter recalled, "and starts screaming at Owsley—whose fault it was *not,* by the way—'You son of a bitch! You dosed my drummer, and he's had to go to the hospital!' And all of a sudden I just saw blood pouring out of her mouth and going all over the room, and, oh, *the horror* of it!" Stanley's companion, Rhoney Gissen, recalled finding Hunter in the street outside the ballroom. "I heard a moan, a guttural utterance as if an animal were in distress," she wrote in her memoir. "I saw a naked human form, flesh and hair lying in the gutter. I bent closer and recognized Robert Hunter's face. He was dirty, distressed, muttering to himself." When Hunter recognized Stanley, he leapt to his feet, threw a headlock on him, and cried, "I will annihilate you, Owsleystein!" Stanley initially wanted to abandon Hunter in favor of a steak at a nearby restaurant, but at Gissen's urging, he helped collect Hunter's clothes and saw him through his dark journey. Hunter later described that evening as the end of his LSD career. "It really did flatten me for a couple of years and made me seriously consider what the wisdom of this drug-taking had been."

Another Hunter lyric, "Casey Jones," added a modern twist to the traditional ballad. In earlier versions of the Casey Jones story, the legendary engineer raced to make up lost time and died on the runaway train. But Hunter's lyric joined two folk tropes, railroading and cocaine use, in the first verse: "Drivin' that train / High on cocaine / Casey Jones, you better / watch your speed." The implicit danger in the first line foreshadows the engineer's spectacular self-destruction, which arrives in the final verse: "Come 'round the bend / You know it's the end / The fireman screams and / The engine just gleams." The song captured the drug culture's dark appeal and inflected that countercultural sublime with a cautionary rhetoric, which critic James Williams has argued is a prominent theme in Hunter's work. That attitude was consistent with the role Hunter assumed as far back as Garcia and Ruppenthal's first LSD experience: in essence, an experienced guide to drug-culture neophytes.

Although Hunter considered "Casey Jones" an antidrug song, he also insisted that he was no one's guardian. The Grateful Dead didn't attempt to be parental, he told journalist David Gans: "We say, 'Do what you want to do.' Like, we don't take a stand for or against drugs. There are individual stands; some people have been through a few things like that, and they're sharing the wisdom . . . that this leads nowhere. Fine. But we're not taking a group stance." Hunter applauded a 12-step support group that met at Dead concerts, and he didn't regard psychoactive drugs as a necessary part of the scene: "I don't think you need to be stoned out of your mind to enjoy the Grateful Dead experience."

Shortly after that song's release, Garcia discussed its production and effects. In his view, "Casey Jones" stressed the unsavory aspects of cocaine use as well as its allure: "It's got a split-second little delay, which sounds very mechanical, like a typewriter almost, on the vocal, which is like a little bit jangly," he said. "I always thought it's a pretty good musical picture of what cocaine is like. A little bit evil. And hard-edged. And also that singsongy thing, because that's what it *is*, a singsongy thing, a little melody that gets in your head." The next year, however, Garcia expressed remorse over the song's reception. When asked how he felt about "putting out that cocaine vibe," he replied, "I'm sorry I did it. We didn't mean for people to go out and start taking a lot of cocaine when we put out that song. It's clearly an anti-coke song. The words aren't light, good-time words—it's just the feeling of it." Garcia often conceded quickly to criticism in his interviews; in fact, he frequently outdid his critics when it came to the Dead's shortcomings. In this case, however, he also explained that "Casey Jones" was more of a tribute to musical tradition. "First of all, there's a whole tradition of cocaine songs, there's a tradition of train songs, and there's a tradition of Casey Jones songs." he said. "It's partly my way of expressing thanks to that whole tradition: to try and add a good song to it." That tradition included Furry Lewis's "Kassie Jones," which Harry Smith had included in his folk anthology.

Despite the antidrug message in "Casey Jones," the mere mention of cocaine limited the song's radio play. One disc jockey in Boston showed Hunter an album with a nail scratch across the "Casey Jones" track. He told Hunter the program director inflicted the damage and instructed the disc jockeys not to play the song because the word *cocaine* was in it. That prohibition came from the Federal Communications Commission, the program director said, adding that they might lose their license if they played the song. A mild profanity in "Uncle John's Band" had the same effect, and Hunter was convinced that radio-industry standards prevented some of his best songs from achieving more commercial success.

In June 1970, Warner Bros. Records released the new album, *Workingman's Dead*. Its title and sepia-tinted album cover, which was art directed by Alton Kelley, signaled the band's new tack. The photograph showed the musicians and Hunter standing in line on a corner in the Hunters Point district of San Francisco, while Kreutzmann, clad in a cowboy hat, lounged in a corner doorway. Weir wore a duster and an oversize belt buckle, and a lunch pail lay at McKernan's feet. The overall effect was Western, vintage, and blue-collar. One reviewer noted that the album cover resembled something from Chris Strachwitz's East Bay label, Arhoolie Records. Founded in 1960 and specializing in blues, Cajun, zydeco, and other American roots idioms, Arhoolie had been part of Garcia's personal music stream since his bluegrass days. The band members in the cover photograph, the reviewer also observed, "look like fine, upstanding proles."

The Dead's new sound took some reviewers by surprise. "Heavens to Lyserge momma," one wrote in UCLA's *Daily Bruin*, "what's the Dead doing playing country?" During live performances, too, fans routinely called for a stronger statement. "Go back to electric!" shouted one fan at the Fillmore. "Relax, man," Garcia said. "It's gonna be all right." At another show, fans urged the Dead to play louder. "No, no, man, you don't understand," Garcia said, "this is the part where we *play* soft, and you *listen* loud!" Appearing with two blues bands in New York City in 1969, the Dead took the stage with Garcia on pedal steel guitar. "Some blues freaks walked out," Robert Christgau reported, "and one ignoramus started catcalling about 'cowboys.' If he only knew. The Dead aren't cowboys, but their style is so eclectic that it doesn't matter." For Gary Lambert, who attended that blues show and eventually worked for the Grateful Dead, the shift was both radical and fearless. It demonstrated the Dead's willingness to go out on a limb, their refusal to resort to rock conventions, and their hunger to expand and improve their music.

At a Fillmore East show in 1971, the Dead performed Merle Haggard's "Okie from Muskogee" with the Beach Boys. Haggard's lyric mocked San Francisco hippies, but the Dead's rendition was no parody; rather, it was another example of the Dead's urge to incorporate as many branches of American roots music as possible into their project. That effort was impeded but by no means thwarted by the music business's generic classifications. In 1946, *Billboard* renamed its "Hillbilly" music chart "American Folk." But only three years later, as folk artists were subjected to scrutiny for their leftist politics, *Billboard* renamed that category "Country & Western." Over time, the audience and politics of country-western music diverged from those of folk music despite their musical similarities. Characteristically, the Dead ignored or blurred those generic distinctions whenever it suited them.

The Dead's folk-country turn reversed the terms of the controversy engendered by Bob Dylan's decision to go electric at the 1965 Newport Folk Festival. With Garcia's coaching, however, Dead fans learned to love the new sound, and back at Warner Bros. Records, Joe Smith was thrilled. When he listened to "Uncle John's Band" for the first time, he heard cash registers ringing. *Rolling Stone* concurred with Smith, calling that song "without question, the best recorded track done by this band." *Workingman's Dead* reached number twenty-seven on the pop chart and went gold four years later. *Rolling Stone* readers voted it the best album of 1970, just ahead of *Déjà Vu*. With the release of *Workingman's Dead*, the band had something to tour behind. In the second half of the year, they played more than thirty shows in and around New York City, which became fertile ground for album sales as well as the nascent taping community.

Despite that success, not all was well with the Dead's operation. Shortly before the band recorded *Workingman's Dead*, concerns about Lenny Hart's management began to surface. Hart had agreed to share office space with the Family Dog near San Francisco's Ocean Beach, but as that plan unfolded, Chet Helms suspected that Lenny was keeping two sets of books. Helms alerted Larry "Ram Rod" Shurtliff, head of the road crew, as well as Jon McIntire and Rock Scully about his suspicion. Lenny Hart quickly moved the Dead's office back to Novato, but in

March 1970, he was caught red-handed. Garcia had worked on the sound track of Michelangelo Antonioni's *Zabriskie Point,* and Carolyn Adams planned to use those earnings to purchase the house she and Garcia had been renting in Larkspur. An office worker told her the check had finally arrived, but when Adams stopped by the office to pick it up, Lenny Hart claimed they hadn't received it. After Adams called a quick meeting to probe the discrepancy, Shurtliff threatened to resign unless Lenny Hart was fired.

Lenny Hart was given a week to put the books in order; instead, he departed with the band's business files and a large portion of its cash reserves. The Dead asked famed San Francisco detective Hal Lipset to investigate. Lipset and Sam Cutler, who had been living with Garcia since Altamont, discovered that Lenny Hart had been squirreling away money from the outset. The following year, a private detective located Hart in San Diego, where he was arrested. In August, Lenny Hart appeared in court in San Rafael and denied the embezzlement charges. The next month, *Rolling Stone* mentioned the case:

> Manager Jon McIntire shook his head. "So much of it's so cut and dry it's amazing how stupid we were," he said. "It was a classic trip: Elmer Gantry coming in. We deserved it. But you wouldn't think he'd fuck his own kid." Mickey Hart left the band shortly after his father had split. "Mickey's still reacting to it," said Scully. "I mean, he was burned by his *father.*"

Lenny Hart eventually pled no contest to two charges of embezzlement. At his sentencing, his attorney described him as a "completely rehabilitated man" and told the judge, "The Lord has touched Mr. Hart." Hart received a six-month sentence, and the Dead recovered $55,000. "When I joined the Grateful Dead," Hart reportedly told his probation officer, "I entered a new world entirely foreign to any previous experience—a lot of money floating around—everyone ripping off each other—I just succumbed to the temptation to take my share." He said he left the group because the Dead started to "get deeper and deeper into drugs and they were getting arrested. . . . I was getting more seriously into religion." In San Diego, he had become an ordained minister in the Assembly of God Church, and after returning to Marin, he lived in a "religious commune" in Novato.

The entire episode devastated Mickey Hart. "Everything turned black for me," he said. "It was more than I could bear. I was almost suicidal." Although he eventually withdrew from the band, the Dead continued to support him. "The band didn't blame me for Lenny's thievery; they made that clear," Hart wrote in his memoir. "They even kept paying me, treating my departure as a leave of absence that would end whenever I managed to pin to the ground the demons I was wrestling."

The embezzlement left the Dead busted but more determined than ever to survive. They began their recovery by assembling a new management team. As the newly appointed band manager, Jon McIntire dealt with the record company, ran the office, and took care of the talent. Sam Cutler, who had been fired by the Rolling Stones after Altamont, became the road manager. Rock Scully accepted a promotional assignment paid for by the record company. For their legal work, the Dead hired Hal Kant, a Beverly Hills lawyer whom they met through a mutual acquaintance. On Kant's advice, the Dead reorganized as a corporation. Ironically, Kant's physical absence added to his authority as a counselor. "I didn't live in San Francisco," he said, "I didn't hang out with them, they were not an important client to me financially, so I could be very independent." The Dead also relocated the office to a brown-shingle house in downtown San Rafael, Marin County's largest city. Set on the corner of Fifth Avenue and Lincoln Avenue, it became their permanent headquarters.

To raise revenue, the Dead rededicated themselves to touring. In 1970, they agreed to play a series of outdoor summer festivals in Canada that would also include the Band, the New Riders of the Purple Sage, the Flying Burrito Brothers, the Janis Joplin Band, Buddy Guy, and Delaney & Bonnie. This time, the promoters had a novel idea: instead of holding a single outdoor festival like Woodstock, the musicians and their associates would board a specially commissioned fourteen-car train, the so-called Festival Express, which would transport them from venue to venue. The Canadian National railroad initially said the trip should proceed from west to east, but one of the festival's promoters flatly refused. Invoking Horace Greeley, he demanded that the train go west. The five scheduled stops, beginning in Montreal and ending in Vancouver, would mimic the historic migration that Greeley encouraged.

The promoters wanted the travel time to be festive, and they equipped one of the bar cars with an organ, a drum kit, and amplifiers. Kenny Gradney, the bassist for Delaney & Bonnie, described the appeal to the musicians. "And just imagine putting a bunch of crazy musicians together and telling them to go have a good time—*try* and have a good time," Gradney said. "Not a problem." Lesh also recalled the festivities fondly. "It was a train full of insane people," he said, "careening across the Canadian countryside, making music night and day, and occasionally we'd get off the train and play a concert."

As a business proposition, the Festival Express was a disaster. Canadian newspapers reported that the promoters laid out $900,000 in expenses—$500,000 of that in talent fees—hoping to make $250,000 on the whole series. But the first event in Montreal was canceled because of scheduling conflicts and security concerns, which were heightened by the mayhem in Altamont. The Toronto concert came off, but activists protested ticket prices—$16 at the gate ($14 in advance), the highest prices ever charged for a rock concert in that city. Although the event featured multiple headliners, the activists argued that the music belonged to the people and should therefore be free. If free wasn't an option, they were willing to discuss a revenue-sharing arrangement. They also demanded free food and marijuana for all spectators and insisted that no police be present. When the promoters ignored those demands, some twenty-five hundred spectators crashed the gates. That led to arrests and violent clashes with Toronto police, whom the protesters routinely referred to as pigs. Some audience members mounted the stage to make political statements, and one pointed his finger and shouted at the Dead, "You're all phonies—you and you and you . . ." Another protester commandeered the microphone and raged about the pigs' violence and the evils of commerce.

Compared to Altamont, the disruption was mild, but the event managers asked Garcia to calm the audience from the stage. His brief address was a masterpiece of hippie cool. "The thing we're trying to do is organize another sort of scene that we can have here," Garcia said, "and we would like, if possible, man, to have like about a half hour of just coolness so that we can work something out that would be an alternative to all this hassling and see if we can avoid people getting hurt." He gently reminded the audience that such events required planning and resources. "You have to remember, man, that somebody put their neck out to put on a festival here," he said. "They didn't have to do it. All this stuff is, like, voluntary in nature." Garcia said the Dead would play a free show at another venue, but when some audience members continued to protest, Garcia's expression betrayed disdain. "You don't have to go for it," he said. "You can believe it or not, but that's where it's at, right now. Be back in a while."

True to Garcia's word, the Dead played a free show at nearby Coronation Park, but later the band members seemed to have little sympathy for the agitators. Back on the train, Weir criticized the violence initiated by the protesters, which he considered unreasonable in light of the show's value and the decency of the police officers he had spoken to personally. The strife at the Toronto event was well publicized. "Festival Express: Bashed Heads and Bad Trips," blared *The Globe and Mail* headline. That bad publicity depressed turnout at subsequent shows, and the promoters canceled the Vancouver concert altogether.

Despite those setbacks, what turned out to be a three-city tour was a peak experience for the Dead. The journey itself furnished most of the highlights. "The train trip wasn't a dream, it was a stone boss reality," McKernan said later. "I'm still on that train." Hunter also relished his week on the locomotive: "Everyone agreed we had just about the best time of our collective lives in that week of nonstop music and partying." Garcia considered it a personal highlight. "It was great. That was the best time I've had in rock 'n' roll. It was our train—it was the musicians' train. There were no straight people. There wasn't any showbiz bullshit. There weren't any fans," he said. "It was like a musicians' convention with no public allowed." In each rail car, the musicians jammed around the clock. "There was the blues car, the country car, the folk car, whatever," Weir recalled. "You could drift from car to car and get involved with any number of jams, some of which really did amount to some pretty heady stuff." Kenny Gradney was even more elated. "It was, I believe, two and half days from Toronto to Winnipeg," he said, "and for any musician that was on this train, it was like heaven." Many of these impromptu sessions were caught on film. One clip featured Janis Joplin, Garcia, Weir, and a very stoned Rick Danko improvising new verses of "Ain't No More Cane," the traditional prison work song that the Band and Bob Dylan recorded during their Basement Tape sessions.

Though tired, Buddy Guy said he slept little because he didn't want to miss any of the festivities. Mickey Hart, who was still struggling with his father's embezzlement, also wanted the full experience. "This train was not for sleeping," Hart said. "It was for a lot of other things, but not for sleeping." Partying was one of those other things. The US musicians thought twice about crossing the border with contraband, and many resorted to alcohol. "Most all of us were new to drinking at that point, too," Weir said. "We'd all been taking LSD or smoking pot or whatever, and this was a new experience for a lot of us. And it worked just fine." Revelry was nothing new for the musicians, but the shared journey created a unique dynamic. "It seemed that time was sort of suspended," John Till of the Janis Joplin Band said. "You know, like usually, the performer wants to get there, get his job done, and get home. In this situation, we wanted it to go on forever." In Calgary, Garcia suggested that the musicians refuse to leave the train, while others considered diverting it to San Francisco. "We could have the whole goddamn city come out to meet us at Union Station," Janis Joplin's road manager said.

Calgary was the end of the line for the Festival Express, but the experience continued to pay off creatively for the Dead. On board, Garcia learned "Goin' Down the Road Feelin' Bad," which Woody Guthrie had recorded; the Dead's version became a concert staple and reinforced their traveling image. Garcia also composed the music for "Ripple," one of the Dead's most beloved songs, while in transit across Canada. "Jerry woke up one morning," Hunter recalled, "sat out on the railroad tracks somewhere near Saskatoon, and put it to music." Hunter's lyric for "Might as Well," first performed in 1976, also grew out of their week on the train.

> *Great Northern Special, were you on board?*
> *You can't find a ride like that no more*
> *Night the chariot swung down low*
> *Ninety-nine children had a chance to go.*

Once again, Hunter combined traditional American idioms and tropes—in this case, gospel music and railroading—to reflect his own experience. Another verse mentioned the sheer variety of musical genres ringing through the railcars.

> *Ragtime solid for twenty-five miles*
> *then slip over to Cajun style*
> *Bar car loaded with rhythm and blues*
> *Rock and roll wailing in the old caboose.*

In the end, the Festival Express transported the Dead in more ways than one. It matched the ecstasy and community of the magical summer at Rancho Olompali, but it also added a new feature: mobility. Kerouac and Cassady had their sedan, Kesey and the Pranksters had the famous bus, but the train was an even richer and more venerated American symbol, especially in country music, and it enabled a larger and more musical party along the way. Like the Dead's Rancho Olompali sojourn, the Festival Express experience was fleeting but significant. Long-distance travel was a fact of life for the Dead, but they embraced that aspect of their operation and made it a central part of their evolving mythology.

As the Dead made their way across Canada, the American social and political scene continued to unravel. Earlier that year, five members of the Chicago Seven were convicted of crossing state lines to incite a riot at the Democratic National Convention in Chicago. In May, National Guardsmen shot and killed students at Kent State University and Jackson State University during antiwar protests; an enraged Neil Young immediately wrote "Ohio" to protest the deaths at Kent State. Despite that turmoil, the Dead were more averse than usual to flamboyant social protest. In one interview, Weir mentioned the Toronto clashes as well as the Dead's impromptu performance at Columbia University's student strike in 1968. "We thought it would be nice for us to go down there [to Columbia] and stir up some shit, nothing political, just lend some energy to the situation," Weir said. "And see how things felt. So we went down and set up, and as soon as the microphones were on . . . there was a mad rush for the microphones because everybody had a very important announcement. And I told about five people in the space of one minute that, no, man, these microphones were for the music and not for politics. And from every single one of the people that I told that to I got some 'lame honky bastard' or 'crass bourgeois son of a bitch.' They just unleashed their political views. And I hate that. And there's a lot of that going down."

In his interviews, Lesh often identified specific causes, but rarely candidates, that he considered righteous. Garcia was even more circumspect. "Protest means dissent," Garcia told *Circus* magazine in the months leading up to the Festival Express. "Dissent means disharmony. Disharmony means nothing gets done. You don't have to go protesting in music. Be the best you can be with your music—the best rubs off." But even in that interview, Garcia mentioned the environment as a major concern. "The big thing now is, 'Danger, danger, poison earth'—and things are getting out of control," he said. "That's the only thing important happening." Two years later, he made a similar point to a British journalist. "I think we're beginning to develop new capacities just in order to be able to save the world from our trips—you know, pollution, etc.—if for nothing else," he said. "Just for survival. The biological news is in one hundred years from now life on earth is finished, so what has to happen is that this organism has to adapt real quick and develop new capacities to stem this flow, to maybe head it off somehow. In this scheme of things, politics and all those things belong to the past. They're meaningless, going down the drain. There aren't going to be power centers in that sense anymore. That's why it's kicking and hollering so loud."

Garcia's environmental concerns also extended to music industry practices. After visiting a record-pressing plant, Garcia claimed that vinyl records created both ecological and labor concerns. "It's time somebody considered other ways of storing music that don't involve polyvinyl chloride," he said. "People stand at these presses, with hot, steaming vinyl coming out of tubes—it's really uncomfortable. I visited a plant recently, and I thought, 'Do I really want to be putting these people through this?'" The same year Garcia made those remarks, press stories indicated that the Dead would help produce and market holographically encoded, pyramid-shaped, miniature records. That story was later described as a hoax, but within a decade, vinyl records were replaced by compact discs.

If Garcia was concerned about environmental issues, he was even more disturbed by the politicization of the Dead's concerts. "Dig: there's a music festival, but because there are people there, radicals say it's a political festival now, not a music festival," he told *Rolling Stone*. "If a musical experience is forcibly transferred to a political plane, it no longer has the thing that made it attractive." Although Bay Area hippies and radicals had begun to take on aspects of each other's project, Garcia saw their efforts as distinct: "The San Francisco energy of a few years back has become air and spread everywhere. It was the energy of becoming free, and so it became free. But the political energy, the Berkeley energy, has assumed a serpentine form, become an armed, burrowing, survival thing."

By Berkeley energy, Garcia probably meant the increasingly militant posture assumed by antiwar activists as the slaughter in Vietnam continued. By that time, Weatherman (later renamed the Weather Underground) had split from Students for a Democratic Society and issued a "Declaration of a State of War" against the United States. Garcia wanted none of it: "Altamont showed us that we don't want to lead people up *that* road anymore, taught us to be more cautious, to realize and respect the boundaries of our power and our space." His motto, he said, was "Accentuate the positive." As Garcia scanned the national landscape, he saw more heads every day, and that proved that the revolution he cared about was well under way. "Today there is no place without its hippies," he said. "*No* place."

Garcia underscored that point in another 1970 interview, whose first question was whether he was very political. "No," Garcia replied. Did he think that rock music was a manifestation of the revolution? "Um, it isn't to me, but I could see that someone could think it is, yeah," Garcia said. "I think that the revolution that's going to make some sort of dent or some change is already over, it's already happened in principle, and the waves of it are now moving away from ground zero at a rate of about, you know, a mile every four years [chuckled] or something like that." The revolution that mattered, he suggested, was already complete and inviolable. "It's already gone, it's already past, and the rest of it is like telling everyone who missed it that it's already happened."

Although the Dead tended to avoid or downplay politics, they played many benefits and were therefore associated in the public mind with specific causes, most of them uncontroversial. One notable exception was a Black Panther Party benefit in March 1971. That event was billed as Revolutionary Intercommunal Day of Solidarity for Bobby Seale, Ericka Huggins, Angela Davis, and Ruchell Magee, all of whom were identified in the promotional material as political prisoners. The party's singers, the Lumpen, were also scheduled to perform; their purpose was to "function as another weapon in the struggle for liberation." The event was arranged to aid the party's legal efforts, but it was also a postbirthday celebration for Huey P. Newton, the Panthers' minister of defense and Supreme Servant of the People. The year before, an appellate court voided Newton's conviction for the voluntary manslaughter of Oakland police officer John Frey. Newton, who was defended by radical attorney Charles Garry, was tried twice more before the Alameda County Superior Court finally dismissed the charges against him.

Despite Newton's hard-won legal victory, his organization's leadership problems were acute. Tried for conspiracy to incite a riot at the 1968 Democratic National Convention, party cofounder Bobby Seale was imprisoned for contempt of court. While serving time, he was tried for the murder of fellow Panther Alex Rackley, whom the party suspected of being an informant. Ericka Huggins was also charged in that case. The alleged crimes of Ruchell Magee and Angela Davis hit closer to the Dead's home. In August 1970, the teenaged brother of Black Panther and San Quentin inmate George Jackson entered a Marin County courtroom. Jonathan Jackson's purpose was to demand the release of the Soledad Brothers, including his brother. After ordering everyone in the courtroom to freeze, Jonathan Jackson distributed guns to the defendant and two witnesses, who were also San Quentin inmates. The armed men marched the judge, the district attorney, and three jurors out of the courthouse to the parking lot, where a van picked them up. A gun battle erupted, leaving the judge, Jonathan Jackson, and two inmates dead; Ruchell Magee, the district attorney, and one of the jurors were seriously wounded. Jonathan Jackson's gun was registered to Angela Davis, for whom he had worked as a bodyguard; she was eventually acquitted.

In October, the Weather Underground bombed the Marin County courthouse in retaliation for the deaths of Jonathan Jackson and the two inmates. Two months after that bombing, Garcia explained the Dead's connection to Newton and the Panthers. "We have some loose semi-association with the Black Panthers because we met Huey Newton and got along well with him," he told *CREEM*. "We don't deal with things on the basis of content, the idea of a philosophy or any of that shit, mostly it's personalities—people. That sort of thing." Weir's recollection was more rueful. "That was another fiasco, I'm afraid," he told Blair Jackson. "We probably paid a lot of legal fees for people who were in jail for things they did."

In the same *CREEM* interview, Garcia was asked whether the Hells Angels were political. No, he replied. Righteous? "Yeah, I think they're pure elementals," he said. "They're something that most modern people don't know what to think about, so they don't know how to deal with the situation when it arises. Like having elementals around—things that you can't control. That's what they are—things that you can't control." In 1972, the Dead played a benefit for the New York chapter, whose apartment had been raided following charges that they had assaulted a Puerto Rican youth on his way home from the grocery store. The raid netted a revolver, a thousand rounds of ammunition, knives, a machete, and a bomb. Once the benefit started, however, the Dead enthusiastically supported the gang. During the show, Weir yelled, "Let's get it on for the Hells Angels of the USA!" *The Village Voice* applauded the general idea but wondered about the specifics. "A venerable tradition; benefits by performing artists to aid the victims of injustice," one writer noted. "How did the bikers enter this category?" The following year, the Dead played a benefit at Winterland for a Bay Area member of the Hells Angels, but they declined to identify him in advance other than to say he was a friend of the band's. That omission landed them bad press in *Rolling Stone* and elsewhere.

Despite those criticisms, no one doubted the Dead's generosity, especially when it involved their tribe. For a 1972 benefit to support the Kesey family dairy in Oregon, only a fraction of the audience purchased tickets, and the band made up the revenue shortfall. Nevertheless, the Dead often resisted the push for free concerts of the sort they had offered in the early days at Golden Gate Park. "There never was a free concert," Garcia told one interviewer. "Money is only a symbol for energy exchange. If energy exchange could be worked out with some other analogue instead of money, I'd be all for it. But if it's going to be strictly an energy rip-off trip, where the musician gets up there and sweats like hell for three hours, and everybody in the front row gets off, and it's all for the purpose of illustrating some philosophical point, fuck it."

Nor did the Dead welcome the idea that music belonged to the people and should therefore be free. "Well, I think the musician's first responsibility is to play music as well as he can, and that's the most important thing," Garcia told *CREEM*. "And any responsibility to anyone else is just journalistic fiction . . . or political fiction. Because that bullshit about the people's music, man, where's that at, and what's that supposed to mean? It wasn't any people that sat with me while I learned to play the guitar. I mean, who paid the dues? I mean, if the people think that way, they can fucking make their own music." Garcia also wondered about who, exactly, the people were. "When somebody says *people*," he said, "to me it means everybody. It means the cops, the guys who drive the limousines, the fucker who runs the elevator, everybody. All that."

After returning from Canada, the Dead began recording again, this time at the Wally Heider Studio in San Francisco's Tenderloin district. The new material featured the Dead at their most soulful. Hunter's goal, he said, was to provide Garcia with "the type of song he could sing with righteous authority." Hunter composed several lyrics in Great Britain, which he visited for the first time before boarding the Festival Express. Fortified by Greek wine, Hunter wrote the lyrics for "Ripple," "Brokedown Palace," and "To Lay Me Down" in one two-hour period. He described that afternoon as "the personal quintessence of the union between writer and Muse, a promising past and bright future prospects melding into one great glowing apocatastasis in South Kensington." The words, he recalled, "seemed to flow like molten gold onto parchment paper."

Hunter spent a great deal of time in England in the early 1970s. Part of the appeal was proximity to the source of the traditional ballads he cherished. Later, when author Carol Brightman asked him about "Lord Randal," a Child ballad, Hunter responded enthusiastically. "Oh, God, yes," he said, "wonderful language, vaguely Elizabethan. I got to *watch* that." But he also challenged Brightman to name a song of his that was based in any specific way on a traditional ballad. His lyrics, he said, came out of his imagination; they carried only "a *sense* of tradition; if you go into it more deeply, it's going to disappear." The England trips also helped consolidate his understanding of himself as a lyricist of the American West. "I am definitely a Westerner," he told Blair Jackson. "I've grown up in Oregon, Seattle, and California, all up and down the West Coast. My grandfather was a cowboy. He could lasso me running across the yard." But Hunter's literary identity was more a choice than a given geographical fact. "I became more aware of myself as a Westerner the more I *wrote* as a Westerner," he told Brightman. In England, he said, he began to define himself that way "in a really comprehensive sense." Garcia's identification with the West was more cinematic; the wide-open spaces and open melancholy of John Ford westerns, he told Blair Jackson, were "an important key to my emotional interior."

Back in Marin County, the Hunter-Garcia partnership was working smoothly. On a walk through Madrone Canyon in 1969, Garcia told Hunter that they were creating a universe, and that Hunter was responsible for the verbal half of it. Living together in Larkspur, Hunter and Garcia composed on the spot, often with other band members. Some of their earlier collaborations had been structurally weak or difficult to perform, but even the new songs that came together quickly were solid and polished. The bridge for "Ripple," Garcia noted, was "a perfect haiku. There's a lot of those kinds of things in our music that people just never get. Hunter is just a fantastic craftsman. He had lots of years speed freaking, you know, to get really crazy about language." Hunter also collaborated with Lesh on "Box of Rain," with Weir on "Sugar Magnolia," and with Dawson and Nelson on "Friend of the Devil," which also featured David Grisman on mandolin. Along with "Ripple," those numbers became favorites in the Grateful Dead songbook.

But the new album's signature song was "Truckin'," a paean to the traveling life. Hunter had decided that the Dead needed a road song, and in the spring of 1970, he joined the musicians on a tour that included stops in Buffalo, New York City, and Florida. While sitting poolside at a Florida hotel, he unveiled his new lyric, and Weir, Lesh, and Garcia worked up the music on acoustic guitars. More straightforward and autobiographical than most Dead lyrics, "Truckin'" mixed Beat adventure with the tedium and hassles of life on the road. Some of those challenges were drug related. One verse wonders about "sweet Jane" and her decline after "living on reds, vitamin C, and cocaine." Two other verses refer to the band's drug arrest in New Orleans the month after Altamont:

Sitting and staring out of the hotel window
Got a tip they're gonna kick the door in again
I'd like to get some sleep before I travel
But if you got a warrant, I guess you're gonna come in.
Busted—down on Bourbon Street
Set up—like a bowling pin
Knocked down—it gets to wearing thin
They just won't let you be.

"Truckin'" reinforced the Dead's outlaw image, but the lyric also linked the Beat preoccupation with mobility to the folk tradition's sense of region and place. At the same time, it explored the tension between dual forms of longing—the itch to travel and the desire for homecoming. On *American Beauty,* the latter urge also found expression in "Brokedown Palace" ("Going home, going home / by the waterside, I will rest my bones"), but the final verse of "Truckin'" features both impulses: "Truckin'—I'm goin' home / Whoa-oh baby, back where I belong / Back home—sit down and patch my bones / and get back Truckin' on." With its reference to the band's "long, strange trip," the lyric also tapped a basic metaphor for human experience and added an entry to the American lexicon. The song was eventually recognized as a national treasure by an act of Congress—"some Dead Head in the House, no doubt," Hunter concluded.

The album-in-progress also reflected a new maturity born of loss. Only ten days after Jimi Hendrix's death in London that summer, Garcia's mother died following a traffic accident in San Francisco. During the same period, Mickey Hart's girlfriend lost a child to a bicycling accident, both of Weir's parents died within a week, and Lesh's father was diagnosed with cancer; before dying in his sleep, his last words were "What are we waiting for? *Let's get this show on the road!*" Lesh's unexpectedly intense grief informed his collaboration with Hunter on "Box of Rain." That lyric captured the surreal quality of everyday life inflected by devastating personal loss. For Lesh, the recording sessions were also a form of consolation. In the studio were Paul Kantner, Grace Slick, and Carlos Santana as well as David Crosby, Stephen Stills, Graham Nash, and Neil Young. Lesh described the scene as "jammer heaven" and the music as "a healing force beyond words to describe."

The band titled the new album *American Beauty*, after the hybrid perpetual rose. That flower was an established part of the Dead's iconography and a long-standing Hunter preoccupation. Always loath to dissect symbols, he was forthcoming about his muses, including "one spirit that's laying roses on me. Roses, roses, can't get enough of those bloody roses," he told David Gans. "It's the most prominent image, as far as I'm concerned, in the human brain. Beauty, delicacy, short-livedness." Among the half dozen songs Hunter named as his favorites in 1978, two included roses in the title: "It Must Have Been the Roses" and "Ramble on Rose." Alton Kelley produced the cover image for *American Beauty* by etching the rose into a mirror with a sandblaster, laying the mirror into a piece of mahogany, and photographing it. The original idea for the back cover was a photograph of the band members brandishing pistols. "They were getting into guns at the time, going over to Mickey's ranch, target shooting," Hunter recalled. "I saw that photo, and that was one of the few times I ever really asserted myself with the band and said, 'No—no pictures of a band with guns on the back cover.' These were incendiary and revolutionary times, and I did not want the band to be making that statement."

American Beauty was another critical and commercial success. Released in 1970, it went gold in 1974. "Our albums went from the bottom of the charts to the upper reaches, consistently," Hunter wrote later. "The songs fit the times and helped to define them." By this time, his lyrics included his favorite Western tropes, including poker, sheriffs, and outlaws. In *Aoxomoxoa*, he had inflected some of those tropes with psychedelic images, as in "Doin' That Rag" ("One-eyed jacks and the deuces are wild / The aces are crawling up and down your sleeve"). In

Hunter's acid-drenched frontier, the deuces were wilder than any card Bill Hickok ever drew, and the ace up the sleeve represented both a sly advantage and a bad trip for the cardsharp. In *American Beauty*, however, the psychedelic dimension was muted. Any verse in "Friend of the Devil," which describes life on the run from a sheriff, could have been plucked from Harry Smith's anthology. As Hunter noted later, "Friend of the Devil" was "the closest we've come to what may be a classic song."

The success of *Workingman's Dead* and *American Beauty* brought several important changes to the Dead's operation. The tours that became their trademark began to focus more on college campuses, including many in the Northeast. Although the musicians had largely avoided higher education, Warner Bros. Records claimed that 75 percent of the band's audience was college educated, and the Dead started to receive many favorable write-ups in Ivy League newspapers. The Grateful Dead's audience, one *Harvard Crimson* piece claimed in 1971, "is the most musically involved and sophisticated of all rock followings." Moreover, the article continued, the Dead had the added virtue of modesty. "Unlike many of their contemporaries in rock music, the Dead play without putting on a show of themselves," the reviewer observed. "The music is enough; the music is what is important, and the Dead play with the rare confidence of men who have found their place in the world."

Lesh understood their show's appeal as a combination of ecstasy, adventure, and community. "To a young person at that time," Lesh wrote in his memoir, "a Grateful Dead show could offer this kind of adventure in a protected environment, gathered together with like-minded people in a community of kindred spirits." That protected environment was designed to accommodate LSD trips. "We played long shows, so those who were tripping could peak and return," Lesh noted. In his view, the Dead concerts offered "a chance to take a chance, to go on an adventure of sorts with a large group of one's peers, and to return to reflect and to tell the tale the next morning." The live shows were still an adventure for the band as well. The second half of the concert, Garcia noted, was partly "inspired by the psychedelic experience as a waveform." The long, open-ended jams were designed for "taking chances and going all to pieces and then coming back and reassembling," he said. "You might lose a few pieces, but you don't despair about seeing yourself go completely to pieces; you let it go."

Another important change was the Dead's expanding sound system. That investment reflected both the band's bottomless appetite for new gear and their commitment to a satisfactory audience experience. The burgeoning sound system, in turn, required a bigger road crew, which was headed by Larry Shurtliff, nicknamed Ram Rod by fellow Oregonian Ken Kesey. Shurtliff first appeared at 710 Ashbury atop a Harley-Davidson motorcycle, and his introduction went straight to the point: "Name's Ram Rod—Kesey sent me—I hear you need a good man." Once hired, Shurtliff drove the band's truck and set up and tore down the equipment for every show. He quickly developed a reputation as a taciturn problem solver. Before one New Year's Eve gig, Hart felt he was too high to play, so Shurtliff strapped him to his drum stool with gaffer's tape. On a truck trip across the Midwest, Hart and crew member Rex Jackson decided to see how long it would take Shurtliff to speak. Passing through their third state, he finally asked, "Hungry?" The band members valued Shurtliff's steady character so highly that when the Grateful Dead incorporated, they named him president, a position he held until the band stopped performing two decades later.

At a 1969 show in Flushing Meadows, New York, Shurtliff and his crew met a local stagehand, Steve Parish, who had recently spent a harrowing week in Rikers Island jail following a minor drug arrest. Sharing hits from a nitrous oxide tank, Parish felt an immediate affinity with the crew, but Garcia's demeanor struck him even more forcefully. "Jerry Garcia stood in the center of the action," Parish recalled, "playing his guitar, a look of pure joy on his face, radiating energy that I'd never felt before from any music or any person." Soon the rangy Parish was working at the Fillmore East, Bill Graham's music venue in the East Village, where he became romantically involved with Candace Brightman, who later directed the Dead's light shows. Before that, Dead fan and future employee Gary Lambert recalled, there was almost no security at the Dead's New York shows. But after someone swiped the band's equipment, Lambert noticed that the crew members started getting bigger.

That summer, Parish traveled to Woodstock, where he hauled heavy equipment for the Dead. With encouragement from Dead roadie Sonny Heard, he moved to San Francisco to work for the band without pay. Parish bunked with Shurtliff, who was staying with Owsley Stanley in the Oakland hills. But Stanley's legal problems made him wary of strangers, and within days Parish landed at Weir's Rucka Rucka Ranch in Marin County, where the band and crew spent many afternoons taking target practice, riding horses and motorcycles, and pranking one another. For the nineteen-year-old New Yorker, mixing with the Oregon cowboys was like "being transported to another era." Even at that point, however, Parish sensed that the Dead were becoming "something they had never really explicitly aspired to be: a hardworking, professional, career-oriented band."

Between their traveling and partying, the crew and band developed a strong bond. That connection also made an impression on Parish: "When I'd been working at the theaters back East, I saw a lot of bands, but I never saw any that displayed the generosity and kindness of the Grateful Dead." The band maintained remarkably egalitarian relationships with the crew, both at home and on the road. Their work was "truly a communal thing between the band and crew. There was no separation." When asked about the crew's status in the organization, Garcia said, "We're dragging them through life; shouldn't they have some say about it? We're all working on the same thing—why should we treat each other any differently?"

The crew was central to the Dead's touring operation, but their roughneck ways didn't always endear them to peace-loving Dead Heads. Weir was also put off by the crew's close connections to the Hells Angels, whose belligerent image occasionally solved problems for the Dead but more often created them. Parish defended the crew by noting the complexity of the Dead's operation: "We had more equipment than other bands, and we had some of the most devoted fans in the world. So we took control of everything: security, setup, and sound. From the moment we arrived in town, the crew was in charge." Parish and his colleagues served as a bulwark against law enforcement officials, theater owners, stagehands, and union officials, many of whom were concerned primarily with work rules rather than the swift assembly and striking of the Dead's elaborate equipment.

The musicians didn't insist on star treatment, but some gatekeeping was required, and the brawny crew protected the band from fans and friends alike. The garrulous Garcia found it especially difficult to turn away visitors. "He'd put up with all these hippies who would come in and lay their trips on him," John Dawson said. "Every fuckin' hippie in the world wanted to talk to Jerry. They all had some cosmic thing that they had to get him to explain to them or they had to explain to him. Everybody wanted to talk to Garcia, man." Despite these claims on his time and attention, Garcia found it easy to empathize with fans. "I used to do all that same stuff, like standing in line for hours for a ticket," he told David Gans.

I did all that shit—drive for hundreds of miles to see someone. I've put in my dues on that level, and I know what it's like. All I have to do is project myself back to that and remember what it's like. That helps. And the other part is that I remember that those people are real people—they're not some kind of half people. There's all kinds of temptations in rock 'n' roll to shine them on and bullshit them, turn into an asshole. But for me, it's important not to—and it's important to maintain some level of contact.

Yet Garcia also realized that he had to pace himself when it came to interacting with his admirers: "There's been times in my life when I burned myself doing that, when I'd sit up all night five nights in a row raving with some hippies."

Garcia relied on Parish to shield him from fans, but he had no desire to live in a celebrity bubble. For his Bay Area side gigs, he typically arrived early to warm up, smoke a joint, and chat with whoever was on hand. He frequently instructed Parish to bring him "somebody weird" to visit with. At other times, weirdness was thrust upon him. Once when Parish and Garcia were strolling the sidewalks of New York City, a car screeched to a stop near them. A passenger emerged, handed Garcia a shoebox, and said, "Take care of this, man. Please, whatever you do, don't lose it." After he departed, Garcia read the note attached to the shoebox: "This is the lizard god, Chonga-Bonga. Don't let him die." When Garcia opened the shoebox, he found an iguana resting on a bed of grass. "Let's go," Garcia told Parish. "We have our orders." The iguana was part of the entourage for weeks until Cutler accidentally scalded it in a bathtub.

In 1968, Bill Graham opened the Fillmore East venue in the East Village of New York City and began an exceptionally busy bicoastal life. Fillmore East became the Dead's New York City home, and they were soon selling more albums in New York than in any other metropolitan area. Back in San Francisco, Graham also began to stage events at the Winterland Arena in Japantown, Formerly known as the Dreamland Auditorium, the building was originally a venue for wrestling and boxing matches as well as musical acts. Remodeled in 1928 and renamed in the late 1930s, Winterland was used primarily as an ice-skating rink. When Graham began promoting events there, it accommodated fifty-four hundred spectators, considerably more than the Fillmore Auditorium and Fillmore West, but it was still intimate enough to suit the Dead, and it quickly became a regular Bay Area venue.

Trouble arose in May 1971, however, when approximately one thousand spectators at Winterland consumed an LSD-laced beverage that circulated during a Dead concert. Dozens of spectators were treated at hospitals, and though no one was actually hospitalized, the San Francisco police chief said that the promoter and Winterland's owner should lose their licenses. Graham was incensed. "You don't just close down an establishment because once, for the first time in five years and thirteen hundred concerts, this happens," he told the press. "Just because there's a train accident, you don't take the trains off the track." *San Francisco Chronicle* critic John Wasserman supported Graham with a sarcastic column: "No, Graham is guilty as charged. In the old days, we'd have lynched him straightaway. . . . And while we're at it, let's send the entire Grateful Dead rock and roll band to the gas chamber."

A week later, Graham announced that he would close both the Fillmore West and Fillmore East venues by the end of that month. "I just don't want to fight anymore," he told the press. The problems were his youthful customers and industry trends. "Young people have changed," he said. "They're different from three or four years ago. The communal, joyful spirit is gone." Graham also found their anti-commercialism and demand for free concerts annoying. "Sure, I have apartments in New York and London and Pacific Heights and a house in Geneva," he told *The San Francisco Examiner*. "But I worked for them. In 1965, I was living in a seventy-two-dollar-a-month flat on Twenty-First Avenue." The bands, too, were spoiled, expecting as much as $60,000 for a single night's work. "It's a question of too much too soon," said Graham. "You build them into stars and they turn and walk away, saying, 'Thanks, but ___ you.'" Graham had had enough. "I'm forty years old, and I've made it big," he told the *Examiner*. "Now I want to take it easy." Graham vowed to remain in the business but to be more selective in the projects he undertook: "I'll do only those things that will make rock respectable again."

On the heels of the Winterland incident, President Richard Nixon made headlines by declaring a war on drugs. The announcement was a response to widespread concerns among white, middle-class voters about drug abuse and the criminality that accompanied it. Although millions of Americans had smoked marijuana, the evidence didn't indicate that drug use had become an epidemic among young people. In 1969, only one out of five high school students had smoked weed, and barely 1 percent smoked it every day. Among college students, a quarter had tried marijuana, and only half of those students had smoked it more than once. As a public health matter, alcohol was by far the greater menace; the number of Americans who died from cirrhosis of the liver was almost twenty times greater than those who died as a result of all other legal and illegal drugs put together. Heroin addition was a significant problem in a handful of cities, but the Nixon administration exaggerated that problem wildly, telling Congress that the nation's heroin addicts stole $2 billion in property per year to support their habits. In fact, the estimated value of *all* stolen property in 1971 was $1.3 billion. Ironically, the federal government's own policies were swelling the ranks of those addicts. When the Pentagon clamped down on marijuana use among military personnel in Vietnam, many soldiers switched to heroin, which was inexpensive, plentiful, and easier to hide. One of that war's unintended consequences was returning thousands of heroin addicts to the States after their military service.

Most of Nixon's drug-war victories came on the public relations front. In 1969, only 3 percent of Americans thought that drugs were the nation's most important problem; a few years later, polls showed that drugs topped the list of national concerns. Nixon's plan included significant resources for drug treatment, which pleased liberals, but its genius lay in the underlying political calculation. The drug crackdown targeted what White House aides privately called "*their* people": young, poor, and black Americans who were unlikely to vote for Nixon anyway. Nixon's metaphor was also a stroke of rhetorical genius. By framing the initiative as a war, he distinguished it from social and public health services, which conservatives tended to oppose, and set the stage for heavy federal spending. Between 1969 and 1974, the federal drug enforcement budget swelled from $65 million to $719 million. The Department of Justice also implemented more aggressive enforcement tools, and its new agency, the Drug Enforcement Administration, took over the task of "scheduling" drugs from public health experts. Marijuana became a Schedule One drug, which meant that it was highly dangerous, had high potential for abuse, and lacked any medical value.

One of the drug war's most ardent supporters was Elvis Presley, who appeared unannounced at the White House bearing a six-page letter scrawled on American Airlines stationery. In that missive, Presley asked to become a "Federal Agent at Large," noting that he was well positioned to help wage the war Nixon had declared. "The drug culture, the hippie elements, the SDS, Black Panthers, etc. do *not* consider me as their enemy, or as they call it, The Establishment," Presley maintained. He had also done his homework: "I have done an in-depth study of drug abuse and Communist brainwashing techniques, and I am right in the middle of the whole thing, where I can and will do the most good." White House aides relieved Presley of his gift to President Nixon—a nickel-plated handgun and ammunition—and ushered him into the Oval Office. Earlier that day, Presley had visited the federal narcotics bureau, which denied his request for a badge. But when Presley asked the president directly, Nixon quickly approved. An exuberant Presley gave the president a bear hug, and Nixon gave the King of Rock and Roll a presidential tie clasp. When the drug-dependant Presley died in 1977, he was still a credentialed Special Assistant in the Bureau of Narcotics and Dangerous Drugs.

The drug war also had a media component. The White House gathered television and film producers and encouraged them to incorporate antidrug themes in their work. Industry groups also lent a hand. In 1973, the National Association of Progressive Radio Announcers tapped musicians and other celebrities to record forty antidrug public service announcements, which were estimated to reach 30 million listeners per day. One of those musicians was Bob Weir, whose announcement warned against heroin use. Weir described his message as "a spot saying, 'Hey, kids, don't do smack.' Heroin is not a groovy drug. . . . Smack slows the planet down." But if Weir was willing to do his part to curb heroin use, the larger drug war meant trouble for Dead Heads. That same year, police arrested thirty-six spectators at the Dead's Nassau Coliseum show, leading the Dead to avoid that venue for years. In the wake of those arrests, one Dead Head told a reporter that smoking pot was worth the risk: "If you're a dedicated Dead freak, you'll take your chances." Another Dead Head said, "I enjoy the Grateful Dead no matter what way I see them. But when people are allowed to smoke together, they get a little closer."

In July 1971, Garcia and Carolyn Adams received a visit at their Stinson Beach home from Jann Wenner, publisher of *Rolling Stone*. Using money from an advance on Garcia's solo album, Adams had purchased the house after an extensive search. "It was an incredible find," she said later. "It was perfect and cost sixty thousand dollars." Although isolated, the property had rustic charm. "It had eucalyptus trees and cypresses and a chicken house that had been converted to a little guest lodge," Adams said, "and then we converted that into a recording studio; George Hunter of the Charlatans, who was an architect, designed it, and Laird Grant built it." Wenner noted the impressive setting: "Their house is surrounded by sea-swept eucalyptus trees, five-foot hedges and large rose bushes, beyond which is a magnificent view of the Pacific Ocean and the Far East, as far as the imagination can take you."

Only four years old, *Rolling Stone* was already an important voice in the rock world, and its growing cachet coincided with the Dead's rising fortunes. Under Wenner and Gleason's leadership, *Rolling Stone* featured political coverage that was less earthshaking than the investigative stories in *Ramparts,* where both men had previously worked. But *Rolling Stone* had something that its muckraking precursor lacked: a reliable advertising base of record companies and other youth-oriented marketers. After running through two private fortunes, *Ramparts* declared bankruptcy for the first time in 1969. Warren Hinckle decamped to start a new magazine, *Scanlan's Monthly,* where he helped create gonzo journalism by pairing Hunter Thompson with illustrator Ralph Steadman for the first time. But *Scanlan's* tanked after only eight issues, and Wenner shrewdly swept in to hire Thompson in 1970. Over the next several years, Thompson and Steadman created their most durable work for *Rolling Stone* and its book division, Straight Arrow Books.

As chief of the magazine's national affairs desk, Thompson added a new and important dimension to *Rolling Stone.* Privately he complained about writing for a magazine preoccupied with what the Jackson Five had for breakfast, but *Rolling Stone* made him a cultural icon. Thompson made no pretense of journalistic objectivity, at least in the discredited sense of reflexively citing an opposing perspective, no matter how absurd. His contempt for Richard Nixon was as obvious as his appetite for alcohol, cocaine, and mescaline. "It is Nixon himself who represents that dark, venal and incurably violent side of the American character that almost every country in the world has learned to fear and despise," Thompson wrote in an article that appeared two days after Nixon's re-election in 1972. "Our Barbie-doll president, with his Barbie-doll wife and his boxful of Barbie-doll children, is also America's answer to the monstrous Mr. Hyde. He speaks for the Werewolf in us; the bully, the predatory shyster who turns into something unspeakable, full of claws and bleeding string-warts on nights when the moon comes too close." Thompson even blamed Nixon for trends in the nation's drug culture. Consciousness expansion "went out with LBJ," he noted in *Fear and*

Loathing in Las Vegas. "And it is worth noting, historically, that downers came in with Nixon."

Like many Haight-Ashbury hippies, Thompson left San Francisco in 1967. Although he eventually established his "fortified compound" outside Aspen, Colorado, he relished his San Francisco years and retained his affection for the Grateful Dead. He listed *Workingman's Dead* among his favorite albums and once declared that if the Dead ever came to his town, he would beat his way in with a tire iron if necessary. In the waning days of George McGovern's unsuccessful presidential bid in 1972, Thompson encouraged the Democratic challenger to appear in public with a Grateful Dead T-shirt, calculating that gesture would guarantee another 1 million votes for the doomed campaign.

Wenner's companion on the drive to Stinson Beach couldn't have been less like Thompson. A tenured law professor, Charles Reich was at the top of his profession. After clerking for Supreme Court justice Hugo Black, Reich practiced law in Washington and New York City before accepting a faculty position at Yale University, where his students included Bill and Hillary Clinton. A lifelong Easterner, Reich spent the summer of 1967 in Berkeley, where he initially described the students as profoundly anti-intellectual, but he was soon crediting their values. His Summer of Love experiences, which included watching Grateful Dead concerts in the park, informed his 1970 manifesto, *The Greening of America*. Random House scheduled a small print run and no publicity for Reich's book, but his mother, the principal of an elite Manhattan nursery school, showed the book to Lillian Ross, whose child was enrolled there. She passed it to William Shawn, editor of *The New Yorker*. He ran excerpts of the book, which quickly became a bestseller.

The Greening of America argued that a social revolution, created by and for the younger generation, was under way. In Reich's view, it was a necessary response to the rise of the corporate state, sweeping technological change, and the threats they posed to nature and humanity. The revolution Reich had in mind wasn't a traditional one, but rather a

A young Jerry Garcia outside the family bar. That world, Garcia said later, "engulfed me like a little community." (USED WITH PERMISSION OF CLIFFORD GARCIA/RED LIGHT MANAGEMENT)

Wally Hedrick, Garcia's mentor at the California School of Fine Arts, introduced him to bohemianism and Jack Kerouac. (NATA PIASKOWSKI/JOHN NATSOULAS, *The Beat Generation Galleries and Beyond*, 1996)

A young Harry Smith in San Francisco. His *Anthology of American Folk Music* captivated Garcia and Robert Hunter as well as Bob Dylan, with whom the peninsula folkies would eventually join forces. (HY HIRSH/HARRY SMITH ARCHIVES)

Impressed by the Beatles and the Rolling Stones, Garcia and Ron "Pigpen" McKernan recruited Phil Lesh, Bob Weir, and Bill Kreutzmann to form the Warlocks, an electric blues band, in 1965. (RYAN/MICHAEL OCHS ARCHIVES/ GETTY)

The Grateful Dead became the house band for Ken Kesey's Acid Tests. "They were our first and best audience," Garcia said later. Like his Beat heroes, Kesey placed a high value on ecstasy, mobility, and community. (JOE ROSENTHAL/ CORBIS)

The Dead's sojourn in Rancho Olompali in the summer of 1966 was ecstatic. "It was a model of how things could really be good," Garcia said. Chet Helms, who promoted the Family Dog concerts and brought Janis Joplin to San Francisco, was one of the Dead's many guests. (ROSIE MCGEE)

The Trips Festival was the largest Acid Test and a showcase for local avant-garde artists. Organizer Stewart Brand said it was "the beginning of the Grateful Dead and the end of everything else." Brand would later publish the *Whole Earth Catalog* and cofound the WELL, a popular online community among Dead Heads. (TED STRESHINSKY/CORBIS)

Ralph J. Gleason of the *San Francisco Chronicle* gave the Dead, the local music scene, and *Rolling Stone* magazine early credibility. (PHOTOGRAPHER UNKNOWN. USED WITH PERMISSION OF THE GLEASON FAMILY.)

Owsley Stanley, the counterculture's most prominent LSD producer, was also the Dead's early patron and sound engineer. (ROSIE MCGEE)

The Dead would always be known as a San Francisco band, but after a drug arrest at 710 Ashbury Street, they moved to Marin County and remained there for decades. (BARNEY PETERSON, *San Francisco Chronicle*/CORBIS)

Alton Kelly and Stanley Mouse found this illustration in a vintage edition of Omar Khayyám's *Rubáiyát*. After they adapted it to promote a Dead concert, skeletons and roses became staples in the band's distinctive iconography.

For many observers, the disastrous free concert at Altamont signaled the end of the counterculture. For others, it was the flip side of the Woodstock coin. (JOHN SPRINGER/CORBIS)

The Dead at Mickey Hart's ranch in 1970. Performing with the New Riders of the Purple Sage, they reached the high point of their folk-and-cowboy period. (*San Francisco Chronicle*/CORBIS)

The Festival Express was another pinnacle for the Dead. "It was a train full of insane people," Phil Lesh recalled, "careening across the Canadian countryside, making music night and day, and occasionally we'd get off the train and play a concert." Garcia, Carolyn Adams, and Delaney Bramlett enjoying a show. (RON "SUNSHINE" MASTRION/ASSOCIATED PRESS)

The Dead at Winterland in 1977. Despite the challenges they faced individually and collectively, their live music that year was exceptional. (ED PERLSTEIN)

With the success of *Workingman's Dead* and *American Beauty*, the Dead hit the road in earnest. Many Dead Heads swelled the progress, and Garcia compared their experience to riding the rails or joining the circus. (ROGER RESSMEYER/ CORBIS)

Bill Graham, Apple cofounder Steve Wozniak, and Mickey Hart at the US Festival. The tech community harbored many Dead Heads, some of whom joined the WELL when it was founded in 1985. (DAVID GANS)

The Dead officially permitted fans to tape concerts starting in 1984. The reproduction and dissemination of tapes, which served as a kind of alternative currency, helped grow and consolidate the Dead Head community. (DAVID GANS)

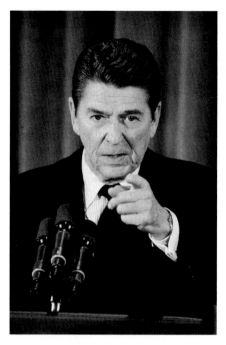

The Dead rarely commented on politicians, but Garcia made an exception for Ronald Reagan. The Dead's first Top Ten hit, "Touch of Grey," can be read as a response to the Age of Reagan. (CHARLES CANCELLARE/CORBIS)

The "Touch of Grey" music video introduced the aging rockers to a new generation of fans. To make it, director Gary Gutierrez drew on the Dead's established iconography. (JAY BLAKESBERG)

The Dead overcame their aversion to stadium shows, which reinstituted an unwelcome separation between musicians and spectators. In 1991, they became the top-grossing touring band in North America. (DAVID McGOUGH)

The Dead supported the Lithuanian basketball team, which had broken away from the Soviet Union, in the 1992 Olympic Games. When Lithuania won the bronze medal, the Dead's gesture was seen as support for political freedom and underdogs in general. (REUTERS /CORBIS)

Jerry Garcia's death was national news, and conservative pundits used the occasion to scold the 1960s counterculture. The Grateful Dead chose to disband, but twenty years later, their community was alive and well. (HERBIE GREENE/*Rolling Stone*)

change in consciousness that would transform politics only as its final act. "It will not require violence to succeed, and it cannot be successfully resisted by violence," Reich predicted. "Its ultimate creation will be a new and enduring wholeness and beauty—a renewed relationship of man to himself, to other men, to society, to nature, and to the land."

During a visit in San Francisco, Reich asked Wenner why *Rolling Stone* had never interviewed Garcia. For Wenner, that interview was "always one of those things we put off into some indefinite future because Jerry was always around and, of course, we'd do it sooner or later." But given his book's thesis, Reich was especially eager to meet Garcia, whom he described as "a symbol of everything that is new and changing and rebellious in America." More specifically, Garcia symbolized the Bay Area youth culture in which Reich placed so much faith. During his visits there, Reich had discovered LSD and marijuana, and though he acknowledged the dangers of their abuse, he described weed as a "maker of revolution" and "a truth serum that repels false consciousness." A forty-two-year-old virgin when his book appeared, Reich also began to explore his sexuality after an encounter with a male prostitute in San Francisco. A few years later, he moved to the city permanently and became a gay activist.

The Stinson Beach colloquy was long and stony. Parking themselves on the lawn overlooking the ocean, the three men turned on the tape recorder, fired up some truth serum, and rambled on for five hours. Later, Reich compared himself to a nervous groupie, and Wenner was at times embarrassed by the professor's "achingly obvious or obviously unanswerable" questions. Weeks later, Reich returned for another two-hour session with Garcia, and Wenner also followed up with his own four-hour chat. After *Rolling Stone* ran the interview in two parts, Reich returned yet again to Stinson Beach on a foggy Sunday morning in March. Once again he started the tape recorder, got high with Garcia, and chatted for five hours. Their "stoned Sunday rap" appeared alongside the interviews in a 1972 book from Straight Arrow. The cover image, shot upside down by *Rolling Stone* photographer Annie Leibovitz, showed Garcia lying on Ocean Beach in jeans, a denim shirt, and boots. In the introduction, Reich claimed that the Dead's body of work reflected "a depth of meaning and a distance into new space that I consider to be one of the supreme achievements in American music." Reich was a legal expert, not a musical one, but his endorsement reinforced Garcia's image as what Wenner called a "spokesman, teacher, and philosopher."

Rolling Stone helped place Garcia and the Dead at the center of the counterculture, which many right-wingers detested. But the conservative movement wasn't monolithic, especially on the question of Nixon's drug war. In a 1972 issue of *National Review,* publisher William F. Buckley ran an article calling for the legalization of marijuana, and he personally endorsed its conclusion. The article maintained that harsh marijuana laws fostered scofflaws, useless bureaucracies, and wasteful public spending. They also interfered with basic freedoms and criminalized the "tribal value" weed had in the counterculture. Some radicals, in fact, celebrated the illegality of marijuana. "Grass teaches us disrespect for the law and the courts," Jerry Rubin maintained. "Make pot legal, and society will fall apart. Keep it illegal, and soon there will be a revolution." Buckley also published a dissenting article by Dartmouth English professor Jeffrey Hart, who celebrated criminalization as a tool for punishing youth culture. Marijuana laws, Hart claimed, "aim to lean on, to penalize the counterculture. They reflect the opinion, surely a majority one, that the counterculture, and its manners and morals, and all its works are *bad*."

But if the counterculture was bad, more and more Americans were wondering about the Establishment's moral credentials. The Vietnam War ground on, and though Richard Nixon was easily reelected in 1972, reports emerged that his campaign operatives had broken into the Democratic National Committee's headquarters. The official investigation revealed both a cover-up and a more extensive pattern of unconstitutional and criminal activity. When the major networks televised the Senate hearings, the testimony riveted millions of Americans, including Garcia. Facing impeachment, Nixon resigned in 1974. His top aides were convicted and served prison time, but Nixon was never prosecuted. His replacement, Gerald Ford, granted the erstwhile champion of law and order a full, free, and absolute pardon for all crimes that he had "committed or may have committed or taken part in" during his presidency.

As Rome burned, the Dead continued to fiddle, and the shows were cooking. "No rock band in this world flies so high and so brilliantly as the Grateful Dead, San Francisco's gift to intelligent, mind-blowing music," the *Philadelphia Daily News* reported. "No wonder Dead fanatics will travel hundreds of miles on a moment's notice to catch a concert that sterile records will never truly capture." Ralph Gleason took in a series of shows in Berkeley and compared the Dead to the jazz greats of Joe Garcia's era. "So now we have come full circle," he wrote in *Rolling Stone*. "The Grateful Dead can play four nights (and they obviously could have played a week) at a concert hall with absolute artistic and commercial success." Gleason also approved of their no-nonsense performance style. "The Dead do not go in for any of the show biz nonsense you see with some Svengali-created groups in which costumes and lighting attempt to create the drama missing from the music. The Dead are very straight ahead in their presentation. To begin with, they are among friends, and they know it." Finally, Gleason admired the Dead's skill, not only with their individual instruments, but also at working the room. "Aside from the individual virtues of the group, they have mastered the ability to control dynamics to a more consistent degree than any other group I know of except the James Brown band," he wrote. "The Dead can come down to whisper and still keep it moving, and this is one of the hardest things to do in group music. That they make it appear to be so effortless is a tribute to their ability."

The Dead's commercial and critical success coincided with several internal changes. They had largely avoided or defused the artistic differences, ego clashes, and legal hassles that afflicted and sometimes dissolved other groups, but as their repertoire became less blues-based, Ron McKernan's role steadily diminished. In 1968, the Dead recruited Tom Constanten to play keyboards on *Anthem of the Sun* and then hired him as a full-time band member. McKernan switched to congas, a difficult transition for him, but he and Constanten became close friends, shared a house in Novato, and roomed together on the road. McKernan even served as Constanten's best man at his first wedding. But as a Scientologist, Constanten was uncomfortable with the band's enthusiastic drug consumption, and the other musicians felt that he didn't always rock to their standards. "He just doesn't boogie," Garcia later told rock critic Robert Christgau. In January 1970, just before the New Orleans drug arrest, Constanten parted ways with the Dead. McKernan returned to keyboards, but his role remained limited while the Dead took their folk-country turn.

In September 1971, McKernan faced an even greater challenge when he entered Novato General Hospital with a perforated ulcer and hepatitis. He had cut back on his drinking when he began to experience early signs of delirium tremens, but at age twenty-five, his juicing had caught up with him. The Dead recruited Keith Godchaux, who was playing with Traffic cofounder Dave Mason, for the keyboard slot and added his wife, Donna, as a backup singer. Keith, who had grown up in the East Bay suburb of Concord, was a gifted pianist but, according to Dennis McNally, "spaced-out, depressive, and extremely vulnerable." Donna, a native of Muscle Shoals, Alabama, had worked on the FAME Studios recordings of Percy Sledge's "When a Man Loves a Woman" and Elvis Presley's "Suspicious Minds." When a frail McKernan returned to the Dead in December 1971, the band kept the Godchauxs on as well.

With McKernan in and out of the lineup, Garcia began to share singing duties with Weir and encouraged him to write songs. "Garcia's mighty tired of it, I'll tell you," Weir told *Crawdaddy!* magazine. Weir's chief songwriting contribution was "Playing in the Band," which he composed with Hunter along with help from Hart. The Dead often used that number to launch the long jams that closed the first set in live performances, but Weir's collaborations with Hunter were famously fraught. Hunter attributed those problems to Weir's habit of altering lyrics without sufficient consultation. "I do enjoy working with Weir once in a while," Hunter said later, "but he uses a lyricist like a whore, I gotta say."

Fortunately for Weir, another option arrived in the form of his boyhood friend John Perry Barlow. Raised on a Wyoming ranch, Barlow attended private school in Colorado with Weir, graduated from Wesleyan University, and successfully pitched a novel to Farrar, Straus & Giroux. Using his advance to travel, he returned to New York and explored its cocaine demimonde. In January 1971, Barlow accompanied Weir and McIntire on an auto trip around Mexico, where they binged on radio and tequila. The following month, Barlow joined the band backstage at a show in Port Chester, New York. There, an exasperated Hunter suggested that Barlow work with Weir. The next week, Barlow contributed his first lyric, "Mexicali Blues," which fictionalized their Mexican adventure and eventually became a concert staple. Over the next year, Barlow and Weir worked up four more songs, all of which appeared on Weir's first solo album. The decision to present *Ace* as a Weir project was almost arbitrary. Although he was the lead singer on every track, the entire Dead crew, including Keith and Donna Godchaux, contributed to the album.

The same month McKernan checked into a hospital, the Dead released a second live album. Kelley and Mouse's skeleton-and-roses illustration was featured on the cover, and the band's first choice for a title was *Skullfuck*. That choice prompted a meeting with Warner Bros. executives at the Continental Hyatt House, known in the music business as the Riot House, located on Sunset Boulevard in West Hollywood.

"There were about a hundred of them: family, friends, hangers-on, in this enormous conference room," Joe Smith recalled. "It went on forever, and I got nowhere. Every time I made a point, some baby would start crying or something. Finally I told them, 'Look. You guys worked a year to make this record. If you call it *Skullfuck*, you'll sell fifteen thousand copies out of head shops. Sears and Wards aren't going to touch it. If you change the name, you might have a gold record.'" The meeting ended with a dull title, *Grateful Dead*, but a large promotional budget.

Because the band was too busy integrating Keith Godchaux to book studio time, many signature songs—including "Ramble on Rose," "Tennessee Jed," "Bertha," and "Wharf Rat"—debuted on the next two live albums. Another such song was "Jack Straw," a cowboy number complete with references to trains and murder. But its first verse became its most controversial:

> *We can share the women*
> *We can share the wine*
> *We can share what we got of yours*
> *'Cause we done shared all of mine*

The lyric's casual sexism matched that of "Mexicali Blues," which depicted a man's drunken liaison with a fourteen-year-old prostitute. But Hunter would remind irony-challenged critics not to identify him with the speaker in "Jack Straw," whose attitude toward women was linked to the violence depicted later in the song.

It was a fair point, but many Hunter characters were difficult to like. One scholar identified a subgenre of Hunter's output as "scoundrel songs," whose speakers were "con men, felons on the lam, gamblers of various sorts, or self-described misanthropes with some obsessive grudge or axe to grind." Even Garcia admitted that he didn't identify with them. "Actually, I relate better to Dylan songs more often than not," he said, but added that Hunter's songs created "*a world*—some kind of mythos or alternative universe that's got a lot of interesting stuff in it." "Brown-Eyed Women" was one such song. Like "Jack Straw," it evoked a world of sin and violence. This time, however, the protagonists weren't cowboys but Appalachian moonshiners. Harry Smith would have recognized the characters and terrain immediately.

> *Daddy made whiskey and he made it well*
> *Cost two dollars and it burned like hell*
> *I cut hick'ry to fire the still*
> *Drink down a bottle and you're ready to kill.*

Another verse suggested a different use for the hickory switch:

> *Delilah Jones was the mother of twins*
> *Two times over and the rest was sins*
> *Raised eight boys, only I turned bad*
> *Didn't get the lickings that the other ones had.*

Composed when millions of American parents were following Dr. Benjamin Spock's enlightened child-rearing theories, "Brown-Eyed Women" transported the listener to a world in which the unbeaten speaker considered himself morally deficient.

Garcia was pleased with *Grateful Dead*'s overall effect. "It's us, man," he said immediately after its release. "Each one of those tracks is the total picture, a good example of what the Grateful Dead really is, *musically*." He then distinguished the live album from the two preceding studio efforts: "For a year we were a light acoustic band, in somebody's head. The new album is enough of an overview so people can see we're like a regular shoot-'em-up saloon band." *Grateful Dead* drew a rare positive review in *CREEM* from Lester Bangs, who had described *Anthem of the Sun* as "a piece of shit." In that review, Bangs detailed the antipathy he felt for the Dead and their music after attending a show in Los Angeles: "I came away from that concert not merely disliking the Dead but hating them and all that they stood for—i.e., self-conscious hipness as a marketable quality and innocuous 'social movement.'" *Grateful Dead* changed all that. "Now their new live album has been released," Bangs wrote, "and I am stunned and turned around." It was "not only great *American* music but a tonal personification of the American *West* both as musical genre and, more importantly, state of mind." Because the Dead had proven they could also play some "mighty rock and roll," Bangs announced that he was, in spite of everything, a Grateful Dead fan.

Grateful Dead was the first Dead album to go gold, and a *Cash Box* cover story ("Grateful Dead: Truckin' Up the Charts") underscored its success. Lesh's first response to news of the gold record was to turn the award into anti-commercial art. "I'm gonna nail it on a tree, fill it with bullet holes, and then nail it on the wall," he said. "Maybe we'll use it for an album cover some day."

Grateful Dead was notable for another reason as well. Inside the gatefold, it included a message to buyers: "Dead Freaks Unite! Who are you? Where are you? How are you? Dead Heads, P.O. Box 1065, San Rafael, California 94901." Many fans responded by sending long and sometimes highly decorated letters, which the office staff saved.

Those fans received irregular newsletters with information about upcoming projects and performance dates, doodles by Hunter and Garcia, and playful parables and characters cooked up by Hunter. But the newsletters also included more substantial updates on the Dead's operation and financial information. By treating their core fans as stakeholders, the Dead put that relationship on a uniquely egalitarian footing. The gatefold message also gave fans a name and collective identity. *Dead Head* was a catchy rhyme as well as a play on *head*, the street term for a drug user. Inspired by the band's ethos and music, many Dead Heads were already following the band on the road, a practice Garcia mentioned in a 1970 interview. "At home, there's always been a certain group of people that don't ever miss a show anyplace we go on the West Coast," Garcia said. "You know—*every* show. That's the kind of fans we have." A similar pattern emerged in the Northeast, where with minimal planning and a bit of couch surfing, Dead Heads could take in several shows, none of them quite the same, in a week's time.

Those tours remained the primary source of revenue for the band's growing tribe. Although that revenue was quickly spent, the overall pattern fit Garcia's idiosyncratic theory of musicians and finance, which he articulated during a filmed conversation on the Festival Express. "Look, man," he told an offscreen interlocutor, "you can't play music and get rich. And I mean, even the cats that get a hundred grand a gig, you know, they don't get fucking rich. It goes *everywhere*. Because musicians essentially aren't in a position where money is what's happening with them. Music is what's happening, and the money *goes* places." Warming to his topic, Garcia continued, "Every musician that gets a lot of bread, man, spends it on their culture, man, on their scene, man. They spend it on dope, they spend it, you know . . . They lay out, man, to other people just like them, man, and it stays in the fucking community, and it moves around real fast. And the reason there are so many heads who are able to live on the street is because there's quite a lot of musicians who make a lot of bread and spend it."

Whether or not all musicians felt or behaved that way, Garcia's remarks accurately described the Dead's approach. In addition to spending money on drugs, especially cocaine, they hired more employees and booked more engagements to cover those salaries and other expenses. In 1968, the band played 115 gigs; the following year, that number rose to 146. But as their fortunes rose, they chose to play fewer shows at larger venues. In 1973, the number of bookings dropped to 73, and most of those shows were at stadiums, arenas, and amphitheaters. Club gigs became rare, though the Dead's many side bands regularly played smaller venues, especially in the Bay Area.

The Dead's next major outing, organized by Sam Cutler, was the grandest road trip of all: a European tour that included twenty-two gigs in seven weeks. On April Fools' Day, the Dead set out for England with forty-nine people and fifteen tons of equipment. The plan was to tape each show and deliver yet another live album to Warner Bros. Records. Starting in London, they made their way through Newcastle, Denmark, Germany, Amsterdam, Luxembourg, and France before returning to London for four shows at the Strand Lyceum. Along the way, the Dead played the Bickershaw Festival near Manchester, one of the larger paydays on the tour. The event drew about forty thousand spectators, only half of whom bought tickets, making it another financial disaster. It also rained three days straight, leading Country Joe McDonald to observe, "God doesn't like festivals." The British headlines featured the precipitation: "The Day the Music Drowned" (*Melody Maker*) and "Bickershaw: Singin' in the Rain" (*New Musical Express*). In the aftermath of Altamont, local law enforcement girded its loins. Police arrested sixteen Hells Angels who were speeding toward the site from Manchester for breach of the peace.

The Dead closed the festival, and a young data-entry clerk named Declan McManus took in the performance from his mud puddle. Long after he began appearing as Elvis Costello, McManus remarked that the Dead's four-hour set was a revelation. "Seeing the Grateful Dead that day on that giant festival stage in a Lancashire field made me realize that being in a band was what I wanted to do," he said. At Bickershaw, too, Weir learned that local musicians played 150 to 200 nights per year. "I got the hint that they thought we were really lazy and just laying back and making money off a big name," Weir said. "Then it occurred to me to ask them how long they play every night—about forty-five minutes. Well, we play about three hours a night, so it works out the same." Even so, the European itinerary left Garcia itching to perform more. "We haven't been playing *enough*," he said. "I'm a music junkie, and I have to play every day. The gigs are too far apart."

The size of the Dead contingent fascinated the European journalists. "You've got what, about forty people with you on this trip?" *Rock* magazine asked Garcia. "Well, we don't always," Garcia replied. "This is almost our whole scene, that is to say, almost the whole Grateful Dead family, Grateful Dead as a social institution, rather than the Grateful Dead as a musical institution." Traveling in two buses, the extended family was anything but stealthy. At the Grand Hotel in Paris, they drew stares even from fellow Americans. "As all the tie-dye and denim and hair gathered in eddies," *Rolling Stone* reported, "the other Americans in Paris began swinging their heads, mouths open. If this was the famous Le Grand Hotel they'd heard about—and were going to spend at least $35 per day to enjoy—then who were all these freaks?"

Rock Scully, who had studied in Switzerland, acknowledged that the Dead family didn't blend in. "We were something of an invasion," Scully said. "Because there were so many of us, we could just take over a hotel or a restaurant. That's the meaning of the big American shoe coming over the rainbow on the [back] cover of *Europe '72*." Kelley and Mouse had already produced the "Rainbow Foot" for Out of Town Tours, a short-lived booking agency run by the Dead family. The illustration for the triple live album also recalled Robert Crumb's *Keep on Truckin'* comic, whose stylized steppers quickly became a visual symbol of—and tagline for—the counterculture's wanderlust and durability. "Most of the people had never been to Europe before," Scully added, "and it was also the longest Dead tour ever, so a group consciousness developed that tended to exclude the surroundings." Scully interpreted the illustration on the album's front cover against that backdrop. Smacking himself on the forehead with an ice-cream cone, the Ice Cream Kid was "the All-American Kid in Europe, in a sense a little spastic about relating to people." The Dead asked Kelley and Mouse to produce T-shirts with both images, thereby becoming the first major band to market its own T-shirts. To handle that business, Kelley and Mouse founded the Monster Company, which they eventually sold to Winterland.

Musically, the Dead were in fine form. "We played great," Lesh recalled. "Keith was coming into his own, really. And I gotta say that Billy played like a young god on [that] tour. I mean, he was everywhere on the drums and just kickin' our butts every which way, which is what drummers live to do." The resulting live album captured that form and appeared that fall to positive notices. *Europe '72* was also another commercial success, going gold before year's end. But even as the Dead extended their streak, the European tour gave Garcia a chance to reflect on the family's lean period. The move to Marin County, he told *Rock* magazine, "made us very clannish, and we had just a pure survival struggle for several years—economical and so forth, trying to keep going, which has been basically what we've been geared to doing. It's only been in this last year that all of a sudden there's been more coming to us than we need." With the success of *Europe '72*, the Dead were stacking their chips for the first time.

McKernan performed on the European tour, but he was thin and weak, and after a Hollywood Bowl concert that June, the band sent him home to recuperate. He lived with family in Palo Alto through the fall. In January, however, he returned to Marin County, where he lived alone. "Pig would call the office—it was just a skeleton crew—and he was really having a hard time with the band on the road and him being out of that," staff member Eileen Law said. "He would call and just want to talk. We felt really bad for him because here was this person that I once thought was a Hells Angel, and now he was this thin little person." Lesh recalled a visit with McKernan, who greeted him with a hug. "I had to be careful not to squeeze too hard," Lesh said. "This once-robust man was now skin and bones."

In March, McKernan's landlady reported that she hadn't seen him recently. A Dead staff member stopped by his Corte Madera apartment and found him lying on the floor. Like Kerouac, he had died of internal bleeding from the esophageal vein, the result of prolonged drinking. He was twenty-seven years old. A shaken Garcia briefly considered folding the band, but the Dead, who had become accustomed to performing without McKernan, decided to continue. "So we went with our strong suit," Garcia said later, "which was kind of a country feel: the American mythos, the Hunter songs. And our other strong suit was weirdness. So we went with our strong suits that didn't involve Pigpen."

As the Dead mourned McKernan and their music took a weird turn, they also continued to explore new and unorthodox ways to organize and run their business. Shortly after Altamont, Garcia quizzed Sam Cutler about the Rolling Stones' business arrangements and found it "wildly impractical" that Mick Jagger made most of the decisions. And because the Dead were deeply skeptical of traditional arrangements, Lesh recalled, they were "constantly besieged with business plans from employees and friends." They certainly never had a master strategy. "It's not possible for the Grateful Dead to have a business plan," Lesh later told *60 Minutes*. "We don't even plan the music." Kreutzmann added, "The stuff we planned the hardest usually turned out the worst." Lesh restated his position in his memoir: "If there ever was a Grateful Dead 'business plan,' it consisted solely of an attitude."

That attitude emphasized tribal self-sufficiency as much as iconoclasm. When asked about their business philosophy in 1972, Garcia laid out his utopian plan:

What we've been trying to do is liberate the music industry, or at least our little part of it, by gradually withdrawing from record companies, gradually withdrawing from the whole scene until we finally have control over the whole range of things we're doing.

Toward that end, the Dead helped launch a set of satellite companies. Sam Cutler started Out of Town Tours, a booking and tour management company, and Bob Weir's girlfriend Frankie (who adopted Weir's surname) formed Fly By Night Travel to handle the band's road arrangements. The Dead also supported Alembic, a company formed to help improve the quality of the band's sound and recordings, and lent Kelley and Mouse funds to start their T-shirt company in 1972. Those companies weren't part of the Dead's core business, and the Dead encouraged their founders to seek out other clients.

The Dead's own tour-heavy business model was still an experiment, and it would be years before their earnings became substantial. The Dead attributed part of their financial challenges to low record sales. Even in 1970, when album sales were spiking, the Dead grumbled about Warner Bros. Records. Asked how he would describe his label's performance, Garcia replied, "Shitty. They have terrible distribution, and they don't sell records." After comparing all record companies to vampires, he toned down the bombast. "I'm not really that far down on Warner Bros. because they've been okay to us," Garcia said. "Warner Bros. has got some good people, but I really don't think they know how to do it."

Joe Smith wasn't thrilled with the Dead's public griping, and he had some complaints of his own. While under contract to Warner Bros. Records, Garcia worked with Merl Saunders and Howard Wales on an album released by Fantasy Records, the Berkeley label headed by Saul Zaentz. "I'd certainly like to hear your side of the story as to how your album is called a 'Garcia Jam' and Jerry's picture is used in conjunction with it," Smith wrote to Zaentz. "We've always had respect for each other's work, and I'd like to avoid any legalities in this matter." Smith sent a copy to Garcia along with a cover letter. "I've been reading your philosophies and attitudes about record companies and their lack of concern about ethics, quality, and responsibility to the customers," Smith wrote. "If your association with Howard Wales and Merl Saunders and the allowing of your name to be so used in the marketing represents your own honesty in our understandings, something got lost in the translation." Referring to Garcia's lamentations about Warner Bros. Records, Smith thought his company could "withstand the press coverage of our alleged folly," but he also opined that Garcia's extracontractual work for Fantasy Records didn't enhance his reputation "as an artist and as a straight ahead guy."

The Dead began to consider alternatives. Several rock bands had already established their own labels. The Beatles, who founded Apple Records in 1968, used Capitol for distribution, and Rolling Stones Records was a subsidiary of Atlantic. Closer to home, Jefferson Airplane tapped RCA for $10 million to establish Grunt Records in 1971. But the Dead were looking beyond a custom label within a larger organization. "We're going to try to set up our own record company," Garcia told a journalist on the European tour, "but it's not going to be a record company in the standard sense that it's not going to be designed for profit, it's going to be designed to sell our records in a way compatible with the way we run our scene." The plan was to be thoroughly alternative. "It would be like families here and there, who would be like distributing our records, selling them," Garcia continued. "The records would be considerably cheaper than regular records in a regular record store—they might not ever be sold in record stores, they might be sold in health-food stores and head shops." The health-food industry, Garcia said, was "entirely a head scene—the farmers are heads, the distributors are heads, the whole thing is incredibly healthy for the whole head economy, which is really a sub-economy in the United States, it doesn't depend on the rest of the straight, American capitalist system." Garcia also compared the Dead's vision to underground newspapers, which were proliferating and reaching large audiences.

On Independence Day 1972, Ron Rakow presented a lengthy written proposal outlining what the Dead's independence might look like. It opened with a statement by Peter Coyote, whom Rakow had sought out for advice. "Look, for all these years we've been working for the record business—we've got this talent; we're just like prizefighters," Coyote observed. "When we get old and die, we're gonna get thrown away, and the Joe Smiths are gonna be there taking in the next." Coyote wondered whether the talent should have some control over where the money went.

> So we decided to come up with an alternate—one that was run the way we wanted to run it—where we could deal with people we enjoyed—where we could get maximum return off our energies—where the distribution system would be people who shared a similar lifestyle. We're looking after our own—that's what we're trying to do—good sound business sense. We're American kids—we understand business; we understand something else: how to live a different life. Why should we support people who make our life difficult?

The answer to Coyote's question was obvious. The Dead should control the revenue they generated and use it to support their own scene.

To emphasize that point, Rakow's proposal included notes from a telephone conversation between Joe Smith and a Dead employee. The notes revealed the band's pique with Warner Bros. Records as well as their bottomless skepticism about major labels in general. They paraphrased Smith on the band's relative significance: "You're not that important—Jethro Tull—important." Such strangeness, Rakow wrote, was due to several factors. The record industry was owned by Wall Street conglomerates, whose only concerns were growth and profit. Most records lost money, which encouraged labels to chisel on the few profitable artists to cover their other losses. Industry leaders didn't listen to their own albums, further disconnecting them from artists and audiences. Their marketing efforts reflected a bygone era dominated by Bing Crosby, Perry Como, and Frank Sinatra. "We inherited a system set up to distribute geriatric music," Rakow noted. "Certainly not religious music. And what we're talking about is religion. It's all the religion I know."

Happily, there was an alternative, which came to Rakow in a vision. "I thought of this program while crawling on my hands and knees, in a peculiar state of mind, through the weeds in Novato," he wrote. "I kept talking to myself, some schizophrenic kind of conversation, where everything that I thought was real far out, my other self would say, real quickly, 'So what?'" Rakow's internal dialogue gave rise to the proposal, which became known as the "So What Papers."

As the Dead pondered Rakow's proposal, they also consulted Clive Davis of Columbia Records. Davis had been eager to sign the Dead for years, and on a trip to San Francisco, he listened carefully to their ideas about starting their own record company. Later, he characterized those ideas as offbeat and naïve. While treating the Dead "with respect that intelligent but misguided people deserve," Davis said, "I really made a very factual case for the warning signals they must consider and solve."

After months of mulling, the Dead launched Grateful Dead Records in April 1973. The musicians would still own Grateful Dead Productions and Ice Nine Publishing Company; Alan Trist, Garcia's boyhood friend, ran the latter, and Hunter maintained a major stake in it. For the new record company, the five musicians (without Hart) received voting shares at 10 percent each, while Rakow, McIntire, Scully, Trist, and Dave Parker had nonvoting shares at the same percentage. (Parker, a member of Mother McCree's Uptown Jug Champions, had since become the Dead's business manager.) Four other wholly owned subsidiaries—Round Records, Round Reels, Round Projects, and Artists Publishing Collective—would be co-owned equally by Garcia and Rakow. Those companies were created to produce side projects, including solo albums. Kant warned against that partnership on the grounds that Round Records' finances would commingle with the Dead's. An angry Garcia reminded Kant that he represented the band, not the record company. Although Garcia quickly apologized for the outburst, he also agreed to hire Rakow's personal attorney to handle Round Records' legal work. In the meantime, Rakow lined up credit from the First National Bank of Boston, hired United Artists Records for manufacturing and distribution, and sold the foreign distribution rights to Atlantic Records for $300,000.

The Dead's new venture received a great deal of press attention. "I've estimated income conservatively and expenses liberally," Rakow told *Rolling Stone*. "We have to satisfy the paranoid viewpoint." In the *San Francisco Chronicle*, Garcia wondered why the Dead should be "providing juice" to Warner's parent company, which began as a parking-lot operation founded by New Jersey gangsters. In his view, running their own business had many virtues and little risk: "We thought it would be groovier to do it ourselves and take a lot of the money the record company made and use it to put out a better product. And we also felt that, even if we [bleeped] up real bad, we could still sell as many records as Warner Bros. could." Besides, the Dead organization maintained, financial security wasn't a priority. "The Grateful Dead exists comfortably but is not a secure financial scene," Rakow said. "As a matter of fact, we have people thinking up ways to guarantee that the Grateful Dead will never be a secure financial scene." That remark was more hippie bravado than a reflection of the Dead's true purpose, which was to help establish a hip economy. Organizations like the Dead would be the intake valve from the straight business world; once the money entered the hippie community, it would circulate quickly but remain in the community.

The Dead's new venture was also covered in the business press, including a laudatory piece in *The Wall Street Journal* titled "The Image Is Hippie, but 'Grateful Dead' Know Business." *Music Retailer* reported that the Dead, with help from First National Bank of Boston, formed a network of eighteen independent distributors throughout the United States. "The Grateful Dead put together a solid presentation of cost and market projections," an assistant vice president of First National told the magazine. "In addition, the independent distributors that committed themselves to handle the Grateful Dead's product are all solid businessmen." First National extended credit to distributors, guaranteed payment to the Dead, and performed bookkeeping and collection duties. The same story noted that returns for *Wake of the Flood,* which sold 420,000 units between October and May, were at 9 percent, well below the industry average. "The returns are built into our cost factor," the First National executive said, "and because the Grateful Dead has developed a cult of its own, we enjoy a steady catalog sale."

Warner Bros. Records wasn't happy. The Dead's first three albums had sold poorly, but the next four were commercially solid if not spectacular. During that period, the company had become a powerhouse. In 1972, it racked up twenty-four gold records—the entire industry produced seventy-five—and its sales increased 50 percent over the previous year. As a result of that success, Joe Smith was named president. It seemed that the Dead's business was on the right track, but Garcia called the band's new arrangements "the most exciting option" for him. "The nice thing would be not to sell out at this point and instead come up with something far-out and different," Garcia said, "which would be sort of traditional with us."

For Garcia, it was never about the money as such. "Jerry was receiving a lot of money from all sorts of sources," a fellow musician noted, "and he'd get a check and just throw it in the glove compartment of his car, and eventually thousands of dollars were sitting in there that he completely forgot about. He just didn't pay attention to money; he was a true hippie in that way." The Dead's loose approach impressed other rock stars as well. "They were having a good time," Pete Townshend noted about their performances. "They enjoyed one another's company. One of them might walk off halfway through and go chat with somebody. It

was slow. It was easy. They were taking their time. They were being al-
most mystical about the process. They were not striving for success.
There was no stress. There was no success ethic. They were moving like
Gypsies across the planet."

That nonchalance, however, masked a serious commitment to the
tribe's survival. Rock Scully described the Dead's new venture as Garcia's "way of reconstituting the lost community of the Haight by other
means." Alan Trist traced the original vision to the Palo Alto period.
"The new paradigm we were all talking about in Palo Alto was still
operative in Jerry's mind, and he wanted it to be that way," Trist said.
"He wanted to have people around who were both his friends and business associates to take care of what needed to be taken care of and interface with the outside world." That effort shaped the organization's hiring.
"We weren't just doing a business," Rakow recalled. "It was a way to
employ people—our friends." The operation already supported seventy-
five people, including thirty employees. "The Grateful Dead always had
a huge overhead because they couldn't have been more generous with
their employees," Hal Kant said, "and they always had a huge number
of people on the payroll."

But the new plan had a major flaw. "The day-to-day requirements of
running a record company," Scully said, "are the very things we've spent
our whole lives avoiding." As Joe Smith told a large audience in 1975,
there was also a mismatch between the band's highly publicized ideals
and their early moves following their independence:

> The Dead dropped out of Warner in order to form their own un-
> derground, nonestablishment label. They told us that no major
> record company could give them the artistic freedom to create
> whatever they wanted, that commercial pressing of records was
> inadequate in quality, that we charge too much money and don't
> distribute directly to the people. Yet when they started their own
> label, they borrowed money from a big East Coast bank, they

press their records at the same plant that Warner does, they distribute through established independents, and their records seem
a little more commercial because they're trying to get singles air-
play and establish their corporate identity. This would seem to
indicate that machinery has arisen that is pretty close to meeting
actual market conditions.

Smith also told *The Wall Street Journal* that the Dead couldn't afford
any major missteps. "One bad record could wipe out all their profit," he
said. "That doesn't happen when artists record for the major record
companies."

If creating a new business was a challenge for the Dead, another was
playing the larger gigs that paid their bills. "I enjoy playing to fifty
people," Garcia told Britain's *Melody Maker* magazine. "The bigger the
audience gets, the harder it is to be light and spontaneous." In October
1970, he had been even more specific about his club preferences. "See,
there's only two theaters, man, they are the only two places that are set
up pretty groovy all around for music and for smooth stage changes,
good lighting, and all that—the Fillmore [East] and the Capitol Theater," he said. "And those are the only two in the whole country. The
rest of the places we play are sort of anonymous halls and auditoriums
and gymnasiums and those kind of places."

The setups at the larger venues compounded that anonymity. The
stages were ten to twelve feet high, and there was more backstage space
and security than was customary at their theater or ballroom shows,
Lesh noted in his memoir. Taken together, the changes helped reestab-
lish the division between the band and audience that the Dead had done
so much to erase.

For Garcia, the Acid Tests and the Fillmore Auditorium concerts
were the templates for the ideal concert experience, but that was difficult

if not impossible to replicate in arenas and amphitheaters. "A lot of times people who don't know how to get it on way outnumber the people who do know how to get it on," Garcia said of their shows in the early 1970s. Outdoor festivals weren't much better. In an interview at the Bickershaw Festival, he wondered openly about the merits of that format. The Dead didn't distinguish themselves at Monterey and Woodstock, and they didn't perform at all at Altamont. Although they relished the Festival Express behind the scenes, the tour was a commercial disaster, as was Bickershaw. So it was perhaps no surprise that Garcia concluded that the festival format itself was a poor vehicle for the Dead.

Even the larger arenas were a trial, as Garcia told one journalist in 1971. "The Grateful Dead have become incredibly popular, and we can't play a small hall anymore without having three thousand people outside waiting to get in," Garcia said.

> Our classic situation for the last six months has been people breaking down the doors and just coming in. And we haven't been able to play small places because our expenses are high and then the prices at the door have to be high. It's a whole upward adjustment that we have to go through. We have to play seven thousand to ten thousand seats to be able to get people in at a reasonable price. Just to do it. It's weird. Here's what we're wondering: Do we really fucking want to do that?

The short answer, it turned out, was yes. Most of the Dead shows at the time fit that description. Stadium shows were even less intimate, but in 1973, the Dead played their first one at Kezar Stadium, which had served as the San Francisco 49ers football field until 1971. Originally scheduled for the Cow Palace, the concert was changed to the stadium at the southeastern corner of Golden Gate Park, just a few blocks from 710 Ashbury.

The geography was right, but the stadium show was a poor substitute for the more intimate and collective experience Garcia valued. Many Dead Heads felt the same way, and some wrote to the band with their concerns. One such letter arrived from Berkeley in May 1973. It protested the band's decision, which made even the Cow Palace ("a fucking livestock exhibition hall") sound good by comparison. The fan predicted the 56,000-seat football stadium would become "a goddamn zoo, what with tens of thousands of sweaty bods crawling all over each other jockeying for position, falling all over picnic baskets and broken booze bottles, and creating general pandemonium." He also questioned the band's motives: "I can't [help] but thinking—I hate to say it—that you're going after the Big Buck."

Dubbed "Dancing on the Green" by Bill Graham, the Kezar show went well. After the New Riders opened, Waylon Jennings gave a strong performance, and the Dead turned on the crowd of twenty thousand. "Superb Sound at Kezar" ran the *Chronicle* headline. A decade after the Beatles played Candlestick Park, the Bay Area stadium show was back, this time under the watchful eye of Bill Graham. For insight on what had become a national trend, *Rolling Stone* turned to Shelly Finkel, who promoted a huge outdoor show that featured the Dead, the Band, and the Allman Brothers at Watkins Glen, New York. Crowd estimates for that show ran to six hundred thousand spectators, easily dwarfing Woodstock. "I think people are beginning to realize that Altamont and all that trouble was just a freak episode," Finkel said. "It was part of that time—the Chicago riots, Mayor Daley, Kent State, all that. You don't see it or feel it anymore. Nobody has trouble with a twenty thousand to twenty-eight thousand audience anymore. On a per-night basis, nothing supplies a hall better than rock concerts. In Los Angeles and Madison Square Garden, it's basketball, then hockey, and then rock [that] brings in the money."

Finkel's claim that nobody had trouble with such shows was incorrect; in fact, the Dead had trouble with it. And if Finkel was right that people "don't see it or feel it anymore," that was precisely the problem. Whatever ecstatic communion the Dead had created at the Fillmore Auditorium or Avalon Ballroom was diluted at stadium shows, whose only justification was the commercial one Finkel offered. "This seems to be the summer of the big kill," Garcia ruefully told the *New York Daily News* after thirty thousand spectators endured torrential downpours to see the Dead in Jersey City. "And if we ever stop traveling long enough, we're going to have to reassess the whole thing."

Stadium shows forced the band to think harder about their core ideals and the tension between them. To maintain their tribe in Marin, the Dead needed the revenue produced by huge gigs; but those shows compromised their relationship with their larger community and undermined ecstasy. "Getting off on the music is a truly high thing and what makes it worthwhile," Garcia told the *Oakland Tribune*. "People will always want to get off, but in a concert situation, it comes down to a compromise. . . . As soon as a concert is announced, so many things come into play that limit that high." As stadium shows became increasingly important to the Dead's enterprise, the musicians and fans accepted them begrudgingly. Eventually, the Dead adapted their performances to make the music more palatable to themselves as well as commercially successful.

The Dead developed a reputation for playing those larger venues regularly, even when they didn't have a new studio album to support. That practice created a new image for the Dead: rock-and-roll workhorses. "The Grateful Dead call themselves the hardest-working band in America today, and it's easy to buy that," a Chicago journalist noted in 1972. Their routine was five or six weeks of one- or two-night stands across the country, two weeks at home, and then out again. "It's a bummer having to work so much," Lesh said. "It would be nice if we could sell a few more records instead of touring so much." Such lamentations sharpened the Dead's reputation for industry as well as itinerancy, and Garcia was often singled out for his busy schedule. Between tours, he often played five nights a week at Bay Area clubs, and in 1972, he also released a solo album. When asked why he decided to record it, Garcia cited finances. "Well, basically it was an economic thing because in Marin County, see—I've got an old lady, and kids and all that scene at home—and in Marin County, there's not too many houses," he told *Rock* magazine.

The Dead's touring and hard work were paying off. They sold merchandise at concerts and kept a larger percentage of the revenue from each album sale. They also built their mailing list. The newsletter announcing the European tour netted four thousand new Dead Heads, and within a year the list swelled to twenty-six thousand names. Over the next three years, that figure surpassed sixty-three thousand, with the majority of fans concentrated in five states: California, New York, New Jersey, Pennsylvania, and Massachusetts.

By 1972, those fans had become sociologically interesting. "Dead freaks plan ahead for Dead concerts," Philip Elwood observed in *The San Francisco Examiner*. "They prepare for hours of music, and since it is they who buy up the tickets, it turns out the Dead audiences not only know all the tunes, they are also collectively freaky." These fans understood the unique nature of the Dead's project. "The Dead are not a 'rock band' anymore," Elwood maintained. "They are an institution that will go down in music history as one of the most important and significant innovating and amalgamating bands of our times. The entire output on the new album indicates this. A visit to Winterland confirms it. The Dead freaks have been right all along."

Attending a Dead show at the Nassau Coliseum on Long Island, Robert Christgau noticed the peaceful vibe. "One remarkable characteristic of a Grateful Dead audience is that its collective wisdom seems to exceed that of the individuals within it—where most crowds always hold the ugly promise of a mob, a Dead crowd can sometimes turn into a kind of community." That attitude was on display when the Dead played the mega-concert at Watkins Glen. Despite its enormous scale, the show came off with few hitches. "It worked out phenomenally," Kreutzmann told Marin County journalist Paul Liberatore. "The head sheriff said they had less trouble with these people than with the Grand Prix." Weir added, "I remember a few dances in Redwood City when we used to go down there to hear Buck Owens that were a lot rougher."

In 1973, *The New York Times* also acknowledged the band's exceptional status. "Their sound is unique, completely unmistakable, something soft and lustrous even at its most hard-driving moments," Patrick Carr wrote. "It owes a great deal to years of electronic fiddling which have culminated in the most polished, custom-fitted, and dynamically 'clear' sound system in current use." The Dead were also "perhaps the most technically proficient and musically integrated band in the world, and it shows in their frequent concerts and on *Europe '72*." Finally, the Dead stood for something besides sex, drugs, and rock and roll. "The Dead embody an ideal of community which is now almost a memory," Carr claimed. "They eschew the inherent madness of the rock scene. They concentrate on music and music alone. They search for ways to cut through the red tape and profit-mongering of the rock business, sometimes successfully. They will still be playing together when their contemporaries have long gone their separate ways, as most of them already have."

Even by that time, however, Carr and other journalists were casting the Dead as symbols of a bygone era. "Time capsules should have a beginning and an end," Carr concluded, "and to many, the Dead are a time capsule representing a period which promised much and delivered precious little. However, the Dead have proved that their appeal and their talents transcend those boundaries; if *Europe '72* is an anachronism, it is one which throbs with a life of its own." Reviewing a show at the Universal Amphitheater, *Los Angeles Times* critic Robert Hilburn also portrayed the Dead as successful holdovers. "Unlike the Jefferson

Airplane, another group from the same period, there is still joy and vitality in the Dead's music," he noted. But Hilburn saw something else as well. "Even more important, perhaps, is the rapport the Dead has with its audience. Because of its history of community involvement and its no-frills stage manner, there is probably less separation between performer and audience at a Dead concert than with any other major rock attraction. There is very much of a feeling of old friends getting together." Assessing the same show, another Southern California journalist was even more explicit about the band's vintage: "To say the least, it is a tribute to the group that they can still manage to sell out their concert appearances after nearly a decade of prominence in the rock field."

A letter to the *Pasadena Union*, however, showed how the pluses Hilburn mentioned left one spectator nonplussed. She found the Dead's live show "disappointing at best," and hoped that John Denver ("a superior musician and songwriter") would prove worthy of the venue's excellent sound system. The Dead's improvisational style and low-key stage presence also left her cold: "The lead guitar needs practice, and the majority of the songs they played sounded unfinished. No creativity or imagination. The Dead are also lacking in stage presence and showmanship. They didn't address the audience once or even acknowledge our presence. During the applause after each number, they turned their backs on the audience and fiddled with the knobs on their amps." If the Dead couldn't put on a better show, she concluded, they should stop performing live.

Even major newspapers were prepared to write off the Dead. A *Washington Post* reviewer claimed that local fans heard "a once-great band gone astray in the musical cosmos, one more case of rock music's popularity-breeds-contempt syndrome." His review veered sharply into elegy: "Gone is Garcia's graceful fluid style of playing. . . . Gone are the magical ways the Dead could make the ambience of a rock concert more like a religious service." Despite the enthusiasm younger listeners brought to such concerts, they were actually witnessing a sad decline. "To older ears," the critic concluded, "the Dead seem somehow to have outlived their usefulness." Covering another gig that same year, a *Village Voice* reviewer portrayed the Dead's backstage scene as an anachronism. "From all outward appearances," she remarked, "the members of the Grateful Dead's 'family' clustered backstage had been caught in a time warp, circa 1967." She credited some aspects of the show but ended the review on a negative note: "A line in 'US Blues,' warns, 'You'd better change your act.' They'd be wise to listen."

The Dead were also invoked, sometimes inaptly, in discussions of social and political issues. The 1960s, a *Los Angeles Times* reporter declared, was "a children's crusade marching to the amplified electronics of the Grateful Dead and reveling in the calamity it caused." Likewise, William F. Buckley Jr. mentioned the Dead to make a point about Senator George McGovern, whose presidential bid had failed the previous year. When McGovern said he had little interest in Texas politician and former Democrat John Connally and his billionaire friends, the conservative columnist objected. "McGovern's aim is to stimulate envy and ignorance and greed, and to generate class envy," Buckley maintained. "I invite him, next time he gives an illustration of unjustified reward, to use not the names of presidents of corporations, but the names of the Rolling Stones, or the Grateful Dead, or Elvis Presley, or Elizabeth Taylor. That would introduce the subject in a soberer way." Though Buckley's claim about the Dead's finances was off base, the symbolism was accurate enough. By 1973, writers could easily press the countercultural icons into political service.

Back in the Bay Area, the Dead began work on their first studio album in three years. After logging almost three hundred hours at the Record Plant in Sausalito, they released *Wake of the Flood* in October. Ron Rakow was well aware of the stakes. "Did you see the crow on our label?" Rakow asked *Rolling Stone* about Rick Griffin's cover illustration. "So many people have had reservations about this company of ours, we decided to put the crow on our album and the labels. That crow's for eating. Either we or a lot of other people are going to have to eat that crow."

In fact, the crow was a raven from the flood story in Genesis, and the portions turned out to be modest. *Wake of the Flood* sold about 450,000 copies in the first four months, roughly the same unit sales Warner Bros. Records managed toward the end of their run with the Dead. "Everything started off real good," said one Grateful Dead Records employee. "We ran it pretty straitlaced, just like the suits would have done." The alternative ideas they had once bandied about—for example, selling their albums from ice-cream trucks—disappeared without a trace. Now the Dead had to reckon with the same commercial challenges that preoccupied the suits, and there was no one else to blame when album sales didn't match their expectations.

Meanwhile, the touring operation continued to evolve. In January 1974, the Dead fired Sam Cutler as road manager. Cutler often compared his work to leading a wagon train through hostile territory, which was "not necessarily the most popular position to be in." He had done much to grow the Dead's business, but he clashed with manager Jon McIntire and undermined his standing with the crew. That wasn't especially difficult to do. McIntire—whom Dennis McNally described as "intellectual, arty, occasionally pretentious, inclined toward hypochondria, utterly nonathletic, and gay"—didn't always mesh well with the crew and its rowdy, macho attitude. But where McIntire was diplomatic and charming, Cutler was polarizing, especially on the decision to establish Grateful Dead Records. "I thought it was a dumb move, a Rakow scam," Cutler recalled. "And I said so."

Cutler was also held responsible for the burgeoning cost of the massive sound system, which after years of tinkering and an estimated cost of $350,000 finally debuted at the Cow Palace in March 1974. Composed of 640 speakers at its peak and weighing seventy-five tons, the

"Wall of Sound" was described by McNally as "an electronic sculpture." It required four semitrailer trucks and a crew of more than twenty to transport and maintain it. That meant higher overhead for an already expensive road operation. The original vision was Owsley Stanley's. In 1968, he coaxed Ron Wickersham away from Ampex to form Alembic, which established a workshop, recording studio, and modest retail space near the Fillmore West. When *Guitar Player* magazine asked why the Dead used so much gear, an Alembic employee replied, "It's not for the volume. Most groups could get three times the volume that the Dead does, but that would be distorted sound. . . . The philosophy of the Dead's system, on the other hand, is that since we have the technology to produce a very high quality of sound, we ought to use it. If you care about music, you've got to care about what the audience hears." Dan Healy, who would mix the Dead's sound for twenty-two years, later credited the band for their audacity. "No other band would have put what amounted to ninety percent of its total earnings into this," he recalled. "There were times when we spent the money on speakers and nobody got paychecks, from Jerry on down. It was a devotion and commitment based on my dream, which may have not even been reliable, but nonetheless people still took a chance on it."

If the Dead's new system was unwieldy, no one doubted its sound quality. Its designers noted that it was quite acceptable at a quarter of a mile without wind and extremely fine up to six hundred feet, or the length of two football fields. That commitment to audio fidelity encouraged audience members to tape live shows, a practice that already had a history. The Pranksters had made recordings of the Acid Tests, Stanley routinely taped the concerts, and Healy continued that practice. Avid fans were also taping shows surreptitiously. The New York taping community became especially active in 1969, and two years later, Les Kippel started the First Free Underground Grateful Dead Tape Exchange in Brooklyn. In 1973, that organization published *Dead Relix,* a fanzine whose name was shortened to *Relix* the following year. When combined with advances in high-fidelity compact cassettes, the Dead's new sound system supercharged the emergent taping community. Fans began trading, copying, stockpiling, cataloging, and commenting on tapes, and many young people's first exposure to the Dead came through those recordings.

Meanwhile, the Dead maintained their studio output. Three days after the "Sound Test" at the Cow Palace, the Dead entered CBS studios on Folsom Street in San Francisco to record another album, *Grateful Dead From the Mars Hotel*. Ironically, the second album on their own label was their slickest yet. The Hunter-Garcia partnership added several first-rate songs to the growing catalog, including "Scarlet Begonias" and "Ship of Fools." The new album also included two lyrics—"Pride of Cucamonga" and "Unbroken Chain"—by Bobby Petersen, Lesh's friend from their College of San Mateo days. Petersen had already contributed "New Potato Caboose" to the debut album, but that song fell out of the live repertoire in 1968. By 1973, Petersen sorely missed McKernan, his drinking and traveling companion, and wrote a poem, "He Was a Friend of Mine," to commemorate him.

> *my eyes*
> *tequila-tortured*
> *4 days mourning*
> *lost another fragment*
> *of my own self*
> *knowing*
> *the same brutal*
> *night-sweats & hungers*
> *he knew*

Petersen's drinking figured in his new lyrics as well; Pride of Cucamonga was a jug wine produced in Rancho Cucamonga, a city at the base of the San Gabriel Mountains in Southern California. "Unbroken

Chain" is widely regarded as a Dead classic, and Lesh would title his memoir, *Searching for the Sound*, after one of its phrases. "Robert Hunter and John Barlow were the lyricists for the Grateful Dead," Peter Conners later observed, "but Bobby Petersen was their poet."

The new album's reception was mixed. *Rolling Stone* called *From the Mars Hotel* "moribund" and gave it three stars on a scale of five. Robert Christgau was more positive. "I realize by now that nobody who can read believes me, but this band really is as great as its word-of-mouth," he wrote. He took Weir and Barlow to task for "Money Money," which was presented as a humorous riff on the expensive tastes of women. For Christgau, it was "one more way for rich Marin hippies to put women down." Nevertheless, he concluded, "The album gives me a happy jolt whenever it drops onto my turntable."

Album sales were fine, with 258,000 units shipped that summer, but by August, the Dead's operation was running on fumes. The main problems were the constant travel and the sheer scale of the touring operation. The urge for mobility that lay at the heart of the Beat project— and the Dead's—was now an exhausting treadmill. The Dead discussed those challenges in their 1974 newsletter, which included an illustration of Dragon Urobouros (Giga Exponentia) eating its own tail. The picture, which also appeared in a *Rolling Stone* profile, showed Greater Demand leading to Larger Halls, which led to More Equipment and Bigger Organization, which led to Larger Overhead, which led to More Gigs, which circled back to Greater Demand. That routine kept everyone busy, but it was physically and emotionally draining. Danny Rifkin, who had joined the crew, spoke for many insiders at a company meeting. "I'm not having any fun anymore," Rifkin said. "I'm thinking I'd like to take some time off and give it a rest and see what it feels like." According to Hal Kant, the Dead "felt that time off would be a revitalizer. They were going to work on their individual projects and sort of reenergize and come back."

The rest of the crew agreed with Rifkin, which struck Weir as ironic.

"We had a crew that was being paid like executives for doing blue-collar work," Weir said. "And they were abusing our generosity." Cocaine abuse was another problem. In Weir's view, the crew members in particular were "drowning in mountains of blow." Lesh recalled that period similarly: "Our crew was twice as large as it needed to be and could be quite surly. Simultaneously, the psychic atmosphere was beginning to cloud up with the emergence of cocaine as the drug of choice among the crew, generating an 'us against the world' mind-set." Lesh also thought cocaine diminished his art. "I hate music when I'm under its influence," he told a journalist in 1974, "so I can't use it, it's just impossible."

Rakow's public comments masked all of those problems. "The company represents a very intense sociological statement," he told a Marin County newspaper in August. "A whole bunch of freaks take over—one year later, we have a $3.5 million to $4 million record company—and we're still freaks." But rumors of a hiatus or even disbanding were rife. "They're breaking up," a source told one San Francisco journalist, "because they've been doing the Grateful Dead for ten years. Other bands wait until they fall apart at the seams." Another story noted that the band had become "increasingly irritated and dislocated while taking the long, tedious road tours that often extend for months and many thousands of miles." Yet another press item quoted a prominent Dead family member, who admitted that the band hadn't really progressed in five years. "And we've been getting away with murder the past two years," that source added. "Say this for the Dead," the *Village Voice* eulogized, "they tried. And say, too, that we will miss them."

In October, the Winterland Arena became the site of a five-night Grateful Dead run that concluded a long tour. The Dead had no other gigs scheduled or studio obligations, and there was a chance that these would be their final live performances. Crew member Rex Jackson encouraged Mickey Hart to join the band for what Bill Graham's company was calling "The Last One." For posterity's sake, the Dead arranged to film the concerts, and the plan was to fashion a documentary for theatrical release. Rakow hired forty-six people to shoot the concerts, including Albert Maysles, who had directed *Gimme Shelter* with his brother David. *The Grateful Dead Movie* soon preoccupied Garcia. "Jerry was very involved with it," one Dead employee said. "From way back, he'd always wanted to make movies." Garcia accepted the suggestion to add an animated sequence, but that segment added significantly to the cost and extended the schedule. Rakow initially budgeted $125,000 for the film's production, but the Dead eventually shelled out $600,000. Garcia called the process "two years of incredible doubt, crisis after crisis." Moreover, the project was "endlessly eating bucks." The rest of the band called the film "Jerry's jerk-off."

Garcia's interest in the film also reflected his disenchantment with the Dead's routine. He even denounced the very idea of success. "Basically, success sucks," he told one interviewer. "And all the other crap that goes with it. We've unconsciously come to the end of what you can do in America, how far you can succeed. And it's nothing, it's nowhere. It means billions of cops and people busted at your gigs. It means high prices and hassling over extramusical stuff. It's unnecessary, so we're into busting it." His personal code of ethics, he said, was "all based on 'fifties artists' evaluations, which were pretty much characterized by a disdain for success, and I've always carried that." Although his attitude was rooted in the San Francisco Renaissance, Garcia's remarks also reflected a more pervasive disillusionment in contemporary American life. By 1974, the nation was exhausted by the divisive war in Vietnam, the Watergate scandal, President Nixon's resignation, and his subsequent pardon. Major studio films such as *The Godfather* and *Chinatown*, which presented high-level corruption and hypocrisy as endemic, picked up where *Easy Rider* left off.

On the brink of the band's hiatus, many fans worried about the prospect of the Dead's absence. One fan letter encapsulated those concerns. "The Dead for many years have given me a strange type of energy and excitement about music that no other musical experience has ever exuded. Your music has been a never-ending source of relaxation and euphoria." The fan acknowledged that times had changed and applauded the Dead's effort to change them.

> The euphoria of the 60s sort of came down to the reality of the 70s. Big money, big business, big hassles, more popularity, all of a sudden things got a lot more complicated. But the Grateful Dead roll on, trying to evolve, not stay in the same model which killed so many other things. New and exciting things were being hatched, a sound system which by far excels any in the music business, a new record company which would allow for creativeness and saneness and bypass a lot of the fucked trips associated [with] big record companies.

His letter closed with a plea to keep the band together: "This may sound camp, but the world needs the Grateful Dead trip."

When the Dead's hiatus finally arrived, many felt the absence keenly. Annie Leibovitz, who became *Rolling Stone*'s chief photographer in 1973, was one of them. In a published conversation with David Felton, she expressed her dissatisfaction with the state of rock music:

> LEIBOVITZ: Let me read you something. (Picks up a recent issue of *Rolling Stone*.) This is Judith Sims writing about Black Sabbath: ". . . There's absolutely nothing sinister about a slightly overweight Ozzy Osbourne galumphing around a stage in bright Superman tights, waving interminable peace signs, and shouting, 'We love you!' while the band thunders along like the grim reaper." This piece is the truth!
> FELTON: So what's your point?
> LEIBOVITZ: My point is, where is Jerry Garcia when you really need him?

Leibovitz's question went far beyond the histrionics of Black Sabbath. For many, Garcia and the Dead answered a felt need for sanity and authenticity, not only in rock music, but also in the culture at large. Although many politicians and pundits pilloried and even demonized the counterculture, the causes they endorsed, most notably the Vietnam War, had brought disaster. As Norman Mailer put it, former secretary of state Dean Rusk was "always a model of sanity on every detail but one: he had a delusion that the war was not bottomless in its lunacy." Now the Watergate revelations indicated that probity was also in short supply at the top of the political food chain.

Although the Dead's hiatus was meant to be a pause in the action, it wasn't an especially restful time for the musicians. Weir toured behind his solo effort, Garcia made the rounds with Merl Saunders and other side bands, Lesh collaborated with Ned Lagin on *Seastones,* and Keith and Donna Godchaux released their own album. During the hiatus, the Dead also recorded *Blues for Allah,* their sixth studio album. It received mixed reviews and marked Mickey Hart's official return to the band.

But if the musicians were busy, the hiatus was a difficult time for Rock Scully. Strung out and with no regular income after the Dead stopped touring, Scully was arrested for his part in an attempt to smuggle three hundred pounds of marijuana from Mexico. He was sentenced to eight months at Lompoc Federal Prison, a minimum-security facility in northern Santa Barbara County. There he became acquainted with another inmate, H. R. Haldeman, President Nixon's former chief of staff, who had received eighteen months for conspiracy and obstruction of justice for his role in the Watergate scandal. Scully described Haldeman as "a mild-mannered, well-spoken company man," except when it came to Nixon, whom Halderman excoriated daily.

One person who didn't sweat the hiatus was Robert Hunter. He recorded two albums for Round Records and even did some "interviews"— actually, correspondence with selected writers—to promote the albums.

When asked what his life had been like recently, he replied, "It's been roses, man. A great thorny field of roses." As for the Dead's achievements, Hunter made them seem inevitable. "There has never been the slightest doubt in my mind that we would accomplish what we've accomplished," he said in a 1975 interview. Hunter also paid homage to Bob Dylan and compared his profession to the Western land rush. "With the exception of the obvious genius who has gone into lyricism in the last decade, it's like the Oklahoma Territory in the 1800s," he noted. "There's room and plenty of it for anyone who wants to make a life of it." When another journalist mentioned Hunter's reputation for writing under the influence of speed, Hunter replied, "Most emphatically not. My six-month sojourn with speed many years ago gave me my first real understanding of my own vulnerable mortality, and I don't require a further lesson." Alcohol had become his drug of choice. "I drink until I realize I'm getting dumb, then I teetotal until I can indulge myself again," he said. "By the end of several weeks of concentrated songwriting, I'm almost a quivering wreck. Then I clean up. I recommend it to no one unless they've been blessed with a cast-iron liver."

The hiatus directly affected the Dead's taping community. Recording concerts remained an underground activity, and quality tapes were still rare; but with the band out of action, the demand for them increased, and over time the supply burgeoned. Between the Dead's live recordings and those of the tapers, more than two thousand Dead concerts were eventually recorded, and many tapes were copied countless times. As a result, the Dead put more music into circulation than any performing group in history. In addition to serving as a currency for fellow Dead fans, the tapes "formed the basis of a culture and something weirdly like a religion," John Barlow said. Later, Garcia acknowledged his own affinity with the tapers. In his youth, he and his friends in the bluegrass community were avid recorders, in part because studio albums were difficult to come by. "Jerry said many times, 'We were just like the Dead Heads are today,'" Sandy Rothman recalled.

It was paradoxical that the Dead, who were so devoted to the moment of performance, spawned so many shrines to memory. "Without a tape," one Grateful Dead taper wrote, "what they played in Lagunitas in '68 is nothing more than past history. With it, however, it becomes a part of my present." Luciano Berio couldn't have said it better. In the Dead's case, the circulation of tapes, which music industry executives considered close substitutes for their products, didn't seem to harm the Dead's album sales. Indeed, taping may have boosted those sales by growing the Dead Head community and furnishing it with an alternative currency.

By early 1976, the Dead announced through their newsletter that they were ready to tour again. Garcia said that his top priority was the survival of the Grateful Dead. "I'm not that taken with my own ideas," he said. "I don't really have that much to say, and I'm more interested in being involved in something that's larger than me." For Lesh, touring defined their identity. "We tour, therefore we are," he wrote later. "We considered ourselves a live band, i.e., playing for live audiences and dancers is what we did best and loved most, and most of our income ultimately came from touring."

But even as the Dead began to reassemble, new management problems arose. When the band's coffers ran low, Rakow tried to borrow money from United Artists, ostensibly to finish the film. In return, he promised six albums—four by the Dead and two solo projects by Garcia and Weir. Rakow also alienated Lesh, who was trying, with Stanley, to finish yet another live album from a pile of disjointed recordings. When Lesh and Stanley told Rakow that the recordings were unusable, Rakow dismissed their objections as "ethereal bullshit." The Dead's core audience, Rakow assured Lesh, would buy the album anyway. Released against Lesh's better judgment, *Steal Your Face* was, according to him, "justly reviled as the perhaps the worst album we ever made."

All of those tensions came to a head in Los Angeles, where Mickey Hart throttled Rakow at a chance meeting on the street. Days later, Rakow received a call from Grateful Dead Records' attorney notifying him that he was fired. Rakow wrote himself checks for $225,000 and called a meeting with Garcia and Lesh. He attempted to justify the payments, but Lesh left the meeting when Rakow said, "You can't fire me, I cut myself a check, I'm splitting, and fuck you." Rakow said the money was rightfully his. Kant considered Rakow's actions embezzlement, but once again, Garcia wanted to settle. In the end, Rakow kept the money in exchange for his interest in the record companies, which folded in August 1976. For the Dead, it was back to square one.

Square one meant touring, and in the summer of 1976, the Dead played a series of gigs at selected small theaters across the country. They offered tickets first to the Dead Head mailing list, a decision that was meant to reward loyalty. But many Dead Heads were unhappy when they learned that their tickets were not in the mail. In an effort to simplify the touring operation, the Dead decided to skip the Wall of Sound and kept many of the various concessions, including the catering, in-house. They also chose two organizations to handle their promotions: Bill Graham Presents took responsibility for everything west of the Rocky Mountains, and Graham's former employee, John Scher, made the arrangements back east. The Dead also began discussions with Arista, a new label headed by Clive Davis, whose roster included Barry Manilow, Melissa Manchester, Aretha Franklin, the Kinks, Rick Danko, and Dionne Warwick. The Dead were still closing down their own record company, but they decided on Arista that fall and made the announcement in January. During the negotiations, Davis asked that the Dead work with producers. "We agreed to do so," Lesh said, "at least for the first few records, since we felt we had temporarily reached the limits of our ability to produce ourselves."

The Dead were pleased with their new outlook. "The sixties model of the Grateful Dead was like very ornate and rococo," Garcia said. "We had this huge entourage with every kind of person involved and an infinite number of capacities. The seventies version is more ecological. It is very efficient, more streamlined, and less cumbersome. This is the new, improved, hassle-free Grateful Dead." That change matched a new political style embodied by California governor Jerry Brown, who succeeded Ronald Reagan in 1974. Touting a book by E .F. Schumacher called *Small Is Beautiful: A Study of Economics as if People Mattered* (1973), Governor Brown called for a new approach to governance. Schumacher, a British economist, claimed that his profession's focus on output and technology was dehumanizing. A more sustainable approach, he argued, was to consider the most appropriate scale for any activity and to reject the idea that more consumption led directly to well-being. Toward this end, Governor Brown also worked with Stewart Brand, who introduced him to iconoclastic environmentalists. Brown's public image, which emphasized his frugality and simple lifestyle, was consistent with this emerging ethic. Instead of moving into the governor's mansion, which was built during the Reagan years, Brown slept on a mattress in his modest Sacramento apartment. He also eschewed the chauffeured limousine, another official perquisite, in favor of a light-blue Plymouth Satellite.

Garcia and Governor Brown seemed to be reading from the same playbook. "The thing of performing at a small level is great," Garcia said during Brown's first term. "At a certain point, if your audience grows so large that you can't accommodate them and live comfortably and have your life be comfortable and what you're doing be meaningful and good . . . the hell with it." Garcia also told Jann Wenner that the Dead's organization was too big if he didn't know everyone by name. Despite the affinity between the Dead's philosophy and Governor Brown's, the band declined his request to endorse his surprisingly effective but unsuccessful 1976 presidential bid. Brown never came to see the Dead perform, Garcia told *People* magazine. "How can we apply the same seriousness to his career?"

The Dead's first posthiatus tour was a critical success. "Grateful Dead Returns in Triumph," declared *The New York Times* following a show at the Beacon Theater. Describing the Dead Head scene outside the venue, reviewer John Rockwell took a step back to gain some perspective: "The question for the outsider, of course, is whether the Grateful Dead is worthy of all this love. Monday's performance would suggest that the answer is yes. This is a remarkably sophisticated ensemble, especially considering the wash of uncritical adulation in which it swims." Rockwell mentioned the Dead's ragged attacks and subpar vocals. "But when it comes to the organic shaping of hours-long sets," he maintained, "this is a band with few peers." In his view, the Dead's music also transcended its generic origins. "Rock from a drug culture normally implies crude psychedelic assaults," he wrote, but the Dead achieved their effects through their musical excellence, "the sort that doesn't need drugs at all." The Dead collected more plaudits in Chicago. One critic endorsed the band's decisions to book small theaters and to offer the first batch of tickets to its faithful followers. "A band does not get rich operating that way," she wrote. "But for a concert experience, you can't beat it."

The small shows didn't last long. In October, more than ninety-three thousand fans turned out for a "Day on the Green" at the Oakland Coliseum, a two-day Bill Graham spectacle that paired the Dead with the Who. By that time, the Dead's record companies were well and truly shuttered, and Weir commented on their folly. "It was kind of absurd, all the business machinations we constructed," he told *Rolling Stone*. "It's not what we do best." The following month, the magazine ran an extensive spread on the Oakland event with photographs by Bob Seidemann and Annie Leibovitz.

It was first-class coverage, but as the Dead resumed touring, even some younger baby boomers regarded them as vestiges. Hippies, psychedelic drugs, and folk rock were still popular but not cutting edge. For the ecstatically minded, reggae music and its sacramental devotion to weed was an increasingly attractive option. Bob Marley and the Wailers scored with "No Woman, No Cry" in 1975 and became *Rolling Stone*'s top band the following year. For the dancers, the new sound was disco, and New Wave bands such as the Talking Heads, Blondie, the Police, and the Pretenders were also attracting large audiences. Glitter rock's extravagant costumes and androgynous posturing contrasted sharply with the Dead's street clothes and low-key showmanship. "I can't stand the premise of going out [onstage] in jeans," David Bowie said, "and looking as real as you can in front of eighteen thousand people. I mean, it's not normal!" With their face paint, pyrotechnics, and blood spitting, Kiss peaked in the late 1970s and eventually racked up twenty-eight gold albums, the most of any American rock band. Alice Cooper's "shock rock" shows also featured fake blood along with guillotines and electric chairs. The Dead were aware of such spectacles but never dreamed of staging them. "Now the appeal has to be extramusical," Weir told one journalist. "The Alice Cooper thing. Soon they'll have geeks up on the stage."

British groups such as the Clash and the Sex Pistols were also challenging music business as usual, and in New York, the Ramones presented themselves as the antidote to the long, improvisational jamming that was the Dead's trademark. Tommy Ramone maintained that musicians "who could not hold a candle to the likes of [Jimi] Hendrix started noodling away. Soon you had endless solos that went nowhere. By 1973, I knew that what was needed was some pure, stripped-down, no-bullshit rock 'n' roll."

In January 1978, the Sex Pistols performed for the final time at Winterland. Amid the chaos, two fans climbed onto the stage and bloodied bassist Sid Vicious's nose. As singer Johnny Rotten left the stage, he asked the agitated crowd, "Ever get the feeling you've been cheated?" The Bay Area had its own batch of punk bands, with the Dead Kennedys receiving the most attention after their 1978 debut at Mabuhay Gardens in North Beach. Waiting outside that venue for a

Dead Kennedys show in 1979, one San Francisco punk described her outlook. "I'm no fool," she said. "I know this is all ritualized violence. I know this is all stupid and pointless. But look. Punkers are anti-rich, anti-class, and anti-racist. They also know they can't change a goddamn thing in this world. So at least we can get good and angry and have a good time doing it." As she spoke, a nearby radio played the last notes of a Grateful Dead song. "That was the Dead," the disc jockey said, "a really positive group." "Positive?" she snorted, kicking her tequila bottle into the street. "Fuck positive."

Other rock acts also sharpened their images on the Dead's reputation. After the Dead closed the Winterland Arena with a successful New Year's Eve show in 1978, the theft of their banners received significant media play. *BAM* magazine quoted Sammy Hagar, the heavy-metal singer who had performed at the Cow Palace the same night. "You couldn't give any of my fans Grateful Dead banners," Hagar said. "If anyone had brought a Grateful Dead banner into my show at the Cow Palace on New Year's Eve, it would have been trampled, stomped, and left with all of the other rubble after the show was over." Despite the anti-Dead hostility Hagar attributed to his fans, he eventually performed with the Dead and became Weir's neighbor and friend in Mill Valley. Decades later, Hagar claimed he had almost joined the Dead at one point, and that his favorite performing style was "a Grateful Dead, jam-band kind of thing."

As musical tastes shifted, San Francisco became less important as a rock capital. Bill Graham's operation was growing, but most Bay Area bands of the 1960s had leveled off, declined, or dissolved, and there were fewer major artists to replace them. Jefferson Airplane, the city's flagship band from the previous decade, released their final album in 1972, more than a year after Marty Balin officially left the band. Some of its members regrouped as Jefferson Starship, which produced several hits but never regained the Airplane's early prominence. In terms of record sales, Santana eventually surpassed all the other Bay Area acts, largely because of its popularity in Spanish-speaking markets, but its US fortunes waxed and waned. The Tubes scored a hit with "White Punks on Dope" in 1975, and the most important new act in the Bay Area was Journey, which achieved liftoff after adding lead singer Steve Perry in 1977. Journey sold millions of records over the next several years, but many critics saw their mainstream appeal as an absurd defeat for San Francisco rock music.

In 1977, two years after Ralph Gleason died of a heart attack, Jann Wenner moved *Rolling Stone*'s headquarters to New York City. Its business managers and an increasing portion of its editorial staff already worked there, but the move was also a sign that San Francisco's moment had come and gone. In the 1960s, Atlantic Records president Ahmed Ertegun had described the San Francisco scene's commercial appeal as sensational. "No other city has anything like it," Ertegun said. "Something like fifteen out of the first nineteen albums recorded by San Francisco bands made the best-seller charts. There's something different about the San Francisco bands, some mystique." A decade later, Wenner told the *San Francisco Chronicle* that the city was "a provincial backwater." Wenner's interest in the Dead's music had also peaked. He found the long jams "too abstract" and preferred the electric blues the Dead played during the Pigpen years. Not everyone was pleased with *Rolling Stone*'s move to New York. Hunter Thompson, whom Wenner had named chief of the national affairs desk, noted a change in the magazine's outlook. "The fun factor had gone out of *Rolling Stone*. It was an outlaw magazine in California. In New York, it was an establishment magazine, and I have never worked well with people like that," Thompson said later. "It became like an insurance office, with people communicating cubicle to cubicle."

Much of the fun factor had also gone out of the Dead. Their operation would never be mistaken for an insurance office, but their collective outlook was hardening. "Part of the deal," said John Barlow, "was that as the Dead Heads became more and more sweetness, light, love, charity, openness, emotional evolution, the darker we were." For Barlow, the Dead and their community invited anthropological comparisons. "We were a totally primitive tribe," Barlow said. "We were like a completely isolated village in Sicily. We had this sort of mafiosi code of honor that was extremely blunt. There was a great deal of loyalty there, but it was a hard loyalty." Bill Graham associate Peter Barsotti agreed. "The thing about the Grateful Dead was that they were like a primitive tribe," he said. "Basically, no one was ever rejected unless they got to the point where they ejected themselves. You could make a hundred mistakes, you could be stupid for your whole life, you could blow it a thousand times, and you were still fine. Mainly it had to do with total subservience of your life to theirs and total acceptance of them as it."

One reason for the darker tone was pharmaceutical. For years, cocaine had been an expensive but manageable habit, but Garcia's decision to begin smoking Persian heroin in 1975 raised new issues. According to Owsley Stanley, Garcia was addicted within a week or so of sampling heroin, and Stanley's attempts to intervene were fruitless. When Stanley told Garcia that he was unpleasant to be around while high, Garcia replied that he valued what the drugs showed him. "I don't think he understood the depth of the changes that occurred in his personality when he was using," Stanley said. Laird Grant also tried to talk to Garcia about his heroin use. "When I found out that he was doing it, we had some very heated words on that," said Grant, who had shot heroin as a teenager. "He was saying that it was cool and he could handle it, and I said, 'That's what they all say.'"

Given Garcia's centrality in the Dead operation, his addiction created a host of problems over and above the threats to his health. Both musically and organizationally, he was the default leader of the Grateful Dead and its community; indeed, that role may have increased the appeal of heroin, which allowed him daily reprieves from his responsibilities. But his heroin use made it decidedly more difficult to sustain the notion that the band shared a single musical mind. "If one guy is on heroin, one guy just snorted a line of coke, and another guy is on acid," Rosie McGee observed, "the one mind can get pretty fucking fragmented."

Carolyn Adams noticed the changes in Garcia's behavior but had no clear strategy for coping with them. "He was starting to become a junkie," she said. "I didn't know what that was. I just knew that it was bad, and that it was wrong, and I couldn't deal with it." Feeling unsupported, Adams issued Garcia an ultimatum: "Basically, I just told him that it was over. Until he got straightened out, I didn't want him to come back to the house." Adams moved to Berkeley and eventually to Oregon, and Garcia joined Rock and Nicki Scully in the Hepburn Heights neighborhood of San Rafael. Garcia's room had a separate entrance, and he became a virtual solitary. "We were kind of his surrogate family," Nicki Scully said, "but he would not go out of his way to come up and be familial. That was not his way. The kind of wall that Jerry built was nothing that required any words. It was never articulated. He never yelled, 'Leave me alone,' at anybody. There was just a palpable wall around him that grew larger and thicker and deeper and more consistent, depending on the deepness of his habit."

Like the man in the Bill Monroe lyric, Garcia was drifting too far from the shore. Rock Scully observed that drift from close range. "Doing any kind of opiate or any kind of drug secretly is isolating," Scully said later. "You end up in a bag you don't want to be in. For Jerry, who was so outgoing, to end up that way was just really depressing." Garcia's drug cocoon also repelled the other band members. "As these things have a habit of doing," Lesh said, "the drug gradually took over his life, first his domestic affairs, and then his music and relationships with the other band members, to the exclusion of all else." Garcia's penchant for altered consciousness had once invigorated the Dead, but now it hampered their creative development. The community he had done so much to foster had become a burden, and the drug adventures that once fueled his innovations now dulled them. "He called that his vacation. His way to take a vacation for a while," Kreutzmann's son Justin recalled. "Because in his mind, with all the pressure from all the overhead, he couldn't stop playing. It must have been a fantastic amount of pressure to have. To be supporting that many people and have everything be so dependent that when he blew a tour, they basically were in financial chaos."

Garcia wasn't the only band member with a drug problem. During the hiatus, Lesh began drinking heavily. In Fairfax, he settled into a routine of "drinking all day, eating dinner, and drinking until the bar closed, whereupon I would then go home with any complaisant female I'd been able to pick up." It was one version of the rock-and-roll lifestyle, but it wasn't pretty. "Thus began my descent into alcoholism," Lesh wrote in his memoir. "Inevitably, I began to wake up in the morning with absolutely no memory of the previous night, but a feeling of dreadful foreboding: What did I do that I don't remember? Whom do I have to apologize to today?" Keith Godchaux was also in the grip of a serious heroin addiction. "Keith was just strung out, nodding, wrecking hotel rooms, and being really crazed," said Dead manager Richard Loren. Donna Jean, a self-described alcoholic, was quarreling openly and melodramatically with Keith; she put his arm in a sling, and he blackened her eyes and knocked out a tooth. "We were wasted," she recalled, "spirit, soul, and body." "The irony was undeniable," Lesh said later. "Drugs had helped us to create our group mind and fuse our music together, and now drugs were isolating us from one another and our own feelings, and starting to kill us off."

Some of that drug culture was on display in *The Grateful Dead Movie*, which finally appeared in 1977. One scene, accompanied by distorted music, showed the road crew pulling on a tank of nitrous oxide. Interviews with Donna and Keith Godchaux were cut from the film because the two were "absolutely flying on acid," Donna said later. But there was much more to the film than drug use. Like the Dead's music, *The Grateful Dead Movie* blurred the boundary between performers and spectators, this time by including behind-the-scenes action as well as comments from fans, concession workers, janitors, and almost every other type of person who participated in the experience. Garcia told *Playboy* that he was pleased with the effort. "Whether or not anyone else will dig it remains to be seen," he said. "At this point, it has to get up and walk on its own two feet. I'm not going to sit here and bullshit about it."

The film's critical reception was generally favorable. One critic compared the movie to a Grateful Dead concert insofar as it was a "sprawling, undisciplined, and unnecessarily long affair," yet he maintained that the band's "dogged determination and shaggy charm" would appeal even to those who "wouldn't know a toke from a riff." The *Los Angeles Times* called the movie one of the rare good rock films and claimed that film was even better entertainment than a Dead concert because it was shorter. The *San Francisco Chronicle* thought the movie would have historical value. "The Grateful Dead will cease to exist someday," John Wasserman wrote, "and their recorded legacy will provide a record only of their music. The *phenomenon* of the group, however, is now secure for posterity, as well. No band could ask for a more accurate and valid documentation."

Despite the challenges the Dead were facing individually and collectively, the spring 1977 tour turned out to be exceptional. Many aficionados later regarded the concert at Cornell University's Barton Hall as the best ever. Even those who preferred other shows, Grateful Dead archivist Nicholas Meriwether noted, admitted that the Cornell show was "an amazing performance in a historic tour." Riding that momentum into the summer, the Dead released their ninth studio album and their first on the Arista label. *Terrapin Station* was a major departure from their earlier efforts—more symphonic, and with a progressive, jazz-rock overlay complete with horns, strings, and the London Chorale. Noting that longtime Dead Heads might not warm up to the album immediately, *Playboy* nevertheless endorsed it. The long, strange trip of the Dead, the article noted, was "getting still stranger and more wondrous."

As predicted, *Terrapin Station* eluded many longtime fans, but mainstream audiences also gave it a wide berth, and most critics thought the album was overproduced. "I can actually remember when these guys used to rock and roll," the *Detroit Free Press* noted. "But that was a long time ago—back when hanging around with the Hell's Angels was still kinda cool. And I remember when the group actually managed to put out a good album (*Workingman's Dead*). But that was a long time ago, too." Detroit had never been a strong market for the Dead, but Garcia later admitted that producer Keith Olsen, who had been selected on the strength of his work with Fleetwood Mac, "put the Grateful Dead in a dress." When asked how he would respond to charges that the Dead sold out, Garcia replied, "Fuck 'em if they can't take a joke."

For Hunter, however, *Terrapin Station* was a benchmark. "There's a lot more where that came from," he told journalist David Gans. "That's another one of those projects that could've gone on and become a triple album, if I'd had my way. I had a lot to say about *Terrapin Station*." Hunter found the title track especially significant. "That song is very meaningful to me," he said. "I wrote it in front of a picture window overlooking the storm-lashed bay. There was lightning in the sky. It was one of those moments when I just *knew* something was going to happen." The album's lyrics, which Hunter said were inspired in part by Walter Scott's border ballads, were the culmination of Hunter's Romanticism. That mood was out of step with other trends in popular music, including disco, which the Dead attempted to channel in "Dancin' in the Streets." But even as *Terrapin Station* failed to please many critics and fans, the Dead were on to bigger and better things.

In September 1978, the Dead undertook their ultimate road adventure. After vacationing in Egypt at the suggestion of Marty Balin, manager Richard Loren thought the Dead would also enjoy it. Lesh, Trist, and Loren traveled to Cairo to arrange a series of performances. It was a propitious time for Middle East relations. The same month the Dead were scheduled to perform, Egyptian president Anwar Sadat and Israeli prime minister Menachem Begin signed the Camp David Accords at the White House. The Dead worked with the Egyptian Ministry of Culture to arrange three concerts at the Sphinx Sound and Light Theater. The proceeds would benefit the Department of Antiquities and the Faith and Hope Society, Madame Sadat's favorite charity. In September 1978, a large Dead contingent set off for Cairo. That group included Bill Graham, Ken Babbs, and Ken Kesey, who had written an article for *Rolling Stone* about the pyramids while the Dead were on hiatus. At Kesey's suggestion, Paul Krassner, who had recently been fired as publisher of *Hustler* magazine, also joined the party. Kesey and Krassner had bonded while working together on *The Last Supplement to the Whole Earth Catalog*.

One of the Dead's most famous fans, Bill Walton, made his own arrangements. Walton's basketball career was at its zenith. After a stellar run at UCLA, he joined the woeful Portland Trail Blazers and quickly led them to an NBA championship in 1977. He was voted the league's Most Valuable Player, but he remained a controversial figure. At UCLA, Walton had been arrested at an antiwar demonstration, and after graduation, he sported a long red beard and ponytail, became a vegetarian, and supported the farmworker and American Indian movements. Along the way, Walton befriended radical sports activist Jack Scott, who had figured in the Patty Hearst saga only a few years before. In 1974, an obscure left-wing group called the Symbionese Liberation Army (SLA) abducted Hearst, the nineteen-year-old granddaughter of media mogul William Randolph Hearst, from her Berkeley apartment. Two months later, Patty Hearst helped the SLA rob a bank San Francisco. Two months after that, Jack Scott secretly drove Hearst to New York and then to rural Pennsylvania. Scott and his wife disappeared for five weeks, and the FBI wiretapped Walton's home. In a 1975 press conference, Walton referred to the FBI as "the enemy" and called for the "rejection of the US government."

The Scotts resurfaced at their lawyer's home in San Francisco, called their own press conference, and took Walton to the Marin County courthouse to show solidarity with the San Quentin Six, who were on trial for murder after an attempted prison escape. That attempt had left six people dead, including inmate George Jackson, who had managed to obtain a pistol. In September, Patty Hearst was arrested in San Francisco, and in its first major investigative story, *Rolling Stone* published the details of Hearst's underground experience. Jack Scott was an unnamed source, and after the Hearst arrest, the Scotts moved into Walton's home in Portland.

Despite his team's success in 1977, Walton was at odds with the Trail Blazers' management, and he made it clear that he wished to be traded. The Golden State Warriors were a great option, Jack Scott told the press; if Walton lived in the Bay Area, he could walk down the street to a Grateful Dead show. (Walton had already persuaded the Portland franchise to replace the traditional pregame organ music with Dead tunes.) As his public feud with management wore on, Walton retained the services of Charles Garry, the radical San Francisco attorney who had represented Huey Newton and Bobby Seale. Walton was reviled by some NBA fans for his outspoken views, but his teammates elected him captain and nicknamed him Chief. The moniker didn't reflect his interest in Native American social problems, *People* magazine reported; rather, Walton's teammates named him after the "quirky, unpredictable giant in *One Flew Over the Cuckoo's Nest*." Walton attributed his unsympathetic press coverage to his countercultural lifestyle. "I wouldn't get bad press if I'd do shaving commercials or underwear commercials or if I wore a suit and tie around," Walton said. "I'd rather associate with the Grateful Dead." With his foot in a cast, Walton made the trek to Egypt. "He was like Murray the K," Paul Krassner said later, "the fifth Beatle. He was also the biggest mascot you've ever seen."

After a long and raucous trip, the Dead contingent landed in Cairo and checked into the Mena House Hotel, where Winston Churchill,

Franklin Delano Roosevelt, and Chiang Kai-shek had issued the Cairo Declaration in 1943. As usual, the Dead family dominated the scene. "The Mena House began to assume an amusing aspect," journalist Michael Watts wrote. "The lobby seemed always to be full of girls with hair down their backs and dressed in tie-dyed shifts and tee-shirts, as though John Sebastian's old wardrobe had been raided." As for the men, they "began turning up in the coffee shop clothed fully as Bedouins, their heads in burnouses, the rest of them shrouded in the ankle-length galabia," Watts reported. "In the beginning it was a laugh; eventually, as each morning you awoke to the sight of the Great Pyramid looking above you, it felt completely natural, quite in keeping with the nature of their pilgrimage." Krassner recalled that the Egyptian tailors had fun measuring Walton for his galabia. Even as the Dead contingent went native, however, Garcia felt surrounded by Western popular culture. "When we were in Egypt," he told the *Houston Chronicle*, "what you heard on every street corner was 'Stayin' Alive.' Everywhere! In the darkest bazaars in the middle of Cairo, there's the Bee Gees and 'Stayin' Alive' blasting out of the bazaar."

In a letter to *Rolling Stone*'s Charles Perry, Kesey described the Dead's first performance. "It was real good global theater, Charlie. And besides being often dramatic, and diplomatic, and historical, it occasionally got downright Biblical." In Krassner's view, the Dead performed "like the pyramids—from the ground up." One by one, the Dead joined the Egyptian musicians onstage, thereby projecting a "sense of respect that filtered down to the audience." Kesey found the music enchanting, the location exotic. He imagined "the Sphinx's jaw dropping to her amazed chest" while both Buddy Holly and Joseph Conrad spun in their coffins.

The Dead were less enthusiastic about their performances. Their plan was to cover the trip's expenses by releasing a live album, but Garcia nixed that idea. The main problem was Godchaux's piano, which was badly out of tune. The piano tuner had quit before the Egypt trip because the crew wouldn't allow his family onstage during a show. The

Dead couldn't find a replacement for him in Egypt, and manager Richard Loren estimated that the snafu cost them half a million dollars. The Dead could have used the money. By that time, they had tasted success, and their other expenses were climbing. "Phil had his Lotus sports car," wrote Dead historian Dennis McNally, "Kreutzmann had his ranch, Mickey wanted equipment for the studio, Keith and Jerry wanted drugs."

Despite that forgone opportunity, the band described the trip as transformational. "I've had about a dozen totally life-altering experiences," Garcia said after his return. "They're kind of before-and-afters. There was the me before I went to Egypt, and there's the me since I've been to Egypt."

Shortly after their return to the United States, the Dead made their first appearance on national television. Then in its fourth season, *Saturday Night Live* was a popular sketch-comedy show and a musical showcase; the other acts that season included Frank Zappa, Van Morrison, James Taylor, the Talking Heads, and the Rolling Stones. The Dead's guest spot arrived courtesy of *SNL* writer Tom Davis. A boyhood friend and comedy partner of fellow Dead Head Al Franken, Davis attended college in California. He was doing improvisational comedy there when he met Garcia and reportedly introduced him to Persian heroin.

With help from Kreutzmann and Hart, Davis overcame Garcia's aversion to television as a showcase for the Dead's music. The band's key reservations were sonic. "On live TV, the technology simply didn't exist then for subtle gradations of sound," Lesh noted, "and what control there was usually rested in the hands of the network sound crew—union lifers to a man—whose background was generally in film, radio, and TV news, and whose experience with music was limited." When Garcia asked the other band members why they were doing this, they said playing *Saturday Night Live* was cool. For the program, the Dead chose to play "Casey Jones"—an ironic selection, given the *SNL* cast's well-known penchant for cocaine—and a Weir medley from *Shakedown Street*, the Dead's new album. Out of their element, the Dead were uncharacteristically nervous but performed well. The main attraction for the band, however, was the postshow party at the Blues Bar, a downtown hole-in-the-wall owned by John Belushi and Dan Aykroyd. "It wasn't open for business yet," Lesh recalled, "so all they had down there was some booze, a jukebox full of blues records, and a whole bunch of cocaine, in which, by that time, we were all indulging."

Despite the national showcase furnished by *Saturday Night Live*, the new album was a critical flop. "With few exceptions," *Rolling Stone* concluded, "*Shakedown Street*, rife with blind intersections, comes across as an artistic dead end." The album went gold, but not until 1987. It was produced by Lowell George, lead guitarist for Little Feat and author of "Willin'," one of the great American road songs. Its chorus invoked weed, whites, and wine, but George's drug appetites, which were notorious even by rock standards, ran toward cocaine and heroin speedballs. Less than a year after *Shakedown Street* appeared, George died of heart failure while touring behind a solo album. He was thirty-four.

Back in the Bay Area, Bill Graham announced that he would no longer book shows at the Winterland Arena. He had subleased the building for eight years, but he told *Rolling Stone* that the five-thousand-seat venue was obsolete. Instead, he would focus on larger Bay Area venues: the Oakland Coliseum, the Greek Theatre in Berkeley, and the Concord Pavilion, which opened in 1975. Graham's announcement received substantial media play, but a few days after the *Rolling Stone* item appeared, a Bay Area news story made Altamont and the Manson Family murders look like child's play.

The Reverend Jim Jones arrived in San Francisco by a circuitous route. He founded his organization, Peoples Temple, in his native state of

Indiana, where he preached the unpopular virtues of racial integration and socialism. Years before Garcia drove to Indiana to meet his hero, Jones left Indiana for Philadelphia to call on his idol, Father Divine, who had built a religious empire worth millions. Jones also visited post-revolutionary Cuba, spent two years in Brazil, and barnstormed the United States in a fleet of buses before establishing a religious community in Ukiah, California, in 1965. Two hours north of San Francisco, Ukiah was the county seat of Mendocino and, as Jones learned from *Esquire* magazine, the southern boundary of the nation's safest place in the event of a nuclear attack. Founding his interracial religious commune in the predominantly Republican hinterlands of Northern California was a challenge, but Jones cultivated local politicians and reporters, and one of his parishioners became an assistant district attorney.

Jones sent busloads of his followers to San Francisco's black neighborhoods to win converts. The Western Addition, which included the Fillmore district, was one such neighborhood. It was also the focus a massive urban-renewal effort, one of the largest in the American West. In 1964, the redevelopment agency used eminent domain to purchase local homes and buy out local businesses in a sixty-block area. Faced with few options, many residents and business owners reluctantly accepted the offers. The agency promised to move residents back into the neighborhood after the project was completed, but new construction proceeded slowly, and the widespread deracination left many residents more receptive to Jones's appeal. His sermons, healings, and gospel music fired their spirits, and the church opened a free medical clinic and distributed free food and clothing to the needy. In 1972, Jones bought the Geary Temple to expand his efforts in San Francisco. Only two doors down from the Fillmore Auditorium, the building had once been owned by Bill Graham, who held rock concerts there and leased studio space to Clive Davis of Columbia Records. Jones also purchased a large parcel of land in Guyana, which he had visited on a stopover in 1961, and founded a branch church and agricultural project there.

For those who were concerned about San Francisco's downtrodden, Peoples Temple was considered a boon, and Jones quickly became a player in city politics during an especially volatile period. Some of that volatility was connected to black nationalist violence. Between October 1973 and April 1974, the so-called Zebra murders—fourteen racially motivated shootings that led to the convictions of four African-American men—terrified many San Franciscans. Led by a black ex-convict, the Symbionese Liberation Army also executed Oakland's black school superintendent as he left a school board meeting in November 1973. Three months later, the SLA kidnapped media heiress Patty Hearst, touching off a media frenzy. In that milieu, Jones became an especially valuable political ally for the city's Democratic Party power structure. Working out of the city's black community, Jones routinely delivered hundreds of polite, punctual, and racially diverse followers to support a wide range of causes. The local state assemblyman, Willie Brown, eventually recruited Jones to help George Moscone in the 1975 San Francisco mayoral race. On Election Day, Jones loaded thirteen buses of volunteers to fan out and vote in the city's various precincts. Moscone won by a mere four thousand votes, and Jones could plausibly claim that his organization's efforts had delivered the victory.

Jones was awarded a coveted spot on the San Francisco Housing Authority, which oversaw public housing and was the city's largest landlord. He used the agency as a source of patronage and was soon hobnobbing with Governor Jerry Brown, Congressman John Burton, and Supervisor Dianne Feinstein. During the 1976 presidential campaign, he also wangled invitations to meet Rosalynn Carter and Walter Mondale. When reporters began to investigate Jones, San Francisco supervisor Harvey Milk came to his aid. "Make sure you're always nice to the Peoples Temple," Milk told one campaign staffer. "They're weird and they're dangerous, and you never want to be on their bad side."

That weirdness took various forms. Jones was above all a skillful manipulator and blackmailer. Several employees routinely rummaged through trash cans of friends and foes alike to find personal information that Jones could turn to his advantage. He went to extraordinary lengths to prevent defectors from exposing his methods to the media or law enforcement. He sexually exploited male and female followers and carefully controlled the private lives of his flock, often dictating sexual practices, arranging marriages, and assembling communalist households to meet his objectives. He subjected temple members to humiliating public criticism and spankings, and he arranged impromptu boxing matches between church members. By these and other methods, Jones consolidated his control over every aspect of his parishioners' lives.

As Peoples Temple grew in numbers and influence, Jones continued to develop his Guyana commune and agricultural project, which he promised would be a paradise. But after reporters in both Indiana and San Francisco began to investigate his operation, Jones fled to Guyana with hundreds of followers. Back in San Francisco, complaints from the communards' families and friends continued, and after a critical magazine piece appeared in 1976, the media pressure on Jones continued to build. Local congressman Leo Ryan flew to Jonestown, Guyana, with a small contingent of staffers and reporters to investigate claims that parishioners were being held there against their will. Toward the end of his visit, Ryan learned that the claims might be true, and the rapturous spirit that Ryan had witnessed upon his arrival turned dark and menacing. As the congressman was preparing to leave, one resident stabbed him; Ryan made it to the runway under his own steam, his bloodied shirt open to the waist. As his party prepared to board the plane, however, Jones's security team opened fire on them, killing Ryan and four others. Jones then directed his followers, who were surrounded by gunmen, to drink Kool-Aid laced with cyanide. The death toll was 918 men, women, and children—the largest single man-made loss of American civilian life at that time.

Radical attorney Charles Garry, who had accompanied Congressman Ryan on the flight from San Francisco, was unharmed. Garry had taken on Peoples Temple as a client and announced that the government was conspiring to destroy it as a viable community organization. Although he later withdrew that charge, Garry continued to represent Peoples Temple along with Mark Lane, best known for his conspiracy theory about the JFK assassination. As the mayhem mounted in Jonestown, armed men recognized the two lawyers and directed them away from the violence. Although both men survived the slaughter, the Jonestown massacre was a repudiation of Garry's most cherished principles and signaled the end of his public career.

Jones's project was even more diabolical for the way it excited and then perverted his community's utopian urges. As his behavior became more erratic and maniacal, his program resembled a distorted version of 1960s social movements. In Guyana, he spoke often about "revolutionary suicide"—he borrowed the phrase from Huey Newton—as well as the possibility of taking refuge in the Soviet Union. He justified his sexual practices in terms of free love, and over time he became a heavy drug user. The back-to-the-land aspect of his project also bore a weird resemblance to hippie efforts, and the Jonestown massacre gave a new and harrowing meaning to the phrase *drinking the Kool-Aid*. Where it once meant joining the psychedelic party, the locution took on a new meaning after the Jonestown massacre: the collective adherence to an unquestioned belief. For many Bay Area residents, not to mention the San Francisco politicians who had made common cause with Jones, the Jonestown massacre was another traumatic reminder that utopian projects sometimes repaid high-minded ideals with catastrophe.

Two weeks after the slaughter in Jonestown, another shock wave hit San Francisco. Dan White, a former police officer and firefighter, had resigned his position as county supervisor in frustration before changing his mind and attempting to regain his seat. Although White and fellow supervisor Harvey Milk had gotten along personally, Milk strongly urged Mayor George Moscone to name a new and more liberal supervisor to White's former seat. On the morning of Monday, November 27, White loaded his .38 Smith & Wesson police revolver with hollow-point bullets and headed for City Hall. He evaded the building's metal detectors, installed after the Jonestown massacre, by crawling through an open basement window. Moscone greeted him sympathetically in the mayor's office, but White pulled his revolver and fired two bullets at point-blank range into Moscone's chest and shoulder. Placing his revolver against Moscone's ear, White fired two more bullets into his brain. Reloading his gun, White walked to Milk's office. He berated Milk for cheating him out of his seat and fired four bullets into Milk. A pale and shaken Dianne Feinstein, then a county supervisor, announced the news to a horrified City Hall press corps.

The loss of George Moscone was incalculable. The son of a San Quentin prison guard, he had been a basketball star at Saint Ignatius Preparatory, the incubator for the city's Catholic elite, before working his way up through the Democratic political machine headed by Phillip and John Burton. Moscone's positions on gay rights and medical marijuana endeared him to San Francisco progressives, and with Jim Jones's help, he earned a razor-thin victory in the 1975 mayoral election and then survived a recall led by his vanquished opponent two years later. But for many San Franciscans, the loss of Harvey Milk was even more dispiriting. The first openly gay supervisor in history, Milk had arrived in San Francisco in 1972, when many hippies and gay men were forsaking the Haight for the Victorian homes of the nearby Eureka Valley neighborhood, which became known as the Castro. Milk opened a camera store on Castro Street and became active in local politics. In 1975, he cut his hair and swore off marijuana and bathhouses; two years later, after election rules were modified to favor neighborhood leaders, he won a seat as a county supervisor. That victory gave hope to the city's growing gay population, but that hope turned to anger and rioting after White was convicted of voluntary manslaughter, not murder. He served only five years in prison and committed suicide shortly after his release.

In the aftermath of the City Hall murders, the media predictably focused on San Francisco's kooky reputation, but the perpetrator was no counterculture figure. As author David Talbot noted, Dan White was a wholesome-looking product of the Catholic Church, US army, and San Francisco police and fire departments. Many residents agreed with the Reverend Cecil Williams of GLIDE Memorial Church, who told his parishioners that George Moscone and Harvey Milk gave their lives for the idea that San Francisco was the most tolerant city in the world. The Jonestown massacre and the City Hall assassinations were horrible, but the combination was catastrophic. The city's carefree optimism of the 1960s was replaced by a gloom that would only deepen as the AIDS crisis devastated San Francisco and the Castro district in particular. A decade after the Summer of Love, San Francisco entered what Talbot, quoting the 1966 Donovan song, called the "season of the witch."

PART 3

COMMUNITY

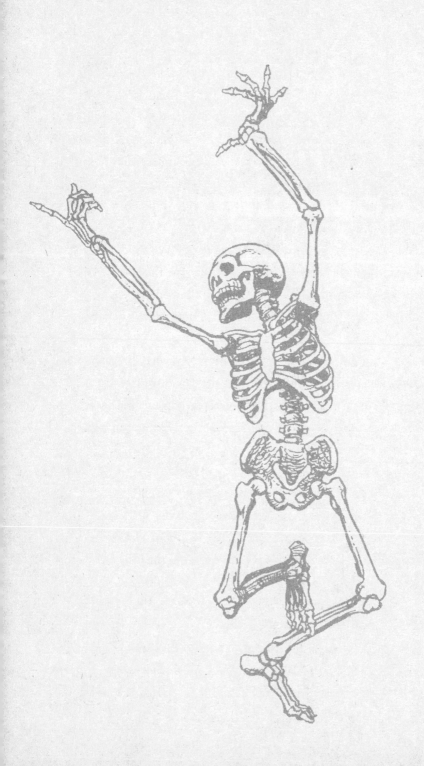

When news of the Jonestown massacre hit, the Grateful Dead were in Washington, DC, where a *Washington Post* headline ("Still Grateful: Their Decade Died, the Dead Did Not") cast them as a durable symbol of the 1960s. The story depicted Rock Scully offering the band a muddled report on Jonestown, but mostly it featured Garcia answering what had become standard questions about drugs, business practices, and the differences between the 1970s and the 1960s. "We were still tilting at windmills," Garcia told the *Post* about their challenges with managers and record companies. "We found ourselves in trouble with the straight world and realized, 'Wow, we're not very good at this.'" Nevertheless, Garcia reported that the Dead and their community were flourishing. "The seventies are depressing all right," he said. "But in the Grateful Dead world, things are snapping right along."

Garcia had a point. The nation was experiencing what President Jimmy Carter called a crisis of confidence, but the Dead were doing as well as ever, despite the fact that the press consistently presented them as yesterday's news. "It seems so long ago," *The Miami Herald* reflected when the Dead came to town in 1977.

> San Francisco's Haight-Ashbury district. The word "psychedelic." Tom Wolfe on what were the "acid tests." And the Grateful Dead. Most of it has disappeared. No one talks about Haight-Ashbury anymore. Psychedelic posters have gone the way of peace pendants. Tom Wolfe writes about a different culture now. But the Grateful Dead aren't gone; not yet.

A steady stream of press accounts recycled phrases that stressed the band's longevity: the Dead were "alive and well," "still truckin' along," "an undying rock institution," and "untouched by age." That emphasis usually implied nostalgia, and even positive concert reviews struck that note. "In a way, the Dead are an anachronism," the *Chicago Tribune* noted. "But if they are not among rock's most 'relevant' acts, they are one of its most durable delights—and chances are they'll still be trucking when a lot of today's trendies are forgotten." Much of the coverage was also faintly condescending. "Apparently, falling in love with the Grateful Dead has become part of growing up, like acne or first sex," the *Chicago Sun-Times* observed. For the media, the Dead had become not only a symbol of the 1960s, but also a monument to that turbulent decade.

A fresher story line featured the Dead Heads, a growing number of whom were following the tours. That phenomenon was unprecedented in American popular music but consistent with the band's artistic roots. Kerouac and Kesey had evoked the romance of the open road, but only so many passengers could fit in Cassady's sedan or Kesey's bus. As the Dead crisscrossed the country playing large venues, they expanded the social space for the expression and transmission of countercultural values. The Dead Heads who swelled that progress were easy to spot and stereotype in the mainstream media. As Blair Jackson noted, they were typically presented as "stoned, tie-dye-wearing, VW-van-driving, stringy-haired, patchouli-scented, weirdly named, monosyllabic crazies who sell veggie burritos and crystals." Jackson conceded that many Dead Heads fit that description, but he maintained that the larger group was always more diverse and included "doctors and dentists and lawyers and geologists, students, computer programmers, jocks, jewelers, organic farmers, Congressional aides, teachers."

The Dead Head community reinforced the band's traveling image, which didn't derive from the sheer number of road gigs but rather from the scale of their operation and following. Louis Armstrong would have considered eighty dates per year a light schedule, but he didn't travel with tons of equipment, employ several dozen workers, feature wanderlust in his numbers, arrive in town with a large cohort of fans, or play for several hours at the local stadium. Following the Dead, Garcia told

Rolling Stone, was more than a musical experience. It was "an adventure you can still have in America, just like Neal on the road. You can't hop the freights anymore, but you can chase the Grateful Dead around. You can have all your tires blow out in some weird town in the Midwest, and you can get hell from strangers. You can have something that lasts throughout your life as adventures, the times you took chances. I think that's essential in anybody's life, and it's harder and harder to do in America."

In a later interview, Garcia also called the tours the modern equivalent of joining the circus. As that remark suggested, the Dead's touring operation followed in the wake of the great nineteenth-century public amusements. Staged by the Ringling Brothers, P. T. Barnum, and James A. Bailey, those exotic circus acts and freak shows did more than any other institution of their time to keep America weird. An offshoot of that tradition was Buffalo Bill's Wild West, whose operation was managed by Bailey and in many ways prefigured the Dead's. After serving as a scout and buffalo hunter on the Great Plains, Cody turned frontier life into a grand entertainment that he never called a show. Three trains moved his cast, animals, support staff, and props. At every venue, the itinerants erected their own tent city, complete with tepees and dining hall, and thereby established their own extravagantly diverse and surprisingly peaceful community. The exhibit's two-acre arena featured electrical works and floodlights, that era's cutting-edge technology, which required a staff of eleven to assemble. In addition to crisscrossing America and achieving critical success in New York City, Buffalo Bill's Wild West toured Europe to great acclaim. Many contemporaries equated Cody's frontier simulacrum with America's essence. When he brought the show to Chicago during the 1893 World's Columbian Exposition, one observer identified it simply as "the American Exposition."

Like Cody, the Dead and their cohort drew liberally from frontier symbols and iconography. The Red Dog Saloon, Native American poster imagery, guns and horses in Marin County, and the Gold Rush–era costumes all linked the San Francisco hippies to the old West and its mythical power. Also reinforcing that image were Hunter's lyrics, the alternative country sound of the New Riders of the Purple Sage, the Dead's two most successful studio albums, and their appearances with Waylon Jennings and Willie Nelson. The name of San Francisco's aborted 1969 free concert, the Wild West Festival, also evoked the frontier and Cody's representation of it. Instead of Cody's tent city, complete with Lakota Indians and Sunday feasts of dog stew, the Dead had a parking-lot culture with vendors selling vegetarian food and trinkets. The Dead's version of the Wild West show also featured the Hells Angels, the twentieth-century equivalent of the old frontiersmen, a point Hunter Thompson underscored in his book about the motorcycle gang. "They're the Wild Bill Hickoks, the Billy the Kids—they're the last American heroes we have, man," Thompson quoted one observer.

Much like Buffalo Bill, whose show attracted fans across the political spectrum, the Dead used politically vague frontier symbols to transcend their era's intense partisan contests. For Cody and his cohort, those contests were connected to the Civil War and its legacy; for the Dead, it was the Vietnam War that divided the country and fueled the counterculture. Paradoxically, Garcia was crystal clear about the Dead's hazy symbolism. "The desire on our fans' part is to have some high moments in your life, some mystery," he said. "So we've made an effort to not contextualize our material. To leave it ambiguous, on purpose. We've talked about being more and more inexact. We have made an effort to make the lyrics as obscure as possible. In a lot of situations, we've eliminated what sense there was in a song in favor of shades of ambiguity. We're not explicit about anything, politics, meaning, anything."

At least two features of the Dead's operation distinguished it from Cody's. First, the Dead drew on Western myth and iconography, but theirs was a psychedelic frontier, not a geographical one. Like Cody, the Grateful Dead spent part of their youth exploring that frontier and then decades re-creating it with their elaborate touring operation. Second, the Dead relied on their audiences to complete, and not merely to witness, the relevant frontier experience. By blurring the line between performers and audience, and by creating a forum for exploring the psychedelic landscape, the Dead issued a standing invitation to anyone who wished to participate in their project. In this sense, Dead scholar Nicholas Meriwether claimed, the Grateful Dead democratized bohemia.

To be sure, that form of bohemia was a historically specific one. "I don't mean to get mystical on you, or nothing like that," Hunter told one interviewer, "but there was a question asked in the early sixties which demanded an answer, and those who demanded an answer naturally came together and recognized one another." That mutual recognition delighted and energized the original San Francisco hippies. Garcia described the 1960s as that "nice thing of discovering kindred spirits—meeting people, and it would be like, 'Oh, you're the weird person from your town? I'm the weird person from my town.'" That acknowledgment was the surest sign that the hippies belonged to something larger than themselves, and it helped grow and consolidate their community.

The Dead's mobility didn't impede efforts to create community, which was never tied to a specific location. To the contrary, their itinerancy powered their community's growth. "We went on a head-hunting mission for twenty-five years," Mickey Hart said later. "We went out there and got this army in tow." Hart's description of that mission also underscored the importance of mobility. "We're in the transportation business," he said. "We move minds." Hart's comment was meant figuratively—the Dead specialized in ecstasy—but to the extent that it also worked at the literal level, it emphasized the links between the Dead's utopian ideals of ecstasy, mobility, and community.

As more and more young people joined or identified with that unique community, some journalists began referring to it as a cult. By that time, the term had a decidedly negative charge, and not only because of Jonestown; critical coverage of Sun Myung Moon's Unification Church was also peaking. The First National Bank of Boston applied that term to the Dead without its negative connotations in 1974, when they noted that their core audience made them a safe business bet. It surfaced again in 1977, when John Rockwell of *The New York Times* described the Dead as "about the most fervently cultish attraction in the history of rock-and-roll." A few days after the Jonestown massacre, *The Philadelphia Inquirer* referred to Dead Heads as "undoubtedly the largest and most enthusiastic cult in rock music." A year later, Rockwell returned to the cult trope in another *Times* story about the Dead: "The Grateful Dead, for some reason or other, has become the New York area's biggest cult rock band." *Rolling Stone* used the same language in 1980, and *Time* magazine adopted the trope in its 1985 profile, which tried to compute the number of Dead Head "cultists."

As the cult meme took hold in the media, sociologists and religious scholars began to study the Dead Head culture more systematically. Sociologist Rebecca G. Adams followed the band on tour, interviewed Dead Heads, and produced a stream of scholarly works about the Dead subculture, which she divided into three major groups: students, hard-core Dead Heads who traveled with the band, and the professional element that Blair Jackson had in mind. Adams also studied the social stigma Dead Heads frequently experienced. Most media observers, however, remained mystified by the Dead's culture and appeal. They criticized the music, especially the albums, and viewed the Dead Head scene with suspicion, scorn, or even pity. Even *Rolling Stone* distanced itself from the Dead. "For the capacity crowd, the Dead's performance seemed as relevant and revelatory as ever," one writer noted. "But to me, the Dead's Sixties metaphysics and musical psychedelia all seemed tame, safe, a bit conservative, and ultimately, redundant." Rock critic Dave Marsh, who had once called *Live/Dead* a great album, began to describe the Dead as meandering, anachronistic, and boring. He later called the Dead "the worst band in creation."

Marsh's work focused primarily on albums, but Dead Heads under-stood that the band's project didn't reduce to vinyl. In the spirit of the Trips Festival, Dead concerts were primarily occasions for the commu-nity to commune. Through social connection and transcendence, Dead Heads could imagine a world that resembled their concert experience. The key to the Dead's success, Rosie McGee felt, was "community—and everybody being high." Some Dead Heads even tried to communi-cate that idea to journalists. "I go see other groups sometimes, but they just put on a show," one youth explained in 1980. "You watch it, dig it, go home. With the Dead, we start partying the afternoon of the show. Everybody hangs out together outside the theater and inside, too. We get high together. We dance together. The party goes on all night. That doesn't happen anywhere else." Audience participation wasn't a happy by-product of a Dead show but rather an indispensable part of its cre-ation. As one reviewer noted, "The Grateful Dead are the precondition, the inspiration, and the symbol, but it's up to the people in the audience to turn it into a *concert*." That description echoed Ralph Gleason's point, made a decade earlier, that the San Francisco bands and their audiences created something together.

Once applied, the cult label proved tenacious. It was true that, like Jim Jones and Peoples Temple, the Dead tapped deep urges for ecstasy and community, but the differences between the two utopian projects were much more striking than the similarities. Unlike Peoples Temple, for example, the Dead community lacked an enthusiastic leader, a role that Garcia consistently rejected. "Some people at the shows think I'm some kind of a fucking prophet or something," he told Laird Grant. "That makes me crazy, man. I'm afraid to say anything because of what people are going to take from it." He connected that fear not to Jim Jones, but rather to another sinister cult leader. "It's like that Manson thing," Garcia said. "You get caught up in that kind of fucking power. I don't want it." Garcia's attitude was consistent with his ambivalence about fame, which he compared to a little dog he took with him every-where. "God, if I could play my music and not have to deal with any of this," he told Grant, "it would be the happiest day of my life."

The Dead's utopian project differed from Jones's in other ways as well. For the most part, the Dead were uninterested in politics or even politically oriented music. The year before the Jonestown massacre, Garcia noted that "New Speedway Boogie," their song about Altamont, was "a totally topical song, and that's *never* been something I've been involved in. It's something I don't even like." Jim Jones's personal and political power was based on his charismatic oratory, but the Dead avoided speeches, pronouncements, and even stage banter. Jones har-nessed the power of spectacle, whereas the Dead steered clear of gaudy showmanship. Jones's community was a residential one, but the Dead's tribe was never tied to an exact location. Above all, Jones loved to con-trol other people, and he took careful measure of how far he could bend people to his will. By all accounts, that kind of power sickened members of the Grateful Dead. Where Jones directed every aspect of his organi-zation and the lives of its members, the Dead were remarkably egalitar-ian, nonhierarchical, and antiauthoritarian—not only in their own organization, but also with their fans. Many Dead Heads and their observers identified freedom and acceptance, not rigid hierarchical control, as the community's bedrock values.

Later scholars described the Dead not as a cult, but rather as "the best example of a popular music subculture with obvious religious di-mensions." In their public remarks, the band actively courted that de-scription. "We used to say that every place we played was church, and that's what it was like," said Lesh. "A pretty far-out church, but that's how we felt." The inner circle also explored nontraditional forms of spir-ituality. In the years preceding the formation of the band, Hunter, Con-stanten, and David Nelson either investigated or accepted the precepts of Scientology. Garcia identified *The Urantia Book,* a two-thousand-page tome that sought to unite religion, science, and philosophy, as one of his favorite esoteric works. But when asked about his religious views, Garcia replied, "I guess music is my religion, in as much as it's my discipline. It's my yoga, it's the thing that I work at, and it's the thing that I measure my achievements against."

Music certainly was Garcia's central concern, but he also claimed the Dead had an ulterior motive: to transform the audience's ordinary reality through "seat-of-the-pants shamanism." That aspect of their project, he said, had "something to do with why the Grateful Dead keep pulling them in." In primitive cultures, he told *Rolling Stone,* the "state of the shaman is a desirable state. In our society, we somehow are trying not to have that. That's a real problem. We need the visions. A lot of what we do is already metaphors for that—movies, television, all that stuff. We want to see other worlds. Music is one of the oldest versions of it." Like most forms of shamanism, the Dead's version emphasized four broad themes: the universe's interconnectedness, altered states of consciousness, sharing those experiences through ritual and symbolism, and employing the insights gained after returning to ordinary consciousness. Many fans, and not only drug-addled youth, were receptive to this part of the Dead's project. Author, professor, and psychotherapist Gary Greenberg, for example, maintained that a Dead show "was not just a concert. It was a place of worship. The band was the high priest, the songs the liturgy, the dancing the prayer, the audience the congregation. Out of these simple ingredients, we created a tradition and enacted a ritual that was at once entirely familiar and thoroughly mysterious."

During his hiatus from the band in the early 1970s, Mickey Hart began to explore the shamanistic aspect of the Dead's music and community. That study blossomed after Hart crossed paths with mythologist Joseph Campbell. "I wanted to find out more about the ecstatic states and trance, and what the difference was," Hart said. "I read all these accounts of how shamans use drums to move in and out of altered states

at will, and I thought, 'Jesus, we move in and out of these altered states
as well. Let's talk about this stuff.'" In 1986, Hart prepared a multimedia
theatrical presentation of shamanic healing rituals from different cultures and eventually coauthored four books on related topics.

Other members of the inner circle were more circumspect about the
religious impulse. In conversation with Hunter in the 1970s, Barlow
remarked that the Dead phenomenon "was turning into a cult, or religion, or something." Hunter agreed. "So far it doesn't have any dogma,"
Barlow continued, "which makes it kind of okay as a religion, but it's
got ritual, it's got iconography, it's got all these characteristics of religion; it just doesn't seem to have a belief system yet." Hunter suggested
that they consciously avoid writing hymns for this quasi-religion. "If it's
going to get a belief system," Hunter said, "it's going to be because of us.
We will provide it. I mean, we are the ones getting up in the bully pul-
pit, and we'll give it a belief system, and we could ride this sucker all the
way to some dark place. But you don't want to do that, and I don't want
to do that." Barlow assented immediately. "No, no, it's already in a dark
place, dude," Barlow told Hunter. "It's scary enough now."

Although Hunter and Barlow avoided dogmatic lyrics, they appreciated the forms of fellowship the Dead fostered. "A lot of what we are
selling is community," Barlow said. "That is our main product, not music." And if that community lacked a formal belief system, it did have
core values, which Dennis McNally enumerated in a 1980 article for
the *San Francisco Chronicle*. Those included the warm sharing of family,
a hippie contempt for commercialism, and a "noisy but peaceful determination to have a good time." When those values were on display,
musicologist Jacob Cohen noted, the Dead community also invited comparisons to nineteenth-century religious camp meetings. Garcia may
have taken a dim view of Bob Dylan's born-again Christianity, but
camp meetings were a different matter. "It would be nice if rock shows
could approach revival meetings," he said in a 1973 interview, "which
happens occasionally when the music is really good."

. . .

Even as the Dead fostered community and strove for transcendence, they struggled with their personal problems. By the early months of 1979, Keith Godchaux's drug and alcohol issues had become critical. He was almost in a vegetative state, Lesh recalled, and his playing "had degenerated to the point where most of us were simply trying to 'lose him onstage,' in Bob's eloquent phrase." At a band meeting, Keith and Donna Godchaux agreed to leave the band. A year and a half later, Keith was killed in an automobile accident while returning home from an all-night party in West Marin.

Within two months of Keith Godchaux's departure from the band, the Dead recruited Brent Mydland as their fourth keyboardist. Born in Germany—his father was an army chaplain—Mydland attended high school in the same East Bay suburb as Godchaux. After graduation, he moved to Los Angeles and played in a band under contract with Arista. He soon met Weir through a mutual friend and joined the Bob Weir Band, where his keyboard virtuosity and high harmonies made him the top candidate to replace Godchaux. Mydland contributed two songs, one of which he cowrote with Barlow, to the Dead's next studio album, *Go to Heaven* (1980). That album, whose cover photograph depicted the band dressed in white disco suits, was widely panned. *Rolling Stone* called it "uninspired fluff," and *Playboy*'s verdict was "mediocrity on the march." Lesh was even less charitable, pronouncing the album "dogshit." Nevertheless, the Dead's fan base put *Go to Heaven* on the charts for twenty-one weeks, peaking at number twenty-three. Dead Heads also turned out for two bookings: a fifteen-show run at the Warfield Theater in San Francisco and eight shows at Radio City Music Hall in New York City. Designed to celebrate the Dead's fifteenth anniversary, the shows were a hot ticket. Dead Heads began lining up for the Radio City Music Hall tickets three days before they went on sale, and some forty-eight thousand tickets were snatched up within hours.

That enthusiasm didn't prevent some journalists from dismissing the Dead with gusto. In 1981, the band played in London, where Paul Morley interviewed Garcia for *New Musical Express*. Morley was openly contemptuous of the grizzled guitarist, who was fifteen years his senior. "You're just part of a perpetuation of bland, blanketing myths," said Morley, who also asked whether it upset Garcia that Morley found him "rusty, crusty, dusty, and fusty." Garcia remained unflappable. "I would be afraid if everyone in the world liked us," he replied. Morley continued to bait Garcia, claiming that the Dead's mood—which he described as relaxed, reasonable, and contained—was wrong for the times. He suggested that American youth should ignore the Dead's music, adding that forty-five minutes of it seemed to go on for two years. "Well, have a nice rest!" Garcia said with a laugh as he departed the interview. The magazine's review of the Dead's performance was less hostile; it concluded that the Dead had "settled into a lazy, but nevertheless elevated level of virtuosity."

Some US journalists saw the Dead as something more than aging rockers. A 1982 *Baltimore Sun* headline ("The Grateful Dead: A Cult Following Keeps These Old Hippies Going") suggested a stale story, but Patrick Ercolano credited the band on two fronts. First, he noted that the Dead weren't recycling their old material for a payday. "The highest compliment one could make about the Dead's Civic Center show was that it was no nostalgia trip," Ercolano wrote. "Yes, the Stones were good in concert last year, but most of their repertoire was ten to eighteen years old." He also noted that the Dead had "something better than fickle mass popularity"—namely, a loyal community that would keep them playing as long as they wanted. "It appears that the Grateful Dead have reached a healthy realization," he concluded. "As long as they plan to be around 'til arthritis sets in, they might as well keep their music changing and growing right along with their audience."

Meanwhile, the Dead's business continued to develop according to its unique precepts. In 1981, the Dead commissioned a report by Alan Trist meant to give their organization more definition and direction. "A Balanced Objective: Overview of Job Definitions" was by no means a conventional business memo. It opened with an *I Ching* result and a Bobby Petersen poem, and Garcia's preface made it clear he didn't want a corporate manual. "This report shows how we really work," he wrote. "We do business the way artists do business." The company was "a legal fiction, not a working reality. It doesn't represent our real work. Just because we have an office doesn't mean we have to feel we have to be office workers, nor identify ourselves as a Corporation because we have a corporation." By making that distinction, Garcia hoped to avoid a conceptual trap: "We need to liberate ourselves from misunderstanding ourselves," he wrote. "We need to protect ourselves from believing that we are essentially a corporate entity." Instead, the organization was "a 24-hour a day living reality. It doesn't matter where we are when we're doing it, we're always doing it." The balance mentioned in the report's title, Trist wrote, had to be struck between "the structural requirements of taking care of its business and the fluid needs of its overall creative process." That balance was threatened by "disharmony in our relationships," whose first cause was "ambiguity about responsibility for essential functions."

The same year, Danny Rifkin replaced Richard Loren as the Dead's manager and made several far-reaching changes. One was establishing a mail-order ticket office that operated out of the Dead's San Rafael headquarters. That change turned out to be a critical part of developing and maintaining the larger Dead community. By allowing fans to purchase tickets through the mail, the Dead rewarded the loyalty of older Dead Heads, some of whom were unwilling to stand in ticket lines for long periods. Throughout the 1980s, about half of the Dead's tickets were sold through the mail, and the results were impressive. In 1985, the Dead played seventy-one concerts, and all but six sold out, generating $11 million in revenue. In his *San Francisco Chronicle* column, Joel Selvin wondered whether the Dead at their two-decade mark held the lifetime record for most concerts played, most tickets sold, and highest box-office revenue. Even a seasoned observer such as Selvin couldn't have known that much bigger numbers were yet to come.

Under Rifkin's management, the Dead also expanded their philanthropic activity. In 1982, they instituted a policy of beginning each tour year with a series of shows to fund various nonprofit organizations. Two years later, they established the Rex Foundation to channel those funds. The foundation was named after Rex Jackson, the Dead crew member and road manager who died in a 1976 automobile accident. Weir served as president of the foundation, and in its first five years, it distributed more than $500,000 to worthy groups. One of the first grantees was the Camp Winnarainbow Scholarship Fund, which helped underwrite a summer camp for seven hundred children, organized by Hugh Romney, who had taken the name Wavy Gravy. The Dead also supported the Society for Epidemiology and Voluntary Assistance, whose acronym (Seva) is the Sanskrit word for service to mankind. Seva was founded in 1978 to alleviate blindness, especially in the developing world, and to improve Native American community health. Having worked with founding physician and epidemiologist Larry Brilliant, Wavy Gravy signed on as a Seva fund-raiser. Gravy's wife became its executive director, and Weir served on the advisory board. The Dead played memorable benefits at the Berkeley Community Theatre in 1981 and in Toronto in 1984, and various band members have continued to play Seva events since then.

As a privately held corporation, the Dead had no fiduciary duty to maximize shareholder value, and that allowed them to avoid narrow legal and profit-maximizing strategies. Over and above their philanthropy, the Dead used their organization to repay kindnesses. After Page Browning died in 1984, Shurtliff proposed that the Dead contribute to his estate. "He was a friend who gave his last $20 many times," the Dead's business minutes note. "Suggested $25k—maybe $5k now and the balance over the course of the year. We will send $5k now and reevaluate in January." The minutes also noted the desire to give more thought to the families of other "deceased brothers," including Sonny

Heard. The Dead had fired the troublesome Heard as a crew member in 1973, but he found a spot on Candace Brightman's lighting crew before returning home to Oregon, where he started a family and was shot in the chest by robbers while defending his home in 1980. The Dead also advanced Bobby Petersen $12,000 against the royalties of his book of poems, which was distributed by the Dead's merchandising arm. Unfortunately, the hard-living Petersen would die in 1987 at age fifty.

At an August 1984 meeting, the organization made a riskier move when it decided to set up a section for tapers at their next concert. The Dead already had a long history with the taping community, but the decision wasn't made lightly. Some insiders wondered whether they should enforce the nontaping rider in their standard contract. "Danny [Rifkin] feels that we should not stop the taping," their minutes read. "Philosophical aspect of this issue is tabled until the next meeting." The Dead were tentatively moving toward an official policy compatible with Garcia's famous remark that the audience could have the music once the band was done with it. By clearing space behind the soundboard for tapers, the Dead blessed a practice that had been part of the Dead Head culture for years. Barlow later said it was "one of the most enlightened, practical, smart things that anybody ever did." It immediately increased the supply of quality tapes, which grew and strengthened the Dead Head community.

During this time, the Dead also hired Dennis McNally as their publicist. McNally was earning a PhD in American history at the University of Massachusetts Amherst when he saw his first Grateful Dead show in 1972. He soon conceived a plan to write a two-volume history of the postwar counterculture; the first book would be a biography of Jack Kerouac, and the second would document the history of the Grateful Dead. When Random House published the Kerouac biography, *Desolate Angel*, in 1979, McNally mailed copies to Garcia and Hunter. He also moved to San Francisco and wrote a piece about the rituals of the Dead's New Year's Eve shows for the *San Francisco Chronicle*. When

Garcia met McNally and learned that he'd authored the Kerouac biography, Garcia rose to shake his hand. McNally felt that the second book had to be the Dead's idea, and Garcia soon suggested it. McNally began collecting the material for what eventually became a bestselling history of the band.

In 1983, McNally accepted an offer from Bill Graham to work as an archivist. The following summer, the band discussed their publicity challenges at their regular meeting. Scully was the official publicist, but he often failed to return telephone calls and was eventually fired. Rifkin had more pressing duties, and the publicity-related calls often fell to an office worker. Garcia recommended McNally for the job because "he knows all of that shit." McNally received his on-the-job training from Garcia. "We don't suck up to the press," Garcia said. "Be nice, of course, but we don't suck up." When McNally asked whether there was anything else he needed to know, Garcia replied, "No, that's about it." He then offered the band's new publicist a joint.

By that time, many journalists had grown up with the Dead and were happy to cover them. The tone of their stories, McNally recalled, was "bemused, confused, but fair." Press accounts focused heavily on the Dead Head culture, whose fanaticism McNally found impressive but boring, and he offered to travel with the band to help reshape its coverage. The crew was leery of that proposal because they saw the touring operation, and the resources that supported it, as their domain. But McNally prevailed, and over the next fifteen years, he missed only two shows. His media work bore fruit in 1987, when *Forbes* ran a cover story on the band. Commenting on that piece, the *Los Angeles Times* summarized the Dead's image at the twenty-two-year mark. "The Dead look like the aging hippies they are, and critics generally have written them off as dinosaurs," the *Times* noted. "They haven't released a record in seven years, but the band—22 years and 1,600 concerts after its birth—have grossed more than $20 million in concert revenues in the last two years due to hard work, rabidly loyal fans, and modern business methods."

Despite McNally's efforts, it wasn't always a lovefest in the publicity department. In 1986, the editor of a Dead-friendly magazine forwarded a letter from a freelancer assigned to interview Brent Mydland. The freelancer's letter noted that Mydland was two hours late for the interview and arrived drunk and high. "Mr. Mydland was unable to speak; albeit he was apologetic and polite (unlike another Grateful Dead band member)," he wrote. "To put it bluntly, I don't have an article." The editor's cover letter indicated that it wasn't an isolated incident. "This is nothing compared to the half dozen phone complaints I got re: Kreutzmann's bad attitude," she wrote. "It really is a shame."

Even without studio recordings, the Dead community was flourishing. Garcia always maintained that the Dead Heads invented themselves, but media efforts aided the community's growth and consolidation. One new outlet was *The Golden Road*, a fanzine founded in 1984 by Blair Jackson and his wife, Regan McMahon. Raised in the suburbs north of New York City, Jackson attended his first show in March 1970 at the Capitol Theatre in Port Chester, one of the Dead's favorite venues. After studying journalism at the University of California, Berkeley, he contributed to *Rolling Stone* and *BAM*, where he became managing editor. In 1983, he wrote *Grateful Dead: The Music Never Stopped*, and the research for that book led to *The Golden Road*, which began as a quarterly. To publicize the new magazine, Jackson and McMahon leafleted at concerts, and circulation peaked at ten thousand. The band liked the magazine and granted Jackson numerous exclusive interviews, excerpts of which appeared in scores of later articles and books. Noting the well-researched articles, set lists, gossip, and tape-trader ads, the *Village Voice* maintained that *The Golden Road* "may well be the slickest, best-written, and least self-conscious fanzine ever produced in honor of any group."

The year after Jackson and McMahon founded *The Golden Road*,

David Gans launched *The Grateful Dead Hour* on KFOG, a San Francisco radio station that had recently dropped its easy-listening format in favor of album-oriented rock (AOR). KFOG was already broadcasting the *Deadhead Hour* on Monday nights, but its host wasn't a Dead Head, and he was busy with other programs. Gans began supplying him with concert tapes he had collected over the previous decade. Writing for *BAM, Mix,* and *Record* (a *Rolling Stone* spin-off), Gans was also amassing material that would soon appear in *Playing in the Band* (1985), which joined Blair Jackson's history as the first critically acclaimed books about the Dead phenomenon. KFOG soon asked Gans to host the Dead show. He wanted to play unreleased live tracks, which deviated from the AOR routine of putting two or three songs into heavy rotation. Gans received permission to explore the Dead's vault for those tracks so long as he didn't broadcast whole sets. When it became clear that the Dead subculture could support such a show, other stations expressed interest in airing it. WHCN in Hartford, home to an energetic Dead Head scene, decided to carry it, as did WNEW in San Diego. Eventually *The Grateful Dead Hour* reached more than eighty radio markets. Back at the mother ship, KFOG began referring to all of its listeners as Fogheads.

The magazine and radio program helped grow and inform the Dead community, but Dead Heads were also pioneers in new media. Seva founder Larry Brilliant, whose company sold computer-conferencing equipment, approached Stewart Brand with the idea of putting the *Whole Earth Catalog* online and allowing users to respond to the items. Brand was receptive but argued that users should create their own online conversations. Thus was born the Whole Earth 'Lectronic Link (WELL), which went live in February 1985. The next year, an advertisement in *The Golden Road* touted "a computer conferencing system/experiment in community-building, operated by Whole Earth in Sausalito." Hosted by David Gans, Bennett Falk, and Mary Eisenhart, the Grateful Dead conference on the WELL was heralded as "a place for Dead Heads from far and near to exchange ideas, make plans, trade tapes, discuss issues, and hang out with kindred spirits." Of the three WELL hosts, Falk was the most technically adept. After receiving a PhD in the philosophy of religion, he drifted into tech support and consulting in Berkeley. He attended Dead shows with Eisenhart, helped Blair Jackson manage *The Golden Road*'s mailing list, and later wrote *The Internet Roadmap*, which went through three editions.

The growth of the WELL community, Eisenhart later noted, reflected the number of Dead Heads who were already exploring or creating new technologies. There were Dead Heads at Apple Computer, and the Boston-based Digital Equipment Corporation (DEC) harbored a community of self-described DEC Heads. Allen Baum had experience with the tech and Dead Head communities on both coasts. Born in New Jersey, he moved to the peninsula when his father accepted a job at SRI. As a student at MIT, Baum lived in the Freak Dorm, met tapers, and began to assemble his own tape collection. Returning to the peninsula, he attended Dead shows as well as the first meetings of the Homebrew Computer Club, an informal group of computing enthusiasts that *Time* magazine later called "the crucible for an entire industry." Baum dragged Steve Wozniak, cofounder of Apple Computer, to his first Homebrew meeting; after that, Wozniak later wrote, "I started designing the computer that would later be know as the Apple I. It was that inspiring." When Wozniak created the US Festival, a megaconcert first held in 1982, the Dead performed along with other leading acts. According to Baum, Steve Jobs also attended at least one Dead concert at the Frost Amphitheatre on the Stanford University campus. He also dated Joan Baez in the early 1980s, when she had a romantic relationship with Mickey Hart as well.

Eisenhart's career also combined an interest in the Dead with high technology. After completing her graduate studies in comparative literature at the University of California, Irvine, she attended a Garcia show in Sonoma County that, she said, "blew the top of my head off." Unable to sleep that night, she wrote a review of the concert and sent it to Blair Jackson at *BAM*. When that magazine launched a spin-off publication, *Micro Times*, she became its editor and recruited Falk to write a regular column on the UNIX operating system. At the WELL, Eisenhart greeted newcomers, started conversations, and made sure they followed the community's precepts.

It was no accident that Dead Heads felt comfortable at the WELL. The founding editor of *Wired* magazine noted that the WELL was designed to be free, profitable, open-ended, self-governing, and communal. Other online providers operated on a public-utility model, channeling information to users, but the WELL cast its participants as content creators. "You own your own words," the log-in screen reminded users when their dial-up service kicked in. That policy was meant to minimize the WELL's liability, but it also reflected the New Communalist movement that Brand had pioneered in the 1960s. Brand's partner in that effort, Ramon Sender, was an early member of the online community. "I felt the energies on the WELL," he said. "It reminded me of the Open Land communes I'd been to in the 1960s." The WELL's early management also reflected the back-to-the-land ethic. Soon after Brand and Brilliant established the service, Brand hired three veterans of the Farm in Tennessee to manage it. In a 1989 *New York Times* article, John Markoff reported that hundreds of hippies, professionals, and computer enthusiasts used the WELL to stay in touch between Dead concerts. He concluded that the self-proclaimed birthplace of the online community movement may owe its success to "the nation's most eclectic counterculture: the Dead Heads."

Dead Heads used new technology to do more than keep in touch between shows. The same year *The New York Times* reported on the WELL, the *Chicago Sun-Times* ran a feature on John Scott, the Dartmouth computer-science student who invented DeadBase. In addition to publishing manuals that contained Grateful Dead set lists, venue information, statistics, opinion, and analysis, DeadBase provided an online database to allow Dead Heads to access that information from home. "DeadBase makes perfect sense," Dennis McNally told the *Sun-Times*. "The Grateful Dead have long moved into the world of the computer, particularly the Macintosh, which we use in the office."

In the summer of 1986, the Dead toured with Bob Dylan and Tom Petty & the Heartbreakers. Petty had established his rock credentials with *Damn the Torpedoes* (1979), which went platinum, but Dylan's career was foundering. Although he recorded steadily, one of his biographers described those years as a prolonged, depressing setback. The Dead couldn't match Dylan's celebrity or Petty's album sales, but their large and steadily growing community guaranteed a healthy turnout. The concerts were scheduled for the largest venues, and ticket sales topped the charts. More than fifty thousand fans attended the show at the Metrodome in Minneapolis, generating more than $1 million in revenue. The two shows at RFK Stadium in Washington, DC, were even more popular. Ticket sales exceeded 108,000 and generated $2.13 million in revenue.

Even so, the heat at RFK Stadium was overwhelming, and Garcia left the stage badly dehydrated. After flying home the next day, he became delirious and passed out in his bathroom. By the time he reached Marin General Hospital, he was in a deep coma brought on by adult-onset diabetes. His temperature soared, and his heart stopped at one point. The doctors resuscitated him, and he was placed on a respirator for two days until he could breathe on his own. Later, the doctors said his blood was so thick that it resembled mud.

Garcia's recollection of the experience resembled an elaborate psychedelic episode. The coma, he said, led him to admire the "incredible, baroque possibilities of mentation."

The mind is so incredibly weird. The whole process of going into the coma was very interesting, too. It was slow onset—it took about a week—and during this time, I started feeling like the vegetable kingdom was speaking to me. It was communicating in comic dialect in iambic pentameter. So there were these Italian accents and German accents, and it got to be this vast gabbling. Potatoes and radishes and trees were all speaking to me. It finally just reached hysteria, and that's when I passed out and woke up in the hospital.

When Garcia regained consciousness, he told Hunter about his visions of spaceships, cockroaches, and monsters taunting him with bad jokes. "Have I gone insane?" he asked. "No," said Hunter. "You've been very sick. You've been in a coma for days, right at death's door. They're only hallucinations, they'll go away. You survived." "Thanks," said Garcia. "I needed to hear that."

The Dead had weathered many health challenges without disturbing their annual migration patterns, but Garcia's crisis brought the operation to an abrupt halt. They hadn't released a studio album since 1980; now they couldn't tour, either. Moreover, Garcia's recovery was slow. Carolyn Adams moved in with Garcia to help, and the entire Dead community rallied behind him. Garcia recalled the support he received and its effects.

I'm not a believer in the invisible, but I got such an incredible outpouring. The mail I got in the hospital was so soulful. All the Dead Heads . . . it was kind of like brotherly, sisterly, motherly, fatherly advice from people. Every conceivable healing vibe was pouring into that place. . . . I really feel that the fans put life back into me.

The Dead had always believed in community; now that community was helping Garcia recover from a grave health crisis.

As Garcia's health returned, he painstakingly relearned the guitar

with the help of Merl Saunders and other collaborators. Saunders recalled the difficulty Garcia had recovering his guitar chops. Fatigue was
one factor, but he also lost his muscle memory and the calluses that
protect the fingers of a regular guitarist. "It came back very slowly,"
Saunders said. "He had to learn chords all over again, and he had a lot
of trouble remembering how to do even the simplest stuff." According
to Saunders, the first song Garcia wanted to relearn was "My Funny
Valentine."

Garcia began to play at small Bay Area venues that fall, but the Dead
didn't perform together until mid-December at the Oakland Coliseum.
Their first song was "Touch of Grey," which had acquired extra significance since its live debut in 1982. One reason was Garcia's brush with
death, which highlighted both his mortality and his resilience. He was
only forty-four, but his grizzled appearance lent verisimilitude to Hunter's song of experience. Older, grayer, not so much defiant as determined to survive, the Dead opened the Oakland show with a song that
reflected their maturation as well as the nation's more conservative
political tone.

That tone was shaped by the ascendancy of Ronald Reagan, another
California utopian. After finishing his second term as California governor, Reagan began his march to the White House, losing the Republican nomination to Gerald Ford in 1976 but vanquishing Democratic
incumbent Jimmy Carter in the 1980 general election. Reagan's basic
vision, like the Dead's, had changed little over the previous two decades. He wanted a smaller federal government, more individual liberty, and victory in the Cold War—exactly as he had declared at the
Cow Palace in 1964. But the political landscape had changed in the
intervening sixteen years, partly as a response to the legacy of Vietnam.
History had been unkind to Reagan's 1965 remark that intervention in
Southeast Asia would be simple and quick. "We should declare war on

Vietnam," Reagan said then. "We could pave the whole country and put parking stripes on it and still be home by Christmas." In the immediate aftermath of that divisive conflict, Reagan pledged that he would never "ask young men to fight and possibly die in a war our government is afraid to win." It was a popular applause line, and four years later, Reagan was still describing the American intervention in Vietnam as "a noble cause." Taken together, his remarks suggested that the problem with America's military intervention in Vietnam lay not in its illegality or catastrophic wrongheadedness, but rather in its timid execution.

As president, Reagan adjusted to a new set of challenges. On his watch, the federal government passed the largest tax increase to that point in US history, including a significant rise in the payroll tax to fund Social Security. He was also handed a foreign-policy setback when a group called Islamic Jihad used truck bombs to kill 241 US marines, sailors, and soldiers in their Beirut barracks during the Lebanese civil war. It was the deadliest single attack on Americans overseas since the Second World War. Reagan withdrew US personnel from the multinational force in Lebanon, thereby breaking his pledge not to commit troops unless the US government had the courage to win a conflict. Yet Reagan also pleased many conservatives by lowering marginal tax rates for the wealthy, hiking military expenditures, deregulating the financial sector, and busting a public-sector union during an air-traffic controllers' strike. By the end of his second term, the elements of the Reagan legend were in place. He was the man, one author noted, who purportedly "won an ideological war at home—reversing a half century of growing government and rising taxes—and then won a cold war abroad, the global conflict between freedom and totalitarian communism, before riding off into the Pacific sunset."

Reagan's biographers often described him as enigmatic. A politician with few close friends, he kept even his inner circle at a distance. But Joan Didion argued that the Reagan mystique was the product of a category error. "Defined as a 'president' or even as 'governor,'" Didion claimed, "Reagan did indeed appear to have some flat sides, some missing pieces. Defined as 'actor,' however, he was from the beginning to the end of his public life entirely consistent, a knowable and in fact quite predictable quantity." Reagan's consistency, Didion argued, could be traced to the studio system that had shaped him. Reagan treated his aides like film-crew members, with whom he bantered amiably but never befriended. His daily appointments resembled a shooting schedule; he even followed the studio practice of drawing a vertical line through the completed task and an arrow pointing to the next one. He regarded his political peers as fellow film principals bonded by what Didion called "the intense but temporary camaraderie of the set." They would "exchange the ritual totems of bonding" and then scatter after the film wrapped. On this point and many others, Reagan was a counterpoint to the Dead, for whom authentic community was a cherished value.

A few Dead Heads, including Ann Coulter and Tucker Carlson, welcomed the nation's turn to the right under President Reagan. Deroy Murdock, now a syndicated columnist and contributing editor at *National Review Online*, noted that his love of freedom made it easy for him to reconcile his politics with his affection for the Dead. Such conservative sentiment, or at least a strain of frontier libertarianism, could also be found within the band's inner circle; John Barlow, a registered Republican, helped coordinate Dick Cheney's 1978 congressional campaign in Wyoming. But Garcia was no Reagan fan. "I didn't like his movies, and I don't like his politics," Garcia said. "I like things wide-open, with question marks hanging over it, everything changing, nothing settled." When a British journalist asked about Reagan's presidency, Garcia was even more dismissive. "Oh! Give me a break!" he exclaimed. "I was shocked when Reagan was elected governor of California! And then, as president, we were embarrassed by the guy. I mean, he wasn't even a good actor."

Most Dead Heads felt the same way. One Massachusetts fan wrote to the band the day after the 1980 election. "*He's* been elected, and never have I felt so far away from the heart and soul of our country," the fan lamented. Reagan "views the past through rose-colored glasses; I say he views the entire world through daguerreotype glasses, yearning for some simpler past that nobody can actually remember." It was certainly true that the Dead's favorite forms of nostalgia were at odds with Reagan's, and the correspondent wondered whether the Dead could bring their California experience with Reagan to bear on the present.

> Reagan was your governor all those Haight-Ashbury years, and you had sort of a minority subculture clearly marching to a different beat than most of California. I think we could be right back to this position again on a larger scale, and I wonder where the hell we fit in.

The fan hoped that the Dead would "read this and think about the parallels between today and Haight-Ashbury."

In 1982, President Reagan declared that illicit drugs were a national security threat. "The mood toward drugs is changing in this country, and the momentum is with us," he maintained. "We're making no excuses for drugs—hard, soft, or otherwise. Drugs are bad, and we're going after them. As I've said before, we've taken down the surrender flag and run up the battle flag. And we're going to win the war on drugs." From a policy perspective, the timing was odd. A National Academy of Sciences (NAS) study, commissioned during the Carter administration but released in 1982, found no convincing evidence that marijuana permanently damaged the brain or nervous system, and the study recommended the decriminalization of possession of small quantities. But the NAS president on Reagan's watch disavowed the report, claiming that its data were insufficient and that its value-laden recommendations should have been left to the political process.

Reagan's drug war had less to do with scientific studies than with the political calendar. With the economy in severe recession, Reagan needed an issue, and he announced his drug initiative three weeks before the midterm elections in 1982. His administration pushed successfully for new laws that allowed the federal government to use military and intelligence assets to detect drug traffickers. The Pentagon was divided over the move. Some, including Defense Secretary Caspar Weinberger, felt that it would distract the military from its core mission and drag it into another unwinnable war. Others welcomed the challenge. "The Latin American drug war is the only war we've got," said one general. The Department of Justice also received broad new powers to confiscate private property upon suspicion, not proof, of drug trafficking. In Humboldt County, California, U-2 planes and helicopters targeted marijuana crops for destruction, families were held at gunpoint at roadblocks, and vehicles and homes were searched without warrants. Even residents who had welcomed the crackdown soon felt that an occupying army controlled their communities. As that crackdown intensified, Nancy Reagan's "Just Say No" campaign became the friendlier face of the Reagan administration's antidrug efforts. Funded by corporate and private donations, that program focused on persuading white, middle-class children to avoid illicit drugs.

As the Reagan administration intensified the drug war, it also lavished benefits on drug companies. "The election of Ronald Reagan in 1980 was perhaps the fundamental element in the rise of big pharma— the collective name for the largest drug companies," wrote a former editor in chief of the *New England Journal of Medicine*. Before that time, pharmaceutical discoveries funded with public money remained in the public domain. Afterward, universities and medical schools, which performed an increasing portion of the basic pharmaceutical research, could patent and license their discoveries. "One of the results," the article continued, "has been a growing pro-industry bias in medical research— precisely where that bias doesn't belong." Starting in 1984, Congress also passed a series of laws that extended patent protections and monopoly rights for brand-name drugs—another bonanza for Big Pharma and a burden for consumers. A thread begun on the WELL in 2000—"Dead Heads and the War on (Some) Drugs"—reflected the Reagan's dual approach to drug production, distribution, and consumption.

Reagan's drug war had a darker dimension as well. In 1996, reporter Gary Webb wrote a series of articles alleging that Nicaraguan drug dealers had sold and distributed powder and crack cocaine in Los Angeles during the 1980s. Moreover, Webb claimed, Reagan administration officials knew that the profits supported the Nicaraguan *contras*, whom the administration actively (and illegally) aided in their efforts to overthrow the leftist Sandinista government. Webb, a reporter for the *San Jose Mercury News*, was immediately attacked. After the paper distanced itself from the story, Webb left the newspaper, wrote a book about the topic, and committed suicide in 2004. Later investigations confirmed the core of Webb's story but criticized him for overstating parts of it. After his death, representatives of *The Washington Post*, the *Los Angeles Times*, and the *Chicago Tribune* admitted that criticisms of Webb had been excessive, and that his story was important. "I still think Gary Webb had it mostly right," the *Chicago Tribune*'s public editor wrote in 2005. "I think he got the treatment that always comes to those who dare question aloud the bona fides of the establishment: First he got misrepresented—his suggestion that the CIA tolerated the *contras'* cocaine trading became an allegation that the agency itself was involved in the drug trade. Then he was ridiculed as a conspiracy-monger."

Garcia turned out to be an unwilling conscript in Reagan's drug war. By January 1985, Garcia's drug use was so disabling that manager Jon McIntire arranged an intervention. Garcia agreed to receive treatment, but while driving to the rehabilitation center in Oakland, he stopped in Golden Gate Park to finish off his drug supply. A police officer noticed the car was unregistered, approached Garcia's parked BMW, and found Garcia trying to hide his stash of heroin and cocaine. Garcia's lawyer argued that he should be sent to counseling sessions, which he attended with Grace Slick. Garcia continued to use drugs, and his health declined alarmingly. His weight ballooned to three hundred pounds, and edema swelled his ankles to the point that his trousers needed to be cut. He began to diet and exercise, but the real wake-up call arrived with his 1986 coma.

Garcia's arrest was a trifle in the drug war, but Reagan's vision was, among other things, a repudiation of the Dead's larger project. This much was clear to Ken Kesey. "The war is not on drugs, the war is on consciousness," he told Paul Krassner. "Nobody has the right to come in and mess with your inside. They don't have any right to tell me what to do inside my head, any more than they have any right to tell women what to do inside their bodies. What's inside is *ours*, and we've got a right to fight for it." But the war on drugs was only part of the tension between Reagan's vision and the Dead's. What Dennis McNally called the Dead Head culture's "hedonistic poverty" was also a rejection of Reagan's cultural politics, just as Kerouac's "barbaric yawp" (a term *Time* magazine borrowed from Walt Whitman) and Ginsberg's howl responded to the age of Eisenhower.

In some ways, too, the Dead community's response to Reagan was a skirmish over who would control the symbols of the American frontier. The Dead had moved on from their High Cowboy period, but their image was firmly linked to their Western provenance and repertoire. Meanwhile, the Reagan team skillfully presented him as a man of the American West: riding horses, clearing brush on his ranch, and appearing on the cover of *Time* magazine in a cowboy hat. As an actor, Reagan had appeared in many westerns and television's *Death Valley Days*. But even in private, Reagan adopted a distinctly Western register. One Secret Service agent noted that Reagan sunbathed at his pool with a reflector every day at 2:00 p.m., no matter how busy his staff was. "That might seem like a vain, sissy thing to do," the agent said, "but Reagan had this cowboy way of describing it. He said he was getting 'a coat of tan.'"

Even President Reagan's grooming habits contrasted sharply with the Dead's. Although Reagan was three decades older than the grizzled Garcia, he had no touches of gray at all. According to Nancy Reagan's unofficial biographer, the Clairol company paid a celebrity hairdresser $20,000 per week to fly to Washington and color her hair; while he was there, he also touched up President Reagan's gray roots. To the end, however, the Reagan team denied the charge. "He never dyed his hair," White House deputy chief of staff Michael Deaver claimed. "He had that wet look, and when I finally got the Brylcreem away from him, people stopped writing about him dying his hair."

The Dead didn't orchestrate a response to Reagan, but in the summer 1984 issue of *The Golden Road,* Blair Jackson and Regan McMahon exhorted Dead Heads to register and vote against the incumbent. "Dead Heads have a reputation of being apolitical," the couple wrote, "and there's no question that many of you have taken your cue on the issue from members of the band, who have professed their utter contempt for the political process through the years." Even so, the couple maintained, it was important to note that Reagan was dangerous, and that his policies would have "two great superpowers clawing at each as they never have before." After noting Walter Mondale's commitments to a nuclear freeze, the environment, and the Equal Rights Amendment, they directly addressed the Dead community's resistance to electoral politics. "Voting doesn't make you any less cool, nor does it mean you're endorsing a political system you think is completely out of touch with the people," they wrote. "Think for a second how Reagan has changed America already. This could well be the most important election of your lifetime." They closed with an apology if their "political rap" offended anyone's sensibilities and offered to publish other viewpoints in the subsequent issue.

By the time that piece appeared, President Reagan's reelection campaign was in high gear. One of its television advertisements declared that it was "morning again in America." But Hunter's first verse of "Touch of Grey" found little to celebrate in that daybreak.

Dawn is breaking everywhere
Light a candle, curse the glare
Draw the curtain, I don't care 'cause
It's all right.

Garcia contributed the second line, which echoed Adlai Stevenson's 1962 comment about Eleanor Roosevelt, who would rather "light a candle than curse the darkness." But for Hunter's world-weary speaker, who resembles Garcia during the darkest days of his addiction, the harsh morning light is as bothersome as the unnamed critic.

I see you've got your list out
Say your piece and get out
Yes, I get the gist of it
But it's all right.

The speaker then refracts another bit of sunny optimism through the prism of jaded middle age.

Sorry that you feel that way
The only thing there is to say
Every silver lining's got a
Touch of grey.

The utopian exuberance of the 1960s is nowhere in sight; instead, the speaker embraces the more modest goal of trying "to keep a little grace." But even that is a challenge, as the next verses make clear.

I know the rent is in arrears
The dog has not been fed in years
It's even worse than it appears
But it's all right.

The cow is giving kerosene
Kid can't read at seventeen
The words he knows are all obscene
But it's all right.

In the face of economic hardship, environmental catastrophe, and educational failure, the speaker's assurances that all is well only highlight the problems. But instead of surrendering to this dystopian scene, he promises to endure: "I will get by / I will survive." That vaunt was a far cry from the Dead's utopian ideals, but a simple pronoun change in the final chorus ("We will get by / We will survive") transformed the song into an anthem. Every Dead Head knew there was a world of difference between *I* and *we,* especially during hard times. At the Oakland Coliseum show, that message resonated powerfully with the crowd. As Garcia swung into the final chorus, Joel Selvin wrote in the *Chronicle* review, "the ecstatic convocation of Dead Heads assembled Monday at the Oakland Coliseum Arena went wild with cheers." The most cherished ideal of all, community, would survive Ronald Reagan, scourge of the hippies.

With the advent of MTV in 1981, videos became a critical part of the music business, and in May 1987, the Dead hired Gary Gutierrez to direct their first one. Gutierrez, who had directed the animated sequence in *The Grateful Dead Movie,* identified "Touch of Grey" as a potential hit single, and he proposed a video that drew on the band's established iconography. He would construct full-size skeletons of the band members, build a rigging over the stage at a live concert, manipulate the puppets like marionettes, then transform the puppets into the real band for the last verse and chorus. When he pitched the idea to Garcia, he drew a laugh. According to Gutierrez, Garcia "couldn't get over the idea because it was so weird."

To produce the video, Gutierrez bought skeletons from a medical-supply company, which the puppeteers customized and dressed to re-semble each band member. After a concert in Monterey, the Dead invited the audience to remain for the making of the video; most of the twenty thousand people did so and cheered the puppets as if they were performing a live concert. When the video was finished, Gutierrez showed it to the Dead at their Front Street rehearsal space in San Ra-fael. "They were really tickled," Gutierrez said. "I really love the mo-ment in the video when skeletons come to life and Jerry shakes his head the way he does and says, 'I will survive.' That shot is a classic image of Jerry."

When Arista released "Touch of Grey" that summer, the video re-ceived heavy play at MTV. For many teenagers, it was their first expo-sure to the middle-aged rockers, and it helped make "Touch of Grey" the band's first top-ten single. McNally recalled breaking that news to the Dead in their dressing room. "I am appalled," Garcia replied. "How low can the American record-buying public go?" The new album, *In the Dark*, went to number six a few weeks later. It became the Dead's first platinum album, and *Shakedown Street* and *Terrapin Station* went gold on the strength of its success. Garcia was genuinely surprised by that reception, which he characteristically deflected. "We're sort of like the town whore that's finally become an institution," he told Blair Jackson. "We're finally becoming respectable."

When Garcia was pressed for a more searching explanation, he sug-gested that, despite Reagan's political success, history was on the Dead's side. "The point is, it happened, there was a revolution, and we won," he said. For Garcia, that outcome was never in doubt. "It was over from the very beginning," he said. "The rest of it is a cleanup operation." The first excursions into psychedelia indicated that there was more to the world than "this drab, dull bullshit." "So you're not joining the Just Say No crowd?" he was asked. "No," Garcia replied. "I think that's much too easy, and it doesn't address the problems. The real problems are cultural."

In Garcia's view, the Reagan era had an expiration date. "It's coming down," he said. "It's on its way down, and nothing they can do—it's too late, really, to do anything about it. Those people are not going to be here that much longer. Reagan can't live forever." Garcia didn't blame the older generation for their fear, and he wished them no ill. They had endured the Depression and the Second World War, and they deserved to be able to "spend their final years in non-anxiety, floating comfortably in a hypothetical America." Unfortunately, Garcia added, "they're creating a second wave of young people who were buying into the same mythos." The Dead were doing the same thing, and in many ways the two mythoi needed and energized each other.

Many new Dead fans were unfamiliar with the show rituals, however, and their rowdiness required the organization to take extra security measures. "They were young kids who saw this incredible party scene," Bill Graham associate Bob Barsotti said. "It fascinated young kids to see this kind of freedom because they'd grown up in the Reagan era with the war on drugs. They equated these ideals with the sixties, but actually it was just a big party scene on Saturday night." Blair Jackson understood the appeal differently. "It's no coincidence that the recent surge in popularity comes at a time when there is a trend toward bohemianism among the young, in part as a reaction against the waning days of the Reagan era," he told Britain's *Q* magazine. "Let's face it, the Grateful Dead scene is an oasis in the desert of American lameness, more now than ever before. It's got something a lot of people want—heart and soul. You can hear it in the music and see it in people's faces—in their smiles, really." When the magazine asked Garcia whether Reagan's America was a fit place to take LSD in, he called that nation a joke, compared it to a rabid dog biting its own leg, and assured his interviewer that the dog wouldn't get its teeth into the Dead.

Some new Dead fans were consciously reacting to the Age of Reagan. Documentary filmmaker Jason Cohn recalled his interest in the Dead during the 1980s:

The way I affiliated with the Dead (and Dead Heads) in high school was less a musical experience than a cultural reaction against Reaganism in all its guises. I wasn't that into the music because I was essentially a Beatles fan, so my musical aesthetic was tuned to that kind of structural precision and poetic beauty rather than the expansive improvisational virtuosity that the Dead represented. But being into the Dead was a cultural marker that said you didn't buy into those ascendant Reaganite values.

Author Peter Conners, who boarded the bus in 1986, also saw the Dead culture as an alternative to Reaganism. If "Touch of Grey" was one expression of that alternative, he thought "Estimated Prophet" was another. Weir and Barlow wrote the lyrics, which highlight California and the prophetic tradition, well before Reagan's election; but Weir's performances in the mid-1980s—which included trippy, extended screeching of the phrase *say no*—seemed to respond to the administration's antidrug campaign. For Conners, that campaign came across as a more general negation; he also felt encouraged to say no to risk, adventure, and nonconformity. Although Conners remained in school, he also regarded his Dead-centered peregrinations as an essential part of his education. The songs about Neal Cassady led him to Ginsberg and Kesey; those writers, in turn, introduced him to Proust and Rimbaud. Similarly, the Dead introduced him to the blues, Django Reinhardt, and the other artists and traditions that fed the Dead's music stream. Following the band, Conners said, resembled the self-directed educational programs of today, and he regards his memoir, *Growing Up Dead*, as "an operating manual for positive ways to use the Dead."

With the success of "Touch of Grey" and *In the Dark*, the Dead found themselves in the brightest spotlight of their collective lives. With the extra revenue, they funded more projects through the Rex Foundation and played more benefits. Along with other headline acts, they raised money and awareness for AIDS prevention and treatment, Greenpeace, El Salvadoran refugees, family farms, and Latino students. Another band based in Marin County, Huey Lewis and the News, performed at some of the same benefits. That band's 1983 album, *Sports*, included four top-ten singles and reached the top of the *Billboard* chart the following year. When Lewis played with the Dead, no one was prouder than his mother, Magda Cregg. A former muralist at the Fillmore West, she was a longtime Dead Head and companion of Beat poet Lew Welch. Her son's stage name was chosen to honor Welch, who acted as his stepfather.

As the Dead's popularity built, new doors opened for them. In 1985, a television producer asked them to write music for a new version of *The Twilight Zone*, the classic science fiction series that originally aired in the early 1960s. Garcia loved the idea. "Man, I *live* in the twilight zone," he told Merl Saunders, the program's musical director. Saunders also recruited Bob Bralove, who helped Stevie Wonder with his synthesizers and digital overdubs. When *The Twilight Zone* work was completed, Bralove joined the Dead on the Dylan tour, wrote songs with Weir and Barlow, and went to Monterey for the "Touch of Grey" video shoot. Immediately after that, he attended a band meeting, where each musician was asked about working with him, and all responded positively. "So hang out with us as long as you're having a good time," Kreutzmann said. "It was that casual," Bralove said, "but very motivating."

Bralove was by no means a Dead Head; in high school, he attended a single show at the Capitol Theatre during the *American Beauty* era. But his innocence turned out to be an asset for the Dead. Bralove didn't know or care how they did things twenty years earlier; instead, he gave them what they literally asked for in the studio. He became the Dead's resident expert on the Musical Instrument Digital Interface (MIDI), a new technology that facilitated communication between electronic instruments and other digital devices. He also produced two albums,

Built to Last (1989) and *Infrared Roses* (1991). The latter was a compilation of the Dead's so-called Drums>Space segments, which featured live improvisations, and the album's first piece, "Crowd Sculpture," also used ambient sounds from the parking lot. *Infrared Roses* was widely regarded as the Dead's most daring and least commercial album since the 1960s.

The Dead's improved fortunes did nothing to simplify their organization. "After 1987," video director and producer Len Dell'Amico said, "it was 'Oh, boy! Now we have a hit. Isn't that great?' *Not!* It just got harder and harder. Bigger hall, bigger questions." Some consideration was given to reducing the scale of their effort. "Then Garcia would say, 'Why don't we not do those stadium shows?'" Dell'Amico recalled. "The unspoken response was that because they had this nut to pay. Hello, fifty employees." Like Anthony Quinn's Bedouin character in *Lawrence of Arabia*, Garcia was a river to his people. "What happened was that the Dead were making so much money, and he had this thing about not walking away," Dell'Amico said. "Because the day he walked away, all these people would lose their job."

If huge concerts were to be the Dead's lot in life, at least they could share it with artists they admired. One of them was Bob Dylan, who was still foundering. By 1987, he wrote later, he felt like "an empty burned-out wreck . . . in the bottomless pit of cultural oblivion." Nevertheless, the Dead were pleased to play with him. "We've always had the utmost respect, fondness, whatever for Dylan's work," Weir said. "I mean, he is the voice of God in my estimation, whether he likes it or not." When Dylan realized which of his songs the Dead wanted to play, however, he regretted the decision to tour with them. In some cases, he couldn't remember his own lyrics. Inventing an excuse to leave their rehearsal in San Rafael, Dylan walked the streets in the rain before noticing a tiny bar with a jazz combo working through some ballads. He found the singer's relaxed, powerful voice inspiring, and he returned to the rehearsal with renewed energy. "I played these shows with the Dead and never had to think twice about it," he recalled. "Maybe they just dropped something in my drink, I can't say, but anything they wanted to do was fine with me."

The six-stop tour drew three hundred thousand fans and grossed $6 million. The show at Sullivan Stadium outside Boston generated $1.3 million, making it the single largest economic event in the history of that venue. "For me, it reached biblical proportions," said Dell'Amico of that tour. "Ninety thousand people. Daytime shows with screens the size of my house. It literally took an eighty-ton crane to put the show in place." *Chronicle* critic Joel Selvin attributed the turnout to the Dead's unexpected commercial success. "The irony of Bob Dylan needing the Grateful Dead to attain any kind of current relevance couldn't be lost on anyone attending the show," he wrote. *Los Angeles Times* critic Robert Hilburn took a different line. He praised the Dead's service to Dylan's songs and described their accompaniment on "Mr. Tambourine Man" as "immaculate, cushioning the song with the understanding of musicians who had lived with the song." He also considered the intersection of the two career trajectories. "The Dead and Dylan will continue on their independent paths," Hilburn concluded. "But there was a magic in their brief crossing that made this an evening to remember—a celebration of two forces that had made it through to the '80s with their spirits intact." That intersection produced an album for Dylan's label that received mixed reviews. It also led to collaborations between Dylan and Hunter. While rehearsing in San Rafael, Dylan came upon two Hunter lyrics that he included on his 1988 album, *Down in the Groove*; much later, after Dylan had regained his footing, he recorded an entire album of songs cowritten with Hunter.

A hit single seemed unlikely after twenty-two years on the job, but a Broadway show strained credulity. Nevertheless, Bill Graham landed Garcia a three-week gig at the Lunt-Fontanne Theatre. That gesture had extra significance for Graham. Arranging Garcia's Broadway gig was a message to John Scher, the Dead's East Coast promoter, that

Graham could operate freely in his counterpart's territory. For help, Garcia recruited musical companions from his youth, including David Nelson and Sandy Rothman. "It was an incredible dream," Rothman said. "I will always consider that to be a pinnacle of anything I ever did in music." All eighteen shows sold out within hours. A full-page advertisement in *Variety* congratulated the band for the biggest first day of sales in the history of Broadway, a record that was eclipsed by *Phantom of the Opera* some six months later. The show was also hard work. Sound checks, matinees, and evening performances kept Garcia at the theater from the early afternoon until after midnight. Yet the Broadway turn added a new and important dimension to Garcia's body of work. "By going on Broadway, he put this stamp of class on rock 'n' roll that had never happened before," Peter Barsotti said. "He didn't even have to change what he was doing to get it. He got to be himself and go to Broadway." A *People* magazine article found that feat amazing: "Without changing musical styles or even—it seems—his clothes, Garcia suddenly found himself in tune with the times. Or vice versa."

There was other evidence that the Dead could do no wrong. Ben & Jerry's ice cream released a new flavor called Cherry Garcia, which became its bestseller. The Dead also hit pay dirt with *So Far*, a fifty-five-minute documentary video that blended live performances with computer animation and found footage. Coproduced by Garcia and Dell'Amico, the video was released in 1987 and quickly found a substantial audience. In December, it ranked fifteenth on *Billboard*'s list of top videocassette sales; that placed *So Far* directly between *Jane Fonda's New Workout* and *Jane Fonda's Workout with Weights*. The Dead's widening appeal was also reflected in the tour numbers. In 1987, they played eighty-four shows in thirty-seven cities and grossed $26.8 million. On the commercial scoreboard, that put the Dead behind only U2, Bon Jovi, and Pink Floyd.

The following September, the Dead sold out eight shows at Madison Square Garden within two hours, producing $2.4 million in revenue.

Yet even as the cash registers rang, mainstream America continued to look askance at the Dead community. *The New York Times*, for example, reported that Dead Heads repelled some commuters at Penn Station: "'Who are these people?' muttered a train-bound woman in a suit to her companion on Thursday, recoiling from a swarm of Grateful Dead fans as if she feared some tie-dye might rub off and kill her. 'They look terrible.'" Dead Heads were unpopular elsewhere as well. As the tours metastasized, complaints about the influx of fans, their campgrounds, and the trash they left behind began to grow. Hartford, Oakland, East Lansing, Ventura, Irvine, and Worcester were sore spots, and a 1989 story in the *Chicago Tribune* outlined the Dead's logistical challenge. "The Grateful Dead is running out of places to play," the story claimed. "The band's cult status crossed over into the mainstream with the release of *In the Dark,* and the Dead's following seemed to nearly double overnight." If their next album was a hit, Weir said, "that's going to be the end of the arena-sized show for us. We'll have to play stadiums only, and a number of those aren't up to having us, either."

In some cases, the Dead Heads prevailed. When a Washington, DC, city council member tried to block the Dead from playing RFK Stadium, a fellow council member appeared at the meeting wearing a Grateful Dead T-shirt to signal her support for the concert. In the end, the Dead were allowed to play the show, and the objecting city council member attended it. "This is so different from what happened the last time they were here," she said. "This is really wonderful. It's like a big picnic. I don't object to people having a good time. How are you going to argue with that?"

Meanwhile, the Dead organization was grappling with the myriad challenges of the mega-Dead period. The main one was creating great music in the enormous settings that were now routine, but security concerns also loomed large. For those and other reasons, Nicholas Meriwether noted later, the Spring 1990 tour had "a monumental quality to it all." On the musical front, the Dead received help from jazz saxophonist Branford Marsalis, who accepted Lesh's invitation to attend the first gig at the Nassau Coliseum. When he stopped in to say hello, Lesh and Garcia implored him to return to the next show with his horn. Even without rehearsal, Marsalis quickly found his groove. "Never did a musician prove his brilliance faster," Dennis McNally noted. After one verse, "Garcia and Marsalis were trading licks as if they were old friends." Marsalis also enjoyed the experience. "Those guys can play *music*," he said. "They're much better than most people give them credit for. They have big ears and real chops, and they've got eighteen thousand tie-dyes dancing along. I've never seen anything like it."

The tour was a success, but graver challenges lay ahead of them. In Garcia's November 1989 interview with *Rolling Stone*, he was asked about President George H. W. Bush's war on drugs. Garcia was dismissive. "It's a joke," he replied. "Greed and the desire to take drugs are two separate things. If you want to separate the two, the thing you do is make drugs legal. It's the obvious solution. Accept the reality that people do want to change their consciousness, and make an effort to make safer, healthier drugs." But hard drugs continued to take their toll on the Dead. In the summer of 1990, Brent Mydland was found dead in his Lafayette, California, home. Recently separated and troubled by the breakup of his family, Mydland overdosed on a cocaine and morphine speedball. "He had a very hard time," said Barlow. "Look at it: when he'd been [in the Dead] for eleven years, he was still the new guy."

The Dead valued Mydland's musical contribution and mourned his death, but they returned to work quickly. Bruce Hornsby, who had performed with the Dead and knew much of their songbook, agreed to fill in while they searched for a full-time replacement. One interviewer asked Hornsby how many Spinal Tap jokes he had heard since the announcement. When the befuddled Hornsby said none, the interviewer explained that many people compared the drummers in *This Is Spinal Tap*, the 1984 mock-documentary film, to the keyboard players in the Grateful Dead because they all died. "So you're not scared?"

the interviewer wondered. "No," said Hornsby. "It seems like a silly question, to be perfectly honest." After a brief round of tryouts, Vince Welnick, formerly of the Tubes, became the Dead's fifth full-time keyboard player, and the touring machine rumbled on.

The same month Mydland died, John Barlow helped launch a new venture. Earlier that year, he had received a visit from an FBI agent investigating the theft and distribution of source code for Apple computers. During the interview, Barlow was struck by the agent's lack of familiarity with computer technology. "I realized right away that before I could demonstrate my innocence," he said, "I would first have to explain to him what guilt might be." He posted a message on the WELL about the incident and was contacted by Mitch Kapor, the founder of Lotus Development Corporation, whose signature product was a hugely successful spreadsheet application for the IBM personal computer. Kapor had had a similar experience, and the two men agreed that advances in computer technology were raising new and important civil liberties issues.

Along with John Gilmore, the fifth employee hired at Sun Microsystems, Barlow and Kapor founded the Electronic Frontier Foundation (EFF), a nonprofit organization designed to advocate for the public interest on digital matters. Having stepped away from his work at the family ranch in Wyoming, Barlow had more time to devote to EFF, and its language and sensibility reflected his outlook and the Grateful Dead culture. The virtual world, he maintained, should remain as free as possible, especially from the government. Borrowing a term from *Neuromancer*, a 1984 William Gibson science fiction novel, Barlow called that domain *cyberspace*, and the term stuck. In their first major case, EFF took on the Secret Service, which had confiscated a small publisher's computers, accessed and deleted all of his e-mail, and eventually returned the equipment without pressing charges. That action hamstrung his business, and the owner maintained that the government had violated his rights as a publisher and the free speech and privacy rights of his users. In that case, the court ruled for the first time that electronic mail deserves at least as much protection as telephone calls.

In 1994, Barlow wrote a long article for *Wired*, the San Francisco magazine touted as the *Rolling Stone* of technology. In fact, the magazine's techno-utopianism was a direct descendant of Stewart Brand's worldview. The first issue of *Wired*, published in 1993, featured six writers who had contributed to Brand's publications. In "The Economy of Ideas," Barlow compared the electronic frontier and the nineteenth-century American West because both showed a "natural preference for social devices that emerge from its conditions rather than those that are imposed from the outside." The piece made no mention of another similarity between those frontiers: the central role of the federal government in creating those communities, or rather their conditions of possibility, in the first place.

Barlow's Western libertarianism found expression in another document he produced in 1996. The occasion for "A Declaration of Independence of Cyberspace" was the passage of the Telecommunications Reform Act, which was the first time Congress included the Internet in broadcasting and spectrum allotment. "Governments of the Industrial World," Barlow began, "you weary giants of flesh and steel, I come from Cyberspace, the new home of Mind. On behalf of the future, I ask you of the past to leave us alone. You are not welcome among us. You have no sovereignty where we gather." Barlow later distanced himself from his declaration, which targeted governments but ignored the monopolistic role corporations would soon play in the digital domain. "We need something—and I think it's governmental—to reregulate the markets and make it free, because the multinationals have taken it away," he told *Reason* magazine in 2004. "Most libertarians are worried about government but not worried about business. I think we need to be worrying about business in exactly the same way we are worrying about the government." By the time that interview appeared, EFF had become one of the premier defenders of free speech, privacy, and consumer rights in the networked world.

In 1991, the Dead were the top-grossing band in North America, generating $34.7 million from seventy-five dates, and the next year looked to be another big one. The Dead arranged to tour with Sting, the former bass player for the Police, who seemed to have little in common with the Dead and their audience. "I'll be playing huge arenas to a completely new audience that likes bands that jam, so we'll have nothing to fear there," Sting said. "Frankly, I'm fascinated by the idea. I know that Branford Marsalis, who's played with us, played with the Dead last year and had a great time."

When the tour arrived at the nation's capital, *USA Today* reported that Senator Albert Gore's wife, Tipper, attended with their twelve-year-old daughter, who wore her mother's KEEP ON TRUCKIN' T-shirt from the 1960s. "Tipper and Al came to a show the last time we were in Washington," Garcia said later. "They're nice people, a nice family. We made every effort not to frighten them." Nineteen days after the concert, Al Gore was chosen as Bill Clinton's running mate. Perhaps the Democrats were finally taking Hunter Thompson's advice and associating themselves with the Grateful Dead. In any case, when the Democratic National Convention began in New York City that summer, one of the hottest souvenirs was a necktie from the J. Garcia Art in Neckwear collection at Bloomingdale's. The ties, which were based on Garcia's paintings, sold for $28.50. "You better believe there are doctors, lawyers, and bankers underneath those tie-dyed T's at the Dead concerts," said a Bloomingdale's employee. The department store reportedly sold at least 180,000 units.

Not everything the Dead touched turned to gold; occasionally they had to settle for the bronze. When a *San Francisco Chronicle* sportswriter introduced the Dead to the Golden State Warriors, the Bay Area's NBA franchise, the band met Sarunas Marciulionis, who left his native Lithuania to become one of the first European players in the NBA. Marciulionis had helped the Soviet Union win a gold medal in the 1988 Olympics, but after Lithuania boldly broke away from Soviet rule, Marciulionis helped organize its national team for the 1992 games in Barcelona. The Lithuanians had plenty of talent but almost no resources, and the Dead quickly contributed $5,000 and their skeleton logo. Donnie Nelson, son of the Warriors' head coach, served as the Lithuanian team's assistant coach, and Mike Fitzgerald, son of the Warriors' owner, furnished tie-dyed T-shirts and warm-ups, which the Lithuanians wore at the European Olympic qualifying tournament.

In Barcelona, the US "Dream Team" easily took the gold medal in men's basketball, but many spectators were put off by the US team's arrogance and lack of sportsmanship. Although Reebok had paid a fortune to outfit the team, some players covered up its logo to protect their lucrative deals with other corporations. Meanwhile, an emotional Lithuanian team beat the Soviets for the bronze medal, and they stole the show with their colorful outfits. The Dead's contribution was a relatively small gesture, but given the Lithuanian experience under Soviet rule, it was also understood as support for political freedom and underdogs in general. Later, the Lithuanian prime minister issued a statement that the country was "very proud to have such a famous band as a sponsor."

As summer turned to fall, the band was forced to cancel its East Coast tour because of Garcia's health. He was never hospitalized, but his doctor put him on a vegetarian diet that helped him lose sixty pounds. By October, he was well enough to play the Oakland Coliseum with his own band. A few days before the Dead's Halloween run, however, they received troubling news: Bill Graham had died in helicopter crash while

shuttling back to Marin from the Concord Pavilion. Along with a host
of major artists and music industry executives, the Dead attended Graham's funeral at Temple Emanu-El in Presidio Heights, where Mickey
Hart spoke. A public event was arranged in Golden Gate Park, and
three hundred thousand people turned out to hear the Dead, Los Lobos, Jackson Browne, Aaron Neville, John Fogerty, Joan Baez, Kris
Kristofferson, Santana, and Crosby, Stills, Nash & Young.

At a press conference, Garcia described Graham as "the guy who
was respectable enough to talk to the rest of the world while we were
out on the fringe." By that time, however, the Dead were at the center of
the live-music business, and Graham would have been the first one to
appreciate their tour numbers for 1992. Although their canceled tour
meant twenty-two fewer performances than the previous year, the Dead
generated nearly as much revenue. The average gross revenue for their
concerts exceeded that of the year's top act, U2, by a substantial margin.
When the 1993 touring season opened, the Dead were honored to play
with jazz legend Ornette Coleman, and their Washington stop led to a
White House visit with Vice President Al Gore. Garcia wore sweat-
pants for the occasion, and Gore showed the band around the White
House before popping over to Tipper's office at the Old Executive Office Building. In New York, the Dead sold out their usual six shows at
Madison Square Garden and grossed almost $3 million.

The Dead's merchandising business was also booming. That fall, the
Dead produced their first *Grateful Dead Almanac,* a catalog that included band news, a community page with Rex Foundation activity,
and other content that harkened back to the early newsletters. Its editor
was Gary Lambert, a New York native who started listening to the
Dead in the late 1960s. In 1974, he moved to the Bay Area with the
intention of working for the Dead or Bill Graham. Mixing studio and
publicity work, he landed a job with Bill Graham Presents in 1983. After helping KPFA with its first Grateful Dead marathon, he and Lesh
pitched a program of adventurous music in 1986. KPFA approved the

program, which David Gans produced, and aired it once a month until 1993. By that time, the Dead's merchandise office had put Lambert in charge of the *Almanac*, whose unpaid circulation soon reached 150,000.

In January 1994, the Grateful Dead were inducted into the Rock and Roll Hall of Fame along with Elton John, Bob Marley, John Lennon, Rod Stewart, the Band, the Animals, and twang guitarist Duane Eddy. Garcia chose not to attend, and the Dead placed a life-size cardboard cutout of him on the dais as they accepted their award. Kreutzmann's remarks mentioned the loss of McKernan, Godchaux, and Mydland, and Lesh offered a shout-out to Dead Heads serving sentences for drug violations. "There's still hope for a miracle in America," Lesh said, and he urged them to keep the faith. The East Coast tour that year included another Capitol Hill visit, this one arranged by Vermont senator Patrick Leahy, who started listening to the Dead when he was a district attorney. In the Senate Dining Room, Leahy introduced the Dead to South Carolina senator and former Dixiecrat Strom Thurmond, who turned ninety-two that year. The interview was weird even by Dead standards. The superannuated senator jerked Garcia out of his chair with his handshake and slapped him on the arm. "Even back when I dropped acid," Garcia remarked, "I never had an experience like that."

In the summer of 1995, even Steve Parish thought Garcia needed treatment as the Dead endured the so-called Tour from Hell. It rained in Pittsburgh, and Garcia received a death threat in Indiana, where five thousand spectators also crashed the gate; fans inside the concert helped by kicking holes in the fence and cheering them on. When local police told the band they wouldn't work the next show, the Dead canceled it— the first time in three decades they had done so for security reasons. In St. Louis, the performance went well, but when Dead Heads at a nearby campground crowded onto a veranda to avoid a rainstorm, it collapsed, sending 108 people to the hospital. Predictably upset by that accident, the Dead were also irked by the chaos in Indiana. "Want to end the touring life of the Grateful Dead?" the band wrote on an Internet message board. "Allow bottle-throwing gate-crashers to keep on thinking they're cool anarchists instead of the creeps they are. Want to continue it? Listen to the rules and pressure others to do so." If part of the Dead's project was to explore the limits of freedom, fan misbehavior and Garcia's health problems pointed up some of those limits.

When the Tour from Hell ended, Garcia returned to the Bay Area and called David Grisman to schedule a recording session. Bob Dylan had arranged a tribute album for Jimmie Rodgers, the legendary Blue Yodeler who, as a railroad brakeman, was said to have scattered marijuana seeds off the back of trains. An enthusiastic Garcia asked Grisman to join him for "Blue Yodel #9," but Garcia wasn't looking well. The next day, he traveled south to the Betty Ford Center in the desert community of Rancho Mirage. It was supposed to be a monthlong program to treat his addiction, but after two hot, unpleasant weeks, he returned to Marin, where he promised his wife, Deborah Koons Garcia, that he would enter another facility. He chose a local substance-abuse clinic called Serenity Knolls, not far from Camp Lagunitas, where the band had bunked in the idyllic summer of 1966. He never made it out alive.

On the morning of August 9, 1995, Paul Liberatore of the *Marin Independent-Journal* was taking a shower when his wife told him he should get to work: Jerry Garcia was dead. It wasn't the first time Liberatore had heard such a report, but this one was authentic. He learned that a counselor had checked Garcia's room early that morning because he could no longer hear Garcia's loud snoring. The counselor found him dead with a smile on his face. As that news spread, Liberatore worked overtime. "I reported my ass off for a week," he said. The Gannett news group owned the Marin newspaper, and because management wanted to attract younger readers, editors had discouraged stories about the Dead. Liberatore tried to reason with them, but at one point an editor threw Garcia's photograph on the floor, saying he wouldn't run it. Liberatore's instincts were confirmed when Garcia's death produced the bestselling issue in the newspaper's history. "The numbers were off the charts for days," he said.

It wasn't only Marin County. The number of users on the WELL quadrupled, causing a slowdown, and Garcia's life, music, and death dominated the Bay Area media. *The San Francisco Examiner* ran three Garcia stories on the front page, three more on the front page of the style section, and two more on the front page of the business section. A *Chronicle* editorial titled "American Beauty" noted that the one word that ran consistently through commentaries on Garcia's life was *integrity*. "In a popular culture that sacrifices every value to mercenary pursuit," the editorial continued, "Garcia never lost the romantic ideals of San Francisco in the 1960s, the special era that spawned his music and nurtured it into the 1990s."

San Francisco mayor Frank Jordan ordered the city's flags to be flown at half-mast, and heartfelt eulogies appeared from the expected sources. Ken Kesey called Garcia "a great warrior, battling for hearts and souls way out on the dangerous frontier." Bob Dylan also praised Garcia and lamented the loss. "To me he wasn't only a musician and a friend, he was more like my big brother who taught and showed me more than he'll ever know," Dylan said. "There are a lot of spaces between the Carter Family, Buddy Holly, and, say, Ornette Coleman, a lot of universes, but he filled them all without being a member of any school. His playing was moody, awesome, sophisticated, hypnotic, and subtle. There's no way to convey the loss. It just digs down really deep." Departing Garcia's funeral, Dylan reportedly told John Scher, "That man back there is the only one who knows what it's like to be me."

In the national media, Senator Patrick Leahy said the news made him feel as if he had been kicked in the stomach. Wearing a black ribbon on his lapel, Governor William Weld of Massachusetts called a news conference to express his grief. He told reporters he discovered the

Dead in the 1960s and listened to *Workingman's Dead* and *American Beauty* the previous night. Only protests from veterans groups persuaded him not to fly the state's flags at half-mast. A lengthy *New York Times* obituary quoted Stewart Brand: "Some of the things the hippies got right came out the strongest and clearest in the Grateful Dead." *Rolling Stone, Entertainment Weekly, Newsweek,* and *People* quickly produced cover articles or special issues. *People* also followed up with a major story on Garcia's funeral and public memorial in Golden Gate Park, where twenty-five thousand fans gathered.

Even the tabloids tried to capitalize on Garcia's demise. The *Globe* reported sloppily that Garcia and his wife, who had been married less than two years, "went through a lot together before he finally died after a lifetime of drug and alcohol abuse." Garcia's death also revived media stereotypes about the Dead Head community. When writer and Dead aficionado Steve Silberman appeared on CNN, he was asked if he "dressed like a Dead Head." "Yes," Silberman replied. "I wear whatever I want."

The following week, the Marin County coroner concluded that Garcia had used heroin within days of his death, but that the drug didn't contribute to the heart attack that killed him. Instead, 85 percent blockage in two of the arteries leading to his heart reduced blood flow to a pinpoint. That finding didn't prevent many pundits from moralizing about drugs, and for some of them, Garcia's death became a referendum on the 1960s. "The band has prospered as the emblem of an era and is complicit in the continuing consequences of the era," George Will wrote in *Newsweek*. "Around it has hung an aroma of disdain for inhibitions on recreational uses of drugs and sex. During the band's nearly 30-year life the costs of 'liberation' from such inhibitions have been made manifest in millions of shattered lives and miles of devastated cities." There's a dark irony in Will's charge. In 2003, he became a full-throated supporter of the US invasion of Iraq, which actually did shatter millions of lives and devastate cities. After most of the damage was done, he blamed the disaster on Vice President Dick Cheney. Almost a decade later, Will wrote a series of columns that seemed to endorse the legalization of drugs, a position Garcia had held for years.

At least Will was corrigible. His former employer at *National Review*, William F. Buckley, also seized on Garcia's death to scold the counterculture, and his brief was even thinner than Will's. In his *National Review* column, Buckley recalled an intern at his magazine who attended a Grateful Dead show and enjoyed it. The intern's work began to drop off, and he later moved to South America to teach English. "Jerry Garcia didn't help this young man," Buckley wrote. "We did not hear again from him, except after an interval of five years or so, when we learned he had married again, this time a native, and gone off to live in the hills. Question before the house: Is Jerry Garcia in some way responsible for this?" According to Buckley, the answer was yes. He asserted that Garcia had "killed, if that's the right word for such as our intern, a lot of people."

Buckley's claim was absurd, even obscene, especially coming from a stout defender of America's bloody intervention in Vietnam. It makes sense only as a symptom of the ideological contest over the nature and meaning of the 1960s. But it wasn't clear that Buckley's view would prevail even at his own magazine. Deroy Murdock, a Dead Head who also wrote for *National Review,* held a less negative view of Garcia. "Jerry Garcia's abuse of his bear-like body should teach all of us a lesson on the value of moderation," he wrote. "But the rest of his life—from the music to which he remained true for over 30 years to the spirit of freedom that still permeates the community he led—amiably embodied an all-American ideal: the pursuit of happiness." Murdock's conclusion was also consistent with Garcia's statements. "We're basically Americans, and we like America," Garcia said. "We like the things about being able to express outrageous amounts of freedom." In this sense, and despite the flak they took from conservatives, the Dead were as American as apple pie—or a lynch mob, as Garcia once remarked pointedly.

Syndicated columnist Mike Barnicle also weighed in against Garcia. "Look," Barnicle wrote, "Jerry Garcia seemed like a nice fellow, and it's unfortunate he died at age 53 because apparently he made some smile and tap their toes, and that's better than a thumb in the eye." But any reverence for Garcia flipped Barnicle's sarcasm switch. "Poor Jerry. Boy, could he play the guitar. And what a fabulous outlook he had on life. Jerry was against the war and for civil rights. Jerry was good. He smiled all the time. No kidding—Jerry was smacked out of his mind." Three years later, Barnicle left *The Boston Globe* amid charges he had fabricated a story about cancer patients and recycled comedian George Carlin's observations without attribution. Barnicle denied the charges, but as the *Globe* considered his future with the newspaper, he received little support from his colleagues, fifty of whom signed a petition calling for tougher treatment after the Carlin incident.

Even President Clinton commented on Garcia's death. "Well, first of all, he was just a great talent," Clinton said in an MTV interview. "I mean, he was really—he was a genius, and I was really pleased to see the Grateful Dead have one more great run around the country, you know, in the last couple of years and see all these young teenagers gravitating to a group that all of us liked twenty or more years ago." Clinton claimed that he enjoyed wearing and giving away Garcia's neckties, but he added that he "would hope that as we mourn him and sort of feel grateful for what he did, young people should say, 'I'm not going to die that way. I'm not going to die in a clinic with a drug addiction.'"

Clinton's DEA chief, Thomas Constantine, saw less need to temper his views. He claimed that the nation could never hope to defeat the scourge of drugs if Americans eulogized Garcia. "And you can't have Jerry Garcia, reportedly a heroin addict, now being extolled as one of the great parts of the American system, and what a wonderful person he was, and things like that," he said. In his remarks that day, Constantine added that he was uncomfortable with the term *war on drugs*. "There has never really been a war on drugs because the American public has never made a commitment to invest the resources that would be required for the struggle," he said. That year, the federal government spent more than $13 billion on drug policy and enforcement—roughly equivalent to $20.4 billion in 2014 dollars.

Garcia's death effectively concluded the project the Dead had launched three decades before. It also dramatized that project's core principles and consequences. A life devoted to ecstasy, mobility, and community was as inviting to a youthful Garcia as it was to the Beats who inspired him. Indeed, Garcia and the Dead lived out those ideals longer and more effectively than Kerouac did. The Dead's core principles were remarkably stable, but the band's success was the product of continuous innovation, experimentation, and adaptation. The Dead scene, David Gans noted, "invented itself on almost every level—musically, technically, and culturally." Over time, the Dead's do-it-yourself ethic became the music industry standard, especially after digital production tools were widely available and bands began to produce and distribute their own music. When digital downloading, streaming, and file sharing started to erode the album-based business model in 2000, the Dead's peripatetic ways also prefigured the tour-heavy business model that's now the norm for popular music.

Musically, the Dead's legacy can still be seen in the jam-band culture carried forward by Phish, Widespread Panic, the String Cheese Incident, Blues Traveler, Spin Doctors, Gov't Mule, and other improvisational bands that draw on American roots music, emphasize live performance over recordings, encourage taping, and make a conscious effort to connect with their fans at the grassroots level. In his book about that culture, Peter Conners offered the Dead as its starting point. "There isn't a band in this book who wouldn't acknowledge some debt to the Grateful Dead," Conners noted. "It's no reach to say that with no Grateful Dead, there would be no jam band scene." The same year Conners's book appeared, the National, a New York–based indie band, announced that their Grateful Dead tribute album would include contributions from Bon Iver, Vampire Weekend, and Kurt Vile. "It's kind of an ambitious project both because of the legacy and of the material," said Aaron Dessner. "We are obsessed enough with the Grateful Dead that it is kind of a monumental idea." Bryce Dessner added that their preoccupation with the Dead began in middle school. "There are all kinds of corners of the musical world that are deeply influenced by the Dead that one wouldn't expect," he said. "So that was part of the idea, but I think it is bigger than that now. Jerry Garcia is a total cat." The same year, pop star John Mayer touted the Dead in a *Rolling Stone* interview.

> I've been listening to the Grateful Dead nonstop. Mark my words, the Grateful Dead are going to make a comeback because of how that music cleanses your palate. When everything is processed and quantized and gridded out—to hear "Tennessee Jed" played with that lope is a real palate-cleanser. They take their time, sometimes too much. This free expressive sort of spirit—I listen and I want to find a mix of that openness. I kind of want to go to that show, if it still existed.

Mayer's comment about "that kind of show" points to a broader cultural effect as well. In addition to inspiring and supporting luthiers, sound engineers, illustrators, and other artists and artisans, the Dead contributed directly to the creation of the San Francisco–style rock concert, whose combination of music, light show, and freestyle dancing has continued to evolve. One can draw a straight line from the Trips Festival to Burning Man, the annual arts festival convened in the northern Nevada desert that drew seventy thousand revelers in 2013. First held on San Francisco's Baker Beach in 1986, Burning Man has emphasized communal self-reliance, radical expression, an aversion to commerce, and leaving no physical trace in the desert after the event. In 2000, *The New*

York Times reported that Burning Man had much in common with a Grateful Dead concert, including "young and formerly young people camping out, enjoying performance art (and maybe various levels of undress and altered states of consciousness), and raging against the machine." Although many Burners would contest the Dead's direct influence on the event, strong family resemblances between the two communities can be traced to the San Francisco art scene to which the Dead made important contributions.

If the Dead's long-term success and influence defied expectations, their lived experience with their core ideals was anything but smooth. Drugs and alcohol took their toll, and their attempts to create a hip economy met with stiff resistance. Yet some of the Dead's most serious challenges came not from external sources but from tensions between their utopian impulses. From the outset, getting high through music meant privileging the moment of performance over studio recordings. That decision entailed heavy touring, which supported the community financially, grew the Dead Head community, and ensured the band's survival. Over time, the Dead found they had to balance their commitments to that larger community and to their family scene in Marin. They did that by playing larger venues, which compromised the ecstatic performances to which they were so committed.

The Dead eventually adapted to the big venues, but faced with constant travel and financial responsibility for an entire organization, Garcia opted for what counterculture historian Theodore Roszak called "counterfeit infinity," which he described as a "frantic search for the pharmacological panacea." That search, Roszak noted in 1968, distracted many young people from what was most valuable in their rebellion and destroyed their most promising sensibilities. Even some drug-war opponents regarded the Dead's statements about expanding consciousness as false promises. Peter Coyote, who has advised the Marijuana Policy Project and compared the drug war to the Inquisition, thought that the pursuit of drug-aided enlightenment "helped kill Jerry." It's easy to fool audiences when you drop in once a year, Coyote said, but real life back home has a way of catching up with artists.

While reflecting on their shared experience in both San Francisco and Marin County, Coyote also recounted a 1968 conversation with Gary Snyder, Kerouac's model for Japhy Ryder in *The Dharma Bums*. When Coyote mentioned the artist's willingness to destroy himself on-stage as a sign of his commitment, Snyder took issue with him. In the days of Verlaine and Rimbaud, Snyder said, bourgeois culture induced artists to seek ecstasy through the systematic derangement of the senses. But in contemporary America, Snyder claimed, the bourgeoisie is socio-pathic, and the artist should model health and sanity. No one ever ac-cused Garcia of modeling good health, but his public remarks in scores of interviews over three decades displayed impressive doses of sanity and insight on a wide range of topics.

Coyote acknowledged that the Dead community was genuine and the key to the band's long-term success. The Grateful Dead, the former Dig-ger felt, were "truest to the ethos of Haight-Ashbury." Likewise, Jann Wenner said the Dead's achievement could be traced to "family values." Others felt that Garcia's freely chosen commitment to the Dead commu-nity was too heavy a burden. "I will remember him as an excellent musi-cian, a very nice guy who was abused by his work," Country Joe McDonald said upon Garcia's death. "It's a much too familiar tale—people who are famous beyond anything but are on a treadmill that prevents them from having normal relationships and getting themselves together."

Garcia saw it differently. The Dead's commitment to community, which had always distinguished them from their peers, was a core value and the key to their success. That commitment was underestimated or misunderstood by most rock critics, who wondered openly how the Dead continued to prosper while their albums floundered and other bands fell by the wayside. Although the Dead's personal relationships could be fractious, the band members understood the value of cohesion. They reveled in each other's eccentricities, Blair Jackson said, and they never trashed each other publicly, which was unique in the rock world. "The members of the Grateful Dead really have a complex relationship," Garcia said in 1989. "At this point, it's gone beyond even blood. The Grateful Dead has been the most intimate kind of relationship I've ever experienced. There is definitely the danger of becoming insular, and we're certainly aware of that on a lot of different levels. But that's kind of what we're after—a kind of community. And we have it."

Epilogue

Four months after Garcia's death, the band members met to ponder their future. Kreutzmann, who had no intention of playing in the Grateful Dead without Garcia, skipped the meeting, but the others spent five hours going over their options. The next day, they announced that they were disbanding.

Despite Garcia's previous health scares, no contingency plans had been made for his death. In the Grateful Dead world, David Gans wrote in 1995, "life as we know it has come to an end, and an immense social and economic network has been thrown into chaos." The touring machine came to an abrupt halt, and many employees were cut from the payroll. But in another branch of the organization, life went on. Gary Lambert converted the fall issue of the *Grateful Dead Almanac* into a tasteful memorial, and the catalog's status was quickly transformed; what had been an afterthought became the organization's main source of revenue. It was a strange transition, Lambert said, in part because the merchandising never stopped. In fact, sales peaked after Garcia's death, as did the number of radio stations airing *The Grateful Dead Hour*.

The organization turned to promoting the post-Dead bands that played under various names. The Other Ones was the most prominent and included Weir, Lesh, Hart, and Bruce Hornsby. In 2000, Kreutzmann joined the band and Lesh dropped out. Two years later, Lesh rejoined and Hornsby dropped out, and their tour was billed as the Grateful Dead Family Reunion with the "Surviving Members of the Grateful Dead." It was the first time Weir, Lesh, Hart, and Kreutzmann had played together since 1995, but Vince Welnick, who was prone to depression, was deeply troubled by his exclusion. In 2003, the group changed its name to the Dead and continued to perform with a shifting lineup.

In 2006, the Grateful Dead signed a deal with Rhino Entertainment, a subsidiary of Warner Music Group specializing in premier reissues. Under the terms of that agreement, Rhino would manage almost every aspect of the Dead's intellectual property for ten years. In return, the band members received guaranteed annual payments roughly equivalent to their earnings in a peak year. They had come a long way financially. Lesh and his wife, Jill, bought a large home in Ross, an upscale community in Marin County, and a house on Stinson Beach once owned by Ralph Gleason. The Dead had also climbed the social ladder. Weir and Hart joined the Bohemian Club, which had long since become an elite private men's club favored by corporate leaders and high-ranking government officials. Its only remaining connection to bohemianism was its requirement that accomplished artists make up 10 percent of its membership. At the Bohemian Grove in Monte Rio, Hart bunked in the Hillbillies Camp, whose members have included George H. W. Bush, Donald Rumsfeld, and Walter Cronkite.

The Dead's contract with Rhino covered unreleased live recordings, videos, merchandise, licensing arrangements, and the official website, which Mary Eisenhart moderated. The agreement didn't include the music publishing operation, Ice Nine, which Alan Trist continued to manage. "In the last couple of years, it became apparent that the business was just too much trouble," Weir told *The New York Times*. "The Grateful Dead of yore was built around being a touring band, and when we stopped touring, the structure wasn't there." A temperature-controlled truck transported the vault tapes—some thirteen thousand live audio and video recordings—from a warehouse in Novato to a facility in the Los Angeles suburb of Burbank.

The local press noted that Weir, Lesh, Kreutzmann, and Hart had been squabbling bitterly over business matters. "I think it was a common thought that if we got rid of the business, we might become friends again," Hart said when the deal was signed. "We might actually play again. We really love each other, and, deep down, we're tied at the heart. Our friendship needs to be renewed, but we could never do it around a boardroom table. Now we have nothing to fight over." Hart's optimism didn't extend to Welnick, who committed suicide in his Sonoma County home a month before the deal was announced. But in 2008, the so-called surviving members of the Grateful Dead made good on Hart's prediction by playing two concerts for Barack Obama's presidential campaign. After Obama was elected, they also played at an official inaugural ball and more than twenty dates that April and May. At one show, Tipper Gore played drums on "Sugar Magnolia."

Rhino continued to market music curated from the Dead's vault. Dick Latvala was in charge of that operation until his death in 1999. David Lemieux succeeded him, and the *Dick's Picks* series became *Dave's Picks*. The most audacious product, perhaps, was *Europe '72: The Complete Recordings*, a box set of seventy-three CDs covering all twenty-two shows on that tour. When Rhino released an exclusive limited edition in September 2011, online buyers snapped up all seventy-two hundred units in four days. That frenzy was a hot topic at *Tales from the Golden Road*, the radio program hosted by David Gans and Gary Lambert on Sirius XM's Grateful Dead channel. While listening to the program, I heard one caller after another take Rhino to task—not for the product's $450 price tag, but for failing to produce enough units to accommodate demand. Rhino hustled to limit the damage, but the company must have been pleased to gross $3.24 million in four days. Although the unit sales were a small addition to the 35 million albums the Dead have sold over the years, the vigorous uptake was a strong signal that the Dead community remained vital.

In August 2013, a music documentary called *Sunshine Daydream* was released and distributed by Rhino Records. Filmed at the 1972 benefit concert for the Springfield Creamery in Veneta, Oregon, the documentary was accompanied by a three-disc CD that debuted at nineteen on the *Billboard* charts. It was the band's second top-twenty album and the first since *In the Dark*. Six months later, *Dave's Picks Volume 9* cracked the Top 40 Albums chart. Both releases were more evidence that, commercially at least, the Grateful Dead were alive and well.

By that time, I was seeking out chances to hear the post-Dead bands. From an October 2011 conversation on the WELL, I learned that former band members might join Bill Kreutzmann's band, 7 Walkers, at the Great American Music Hall in San Francisco. Sure enough, Mickey Hart came out with Kreutzmann's band and began a long, rhythmic dialogue with his former partner. After a few minutes of watching it, I was convinced that I had wasted my time on the planet. An extra microphone stood in the middle of the stage, and a few numbers into the first set, Bob Weir shambled out. It was the first time since 2009 that the three former Dead members had played together. In the first set, the band ripped through "Mister Charlie," "New Speedway Boogie," "Big Railroad Blues," "Bird Song," "Wang Dang Doodle," "Deal," and "Sugaree." It was an embarrassment of riches for the average fan, who could stroll up to the ticket booth, plunk down $25, and wander up to the front of the stage. The audience was noticeably long in the tooth, but the show was otherwise the closest possible approximation I could find to the old Fillmore and Avalon events.

By that time, Weir had founded the Tamalpais Research Institute

(TRI), which was built to broadcast HD video and audio streaming from a high-tech studio in San Rafael. Casting the facility as the "ultimate playpen for musicians," Weir used the 11,500-square-foot facility as a rehearsal studio until April 2011, when TRI broadcast a live performance of Furthur, the band Weir and Lesh had formed in 2009, over the Internet. "A lot of guys when they have a little success in life, they go out and buy a yacht or a fancy car or something," Weir told Joel Selvin. "What I did was go out and buy a flying saucer."

I also made several visits to Terrapin Crossroads, which Phil and Jill Lesh opened in 2012. The previous year, Lesh wrote on the Furthur website that they were "taking the first steps to make a longtime dream—a permanent musical home—come true." The goal was "to create a vibrant community gathering place: beautiful, comfortable, welcoming— for members of the community to commingle and enjoy good music." The original plan was to remodel the Good Earth restaurant in Fairfax, but after meeting resistance from residents, the Leshes chose to remodel a restaurant in the canal district of San Rafael. Lesh described the genesis of that decision on his website.

I was recently rereading Bob Dylan's *Chronicles,* and Jill and I started reminiscing about the 1987 rehearsal sessions with Bob that took place at Club Front, the Grateful Dead San Rafael studio/boys' club from the late seventies until the mid-nineties. We were having lunch in the area one afternoon and decided to take a drive by the old studio. While we were driving around we went by the Seafood Peddler restaurant, where Furthur did some rehearsal shows a couple years ago in their Palm Ballroom. We pulled into the rear parking lot and we saw a large painted Grateful Dead logo with the words "Buckle Up Kids" above it. We looked at each other and both had the same flash—that the Seafood Peddler had the foundation for us to realize our long-held dream of finding a place in Marin County to make music.

On my first visit to Terrapin Crossroads, I heard the Terrapin Family Band with Lesh's sons, Brian and Grahame. They opened with the Rolling Stones' "Miss You" from the *Some Girls* album of 1978, played several bluegrass numbers, and ended with a superb version of "The Weight" by the Band. About fifty people were in the bar, and I spotted Phil Lesh sitting at a café table near the soundboard. Although he had received a liver transplant in 1998, he looked well at age seventy-three. He was clearly enjoying himself as he worked on a plate of pasta, sang along, and laughed during the performance.

A Dead sighting the following year was more serendipitous. In August, I attended the final stop on the Americanarama tour featuring Bob Dylan, Wilco, My Morning Jacket, and Ryan Bingham. The venue was the Shoreline Amphitheater on the peninsula, not far from the Dead's original home and even closer to Google headquarters. Halfway through My Morning Jacket's set, the band invited Bob Weir to join them for "Knockin' on Heaven's Door." During Wilco's set, Weir came out for "Saint Stephen" and "Dark Star." Into the latter song, they dropped "California Stars," the Woody Guthrie song Wilco had put music to in 1998. The audience, especially the older hippies, went bananas. The two sets featured five Dead songs, two Dylan numbers, and one Springsteen tune before Dylan took the stage and marched through his set.

The following month, Robert Hunter received a lifetime achievement award from the Americana Music Association in Nashville. After the dissolution of the Grateful Dead, Hunter wrote songs for or with Bob Dylan, Jim Lauderdale, Little Feat, Los Lobos, Bruce Hornsby, New Riders of the Purple Sage, 7 Walkers, Furthur, and Mickey Hart. In October 2013, he also played eight solo shows on the East Coast and gave an exclusive interview to *Rolling Stone* to promote them. He cited medical expenses as one reason for the tour. "Last year I managed to have a nice hospitalization that should have been fatal. I had a spinal abscess," he said. "It was a honey. They had me on morphine for about a month. I had never had the distinction of being involved with that

[drug] before. It was the strangest world. I couldn't tell delusions from reality. I was calling my mom in the middle of the night saying they were going to execute me."

The same month Hunter received his award, I attended my first Furthur concert. It was the last show in a three-night stand at the Greek Theatre in Berkeley, one of the Dead's sacred sites. I didn't like my chances for landing tickets and had resigned myself to missing the shows. But two nights before the first concert, I pledged to KPFA during David Gans's program, *Dead to the World*, and acquired a pair of tickets to the Sunday show. My girlfriend couldn't go, and a colleague's husband volunteered to accompany me. Outside the venue, Jeff (not his real name) and I encountered many of the Dead Head hallmarks—a drum circle, a cascade of tie-dye, and dreadlocked waifs with index fingers pointed skyward, hoping for a miracle ticket. Inside, Bill Walton was quite noticeably on the scene, as was John Barlow. Lesh had already announced that Furthur were going on hiatus at the end of the year, and many suspected that this might be their final show in the Bay Area. That announcement gave the event extra piquancy, and Blair Jackson, who attended all three shows at the Greek, told me the Sunday concert was the closest thing he had seen to a Dead show since 1995.

Jeff and I agreed beforehand that some age-appropriate psychoactivity was in order, and we ingested half our supply as the show began. By the middle of the first set, I could see he was transported. Inspired by the Lawrence Berkeley National Laboratory, which sits atop the hill behind the Greek Theatre, Jeff's conversation turned to the Voyager spacecraft, which originally launched in 1977 and produced extraordinary photographs of Jupiter, Saturn, Uranus, and Neptune. "I bet some of those guys are here right now," he said of the spacecraft's computer programmers. "I really hope so." As we chatted, two young parents near us were enjoying the show while their girls played with dolls. The father offered us a bowl of marijuana; we declined and fell silent as we tried to imagine bringing our young daughters to such an event. Years earlier, I had misgivings about taking my teenage daughters to a Train concert at the Fillmore Auditorium, where thick clouds of pot smoke were routine.

During the first set, my attention turned to a section of deaf spectators and a woman who was signing the lyrics for them. She incorporated her signing into her dance, which transfixed me. I glanced periodically at Walton, who was scanning the audience. The rounded shape of the Greek Theatre made that activity especially rewarding, and the sight of eighty-five hundred spectators moving in rhythm was one of the show's chief pleasures. Again I watched the drummer with unvarnished envy. Finally, I admitted to Jeff that I wanted to become a drummer. He looked at me with a mixture of exasperation and disappointment. "Man, you're *already* a drummer," he said. "Don't you know that? We're *all* drummers."

We ingested the rest of our contraband, and Jeff went for a long walk. During the intermission, I chatted with a pleasant older couple sitting next to us. Surprisingly, I kept up my end of the conversation while the pattern on her purse began to roil and glisten like a snake. Jeff returned after the intermission, and we let the music wash over us. Both sets consisted entirely of Dead songs with two exceptions, the Beatles' "Strawberry Fields" and Ryan Adams's "Let It Ride." Toward the end of the second set, everyone was dancing, and as a lengthy version of "Franklin's Tower" built to a crescendo, I could feel the music in my bones. It had been ages since I had so thoroughly lost my mind and come to my senses. My improvised dance, adjusted to accommodate the tight space, felt completely natural. Even so, it occurred to me that I might be embarrassing Jeff. When I glanced his way, he was swaying from side to side, occasionally sweeping his left arm across his torso. Finally, he turned to me and said, "I really feel like I could play tennis left-handed right now." Although we never followed up on that hunch, our afternoon together felt like a gratuitous grace, and I accepted it thankfully.

Acknowledgments

This project benefited enormously from my association with the Grateful Dead Scholars Caucus and its organizer, Nick Meriwether. At our annual meetings, I've met and learned from musicologist Graeme Boone, sociologist Rebecca Adams, literary scholar Ulf Olsson, and management professor Barry Barnes. My other teachers there include Melvin Backstrom, Gary Burnett, Jake Cohen, Michael Parrish, Sue Reitz, Jay Williams, Brent Wood, and Christian Crumlish, the father of Bobby Petersen studies. Jesse Jarnow, another Caucus member, was an enthusiastic source of references and historical detail; I eagerly await his forthcoming book. Nick, Ulf, David Gans, and Rosie McGee read my draft manuscript, as did Reed Malcolm, my colleague at the University of California Press. I'm grateful for their interest, expertise, corrections, and suggestions.

As I was researching the book, David Gans introduced me to Rosie McGee, who was writing her memoir, *Dancing with the Dead*. It was a valuable resource, but Rosie's conversation also provided me with background information that I couldn't have acquired from my reading, interviews, or archival work. I'm grateful to David for the introduction and to Rosie for her friendship and support. I reviewed her book for *Dead Studies* along with Rhoney Gissen Stanley's memoir, *Owsley and Me*. Both Rosie and Rhoney attended the 2014 meeting of the Grateful Dead Scholars Caucus, where Rhoney alerted me to aspects of the Reagan drug war that I had previously overlooked. I thank her for that pointer and for her other contributions to our sessions.

For their thoughts and reflections, I also thank Allen Baum, Bob Bralove, Jason Cohn, Peter Conners, Peter Coyote, Mary Eisenhart, Bennett Falk, David Gans, Toby Gleason, Blair Jackson, Paul Krassner, Gary Lambert, Paul Liberatore, Rosie McGee, Dennis McNally, Jann Wenner, and Baron Wolman. Alan Trist replied to my questions about the Dead, and Kim Stanley Robinson enlightened me about the mid-century science-fiction scene in the Bay Area. The sources section is a master list of my intellectual debts, but I would single out David Gans, Blair Jackson, Dennis McNally, and Nick Meriwether for the quality, quantity, and utility of their work on the Grateful Dead over the years. As my endnotes make clear, I also found Robert Greenfield's books on Bill Graham and Jerry Garcia extremely useful.

My agent, Andy Ross, made this project possible. I thank him for his advocacy and for his years of stewardship at Cody's Books, which ranks with Kepler's and City Lights as the Bay Area's key independent bookstores in the second half of the twentieth century. I also thank Marc Resnick at St. Martin's Press for his early interest in the project and his enthusiastic support throughout. Editorial assistant Jaime Coyne deftly shepherded the project through production including superb work on the photo insert. Steven Henry Boldt copyedited the manuscript assiduously and alerted me to various errors and lapses; those that remain are mine alone.

The University of California libraries helped me immensely. At UC Santa Cruz, I benefited from the Grateful Dead Archive as well as Nick's and Laura McClanathan's interest, support, and hospitality. I also appreciate the services provided by the UC Berkeley libraries. Their vast collection of books and periodicals—and tantalizing bits of Ralph J. Gleason's correspondence—were a boon to me. Jeff Gundersen, librarian at the San Francisco Art Institute, also furnished me with a useful file of materials on Wally Hedrick, Jerry Garcia, and the California School of Fine Arts.

My brother Rod generously shared his memories of the Bay Area shows he attended in the 1960s and 1970s. As always, my daughters, Ashley and Mary Richardson, were an important source of encouragement, and Ashley also served as my endnote wrangler. Beth Tudor deserves no end of credit for her support, patience, advice, and companionship. My time in Santa Cruz with Ashley, Mary, and Beth was my little summer of love.

Notes

INTRODUCTION

Pages 2–7

2 "We're basically Americans": Eisenhart 1987.

2 "Nobody's making any real": Garcia et al. 1972, xix.

3 "The Grateful Dead is not for": Garcia et al. 1972, 100.

7 "Those flowers": Cutler 2010, 220–21.

PART 1: ECSTASY

Pages 11–146

11 "I had always wanted to do psychedelics": Greenfield 1996, 55.

11 Yeats reported that: Dunaway 1989, 286.

12 As his daily concerns evaporated: Dunaway 1989, 289.

13 "All I am suggesting": Huxley 1954, 73.

14 "I think it had a dirt floor": Jackson 1999, 55.

14 "The clarinet had that lovely": Jackson 1999, 8.

15 "I've always wanted to be able": McNally 2002, 14.

15 By the time Garcia's opened: Issel and Cherny 1986, 59.

15 "We were aware that the bulk of the people": Issel and Cherny 1986, 109.

17 "Like the drifters who rode west": Thompson 1966, 58.

17 "We knew about the beatniks": Greenfield 1996, 10–11.

17 Poet Kenneth Rexroth: Davidson 1989, 11.

18 The earlier San Francisco literature: Foley 2001, 8.

18 "Local and itinerant poets": Caples et al. 2013, xix.

19 "West Coast of those days": Davidson 1989, 29.

19 "You sensed that everybody": Jarnot 2012, 125.

19 "My view of the Dionysian": Davidson 1989, 49.

19 Responding to a heckler: Jarnot 2012, 135.

20 "Only by chancing the ridiculous": Green and Levy 2003, ix.

20 "We had been trying for a whole decade": Meltzer 2001, 41–42.

20 The Beat poets were "wild-ass carpetbaggers": Caples et al. 2013, xix.

21 "I was a young writer and I wanted to take off": Kerouac 1957, 8.

21 Moriarty was "a sideburned hero of the snowy West": Kerouac 1957, 7–8.

21 But for all their high spirits: Kerouac 1957, 117.

21 Later Sal admits: Kerouac 1957, 126.

21 "This madness would lead nowhere": Kerouac 1957, 128.

22 "We were all delighted": Kerouac 1957, 134.

22 "My mother remarried": Garcia et al. 1972, 2.

23 "We'd hang out in front of the Anxious Asp": Jackson 1999, 23.

24 "This was when they were coming": Wally Hedrick, Smithsonian interview, 1974.

24 Reviewing his work of that period: Solnit 2004.

24 "There is, no doubt": Hedrick file, SFAI archive.

25 Years later, Garcia gave the same advice: Greenfield 1996, 99.

25 Garcia learned from Hedrick: McNally 2002, 24.

25 "Wally and Jay's house": Hedrick file, SFAI archive.

25 "I like to hear every note": Jackson 1999, 75.

25 "This big limo pulled up": Greenfield 1996, 13–14.

26 McClure ingested: Smith 1995, 247.

26 Influenced by their example: Ellingham and Killian 1998, 50.

26 "There was no market for art": Bruce Conner, Smithsonian interview, 1974.

28 "Then in the next couple of years": Jack Kerouac Collection audiotape booklet.

29 "I wanted to do something": DeCurtis 1993.

29 "I wanted so badly": Jackson 1999, 25.

29 "That's where my life began": Troy 1994, 27.

30 But there was nothing: Hajdu 2001, 10.

30 "It not was merely": Hajdu 2001, 12.

30 When Dylan arrived in New York: Smith 2011.

31 Paul Kantner and David Freiberg: Parrish 2014.

32 "When Joan Baez's first record came out": Gleason 1969, 309.

32 "When I got into folk music": Gleason 1969, 327.

32 "It could have been at some longshoremen's hall": Cohen 1968, in Perchuk and Singh 2010.

33 He also explored avant-garde film: Igliori 1996, 25–26.

33 In his view, anything that "changed consciousness": Cohen 1968, in Perchuk and Singh 2010.

33 Smith later noted its: Cohen 1968, in Igliori 1996.

33 "We would visit her apartment": Jackson 1999, 39.

34 "For me it was the Harry Smith anthology": Jackson 1992, 210–11.

34 For a young Bob Dylan: Marcus 2011, 30.

35 "I have *never* had better acid": Brown et al. 2009, 19.

35 "I couldn't figure out why they were paying me": Mikkelsen 2013.

35 "I do not contend that driving people crazy": Lee and Shlain 1985, 37.

36 "God," Garcia said: McNally 2002, 43.

36 A Berkeley native and jazz trumpeter: Lesh 2005, 14.

37 Precisely because music didn't endure: Berio 2006, 63.

38 The purpose of *City Scale*: Bernstein 2008, 64.

39 "He would walk around the Chateau": Lesh 2005, 30.

39 "I'd go over there and see these charts": Greenfield 1996, 64.

39 "Ken was a competitive writer": McMurtry 2009, 22.

40 A popular teacher whose work and outlook: Fradkin 2009, 131.

40 "Eight o'clock every Tuesday morning": Kesey 2002, vii.

41 "Everybody I knew had read *On the Road*": Gibney and Ellwood 2011.

41 Vic Lovell, the psychologist to whom: Stone 2007, 94–95.

41 It was just as well, Kesey said: Brightman 1998, 21–22.

41 "Many of the bands came around": Stone, in George-Warren 1995.

42 The alcoholic Kerouac: Gibney and Ellwood 2011.

43 "I thought this was as American as you could get": Gibney and Ellwood 2011.

44 "Everybody looks like animals": Greenfield 1996, 57.

44 "Everything was okay": Greenfield 1996, 57.

45 Monroe's band, the Blue Grass Boys: Smith 2000, x–xi.

45 Garcia cut his hair: Jackson 1999, 62; McNally 2002, 71.

46 Bruce kept those lawyers busy: Krassner 1993, 67.

46 The accompanying note: Krassner 1993, 77.

47 "I learned so much, it was incredible": McNally 2002, 73.

47 Weir taped Kaukonen's coffeehouse performances: Gleason 1969, 312.

47 "The Beatles were why we turned from a jug band": Jackson 1999, 67.

48 It hit him like "a big soft pillow": Lesh 2005, 40.

48 "I was twenty-four years old": Lesh 2005, 34.

48 Lesh recalled, "Things started": Lesh 2005, 36.

48 Much to the disappointment: Greenfield 1996, 67.

49 "Listen, man," Garcia said: Lesh 2005, 46–47.

49 "Jerry took a real leap there": Greenfield 1996, 65.

49 "Pigpen was the only guy in the band": Jackson 1992, 29.

50 "That's the first time I had the experience of being high": McNally 2002, 21.

50 As the band's front man: Scully and Dalton 1996, 29.

50 "When LSD hit the streets": McNally 2002, 104.

51 "When I first saw the Warlocks": Private correspondence, Grateful Dead Archive.

51 By the fifth set: McNally 2002, 88.

51 "That's what's wrong with the Cow Palace shows": Gleason 1969, 3.

52 "George was the first hippie I ever saw": Grushkin 1999, 68.

52 "We completely decorated the place": Sculatti and Seay 1985, 33.

53 "About four hundred or five hundred people showed up": Weller 2012.

53 According to Ralph Gleason: Gleason 1969, 6.

53 "They entered into the occasion": Gleason 1969, 8.

54 "Lady, what this little séance": McNally 2002, 96.

54 "You guys will never make it": Lesh 2005, 61.

55 The *San Jose Mercury*: Lesh 2005, 66.

55 "Actually, Jerry didn't love that scene": Greenfield 1996, 71.

55 "The idea of dealing with motorcycle gang members": Greenfield 1996, 71.

55 "We were younger than the Pranksters": Greenfield 1996, 73.

55 "They were our first and best audience": Saffra and Talbot 1987.

56 "When it was moving right": Lydon 1969.

56 As one insider noted later: Scully and Dalton 1996, 45.

56 "Everything else on the page went blank": McNally 2002, 100.

57 But when they arrived: Graham and Greenfield 1992, 124.

57 "The band went on": Greenfield 1996, 77.

58 "We'd never seen anyone play like that before": Greenfield 1996, 74.

58 "We'll have to wipe the mikes": Selvin 1999, 45.

58 "Garcia sort of put down his guitar": Greenfield 1996, 77.

59 "Kesey was the kind of guy": Gans 1993, 299.

59 "I was standing in the hall": Greenfield 1996, 74.

59 Lesh said they also lacked a sound engineer: Gans 1993, 307.

59 Festooned with movie screens: Scully and Dalton 1996, 14.

59 "Close up, the bizarre nature": Scully and Dalton 1996, 19.

60 It was, according to one music scholar: Bernstein 2008, 5

60 "It was the beginning of the Grateful Dead": Bernstein 2008, 243–44.

60 "Nothing. A bust, a bore": Gleason 1969, 18.

60 "The truth about the Trips Festival": Gleason 1969, 21–22.

61 "And so the Grateful Dead was blasting away": Bernstein 2008, 248.

61 "I remember the Merry Pranksters were there": Graham and Greenfield 1992, 136.

61 "There was a guy standing there in a space suit": Graham and Greenfield 1992, 139.

62 Wandering around the venue: Graham and Greenfield 1992, 139.

62 "I had some sense": Graham and Greenfield 1992, 139–40.

63 "I just thought it was the most touching thing": Graham and Greenfield 1992, 140–41.

63 "Thousands of people, man": Lydon 1969.

63 Recounting a twenty-minute version: Gleason, September 1966.

64 In Gleason's view: Gleason 1969, 26.

64 "Considering that I personally": Jackson 1999, 109.

64 "I went to shows every night": Jackson 1999, 109.

64 "The best thing about it": Jackson 1999, 110.

64 "I was thinking, 'This is hell'": Brown et al. 2009, 18.

65 "Hey, you're messing with ancient stuff": Gans 1993, 307.

66 "It was patronage in the finest sense": Gans 1993, 292.

66 He hadn't had any "plant food": Gans 1993, 291.

66 "We were mostly just bullshitting each other": Greenfield 1996, 84–85.

67 First, it would be intangible: McNally 2002, 132.

67 "This isn't strictly recreational": McNally 2002, 132.

67 Rock Scully noticed: Greenfield 1996, 87.

67 "I want to make enough money": Greenfield 1996, 129.

67 "For any reader of science fiction": Kaler, in Meriwether 2012.

68 Boucher was also Dick's mentor: Sutin 1989, 70.

68 Frank Herbert, Jack Vance: Kim Stanley Robinson, private correspondence.

68 "We both loved science fiction": Blair Jackson, personal correspondence.

68 "It's one of the few Vonnegut books": Eisenhart 1987.

69 Later, he returned to Austin: Eisenhart 1987.

71 Although they were often required: Selz 2006, 107.

71 In effect, local San Francisco artists: Cushing 2012.

71 Rock posters also exerted: Selz 2006, 106.

71 "You can throw anything at it": Jackson 1999, 104.

72 "I was just thumbing through some books": Jackson 1984.

72 "We didn't really know what it was going to look like": Jackson 1984.

72 Initially unaware of the illustration's provenance: McNally 2002, 157.

73 "It was sheer panic": AMC 1995.

73 "Some of the scarier [trips] were the most memorable": Alderson 2008.

73 One anthropologist noted that: Silverman, in Tuedio and Spector 2010.

74 "It was a really fun place": Greenfield 1996, 88.

74 "It was the height of our folly": Greenfield 1996, 88.

74 "Two or three hundred people would come": Jackson 1999, 104–5.

75 Olompali was "completely comfortable": Jackson 1999, 105.

75 The experience "effectively opened out": Gans 1993, 76–77.

75 "Psychedelics were probably the single most significant": Jackson 1999, 106.

75 "Jerry freaked out": Greenfield 1996, 89–90.

76 During one of Lesh's trips that summer: McNally 2002, 147.

76 "Every time we'd make another batch": Lee and Shlain 1985, 147.

77 "Everywhere they turn": Scully and Dalton 1996, 56–59.

78 Behind the scenes: Rosenfeld 2013.

80 Responding to the dog whistle: McWilliams 1966.

80 In the spring of 1966: Lee and Shlain 1985, 150.

81 "Their signs say": Cannon 2003, 285.

82 "Neal, man!": Goodwin 1971.

82 "I think Cassady just went where the juice was": Greenfield 1996, 100.

82 "The reason they lived at 710": Greenfield 1996, 101.

83 "Suddenly they were the stars": Jackson 1999, 113.

83 "Jerry was a leader": Greenfield 1996, 99.

83 When Joe Smith traveled to San Francisco: Sculatti and Seay 1985, 150–51.

84 "You've got to sign them": Sculatti and Seay 1985, 151.

84 "I was talking to all of them": Sculatti and Seay 1985, 151.

84 Smith refused, and the band signed anyway: Jackson 1999, 117; McNally 2002, 173.

85 "I just want to say what an honor": Goodman 1997, 43.

85 "So we went down there": Jackson 1999, 122.

85 Although the songs reflected: Lesh 2005, 99.

86 According to Joe Smith: Sculatti and Seay 1985, 121.

87 "I find the San Francisco groups": Meriwether 2011, 78–79.

88 "I am not now, and never have been": Gleason tape recording, Grateful Dead Archive.

88 The other strain, Hinckle argued: Hinckle 1967.

89 In the middle of that scene: Rorabaugh 1989, 97–98.

89 Their work, Digger Peter Coyote later said: Coyote interview.

90 "The danger in the hippie movement": Hinckle 1967.

90 As Garcia would later say: Garcia et al. 1972, 100–101.

90 Garcia cast his last vote: McNally 2002, 75, 442.

90 "I remember once being at a be-in": Carroll 1982.

91 "For me, the lame part of the sixties": Goodman 1989.

91 In 1972, for example: Garcia et al. 1972, 93.

91 "We inherited the evil and wars": McNally 2002, 192.

91 "You know, we're not going to stop this war": Wolfe 1968, 223–24.

91 There were tensions galore: Gitlin 1987, 213.

92 Gleason was a man of the left: Hoffman collection, September 2, 1963, Bancroft Library.

92 "I don't think there is any possibility whatsoever": Meriwether 2011, 76.

93 "What we're thinking about is a peaceful planet": Lydon 1969.

94 "To get really high is to forget yourself": Garcia et al. 1972, 100.

94 "I'm not talking about unconscious": Garcia et al. 1972, 100.

94 In his 1966 bestseller, Hunter Thompson wrote: Thompson 1966, 245.

94 "Tiny hurts people": Thompson 1966, 179.

95 Those songs urged young people: Jackson 1992, 216.

95 "We thought culture was much more important": Dolgin and Franco 2007.

96 "There's a kid in Iowa, Kansas, in the summer of '67": Christensen 2007.

96 "And before that, rock-and-roll songs were three minutes": Dolgin and Franco 2007.

97 "And the audience wants to be transformed": Henke 1991.

98 Joan Didion described Morrison as a twenty-four-year-old UCLA graduate: Didion 1979, 22.

98 "We live entirely, especially if we are writers": Didion, 1979, 11.

98 "The only problem was that my entire education": Didion 1979, 12–13.

98 As historian David Farber noted, the counterculture posed: Farber 1994, 168.

98 "When it has to deal with uptight New York or plastic Los Angeles": Christgau 1968.

99 "For the millions of people down there": Gleason 1969, 324–25.

100 "The Dead's shorter arrangements": Hansen 1967.

100 "If the Who had not done": Hansen 1967.

101 "Very, very appealing": Silberman 1992.

101 "Joyce was my primary influence": Jackson 1999, 134.

101 "I can still recite the first page": Silberman 1992.

102 "It opened up everything": Jackson 1999, 134.

102 Although that song became Dylan's most popular: Marqusee 2005, 208.

102 The Basement Tape sessions were: Marcus 2011, 86–87.

102 "In 1959 and 1960": Marcus 2011, 88.

102 "The trip took six weeks": Hunter 1993, v.

103 "They were rehearsing in the hall": Jackson 1999, 135.

103 "The reason the music is the way it is": Jackson 1999, 136.

103 He composed them: Jackson 1992, 214.

104 "I had a cat sitting on my belly": Gans 1993, 24.

104 He later joked: Hunter 1993, 35.

104 "Some songs are trying to make sense": Gans 1993, 25.

105 Because of his background in folk music: Tamarkin 1980.

105 When those lyrics worked: Jackson 1992, 209.

105 The car broke down: Hunter 1993, 7.

105 Those opportunities were scarce: Trist and Dodd 2005, xiv.

105 "My own improbable dream": Trist and Dodd 2005, xi.

106 He realized that his: Trist and Dodd 2005, xiv.

106 The result was "an ever-changing": Fauth, in Dodd 1995–2002.

106 "I like a diamond here, a ruby there": Gans 1993, 26.

106 His entire project: Trist and Dodd 2005, xiv.

106 His method was to channel: Trist and Dodd 2005, xvii.

107 "He loves the mournful, death-connected ballad": Jackson 1992, 117–18.

107 "I keep doing them": Jackson 1992, 121.

107 "Most songs are basically love songs": Henke 1991.

107 Brent Wood estimates that nearly three-quarters: Wood 2013, 50.

107 "Even before the summer of '67": *Rolling Stone*, July 12–26, 2007.

108 "By the end of '66": Thompson 1979, 155.

108 "It was too many people": Jackson 2012.

108 When asked whether the youth influx: Peacock 1972.

108 One of those women: Talbot 2012, 132–33.

109 "We're getting rid of all these possessions": Taylor 1996.

109 Rock Scully noted that their home: Scully and Dalton 1996, 74.

109 Some nights he slept on her sofa: Talbot 2012, 29.

109 "The sun was shining": Talbot 2012, 25.

110 The marijuana laws, Rifkin claimed: *San Francisco Chronicle*, October 6, 1967.

110 The three women: "The Very Grateful Dead," *San Francisco Chronicle*, June 25, 1968.

111 "I feel this incredible hot rush": Scully and Dalton 1996, 132.

112 "After about an hour": Press file, 1973, Grateful Dead Archive.

112 "I get in a group": McNally 1979, 333.

113 "Twenty years of fast living": Wills 2012, 28.

113 Back in San Francisco, Ron Rakow: McNally 2002, 247.

113 "He'd been in the world where I came from": Graham and Greenfield 1992, 239.

114 "I had a little problem in December": Gans 1993, 321.

114 That much was foreseen by Janis Joplin: Scully and Dalton 1996, 142.

114 "Ron Rakow was a wheeler-dealer": Graham and Greenfield 1992, 238.

114 "The band had so many guests?": Graham and Greenfield 1992, 239.

115 Graham's lease on the Fillmore Auditorium: *Rolling Stone*, April 27, 1968.

115 The chairman of that august body: Gleason 1969, 61.

115 His book, which found its way to 710 Ashbury: McNally 2002, 274.

115 Lesh later noted that *Anthem:* Lesh 2005, 128.

115 "I've always felt that as an artistic statement": Lesh 2005, 130.

116 "Both of us were seekers": Lesh 2005, 130.

116 *Anthem of the Sun* was: Blumenberg 1968.

116 Likewise, *Rolling Stone* called the album: Miller 1968.

116 Both of his parents were drummers: McNally 2002, 223.

117 "The din was incredible": Hart and Stevens 1990, 96.

117 That trend gave rise: McNally 2002, 275.

118 The police brutality: Gibney and Ellwood 2008.

118 "I went from a state of Cold Shock": Thompson 2003, 78.

118 "I went to the Democratic convention": McKeen 2008, 125.

118 "A motion?": McNally 2002, 277.

119 Capitalizing on a wave: Walker 2007, 94.

120 "He urges hippies to move out of the cities": Thompson 1967.

121 He was promptly evicted: Gravy 1993, xx.

121 Two members who escaped arrest: Schou 2010, 170.

122 "To get back to something": Turner 2006, 147.

122 "Stephen Gaskin gets people high": Fairfield 2010, 43.

122 According to one founding member: Miller 1999, 73.

122 When they arrived at the property: Coyote 1998, 150.

123 Sponsored by the *San Francisco Oracle*: Conners 2010, 281–82.

124 "Having a baby, having a family": Fairfield 2010, 78.

124 "We looked down our noses at them": Boal et al. 2012, 131.

124 "Then the horses escaped": Boal et al. 2012, 131.

125 One scholar described the catalog's: Kirk 2007, 5.

125 In his view: PlentyMag.com 2009.

125 "Ready or not, computers are coming to the people": Brand 1972.

127 One *Green Acres* actor recalled 1971: Farber 1994, 54–55.

128 "The only thing you'd notice": McNally 2002, 308.

128 "Maybe half of Mill Valley": *Rolling Stone,* September 17, 1970.

129 "Sure, we argue, just like any blood family": O'Haire 1970.

129 Lesh added that they weren't making top scale: Robinson 1970.

130 "I want to thank you for your special gift": McNally 2002, 286.

133 Weir was essentially electrocuted: McNally 2002, 332.

133 "Consciously or subconsciously, by their free concerts": Gleason, June 29, 1969.

134 The strike was called off: Selvin 1999.

134 That beauty was enhanced by the Dead: Gleason, July 12, 1969.

135 "The forces of 'law and order'": Truscott 1969.

135 "But if rock is music that makes you dance": Christgau 1969.

136 His article began with a suggestive passage: Lydon 1969.

136 "The Grateful Dead are the Grateful Dead": Gleason, March 3, 1969

137 Journalist Lenny Kaye: Kaye 1970.

137 "Finally, a great album from the Dead": Marsh 1970.

138 There they visited the Hog Farm commune: Krassner 1993, 194.

138 He then dropped to his knees: Bugliosi 1974, 335.

138 Manson's orders were to kill everyone on-site: Bugliosi 1974, 346.

138 When Tate begged for her and her unborn baby's lives: Bugliosi 1974, 125.

139 Later, she told a fellow inmate: Bugliosi 1974, 126.

139 "There doesn't really seem to be time": Gleason, November 28, 1969.

140 "If you're going to Sears Point Raceway": Gleason, December 5, 1969.

140 "Behind it all was a long torturous tale": Gleason, December 5, 1969, "Bad Vibes for Rolling Stones."

141 As organizers frantically prepared for the event: McNally 2002, 345.

141 "Dawn broke at Altamont on December 6, 1969": Cutler 2010, 165.

141 "I remember filling up a bottle of cheap wine": Schou 2010, 176.

141 "Before me was the ugly truth": Cutler 2010, 170.

142 "I had my eyes closed": Tamarkin 2003, 214.

142 Animal immediately knocked him out again: Cutler 2010, 172–73.

142 "It wasn't just the Angels": Goodwin 1971.

000 "Woodstock, held in high summer": Lesh 2005, 165–66.

143 "It seemed entirely appropriate": Talbot 2012, 140–41.

144 "This is a wonderful, fervent loss of self": Jackson 1986.

144 "The reality was that when we beat a hasty retreat": Stern, in Editors of *Ramparts* 1971.

144 "I think we have to remember": Gleason, December 19, 1969.

145 "If the name 'Woodstock' has come to denote": Gleason 1970.

145 "Clearly, nobody is in control": McMillian 2011, 1–2.

PART 2: MOBILITY

Pages 149–244

149 "We were into a much more relaxed thing": Jackson 1999, 181.

149 "He had the full beard": Greenfield 1996, 123.

149 Weir began contributing country-western cover songs: Trist and Dodd 2005, xxiii.

149 Lesh favored experimental, open-ended jams: McNally 2002, 319.

150 "The electric side was so fun and so stimulating": McNally 2002, 319.

150 "I was very much impressed with the area [Robbie] Robertson": Jackson 2013.

150 "That's really the way to do a recording": Wenner 1969.

150 *Rolling Stone* later maintained that Dylan's effort: Gilmore 2013.

150 "He took [rock music] out of the realm": Jackson 1992, 220.

150 "Hearing those guys sing": Jackson 1992, 224.

150 "Crosby, Stills and Nash came along and changed us": Jackson 1983, 106.

151 "There wasn't any money involved": Greenfield 1996, 120.

151 "We gave them an opening act for cheap": Greenfield 1996, 123.

152 "Jerry would be onstage all night long": Greenfield 1996, 124.

152 "In the first days," Dawson said: Greenfield 1996, 125.

152 Assuming that the San Francisco hippies: McNally 2002, 351.

153 "Every night I was coming home from the studio": Krassner 1985.

153 "Janis Joplin came in while I was starting to rush": Jackson 1992, 115.

153 When Hunter recognized Stanley: Stanley 2012, 193.

154 "It really did flatten me": Jackson 1992, 115.

154 The song captured the drug culture's dark appeal: Williams 2012.

154 "I don't think you need to be stoned": Gans 1993, 284.

154 "It's got a split-second little delay": Garcia et al. 1972, 69–70.

155 "First of all, there's a whole tradition of cocaine songs": Goodwin 1971.

155 That prohibition came from the Federal Communications Commission: Gans 1993, 280.

156 The band members in the cover photograph: Reitman 1970.

156 "Heavens to Lyserge momma": Lynn 1970.

156 "No, no, man, you don't understand": McClanahan 1972.

156 "Some blues freaks walked out": Christgau 1969.

156 It demonstrated the Dead's willingness to go out on a limb: Lambert interview.

157 Over time, the audience and politics of country-western music: Backstrom 2014.

157 *Rolling Stone* concurred with Smith: Zwerling 1970.

158 "Manager Jon McIntire shook his head": Fong-Torres 1971.

159 In San Diego, he had become an ordained minister: Press file, 1972, Grateful Dead Archive.

159 "Everything turned black for me": McNally 2002, 361.

159 "The band didn't blame me for Lenny's thievery": Hart and Stevens 1990, 145.

159 "I didn't live in San Francisco": McNally 2002, 423.

160 "And just imagine putting a bunch of crazy musicians together": Smeaton 2004.

160 "It was a train full of insane people": Smeaton 2004.

161 Some audience members mounted the stage: Dalton and Cott 1970.

161 "You don't have to go for it": Smeaton 2004.

162 "The train trip wasn't a dream": Jackson 1999, 193.

162 Hunter also relished his week on the locomotive: Hunter 1993, 149.

162 "It was great": Jackson 1999, 193.

162 "It was, I believe, two and half days from Toronto to Winnipeg": Smeaton 2004.

162 "It seemed that time was sort of suspended": Smeaton 2004.

163 "We could have the whole goddamn city": Dalton and Cott 1970.

163 "Jerry woke up one morning": Jackson 1992, 220.

164 "We thought it would be nice for us": *CREEM*, December 1970.

165 "The big thing now is, 'Danger, danger, poison earth'": Harris 1970.

165 "I think we're beginning to develop new capacities": Watts 1972.

165 "It's time somebody considered other ways of storing music": Lake 1974.

166 "The San Francisco energy of a few years back": Lydon 1970.

166 "Today there is no place without its hippies": Lydon 1970.

166 "It's already gone, it's already past": *Hard Road,* July 20, 1970.

168 "We have some loose semi-association with the Black Panthers": Robinson 1970.

168 "That was another fiasco, I'm afraid": Jackson 1992, 73.

168 "Yeah, I think they're pure elementals": Robinson 1970.

169 "A venerable tradition": Alioto 1972.

169 "Money is only a symbol for energy exchange": Goodwin 1971.

169 "And any responsibility to anyone else is just journalistic fiction": Robinson 1970.

170 Hunter's goal, he said, was to provide Garcia: Trist and Dodd 2005, xxiii.

170 The words, he recalled, "seemed to flow": Trist and Dodd 2005, xviii–xix.

170 "I am definitely a Westerner": Jackson 1992, 119.

170 In England, he said, he began to define himself that way: Brightman 1998, 65–66.

171 Garcia's identification with the West was more cinematic: Jackson 1992, 223.

171 On a walk through Madrone Canyon in 1969: Hunter 1996.

171 The bridge for "Ripple," Garcia noted: Garcia et al. 1972, 54.

172 The song was eventually recognized as a national treasure: Trist and Dodd 2005, xxiii.

172 During the same period, Mickey Hart's girlfriend lost: Lesh 2005, 189.

173 Lesh described the scene as "jammer heaven": Lesh 2005, 190.

173 Always loath to dissect symbols: Gans 1993, 26.

173 Among the half dozen songs Hunter named as his favorites: Brown et al. 2009, 20.

173 "They were getting into guns at the time": Gilmore 1987.

173 "Our albums went from the bottom": Trist and Dodd 2005, xxiii.

174 As Hunter noted later, "Friend of the Devil": Brown et al. 2009, 20.

174 "Unlike many of their contemporaries in rock music": Beckett 1971.

174 "To a young person at that time": Lesh 2005, 192.

174 In his view, the Dead concerts offered: Lesh 2005, 192.

175 The long, open-ended jams were designed: Jackson 1999, 318.

175 Passing through their third state: Selvin 2006.

175 "Jerry Garcia stood in the center of the action": Parish 2003, 33.

176 For the nineteen-year-old New Yorker: Parish 2003, 47.

176 Even at that point, however, Parish sensed: Parish 2003, 49.

176 Their work was "truly a communal thing": Parish 2003, 63.

176 When asked about the crew's status in the organization: Gans 1993, 57.

177 "We had more equipment than other bands": Parish 2003, 123–24.

177 "He'd put up with all these hippies": Greenfield 1996, 163.

177 "I did all that shit—drive for hundreds of miles": Gans 1993, 236.

178 "There's been times in my life when I burned myself": Gans 1991, 236.

178 He frequently instructed Parish to bring him "somebody weird": McNally 2002, 399.

178 The iguana was part of the entourage: Parish 2003, 96–97.

179 "No, Graham is guilty as charged": Wasserman 1971.

179 "I just don't want to fight anymore": Wasserman 1971.

179 "Young people have changed": Webb 1971.

180 "I'll do only those things": Eichelbaum 1971.

180 In 1969, only one out of five: Baum 1996, 20.

180 Among college students: Baum 1996, 39.

180 As a public health matter, alcohol was by far: Baum 1996, 20.

180 In fact, the estimated value of *all* stolen property: Baum 1996, 58.

180 The drug crackdown targeted what White House aides: Baum 1996, 20.

181 Between 1969 and 1974, the federal drug enforcement: Baum 1996, 75.

181 Marijuana became a Schedule One drug: Baum 1996, 110.

181 "I have done an in-depth study: Baum 1996, 46.

181 When the drug-dependant Presley died in 1977: Baum 1996, 47.

182 Weir described his message as: Tilley 1973.

182 Another Dead Head said: Fluhrer 1973.

182 "It was an incredible find": Jackson 1999, 212.

182 "It had eucalyptus trees and cypresses": Jackson 1999, 212.

182 "Their house is surrounded by sea-swept eucalyptus trees": Garcia et al. 1972, ix.

183 "Our Barbie-doll president, with his Barbie-doll wife": Thompson 1972.

183 Consciousness expansion "went out with LBJ": Thompson 1971, 202.

184 A lifelong Easterner, Reich spent the summer: Citron 2007/8.

185 "Its ultimate creation will be a new and enduring wholeness": Reich 1970, 4.

185 For Wenner, that interview was: Garcia et al. 1972, vii.

185 But given his book's thesis, Reich was especially eager: Garcia et al. 1972, xi.

185 During his visits there, Reich had discovered LSD: Reich 1970, 259–60.

185 Later, Reich compared himself to a nervous groupie: Garcia et al. 1972, ix.

186 In the introduction, Reich claimed that: Garcia et al. 1972, xvii.

186 Reich was a legal expert, not a musical one: Garcia et al. 1972, ix.

186 "Grass teaches us disrespect for the law": Rubin 1971.

186 Marijuana laws, Hart claimed: Hart 1972.

187 "No wonder Dead fanatics will travel hundreds of miles": Takiff 1972.

187 "Aside from the individual virtues of the group": Gleason, September 28, 1972.

188 "He just doesn't boogie": Christgau, April 14, 1974.

188 Godchaux was a gifted pianist: McNally 2002, 411.

188 "Garcia's mighty tired of it, I'll tell you": McKaie 1972.

189 "I do enjoy working with Weir once in a while": Gans 1993, 27.

190 "There were about a hundred of them": Sculatti and Seay 1985, 173.

190 "We can share the women": Trist and Dodd 2005, 167.

190 One scholar identified a subgenre: Wallach 2011.

190 "Actually, I relate better to Dylan songs": Jackson 1999, 234.

191 "Delilah Jones was the mother of twins": Trist and Dodd 2005, 162.

191 "For a year we were a light acoustic band: Jackson 1999, 218.

192 Because the Dead had proven they could also play: Bangs 1971.

192 "I'm gonna nail it on a tree": Van Matre 1972.

193 "At home, there's always been a certain group": Jackson 1999, 218.

193 "Every musician that gets a lot of bread": Smeaton 2004.

195 "We haven't been playing *enough*": Hopkins 1972.

195 "Well, we don't always": Peacock 1972.

195 "As all the tie-dye and denim and hair gathered": Hopkins 1972.

195 Smacking himself on the forehead with an ice-cream cone: Perry 1973.

196 "We played great": Jackson 1999, 229–30.

196 The move to Marin County, he told *Rock* magazine: Peacock 1972.

196 "Pig would call the office": Jackson 1999, 232.

196 "I had to be careful not to squeeze too hard": Lesh 2005, 213.

197 "So we went with our strong suit": Jackson 1999, 240.

197 Shortly after Altamont, Garcia quizzed: Cutler 2010, 193.

197 Kreutzmann added, "The stuff we planned": Leung 2003.

197 "If there ever was a Grateful Dead 'business plan'": Lesh 2005, 211.

197 "What we've been trying to do is liberate the music": Peacock 1972.

198 "I'm not really that far down on Warner Bros.": McNally 2002, 495.

199 The health-food industry, Garcia said: Peacock 1972.

201 While treating the Dead "with respect": McNally 2002, 496.

202 "I've estimated income conservatively": Perry 1973.

202 "The Grateful Dead exists comfortably": Wasserman 1973.

202 The Dead's new venture was also covered: Kates 1974.

203 "The returns are built into our cost factor": *Music Retailer*, May 1974.

203 "The nice thing would be not to sell out": McNally 2002, 452.

203 "Jerry was receiving a lot of money from all sorts": Jackson 1999, 241.

203 "They were having a good time": Greenfield 1996, 186.

204 "The new paradigm we were all talking about": Greenfield 1996, 171.

204 "We weren't just doing a business": Jackson 1999, 246.

204 "The Grateful Dead always had a huge overhead": Greenfield 1996, 181.

204 "The day-to-day requirements": Scully and Dalton 1996, 229.

204 "The Dead dropped out of Warner": Freedland 1975.

205 "One bad record could wipe out all their profit": Kates 1974.

205 "I enjoy playing to fifty people": Lake 1974.

205 "See, there's only two theaters, man": Itkowitz 1970.

205 The stages were ten to twelve feet high: Lesh 2005, 218.

205 "The amount of security and backstage space": Lesh 2005, 218.

206 "Our classic situation for the last six months": Fedele 1971.

207 "First of all, a 56,000-seat football stadium": Grateful Dead Archive.

207 "I think people are beginning to realize": Hamilton 1974.

208 "This seems to be the summer of the big kill": Pousner 1974.

208 "Getting off on the music is a truly high thing": Cowan 1973.

208 "It's a bummer having to work so much": Van Matre 1972.

209 "The Dead are not a 'rock band' anymore": Elwood 1972.

209 "One remarkable characteristic of a Grateful Dead audience": Christgau 1973.

210 "It worked out phenomenally": Liberatore 1973.

210 "The Dead embody an ideal of community": Carr 1973.

210 "Time capsules should have a beginning and an end": Carr 1973.

210 "Even more important, perhaps": Hilburn 1973.

211 "To say the least, it is a tribute to the group": Sharpe 1973.

211 "The lead guitar needs practice": Press file, 1973, Grateful Dead Archive.

211 "To older ears," the critic concluded: Zito 1973.

212 She credited some aspects of the show: Werner 1974.

212 The 1960s, a *Los Angeles Times* reporter: Martinez 1973.

212 "McGovern's aim is to stimulate envy": Buckley 1973.

212 "So many people have had reservations": Perry 1973.

213 "Everything started off real good": Greenfield 1996, 176.

213 Cutler often compared his work: McNally 2002, 363.

213 McIntire—whom Dennis McNally described as: McNally 2002, 363.

213 "I thought it was a dumb move, a Rakow scam": McNally 2002, 468.

213 Composed of 640 speakers at its peak: McNally 2002, 470.

214 When *Guitar Player* magazine asked why: Aiken 1973.

214 "No other band would have put": Liberatore 2007.

216 "Robert Hunter and John Barlow": Meriwether 2014, 84.

216 For Christgau, it was: Christgau August 2, 1974.

216 "I'm not having any fun anymore": McNally 2002, 475.

216 According to Hal Kant, the Dead: Greenfield 1996, 181.

217 "We had a crew that was being paid": McNally 2002, 475.

217 "Our crew was twice as large": Lesh 2005, 218.

217 "I hate music when I'm under its influence": Childs 1974.

217 "The company represents a very intense sociological statement": Johnson 1974.

217 "They're breaking up": Ward 1974.

217 Another story noted that the band: Elwood 1974.

217 "And we've been getting away with murder": Selvin 1974.

217 "Say this for the Dead": Stokes 1974.

218 "Jerry was very involved with it": Greenfield 1996, 174.

218 The rest of the band called the film: McNally 2002, 499.

218 His personal code of ethics: Lake 1974.

218 "This may sound camp": Correspondence file, 1974, Grateful Dead Archive.

219 "Let me read you something": Felton 1975.

220 As Norman Mailer put it: Mailer 2008, 162.

220 Scully described Haldeman: Scully and Dalton 1996, 260.

221 "With the exception of the obvious genius": Snyder-Scumpy 1975.

221 "I drink until I realize I'm getting dumb": George 1974.

221 Recording concerts remained an underground activity: Getz and Dwork 1998, xv.

221 As a result, the Dead put more music: Paumgarten 2012.

221 In addition to serving as a currency for fellow Dead fans: McNally 2002, 386.

221 "Jerry said many times": Greenfield 1996, 43.

222 "Without a tape," one Grateful Dead taper wrote: McNally 2002, 385.

222 "I'm not that taken with my own ideas": McNally 2002, 489.

222 "We tour, therefore we are": Lesh 2005, 252.

222 When Lesh and Stanley told Rakow: McNally 2002, 490.

222 Released against Lesh's better judgment: Lesh 2005, 222.

223 He attempted to justify the payments: Lesh 2005, 227.

223 "We agreed to do so": Lesh 2005, 228.

223 "The sixties model of the Grateful Dead": Adamson 1976.

224 Toward this end, Governor Brown: Kirk 2007, 187.

224 "At a certain point, if your audience grows": Arrington 1977.

224 Garcia also told Jann Wenner: Wenner interview.

224 "How can we apply": *People,* July 12, 1976.

225 "Rock from a drug culture": Rockwell 1976.

225 "A band does not get rich": Van Matre 1976.

225 "It was kind of absurd": Wiseman 1976.

226 "I can't stand the premise of going out": Baruma 2013.

226 "Now the appeal has to be extramusical": Takiff 1973.

226 Tommy Ramone maintained that musicians: Ramone 2007.

227 "That was the Dead": Bauer 1979.

227 "You couldn't give any of my fans Grateful Dead banners": *BAM,* February 2, 1979.

227 Despite the anti-Dead hostility: Jambands.com 2013; Eisen 2013.

228 "No other city has anything like it": Gleason 1969, 68.

228 He found the long jams "too abstract": Wenner interview.

228 "The fun factor had gone out of *Rolling Stone*": McKeen 1991, 105–9.

228 "We were a totally primitive tribe": Greenfield 1996, 173.

229 "The thing about the Grateful Dead was": Greenfield 1996, 173.

000 "Jerry was still under a black cloud": Lesh 2005, 230.

229 "I don't think he understood the depth": Greenfield 1996, 184.

229 "When I found out that he was doing it": Greenfield 1996, 185.

229 "If one guy is on heroin": McGee interview.

230 "Basically, I just told him that it was over": Greenfield 1996, 190.

230 "We were kind of his surrogate family": Greenfield 1996, 195.

230 "Doing any kind of opiate": Greenfield 1996, 202.

230 "As these things have a habit of doing": Lesh 2005, 230.

230 "He called that his vacation": Greenfield 1996, 205.

231 "Thus began my descent into alcoholism": Lesh 2005, 225–26.

231 "We were wasted": Greenfield 1996, 193.

231 "The irony was undeniable": Lesh 2005, 251.

231 Interviews with Donna and Keith Godchaux: *Golden Road,* Spring 1985.

232 "Whether or not anyone else": "Ready When You Are, J.G.," *Playboy,* September 1977.

232 One critic compared the movie: Rohter 1977.

232 The *Los Angeles Times* called the movie: Hunt 1977.

232 "The Grateful Dead will cease to exist": Wasserman 1977.

232 Even those who preferred other shows: Meriwether 2012, "Revisiting Cornell '77."

233 "I can actually remember when these guys": Duffy 1977.

233 Detroit had never been a strong market for the Dead: McNally 2002, 505.

233 When asked how he would respond: Block 1977.

233 "That song is very meaningful to me": Gans 1993, 270.

235 The moniker didn't reflect: Berkow 1977.

235 "I wouldn't get bad press": Diaz 1978.

235 With his foot in a cast: Krassner interview.

236 "In the beginning it was a laugh": Watts 1978.

236 "When we were in Egypt": Adamson 1979.

236 One by one, the Dead joined the Egyptian musicians: Krassner interview.

236 He imagined "the Sphinx's jaw": Private correspondence, Grateful Dead Archive.

237 The Dead couldn't find a replacement for him: Greenfield 1996, 189.

237 "Phil had his Lotus sports car": McNally 2002, 524.

237 "I've had about a dozen totally life-altering experiences": Vaughan 1987.

237 "On live TV, the technology simply didn't exist": Lesh 2005, 246.

238 "It wasn't open for business yet": Lesh 2005, 247.

238 "With few exceptions," *Rolling Stone* concluded: Von Tersch 1979.

238 He had subleased the building for eight years: *Rolling Stone,* November 16, 1978.

240 "Make sure you're always nice to the Peoples Temple": Talbot 2012, 282.

244 As author David Talbot noted, Dan White: Talbot 2012, 333.

244 Many residents agreed with the Reverend Cecil Williams: Talbot 2012, 334.

PART 3: COMMUNITY

Pages 247–303

247 "The seventies are depressing all right": Darling 1978.

247 "San Francisco's Haight-Ashbury district": Reddicliffe 1977.

248 "In a way, the Dead are an anachronism": Van Matre 1979.

248 "Apparently, falling in love with the Grateful Dead": Wald 1978.

248 Jackson conceded that many Dead Heads fit: Shenk and Silberman 1994, 61.

249 It was "an adventure you can still have in America": Goodman 1989.

249 In a later interview, Garcia also called the tours: DeCurtis 1993.

249 When he brought the show to Chicago: Warren 2005, 420.

250 "They're the Wild Bill Hickoks, the Billy the Kids": Thompson 1966, 51.

250 Much like Buffalo Bill: Warren 2005, 546.

250 "The desire on our fans' part": Watrous 1989.

251 "I don't mean to get mystical on you": Snyder-Scumpy 1975.

251 Garcia described the 1960s as: Darling 1978.

251 "We went on a head-hunting mission for twenty-five years": Brightman 1998, 3.

251 "We're in the transportation business": McNally 2002, 538.

252 It surfaced again in 1977: Rockwell 1977.

252 A few days after the Jonestown massacre: Lloyd 1978.

252 "The Grateful Dead, for some reason or other": Rockwell 1979.

252 *Rolling Stone* used the same language in 1980: Skow 1985.

252 "For the capacity crowd, the Dead's performance": Goldberg 1980.

252 He later called the Dead "the worst band in creation": Marsh 1989.

253 The key to the Dead's success: McGee interview.

253 "I go see other groups sometimes": Jackson 1980.

253 As one reviewer noted, "The Grateful Dead": Spitzer 1980.

253 "God, if I could play my music": Greenfield 1996, 250–51.

254 The year before the Jonestown massacre: Block 1977.

254 Later scholars described the Dead not as a cult: Sylvan 2002, 83.

254 "We used to say that every place we played was church": Platt 1993.

255 But when asked about his religious views: Lake 1974.

255 That aspect of their project: Henke 1991.

255 In primitive cultures, he told *Rolling Stone*: Goodman 1989.

255 Like most forms of shamanism: Reist, in Weiner 1999.

255 "Out of these simple ingredients": Gans 1995, 42–43.

255 "I wanted to find out more about the ecstatic states": Jackson 1992, 198.

256 "No, no, it's already in a dark place, dude": Barlow 2012.

256 "A lot of what we are selling is community": McNally 2002, 386.

256 Those included the warm sharing of family: McNally 1980.

256 When those values were on display: Cohen, in Meriwether 2012.

256 "It would be nice if rock shows": Cowan 1973.

257 He was almost in a vegetative state: Lesh 2005, 248.

257 Lesh was even less charitable: McNally 2002, 531.

258 "Well, have a nice rest!": Morley 1981.

258 The magazine's review of the Dead's performance: Bohn 1981.

258 "The highest compliment one could make": Ercolano 1982.

261 The Dead had fired the troublesome Heard: Parish 2003, 215–16.

261 Barlow later said it was "one of the most enlightened": McNally 2002, 386.

262 Garcia recommended McNally for the job: McNally 2009.

262 The tone of their stories, McNally recalled: McNally interview.

262 "The Dead look like the aging hippies they are": Steigerwald 1987.

263 "This is nothing compared to the half dozen phone complaints": Press file, 1986, Grateful Dead Archive.

263 Noting the well-researched articles: Gehr 1987.

265 He attended Dead shows with Eisenhart: Falk interview.

265 Returning to the peninsula, he attended Dead shows: McCracken 2013.

265 Baum dragged Steve Wozniak, cofounder of Apple Computer: Wozniak 2006, 150.

265 According to Baum, Steve Jobs also attended: Baum interview.

266 The founding editor of *Wired* magazine noted: Turner 2006, 143.

266 "I felt the energies on the WELL": Turner 2006, 146.

266 He concluded that the self-proclaimed birthplace: Markoff 1989.

267 "DeadBase makes perfect sense": Bazinet 1989.

267 Although he recorded steadily: Wilentz 2010, 210.

267 "The mind is so incredibly weird": Jackson 1999, 348.

268 "Have I gone insane?": Hunter 1996.

268 "I'm not a believer in the invisible": Gilmore 1987.

269 "It came back very slowly": Jackson 1999, 351.

269 "We should declare war on Vietnam": Cannon 1991, 197.

270 In the immediate aftermath of that divisive conflict: Cannon 1991, 335.

270 It was a popular applause line: Cannon and Cannon 2008, 122.

270 He was the man, one author noted: Bunch 2009, 8.

270 "Defined as a 'president' or even as 'governor,'": Didion 2001, 109.

271 They would "exchange the ritual totems of bonding": Didion 2001, 110.

271 "I didn't like his movies, and I don't like his politics": McNally 2002, 545.

271 "Oh! Give me a break!": Sutherland 1989.

271 The fan hoped that the Dead would: Correspondence file, 1980, Grateful Dead Archive.

272 But the NAS president on Reagan's watch disavowed the report: Baum 1996, 162.

273 "The Latin American drug war is the only war we've got": Baum 1996, 167.

273 Starting in 1984, Congress also passed a series of laws: Angell 2004.

274 "I still think Gary Webb had it mostly right": Wycliff 2005.

275 "The war is not on drugs, the war is on consciousness": Krassner 1993, 213.

275 "That might seem like a vain, sissy thing to do": Kelley 1991, 238.

276 According to Nancy Reagan's unofficial biographer: Kelley 1991, 292.

276 "He never dyed his hair": Bedard 2010.

277 "I know the rent is in arrears": Trist and Dodd 2005, 313–15.

278 As Garcia swung into the final chorus: Selvin 1986.

278 According to Gutierrez, Garcia "couldn't get over the idea": Greenfield 1996, 235.

279 "They were really tickled": Greenfield 1996, 236.

279 "I am appalled": *Q,* February 1988.

279 We're sort of like the town whore": Jackson 1999, 368.

280 Unfortunately, Garcia added, "they're creating a second wave": Eisenhart 1987.

280 "They were young kids who saw this incredible party scene": Greenfield 1996, 250.

280 When the magazine asked Garcia whether Reagan's America: *Q,* February 1988.

281 "The way I affiliated with the Dead": Cohn, private correspondence.

281 Following the band, Conners said, resembled: Conners interview.

282 "Man, I *live* in the twilight zone": McNally 2002, 552.

282 "So hang out with us as long as you're having a good time": Bralove interview.

283 "After 1987": Greenfield 1996, 249.

283 "Then Garcia would say": Greenfield 1996, 250.

283 "What happened was that the Dead were making": Greenfield 1996, 249.

283 By 1987, he wrote later, he felt like "an empty burned-out wreck": Dylan 2004, 147.

283 "We've always had the utmost respect": Sutherland 1989.

283 "I played these shows with the Dead": Dylan 2004, 151.

284 "Ninety thousand people": Greenfield 1996, 239.

284 "The irony of Bob Dylan needing the Grateful Dead": Selvin 1987.

284 "The Dead and Dylan will continue on their independent paths": Hilburn 1987.

285 "It was an incredible dream": Greenfield 1996, 244.

285 "By going on Broadway, he put this stamp": Greenfield 1996, 245.

285 "Without changing musical styles": *People,* December 28, 1987.

286 "'Who are these people?'": Lyall 1988.

286 If their next album was a hit, Weir said: Rense 1989.

286 "This is so different from what happened the last time they were here": Levine 1989.

286 For those and other reasons: Meriwether 2014.

287 "Never did a musician prove his brilliance faster": McNally 2002, 581–82.

287 "Those guys can play *music*": Pooley 1990.

287 "It's a joke": Goodman 1989.

287 "He had a very hard time": Goodman 1990.

287 "So you're not scared?": Press file, 1990, Grateful Dead Archive.

289 In "The Economy of Ideas," Barlow compared the electronic frontier: Barlow 1994.

289 "Most libertarians are worried about government": Dougherty 2004.

290 "I'll be playing huge arenas": Morse 1992.

290 "Tipper and Al came to a show": *Boston Globe,* December 12, 1992.

290 Nineteen days after the concert: Hall 1992.

290 "You better believe there are doctors": Gannett News Service, July 7, 1992.

292 At a press conference, Garcia described Graham: McNally 2002, 590.

293 "There's still hope for a miracle in America": McNally 2002, 607.

293 "Even back when I dropped acid": Corliss 1995.

295 "The numbers were off the charts for days": Liberatore interview.

295 "In a popular culture that sacrifices every value": *San Francisco Chronicle*, August 11, 1995.

295 Departing Garcia's funeral, Dylan reportedly told John Scher: Junod 2014.

295 In the national media, Senator Patrick Leahy said the news: Kuklenski 1995.

296 Only protests from veterans groups: Connolly 1995.

296 "Some of the things the hippies got right": Markoff 1995.

296 The *Globe* reported sloppily: *Globe,* August 23, 1995.

296 "Yes," Silberman replied: Gans 1995, 41.

296 Instead, 85 percent blockage in two of the arteries: Mead 1995.

296 "The band has prospered as the emblem of an era": Will 1995.

297 He asserted that Garcia had "killed, if that's the right word": Buckley 1995.

297 "Jerry Garcia's abuse of his bear-like body": Murdock 1995.

298 "Poor Jerry. Boy, could he play the guitar": Barnicle 1995.

298 "There has never really been a war on drugs": Golden 1995.

299 The Dead scene, David Gans noted: Gans 1993, 4.

299 "[T]here isn't a band in this book": Conners, 2013, xvi–xvii.

300 "There are all kinds of corners of the musical world": Greenhaus 2013.

300 "I've been listening to the Grateful Dead nonstop": Doyle 2013.

300 In 2000, *The New York Times* reported that Burning Man: Ellin 2000.

301 That search, Roszak noted in 1968, distracted many young people: Roszak 1969, 155.

301 The Grateful Dead, the former Digger felt: Coyote interview.

302 Likewise, Jann Wenner said the Dead's achievement: Wenner interview.

302 "I will remember him as an excellent musician": 1995, Grateful Dead Archive.

302 They reveled in each other's eccentricities: Jackson interview.

303 "The members of the Grateful Dead really have": Goodman 1989.

EPILOGUE

Pages 305–312

305 In the Grateful Dead world, David Gans wrote in 1995: Gans 1995, 17.

305 It was a strange transition, Lambert said: Lambert interview.

305 "In the last couple of years, it became apparent": Light 2006.

306 "I think it was a common thought": Liberatore 2006.

307 "A lot of guys when they have a little success in life": Selvin 2011.

309 "Last year I managed to have a nice hospitalization": Browne 2013.

310 That announcement gave the event extra piquancy: Jackson interview.

Sources

Adamson, Dale. Untitled. *Houston Chronicle,* January 7, 1979.

———. "Jerry Garcia Says the Grateful Dead Aren't Dead—They Are Just De-Controlled." *Houston Chronicle,* March 28, 1976.

Aiken, Jim. "Grateful Dead: Wired for Sound." *Guitar Player,* July/August 1973.

Albright, Thomas. *Art in the San Francisco Bay Area, 1945–1980.* University of California Press, 1985.

Alderson, Jeremy. "Q&A with Jerry Garcia: Portrait of an Artist as Tripper." *Relix,* 2008. http://www.relix.com/articles/detail/q-a-with-jerry-garcia-portrait-of-an-artist-as-a-tripper.

Alioto, Ann. "The Grateful Hell's Angels." *Village Voice,* March 30, 1972.

AMC. "Jerry Garcia—The Movie That Changed My Life." 1995. http://www.youtube.com/watch?v=qeW-kdQ46ys.

Anderson, Roger. "Deadhead Redux." *East Bay Express,* October 21, 1988.

Angell, Marcia. "The Truth About the Drug Companies." *New York Review of Books,* July 14, 2004.

Arrington, Carl. "The Dead Rock On in the '70s." *New York Post,* May 7, 1977.

Avlon, John P. "Jerry Garcia's Conservative Children." *New York Sun,* August 9, 2005. http://www.nysun.com/opinion/jerry-garcias-conservative-children/18288/.

Backstrom, Melvin. "'Sing Me Back Home': Country Music and the Counterculture." Paper presented at the Southwest Popular/American Culture Association Conference, 2014.

Bangs, Lester. "How I Learned to Stop Worrying and Love . . ." *CREEM,* December 1971.

Barlow, John Perry. "Thinking About the Dead: Amateur Anthropology, the Human Comedy, and Making Good Ancestors." In Meriwether 2012, 19–23.

———. "The Economy of Ideas." *Wired,* March 1994.

Barnicle, Mike. "Jerry Garcia: Junkie, Man." *San Francisco Chronicle,* August 16, 1995.

Baruma, Ian. "The Invention of David Bowie." *New York Review of Books,* May 23, 2013.

Bauer, Bernard. "Punk Is a Four-Letter Word." *San Francisco Sunday Examiner & Chronicle,* January 7, 1979.

Baum, Dan. *Smoke and Mirrors: The War on Drugs and the Politics of Failure.* Little, Brown, 1996.

Bazinet, Kenneth R. "Computer Ace Links Rock Fans to Grateful Dead Data." *Chicago Sun-Times,* March 3, 1989.

Beckett, William S. "Come Hear Uncle John's Band." *Harvard Crimson,* January 7, 1971.

Bedard, Paul. "Ronald Reagan's Hollywood Tips for Staying Youthful." *U.S. News & World Report,* September 20, 2010. http://www.usnews.com/news/blogs/washington -whispers/2010/09/20/ronald-reagans-hollywood-tips-for-staying-youthful.

Berio, Luciano. *Remembering the Future.* Harvard University Press, 2006.

Berkow, Ira. "Bill Walton Leaves the Radical Left's All-Star Team and Makes the One in Pro Basketball." *People,* February 28, 1977.

Bernstein, David W., ed. *The San Francisco Tape Music Center: 1960s Counterculture and the Avant-Garde.* University of California Press, 2008.

Block, Adam. "Garcia '77." *BAM Magazine,* December 1977.

Blumenberg, Ben. "Grateful Dead: Smooth and Manifold." *Boston After Dark,* September 18, 1968, 27.

Boal, Iain, Janferie Stone, Michael Watts, and Cal Winslow, eds. *West of Eden: Communes and Utopia in Northern California.* PM Press, 2012.

Bohn, Chris. "Dead: Alive If Not Kicking." *New Musical Express,* March 28, 1981.

Brand, Stewart. "Spacewar: Fanatic Life and Symbolic Death Among the Computer Bums." *Rolling Stone,* December 7, 1972.

Brandelius, Jerilyn. *Grateful Dead Family Album.* Warner Books, 1989.

Brightman, Carol. *Sweet Chaos: The Grateful Dead's American Adventure.* Clarkson Potter, 1998.

Brown, Toni, with Lee Abraham and Ed Munson. *Relix: The Book.* Backbeat Books, 2009.

Browne, David. "Grateful Dead Lyricist Robert Hunter Set for Rare Tour." *Rolling Stone,* September 25, 2013.

Buckley, William F., Jr. "Jerry Garcia, R.I.P." *National Review,* September 25, 1995.

———. "Is Rock Musicians' Wealth Evil, Too, George?" *National Review,* February 1973.

Bugliosi, Vincent, with Curt Gentry. *Helter Skelter: The True Story of the Manson Murders.* W. W. Norton, 1974. Reprint, 2001.

Bunch, Will. *Tear Down This Myth: How the Reagan Legacy Has Distorted Our Politics and Haunts Our Future.* Free Press, 2009.

Cannon, Lou. *Governor Reagan: His Rise to Power*. PublicAffairs, 2003.

———. *President Reagan: The Role of a Lifetime*. Simon and Schuster, 1991.

Cannon, Lou, and Carl M. Cannon. *Reagan's Disciple: George W. Bush's Troubled Quest for a Presidential Legacy*. PublicAffairs, 2008.

Caples, Garrett, Andrew Joron, and Nancy Joyce Peters. *The Collected Poems of Philip Lamantia*. University of California Press, 2013.

Carr, Patrick. "The Grateful Dead Makes a Real Good Hamburger." *New York Times*, March 8, 1973.

Carroll, Jon. "A Conversation with Jerry Garcia." *Playboy Guide: Electronic Entertainment*, Spring/Summer 1982.

CBS News. *The Hippie Temptation*. August 1967.

Childs, Andy. "A Conversation with Phil Lesh." *Zigzag*, September 1974.

Christensen, Eric. *The Trips Festival Movie*. The Trips Festival, LLC, 2007.

Christgau, Robert. Review of *From the Mars Hotel*. *Newsday*, August 2, 1974.

———. "Steely Dan's Boogie Has Its Own Boom." *Newsday*, April 14, 1974.

———. "Grateful Dead—Very Much Alive." *Newsday*, March 16, 1973

———. "The Grateful Dead Are Rising Again." *New York Times*, July 27, 1969.

———. "Anatomy of a Love Festival." *Esquire*, January 1968.

Citron, Rodger D. "Charles Reich's Journey from the *Yale Law Review* to the *New York Times* Bestseller List: The Personal History of *The Greening of America*." *New York Law School Law Review* 52 (2007/8): 387–416.

Cohen, Jacob A. "Nomadic Musical Audiences: A Historical Precedent for the Grateful Dead." In Meriwether 2012, 237–46.

Cohen, John. "A Rare Interview with Harry Smith." *Sing Out!* 19, no. 1 (April/May 1969).

Conners, Peter. "'Sink Like a Stone, Float Like a Feather': The Poetics of Bobby Petersen." In Meriwether 2014.

———. *JAMerica: The History of the Jam Band and Festival Scene from the Grateful Dead to Phish, from H.O.R.D.E. to Bonnaroo, and Beyond*. Da Capo, 2013.

———. *White Hand Society: The Psychedelic Partnership of Timothy Leary and Allen Ginsberg*. City Lights Books, 2010.

———. *Growing Up Dead: The Hallucinated Confessions of a Teenage Deadhead*. Da Capo, 2009.

Connolly, Robert. "A Subdued Weld Takes Guitarist's Death Hard." *Boston Herald*, August 10, 1995.

Corliss, Richard. "The Trip Ends." *Time*, August 21, 1995.

Cowan, Peter. "Grateful Dead Is Playing a New Game." *Oakland Tribune*, December 7, 1973.

Coyote, Peter. *Sleeping Where I Fall*. Counterpoint, 1998.

Cushing, Lincoln. *All of Us or None: Social Justice Posters of the San Francisco Bay Area*. Heyday, 2012.

Cushway, Philip, ed. *Art of the Dead*. Counterpoint, 2012.

Cutler, Sam. *You Can't Always Get What You Want: My Life with the Rolling Stones, the Grateful Dead and Other Wonderful Reprobates*. Random House Australia, 2008. Reprint, ECW Press, 2010.

Dalton, David, and Jonathan Cott. "The Million Dollar Bash." *Rolling Stone*, September 3, 1970.

Darling, Lynn. "Still Grateful: Their Decade Died, the Dead Did Not." *Washington Post*, November 24, 1978.

Davidson, Michael. *The San Francisco Renaissance: Poetic and Community at Midcentury*. Cambridge University Press, 1989.

DeCurtis, Anthony. "The Music Never Stops: The *Rolling Stone* Interview with Jerry Garcia." *Rolling Stone*, September 2, 1993.

Diaz, George. "See, Bill Marches to the Beat of a Different Drummer." *Miami Herald*, September 15, 1978.

Didion, Joan. *Political Fictions*. Alfred A. Knopf/Random House, 2001.

———. *The White Album*. Simon and Schuster, 1979. Reprint, Noonday Press/Farrar, Straus and Giroux, 1990.

Dodd, David G. *The Annotated Grateful Dead Lyrics*. 1995–2002. http://arts.ucsc.edu/gdead/agdl.

Dodd, David G., and Diana Spaulding, eds. *The Grateful Dead Reader*. Oxford University Press, 2000.

Dolgin, Gail, and Vicente Franco. *Summer of Love*. WGBH Educational Foundation, 2007.

Dougherty, Brian. "John Perry Barlow 2.0: The Thomas Jefferson of Cyberspace Reinvents His Body—and His Politics." *Reason*, August/September 2004.

Dougherty, Timothy. "Got Their Chips Cashed In: Grateful Dead Is Weird but Profitable Corporation." *Marin Independent-Journal*, July 19, 1988.

Doyle, Patrick. "Q&A: John Mayer on His New Voice, Summer Tour and Dating Katy Perry." *Rolling Stone*, January 30, 2013.

Duffy, Mike. "Dedicated Dead Heads Shouldn't Be Grateful." *Detroit Free Press*, August 9, 1977.

Dunaway, David King. *Huxley in Hollywood*. Harper and Row, 1989.

Dylan, Bob. *Chronicles: Volume One*. Simon and Schuster, 2004.

Editors of *Ramparts*. *Conversations with the New Reality: Readings in the Cultural Revolution*. Canfield Press, 1971.

Eichelbaum, Stanley. "Bill Graham's Postscript to Fillmore East." *San Francisco Examiner*, June 30, 1971.

Eisen, Benjy. "Q&A: Sammy Hagar on New Album and 'Re-Tarnishing' Van Halen." *Rolling Stone*, August 12, 2013.

Eisenhart, Mary. Transcript, Jerry Garcia interview, November 12, 1987. http://www.yoyow.com/marye/garcia4.html.

Ellin, Abby. "Preludes: Out on the Road to Burning Man." *New York Times*, September 17, 2000.

Ellingham, Lewis, and Kevin Killian. *Poet Be Like God: Jack Spicer and the San Francisco Renaissance*. Wesleyan University Press, 1998.

Elwood, Philip. "Dead Have a Lot of Living to Do." *San Francisco Examiner*, October 15, 1974.

———. "Long Live the Grateful Dead." *San Francisco Examiner*, December 12, 1972.

Ercolano, Patrick. "The Grateful Dead: A Cult Following Keeps These Old Hippies Going." *Baltimore Sun*, April 20, 1982.

Fairchild, Richard. *The Modern Utopian: Alternative Communities of the '60s and '70s*. Process Media, 2010.

Farber, Michael. *The Age of Great Dreams: America in the 1960s*. Hill and Wang, 1994.

Fauth, Jurgen. "The Fractals of Familiarity and Innovation: Robert Hunter and the Grateful Dead Concert." In Dodd 1995–2002.

Fedele, Frank. "Fuck No, We're Just Musicians: An Interview with Jerry Garcia." *ORGAN*, December 1971.

Felton, David. "As We Knew It." *The City*, September 30, 1975.

Fluhrer, David. "Risking Their Liberty for the 'Dead.'" *Newsday*, September 9, 1973.

Foley, Jack, ed. *The "Fallen Western Star" Wars: A Debate About Literary California*. Scarlet Tanager Books, 2001.

Fong-Torres, Ben. "Grateful Dead Bust Their Dad." *Rolling Stone*, September 2, 1971.

Fradkin, Philip. *Wallace Stegner and the American West*. University of California Press, 2009.

Freedland, Nat. "The Artist: Million $ Asset." *Billboard*, January 18, 1975.

Gans, David. *Not Fade Away: The Online World Remembers Jerry Garcia*. Thunder's Mouth Press, 1995.

———. *Conversations with the Dead: The Grateful Dead Interview Book*. Carol, 1993.

Gans, David, and Peter Simon. *Playing in the Band: An Oral and Visual Portrait of the Grateful Dead*. St. Martin's Press, 1985.

Garcia, Jerry, Charles Reich, and Jann Wenner. *Garcia: A Signpost to New Space*. Straight Arrow Books, 1972. Reprint, Da Capo Press, 2003.

Gates, David. "Requiem for the Dead." *Newsweek*, August 21, 1995.

Gehr, Richard. "The Dead Zone." *Village Voice*, April 21, 1987.

George, Art. "Rock's Howard Hughes Speaks Out, Sort Of." *Oakland Tribune*, June 23, 1974.

George-Warren, Holly, ed. *Garcia*. Little, Brown, 1995.

Getz, Michael M., and John R. Dwork. *The Deadhead's Taping Compendium*. Vols. 1–3. Owl Books, 1998, 1999, and 2000.

Gibney, Alex, and Alison Ellwood. *Magic Trip: Ken Kesey's Search for a Kool Place*. Magnolia Pictures, 2011.

———. *Gonzo: The Life and Work of Dr. Hunter S. Thompson*. BBC Storyville, 2008.

Gilmore, Mikal. "Dylan's Lost Years." *Rolling Stone,* November 12, 2013.

———. "The New Dawn of the Grateful Dead." *Rolling Stone,* June 16, 1987.

Gitlin, Todd. *The Sixties: Years of Hope, Days of Rage.* Bantam, 1987.

Gleason, Ralph J. "Perspectives: Full Circle with the Dead." *Rolling Stone,* September 28, 1972.

———. "Where Have All the Free Concerts Gone?" *Rolling Stone,* September 10, 1972.

———. "Aquarius Wept." *Esquire,* August 1970.

———. "Who's Responsible for Murder?" *San Francisco Chronicle,* December 19, 1969.

———. "Bad Vibes for Rolling Stones." *San Francisco Chronicle,* December 5, 1969.

———. "The Rolling Stones Are Right On." *San Francisco Chronicle,* December 5, 1969.

———. "A Few Guesses on the Rolling Stones." *San Francisco Chronicle,* November 28, 1969.

———. "Perspectives: A Reunion at Winterland." *Rolling Stone,* July 12, 1969, 28, 30.

———. "The Fascinating Free Concert Phenomenon." *San Francisco Chronicle,* June 29, 1969.

———. "A Delightful Show at the Fillmore West." *San Francisco Chronicle,* March 3, 1969.

———. *The Jefferson Airplane and the San Francisco Sound.* Ballantine, 1969.

———. "All That Jazz and Rock Paid Off." *San Francisco Chronicle,* September 11, 1966.

———. "An Old Joint That's Really Jumpin'." *San Francisco Chronicle,* July 15–17, 1966.

Goldberg, Michael. "The New Year's Dead." *Rolling Stone,* February 21, 1980.

Golden, Arthur. "DEA Chief Condemns Eulogies for Garcia." Press file, Grateful Dead Archive, August 12, 1995.

Goodman, Fred. *The Mansion on the Hill: Dylan, Young, Geffen, Springsteen and the Head-On Collision of Rock and Commerce.* Jonathan Cape, 1997.

———. "Brent Mydland: 1952–1990." *Rolling Stone,* September 6, 1990.

———. "The *Rolling Stone* Interview: Jerry Garcia." *Rolling Stone,* November 30, 1989.

Goodwin, Michael. "Jerry Garcia at 700 MPH." *Flash,* Issue 0, 1971.

Graham, Bill, and Robert Greenfield. *Bill Graham Presents: My Life Inside Rock and Out.* Doubleday, 1992. Reprint, Da Capo, 2004.

Gravy, Wavy. *Something Good for a Change: Random Notes on Peace Thru Living.* St. Martin's Press, 1993.

Green, Jane, and Leah Levy. *Jay DeFeo and The Rose.* University of California Press/Whitney Museum of American Art, 2003.

Greenfield, Robert. *Dark Star: An Oral Biography of Jerry Garcia.* William Morrow, 1996. Reprint, HarperCollins, 2009.

Greenhaus, Mike. "The National to Enlist Members of Vampire Weekend, the War on Drugs, Bon Iver, and Kurt Vile for Grateful Dead Tribute Album." *Relix,* August 1, 2013.

Grushkin, Paul. *The Art of Rock Posters from Presley to Punk.* Abbeville Press, 1999.

Hajdu, David. *Positively 4th Street: The Lives and Times of Joan Baez, Bob Dylan, Mimi Baez Farina, and Richard Farina.* Farrar, Straus and Giroux, 2001.

Hall, Mimi. "Tipper Gore's Balancing Act." *USA Today,* August 3, 1992.

Hamilton, David. "Rock & Road: Hot Money in the Summertime." *Rolling Stone,* June 20, 1974.

Hansen, Barry. "First Annual Monterey Pop Festival." *Down Beat,* August 10, 1967, 23–26.

Harris, David. *Circus,* March 1970, 32–35.

Hart, Jeffrey. "Marijuana and the Counterculture." *National Review,* December 8, 1972.

Hart, Mickey, with Jay Stevens. *Drumming at the Edge of Magic: A Journey into the Spirit of Percussion.* HarperSanFrancisco, 1990.

Henke, James. "Alive and Well with Jerry Garcia: The *Rolling Stone* Interview." *Rolling Stone,* October 31, 1991. Reprint in George-Warren 1995, 180–89.

Herbst, Peter. "A Message from Jerry Garcia: Nothing Exceeds Like Success." *Boston After Dark,* November 19, 1974.

Hilburn, Robert. "Grateful Dead, Dylan: Ending on a High Note." *Los Angeles Times,* July 28, 1987.

———. "A Mellow Opener for the Amphitheater." *Los Angeles Times,* July 3, 1973.

Hinckle, Warren. *If You Have a Lemon, Make Lemonade: An Essential Memoir of a Lunatic Decade.* G. P. Putnam's Sons, 1974.

———. "The Social History of the Hippies." *Ramparts,* March 1967.

Hopkins, Jerry. "The Beautiful Dead Hit Europe." *Rolling Stone,* June 22, 1972.

Hunt, Dennis. "A Lively Forum for the Grateful Dead." *Los Angeles Times,* July 19, 1977.

Hunter, Robert. "Letter to JG." Hunter archive, 1996. http://www.hunterarchive.com /files/mailpages/lettertoJG.html.

———. *A Box of Rain: Lyrics 1965–1993.* Penguin, 1993.

Huxley, Aldous. *The Doors of Perception.* Harper and Brothers, 1954. Reprint, First Harper Perennial Modern Classics, 2009.

Igliori, Paola. *American Magus Harry Smith: A Modern Alchemist.* In and Out Press, 1996.

Issel, William, and Robert W. Cherny. *San Francisco, 1865–1932: Politics, Power, and Urban Development.* University of California Press, 1986.

Itkowitz, Jay B. "Interview with Jerry Garcia." *Action World* 2, no. 5 (November 1970).

Jackson, Blair. "With *Workingman's Dead,* the Dead Shifted from Uncommercial Jam Band to One of the World's Most Popular Acts." *Guitar World,* November 4, 2013. http://www.guitarworld.com/workingman-s-dead-grateful-dead-shifted-uncom mercial-jam-band-one-worlds-most-popular-acts?page=0,1.

———. "*Dancing with the Dead* Captures the Early Scene with Stories and Photos." Dead.net, 2012. http://www.dead.net/features/blair-jackson/blair-s-golden-road-blog -dancing-dead-captures-early-scene-stories-and-photos.

———. *Grateful Dead: The Illustrated Trip.* DK Pub, 2003.

———. *Garcia: An American Life*. Viking Penguin, 1999.

———. *Goin' Down the Road: A Grateful Dead Traveling Companion*. Harmony, 1992.

———. "Mythologist Campbell on the Dead." *Golden Road,* Summer 1986.

———. "The Magical World of Alton Kelley." *Golden Road,* Summer 1984.

———. *Grateful Dead: The Music Never Stopped*. Delilah Books, 1983.

———. "Dead Heads: A Strange Tale of Love, Devotion, and Surrender." *BAM Magazine,* April 4, 1980.

Jambands.com. "Sammy Hagar Says That Bob Weir and Mickey Hart Wanted Him to Play in the Grateful Dead." October 29, 2013. http://www.jambands.com/news /2013/10/29/sammy-hagar-says-that-bob-weir-and-mickey-hart-wanted-him-to -play-in-the-grateful-dead#.UnExDmPLwVk.

Jarnot, Lisa. *Robert Duncan: The Ambassador from Venus*. University of California Press, 2012.

Johnson, Nels. "An Idea Worth Many Millions." *San Rafael Independent-Journal,* August 16, 1974.

Junod, Tom. "Seven Questions for Bob Dylan." *Esquire,* February 2014.

Kaler, Michael. "How the Grateful Dead Learned to Jam." In Meriwether 2012.

Kates, Marcy. "The Image Is Hippie, but 'Grateful Dead' Also Know Business." *Wall Street Journal,* November 22, 1974.

Kaye, Lenny. *Live/Dead* review. *Rolling Stone,* February 7, 1970.

Kelley, Kitty. *Nancy Reagan: The Unauthorized Biography*. Simon and Schuster, 1991.

Kerouac, Jack. *The Dharma Bums*. Viking Press, 1958. Reprint, Penguin, 1976.

———. *On the Road*. Viking Press, 1957. Reprint, Penguin, 1976.

Kerr, Mary. *San Francisco's Wild History Groove*. CA Palm, 2011.

Kesey, Ken. *One Flew Over the Cuckoo's Nest*. Viking Press, 1962. Reprint, Penguin Classic, 2002.

Kirk, Andrew G. *Counterculture Green: The* Whole Earth Catalog *and American Environmentalism*. University Press of Kansas, 2007.

Krassner, Paul. *Confessions of a Raving, Unconfined Nut: Misadventures in the Counter-Culture*. Simon & Schuster, 1993.

———. "Interview: Jerry Garcia." *Realist* 99 (September/October 1985).

Kuklenski, Valerie. "Garcia Death Sparks Memories." Press File, Grateful Dead Archive, Auust 9, 1995.

Lake, Steve. "Rock 'n' Roll Misfit." *Melody Maker,* September 14, 1974.

Lang, Raymond. "Four Explosions: The Grateful Dead." *Daily Californian,* January 20, 1970.

LaValley, Albert J., ed. *The New Consciousness: An Anthology of the New Literature*. Pennsylvania State University, 1972.

Lee, Barbara, and Paul S. Hersh. "A Personal Interview with Robert Hunter." *Centerstage,* March 1978.

Lee, Martin A., and Bruce Shlain. *Acid Dreams: The Complete Social History of LSD: The CIA, the Sixties, and Beyond*. Grove Press, 1985.

Lescaze, Lee. "Reagan Calls for Reforms to Fight Mounting Crime." *Spokesman-Review*, September 29, 1981.

Lesh, Phil. *Searching for the Sound: My Life with the Grateful Dead*. Little, Brown, 2005.

Leung, Rebecca. "Bringing Back 'The Dead': Surviving Members Talk About the Event That Tore the Group Apart." CBS News, November 11, 2003. http://www.cbsnews .com/news/bringing-back-the-dead/.

Levine, David. "The Peaceable Kingdom: Neighborhood Stays Calm as Deadheads Party at RFK." *Washington Post*, July 13, 1989.

Liberatore, Paul. "Dan Healy: Sound Mix Master for the Grateful Dead." *Marin Independent-Journal*, November 3, 2007.

———. "Only the Memories Remain: Grateful Dead's Recordings Moved." *Marin Independent-Journal*, August 4, 2006.

———. "Group Plays Famous Eastern Gig." *San Rafael Independent-Journal*, August 17, 1973.

Light, Alan. "A Resurrection, of Sorts, for the Grateful Dead." *New York Times*, July 10, 2006.

Lloyd, Jack. "Grateful Dead's Mellower, but Fans' Devotion Is Not." *Philadelphia Inquirer*, November 23, 1978.

Lyall, Sarah. "'The Dead' and Their Undying Fans." *New York Times*, September 24, 1988.

Lydon, Michael. "An Evening with the Grateful Dead." *Rolling Stone*, September 17, 1970.

———. "Good Old Grateful Dead." *Rolling Stone*, August 23, 1969.

Lynn, Bob. "The Dead—After the Apocalypse." *Daily Bruin*, July 17, 1970.

Maier, Peter. "When Did Ronald Reagan Have Alzheimer's? The Debate Goes On." CBS News, February 6, 2011. http://www.cbsnews.com/8301-503544_162-20030791 -503544.html.

Mailer, Norman. *Miami and the Siege of Chicago*. New York Review Books, 2008.

Marcus, Greil. *The Old, Weird America: The World of Bob Dylan's Basement Tapes*. Picador, 2011. First published in 1997 as *Invisible Republic* by Henry Holt.

Markoff, John. "Sadness from the Streets to High Offices." *New York Times*, August 10, 1995.

———. "Whole Earth State-of-Art Rapping." *New York Times*, August 15, 1989.

Marqusee, Mike. *Wicked Messenger: Bob Dylan and the 1960s*. Seven Stories Press, 2005.

Marsh, Dave. "Dylan and the Dead." *Playboy*, June 1989.

Martinez, Al. "1960s: Where Have All the Protests Led?" *Los Angeles Times*, May 7, 1973.

McClanahan, Ed. "Grateful Dead I Have Known." *Playboy*, March 1972.

McCracken, Harry. "For One Night Only, Silicon Valley's Homebrew Computer Club Reconvenes." *Time*, November 12, 2013.

McKaie, Andy. "Bob 'Ace' Weir: Inside Straight on the Dead's Full House." *Crawdaddy!*, September 1972.

McKeen, William. *Outlaw Journalist: The Life and Times of Hunter S. Thompson.* W. W. Norton, 2008.

———. *Hunter S. Thompson.* Twayne Publishers, 1991.

McMillian, John. *Smoking Typewriters: The Sixties Underground Press and the Rise of Alternative Media in America.* Oxford University Press, 2011.

McMurtry, Larry. *Literary Life: A Second Memoir.* Simon and Schuster, 2009.

McNally, Dennis. "The Grateful Dead in the Academy." *Dead Letters: Essays on the Grateful Dead Phenomenon* 4 (2009): 13–28.

———. *A Long, Strange Trip: The Inside History of the Grateful Dead.* Broadway, 2002.

———. "Meditations on the Grateful Dead." *San Francisco Sunday Examiner and Chronicle,* September 28, 1980.

———. *Desolate Angel: Jack Kerouac, the Beat Generation, and America.* Random House, 1979; Reprint, Da Capo Press, 2003.

McWilliams, Carey. "How to Succeed with the Backlash." *Nation,* October 31, 1966.

Mead, Tyra. "Heroin Use Didn't Kill Jerry Garcia." *San Francisco Chronicle,* August 30, 1995.

Meltzer, David, ed. *San Francisco Beat: Talking with the Poets.* City Lights Books, 2001.

Meriwether, Nicholas. "The Promise of Magic, and the Rest of Spring 1990." Liner-note manuscript.

———, ed. *A Rare and Different Tune: The Seventeenth Annual Grateful Dead Scholars Caucus.* Dead Letters Press, 2014.

———, ed. *Reading the Grateful Dead: A Critical Survey.* Scarecrow Press, 2012.

——— "Revisiting Cornell '77." http://rockhall.com/story-of-rock/features/all-featured /7745_grateful-dead-live-at-barton-hall-1977-concert/.

———, ed. *Dead Studies.* Vol. 1. Grateful Dead Archive/UC Santa Cruz Libraries, 2011.

Mikkelsen, Randall. "Grateful Dead Songwriter Hits the Road for Rare Tour." *Washington Post,* September 21, 2013.

Miller, Jim. *Anthem of the Sun* review. *Rolling Stone,* September 28, 1968.

Miller, Timothy. *The 60s Communes: Hippies and Beyond.* Syracuse University Press, 1999.

Morley, Paul. "What a Long Predictable Trip It's Become." *New Musical Express,* March 28, 1981.

Morse, Steve. "Sting Lightens Up, Brings a 'Ragbag of Styles' to Latest Disc." *Boston Globe,* February 28, 1992.

Murdock, Deroy. "Garcia Was a Monument to Human Freedom." *Detroit News,* August 17, 1995.

O'Haire, Pat. "Living Dead." *New York Daily News,* November 10, 1970.

Parish, Steve, with Joe Layden. *Home Before Daylight: My Life on the Road with the Grateful Dead.* St. Martin's Press, 2003.

Parrish, Michael. "South Bay Folk Roots of the San Francisco Sound." Paper presented at the Southwest Popular/American Culture Association Conference, 2014.

Paumgarten, Nick. "Deadhead: The Afterlife." *New Yorker,* November 26, 2012.

Peacock, Steve. "Jerry Garcia in London." *Rock,* April 1972.

Perchuk, Andrew, and Rani Singh, eds. *Harry Smith: The Avant-Garde in the American Vernacular.* Getty Research Institute, 2010.

Perry, Charles. "A New Life for the Dead." *Rolling Stone,* November 22, 1973.

Platt, John. "Reddy Kilowatt Speaks: An Interview with Phil Lesh." *Spiral Light* 30 (November 1993).

PlentyMag.com. "The *Whole Earth Catalog* Effect." May 9, 2009. http://www.mnn.com /lifestyle/arts-culture/stories/the-whole-earth-catalog-effect.

Pooley, Eric. "Raising the Dead." *New York,* April 16, 1990.

Pousner, Michael. "It's Back, Folks—the Sound of the '60s!" *New York Daily News,* August 12, 1974.

Powers, Charles T. "Communes: New Mexico's Stoned Society." *Los Angeles Times,* March 17, 1970.

Rainier, Pat. "Interview with Jerry Garcia of the Dead." *Tennessee Roc,* August 1970.

Rakow, Ron. "A Dead Anecdote." Press file, Grateful Dead Archive, April 1974.

Ramone, Tommy. "Fight Club." *Uncut,* January 2007.

Raphael, Ray. *Cash Crop: An American Dream.* Ridge Times Press, 1985.

Reddicliffe, Steven. "The Dead Still Very Much with Us with a Grateful, Faithful Following." *Miami Herald,* May 22, 1977.

Reich, Charles. *The Greening of America.* Random House, 1970.

Reist, Nancy. "Clinging to the Edge of Magic: Shamanic Aspects of the Grateful Dead." In Weiner 1999, 183–90.

Reitman, David. Review of *Workingman's Dead. Rock,* July 6, 1970.

Rense, Rip. "Dead Reckoning: New Album May Further Imperil the Band's Live-Concert Plans." *Chicago Tribune,* October 29, 1989.

Richardson, Peter. *A Bomb in Every Issue: How the Short, Unruly Life of* Ramparts *Magazine Changed America.* New Press, 2009.

Robinson, Lisa. "*CREEM* Interview with the Grateful Dead." *CREEM,* December 1970.

Rockwell, John. "Rock: The Grateful Dead Open Series at Garden." *New York Times,* September 6, 1979.

———. "Grateful Dead Play the Palladium with the Special Winning Blend." *New York Times,* May 1, 1977.

———. "Grateful Dead Returns in Triumph." *New York Times,* June 16, 1976.

Rohter, Larry. "A Movie to Make 'Dead Heads' Grateful." Press file, 1977, Grateful Dead Archive.

Rorabaugh, W. J. *Berkeley at War: The 1960s.* Oxford University Press, 1989.

Rosenfeld, Seth. *Subversives: The FBI's War on Student Radicals, and Reagan's Rise to Power*. Farrar, Straus and Giroux, 2013.

Roszak, Theodore. *The Making of a Counter Culture: Reflections on the Technocratic Society and Its Youthful Opposition*. Doubleday, 1969. Reprint, University of California Press, 1999.

Rubin, Jerry. "Keep Pot Illegal." In Editors of *Ramparts* 1971, 36–38.

Saffra, Joan, and Stephen Talbot. *Further! Ken Kesey's American Dreams*. KQED, 1987.

Sargent, Lyman Tower. *Utopianism: A Very Short Introduction*. Oxford University Press, 2010.

Schou, Nicholas. *Orange Sunshine: The Brotherhood of Eternal Love and Its Quest to Spread Peace, Love, and Acid to the World*. St. Martin's Press, 2010.

Sculatti, Gene, and Davin Seay. *San Francisco Nights: The Psychedelic Music Trip, 1965–1968*. St. Martin's Press, 1985.

Scully, Rock, and David Dalton. *Living with the Dead: Twenty Years on the Bus with Garcia and the Grateful Dead*. Little, Brown, 1996.

Selvin, Joel. "Grateful Dead's Bob Weir Debuts TRI Studios on Web." *San Francisco Chronicle*, June 6, 2011.

———. "Lawrence 'Ramrod' Shurtliff: 1945–2006." *San Francisco Chronicle*, May 18, 2006.

———. *Summer of Love: The Inside Story of LSD, Rock & Roll, Free Love and High Times in the Wild West*. Cooper Square Publishers, 1999.

———. "The Night of the Living Dead: Dylan Was Just Along for the Ride." *San Francisco Chronicle*, July 27, 1987.

———. "The Dead Roar Back to Life." *San Francisco Chronicle*, December 17, 1986.

———. "Getting Straight with the Dead." *San Francisco Chronicle*, October 18, 1974.

Selz, Peter. *Art of Engagement: Visual Politics in California and Beyond*. University of California Press, 2006.

Sharpe, Keith. "'Spontaneous Confusion' with the Grateful Dead." *Thousand Oaks News Chronicle*, July 5, 1973.

Shenk, David, and Steve Silberman. *Skeleton Key: A Dictionary for Deadheads*. Doubleday, 1994.

Silberman, Steve. "Standing in the Soul: Robert Hunter Interview." *Poetry Flash*, December 1992.

Silverman, Eric. "'Mysteries Dark and Vast': Grateful Dead Concerts and Initiation into the Sublime." In Tuedio and Spector 2010, 214–31.

Skow, John. "In California: The Dead Live On." *Time*, February 11, 1985.

Smeaton, Bob. *Festival Express*. THINKfilm, 2004.

Smith, Casper Llewellyn. "Bob Dylan Visits Woody Guthrie." *Guardian*, June 15, 2011.

Smith, Richard Candida. *Utopia and Dissent: Art, Poetry, and Politics in California*. University of California Press, 1995.

Smith, Richard D. *Can't You Hear Me Callin': The Life of Bill Monroe, Father of Bluegrass*. Little, Brown, 2000.

Snyder-Scumpy, Patrick. "Robert Hunter, Dark Star." *Crawdaddy!*, January 1975.

Solnit, Rebecca. "Inventing San Francisco's Art Scene." *San Francisco Chronicle*, January 24, 2004.

———. *Secret Exhibition: Six California Artists of the Cold War Era.* City Lights, 1990.

Spitzer, John. Grateful Dead concert review. *Ithaca Journal*, May 8, 1980.

Stanley, Rhoney Gissen. *Owsley and Me: My LSD Family.* Monkfish Book Publishing, 2012.

Steigerwald, Bill. "*Forbes* Focuses on the Dead and Their $20 Million." *Los Angeles Times*, May 15, 1987.

Stern, Sol. "Altamont: Pearl Harbor to the Woodstock Nation." In Editors of *Ramparts* 1971, 45–68.

Stewart, Jon. "Communes in Taos." In Editors of *Ramparts* 1971, 206–20.

Stokes, Geoffrey. "Death of the Dead?" *Village Voice*, October 31, 1974.

Stone, Robert. *Prime Green: Remembering the Sixties.* Ecco/HarperCollins, 2007.

———. "End of the Beginning." In George-Warren 1995, 32–34.

Sutherland, Steve. "Grateful Dead: Further Ahead." *Melody Maker*, May 13, 1989.

———. "Grateful Dead: Acid Daze." *Melody Maker*, May 6, 1989.

Sutin, Lawrence. *Divine Invasions: A Life of Philip K. Dick.* Harmony Books, 1989.

Sylvan, Robin. *Traces of the Spirit: The Religious Dimensions of Popular Music.* New York University Press, 2002.

Takiff, Jonathan. "A Dinner Date with the Grateful Dead Is Less Than a Trip." *Philadelphia Daily News*, September 21, 1973.

———. "Grateful Dead Leaves 'Em Alive, Thankful." *Philadelphia Daily News*, September 22, 1972.

Talbot, David. *Season of the Witch: Enchantment, Terror, and Deliverance in the City of Love.* Free Press, 2012.

Tamarkin, Jeff. *Got a Revolution! The Turbulent Flight of Jefferson Airplane.* Atria, 2003.

———. "The *Relix* Interview: Jerry Garcia, Part I." *Relix*, August 1980.

Taylor, Michael. "Obituary—Ron Thelin." *San Francisco Chronicle*, March 22, 1996.

Thomas, Fred. "*Sunshine Daydream*." *AllMusic*. Retrieved February 13, 2014.

Thompson, Hunter S. *Kingdom of Fear: Loathsome Secrets of a Star-Crossed Child in the Final Days of the American Century.* Simon and Schuster, 2003.

———. *The Great Shark Hunt.* Summit Books, 1979.

———. "Ask Not for Whom the Bell Tolls: Re-Elect the President." *Rolling Stone*, November 9, 1972.

———. *Fear and Loathing in Las Vegas: A Savage Journey to the Heart of the American Dream.* Random House, 1971.

———. "The 'Hashbury' Is the Capital of the Hippies." *New York Times Magazine*, May 14, 1967.

———. *Hell's Angels: A Strange and Terrible Saga.* Ballantine, 1966. Reprint, 1996.

Tilley, Kathy. "Rock Musician Trips on Music." *Atlanta Constitution*, December 14, 1973.

Trachtenberg, Jay. "Kingfish Keeping Dead Spirit Alive." *Santa Barbara News & Review*, March 28, 1976.

Trist, Alan, and David Dodd, eds. *The Complete Annotated Grateful Dead Lyrics*. Free Press, 2005.

Troy, Sandy. *Captain Trips: A Biography of Jerry Garcia*. Thunders Mouth Press, 1994.

Truscott, Lucian, IV. "No Favors." *Village Voice*, June 26, 1969.

Tuedio, Jim, and Stan Spector, eds. *The Grateful Dead in Concert*. McFarland, 2010.

Turner, Fred. *From Counterculture to Cyberculture: Stewart Brand, the Whole Earth Network, and the Rise of Digital Utopianism*. University of Chicago Press, 2006.

Van Matre, Lynn. "Jerry Garcia Keeps the Spirit of Grateful Dead Alive." *Chicago Tribune*, July 5, 1981.

———. "Grateful Dead—a Grateful Touch of the Familiar." *Chicago Tribune*, December 4, 1979.

———. "Rare Trip with the Grateful Dead." *Chicago Tribune*, June 28, 1976.

———. "The Grateful Dead: Haven't Changed Much." *New Sound*, January 1972.

Vaughan, Chris. "Dead Fingers Talk." *Spin* 3, no. 4 (July 1987).

Von Tersch, Gary. *Shakedown Street* review. *Rolling Stone*, March 8, 1979.

Wald, Eliot. "The Living Culture and Traditions of the Grateful Dead." *Chicago Sun-Times*, May 18, 1978.

Walker, Richard A. *The Country in the City: The Greening of the San Francisco Bay Area*. University of Washington Press, 2007.

Wallach, Rick. "Sublimated Sexual Anxiety in the 'Scoundrel Songs' of the Grateful Dead." Paper presented at the Southwest/Texas Popular Culture Association/American Culture Association Conference, 2011.

Ward, Ed. "Obituary: The Grateful Dead, 1965–1974?" *City*, October 15, 1974.

Warren, Louis S. *Buffalo Bill's America: William Cody and the Wild West Show*. Alfred A. Knopf, 2005.

Wasserman, John. "Grateful Dead Film a Unique Experience." *San Francisco Chronicle*, July 22, 1977.

———. "The Expansion of the Grateful Dead." *San Francisco Chronicle*, October 12, 1973.

———. "On the Town." *San Francisco Chronicle*, June 4, 1971.

Watrous, Peter. "Touch of Gray Matter: The Grateful Dead Are Different from You and Me." *Musician*, December 1989.

Watts, Michael. "Dead on the Nile." *Melody Maker*, September 23, 1978.

———. "Honour the Dead." *Melody Maker*, April 15, 1972.

Webb, Mike. "Graham: 'Joyful Spirit Is Gone,'" August 12, 1971.

Weiner, Robert G., ed. *Perspectives on the Grateful Dead: Critical Writings*. Greenwood Press, 1999.

Weller, Sheila. "LSD, Ecstasy, and a Blast of Utopianism: How 1967's 'Summer of Love' All Began." *Vanity Fair,* July 2012.

Wenner, Jann. "Bob Dylan's First *RS* Interview." *Rolling Stone,* November 29, 1969.

Werner, Laurie. "Grateful Dead: Professionalism?" *Village Voice,* August 15, 1974.

Whitman, Walt. *Democratic Vistas, and Other Papers.* W. B. Gage, 1988.

Wilentz, Sean. *Bob Dylan in America.* Doubleday, 2010.

Will, George. "About the 'Sixties Idealism.'" *Newsweek,* August 21, 1995.

Williams, James. "Caution! The Lyrics of the Grateful Dead." Paper presented at the Southwest/Texas Popular Culture Association/American Culture Association Conference, 2012.

Wills, David S. *Beatdom #6.* Beatdom Books, 2012.

Wiseman, Rich. "Random Notes." *Rolling Stone,* October 31, 1976.

Wolfe, Tom. *The Electric Kool-Aid Acid Test.* Farrar, Straus and Giroux, 1968. Reprint, Ballantine, 1999.

Wood, Brent. "Mystery Dances: How Jerry Garcia and the Grateful Dead Reinvented Musical Tragedy." Unpublished manuscript, 2013.

Wozniak, Steve, with Gina Smith. *iWoz: Computer Geek to Cult Icon: How I Invented the Personal Computer, Co-founded Apple, and Had Fun Doing It.* W. W. Norton, 2006.

Wycliff, Don. "Dangers of Questioning Government Actions." *Chicago Tribune,* January 6, 2005.

Zito, Tom. "The Dead Gone Astray." *Washington Post,* March 28, 1973.

Zwerling, Alex. Review of *Workingman's Dead. Rolling Stone,* July 23, 1970.

Index

ABOUT THE AUTHOR

Peter Richardson teaches humanities and American studies at San Francisco State University. His previous books include *A Bomb in Every Issue: How the Short, Unruly Life of* Ramparts *Magazine Changed America* (2009) and *American Prophet: The Life and Work of Carey McWilliams* (2005). *A Bomb in Every Issue* was an Editors' Choice at *The New York Times*, a Top Book of 2009 at *Mother Jones*, and a Notable Bay Area Book of the Year at the *San Francisco Chronicle*. Writing for *The Nation*, Mike Davis described *American Prophet* as a superb biography.

Richardson's work has also appeared in the print or online editions of *The New York Times*, the *Los Angeles Times Book Review*, *Mother Jones*, *Truthdig*, *The American Conservative*, *California History*, and many scholarly journals. In 2013, he received the National Entertainment Journalism Award for Online Criticism.

Richardson was the founding editorial director of PoliPoint Press, where he acquired books on progressive politics and current affairs. Before that, he was an editor at the Public Policy Institute of California, an associate professor of English at the University of North Texas, and an editor at Harper & Row, Publishers. He received a Ph.D. in English from the University of California, Berkeley, in 1991, and a B.A. in economics from the University of California, Santa Barbara, in 1981. He lives in Richmond, California.